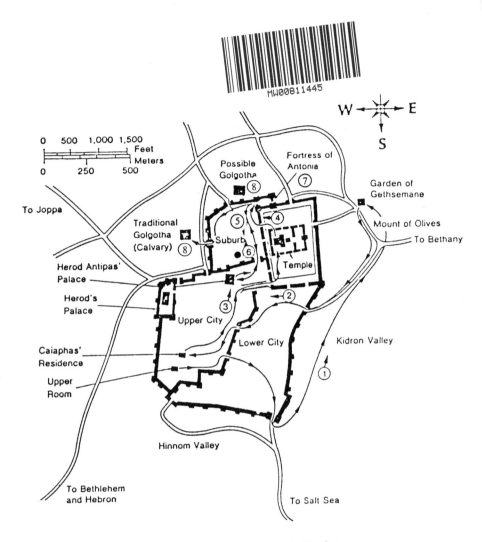

Map of Jerusalem at the Time of Christ

#1--After leaving the upper room where the Last Supper was held, Jesus walked with his disciples to the Mount of Olives and prayed in the Garden of Gethsemane.

#2--Jesus was arrested and taken to Annas and then to Caiaphas.

#3--After his first trial before the Sanhedrin during the night, Jesus had to be tried again after day-break to make it legal.

#4--Next, he was taken to Pontius Pilate.

#5--Pilate sent Jesus to Herod Antipas.

#6--Herod returned Jesus to Pilate.

#7--Pilate finally handed Jesus over to scourging at the Fortress of Antonia.

#8--He was then sent to Golgotha for crucifixion (two possible locations).

Days of the
LIVING
CHRIST

THE GENTLE HEALER
by Greg K. Olsen

Days of the
LIVING CHRIST

VOLUME TWO

W. CLEON SKOUSEN

ENSIGN PUBLISHING CO.
SALT LAKE CITY, UTAH

ISBN 0-916095-47-9

The Ensign Publishing Co.
Salt Lake City, Utah

Distributed by:
Sounds of Zion
6973 S. 300 W., Midvale, Utah 84047

Cover design by:
James Fedor

1st Printing, January 1993
2nd Printing, May 1994

This Book Is In Honor of

JEWEL ALMIRA PITCHER SKOUSEN

Loving wife, mother of eight,
co-editor, and proofreader,
without whose help and encouragement
this book might never have been completed.

THIS BOOK IS DEDICATED TO:

THE JEWS

Whom Jesus loved because they were his own people, and because they assisted him in going through his assigned ordeal of providing a redemptive sacrifice for all mankind.

THE ARABS

Who are the seed of Abraham, and on whom Jesus has already laid claim. Isaiah names the lands occupied by the great Arab nations in the latter days, and says they will be blessed by the Lord, and be called "my people," and "the work of my hands," at the very same time Israel becomes "mine inheritance."[1]

THE GENTILES

Among whom Jesus has already raised up the descendant of the Patriarch Joseph whom the Jews have been expecting as their "Messiah ben Joseph." Through him the prophetic "Ensign" has been raised up.[2] Israel has been promised that in the latter days the Gentiles will assist them in returning to the land of their former inheritances.[3]

THE LAMANITES—THE AMERICAN ISRAELITES

Isaiah called these American Israelites a people "scattered and peeled," and inhabiting a great land "beyond the rivers of Ethiopia" (Africa).[4] Isaiah knew their land would be among "the islands of the sea," and the ancient American prophets knew Isaiah was looking at the western hemisphere where they dwelt.[5]

The Lamanites represent three royal bloodlines—Ephraim and Manasseh (of the tribe of Joseph), and the people of Mulek (of the tribe of Judah), Mulek being a direct descendant of King David.[6]

---

[1]Isaiah 19:25.
[2]Isaiah 11:12.
[3]Isaiah 49:22.
[4]Isaiah 18:1-2.
[5]2 Nephi 10:19-22, *Book of Mormon*, hereafter cited as B. of M.
[6]Helaman 8:21, B. of M.

Contents – Volume 2

Preface

In Volume One we traced the Savior's life from his birth to the critical time when he had only six more months of life on earth. Those last tempestuous six months are in this second volume.

The highlights in Volume One commence with the Savior's birth when some interesting and unusual events occurred both in Judea and in America.

Then we discussed what it must have been like for Mary as she undertook to raise Jesus along with four half-brothers and at least two half-sisters. We also reflected on the feelings of the four half-brothers who rejected Christ during his ministry. Later on, we discovered what happened to them.

Before Jesus was taken to the temple at the age of twelve we find that he had apparently received extensive heavenly training without the knowledge of Mary or Joseph. Later, when John the Baptist appeared on the scene there were many things about him the Jews would never have suspected.

After Jesus was baptized he went into the wilderness to receive further instructions. We learned some interesting things about the three great temptations, and how the Holy Ghost arranged the setting for two of them so Satan could have his "equal opportunity" and Jesus could get on with his ministry.

We learned some new details connected with the Savior's first miracle when he changed water into wine, and discussed the "God-science" connected with the performing of miracles.

Then there was the extremely important question as to why the Jews had been selected to help Jesus get through the ordeal of his torturous redemptive sacrifice. We also learned the things the Jews had been taught in their schools which caused most of them to reject Jesus as an impostor in spite of his many miracles.

As we followed Jesus through his ministry we contemplated the hundreds of miracles he performed. The initial outpouring of miracles occurred right after the first cleansing of the temple, and we saw that he had to hide himself so the people would not acclaim him their King-Messiah and thereby defeat the purpose of his mission. We noted that his miracles included every kind of healing from cleansing lepers to raising the dead. In certain instances—such as raising Lazarus from the dead—he asked the Father's permission, and we noted that when it was granted, he wept because of his gratitude for the Father's love and support in granting his request.

From the time Jesus began selecting his apostles, he taught them and trained them for their great mission. He prayed all night before he ordained them and then he gave them the famous Sermon on the Mount. This is the most simple and practical philosophy of life ever recorded.

At times great throngs from all over the country followed Jesus to hear his teachings and observe his astonishing power to do unbelievable things. Nevertheless, his mission was not to raise up a multitude of admiring curiosity seekers, and he therefore cleansed their ranks every so often by teaching doctrines that sent them away holding their ears and crying out, "Blasphemy! Blasphemy!" On one occasion he asked the apostles if they too were going to run away.

Jesus taught his apostles the divine art of story telling by introducing them to many beautiful parables. It is difficult to remember abstract principles, but it is easy to remember the moral of a good story. Each of these simple narratives contained many esoteric or hidden teachings which Jesus later explained to his apostles after the crowds had gone.

We saw that Jesus sometimes created such great hostility among those who opposed him that on at least four occasions he had to veil the eyes of those who tried to stone him or throw him over a cliff. On these occasions he could hide himself and quietly walk out from among them. As we shall see in Volume Two, it was astonishing to the apostles that Jesus did not use this power when Judas and the soldiers of the high priest came to arrest him.

But this is getting ahead of our story. It is time to move on to the unfolding of the narrative in this second volume.

CHAPTER 26

JESUS BEGINS THE LAST SIX MONTHS OF HIS MORTAL LIFE

When the Feast of the Tabernacles came to a close during the early part of October, Jesus knew that his mortal life would only extend into the future about another 180 days. In a sense, the shadow of the cross and his rendezvous with an eternal destiny lay directly over the horizon.

Of course, the Savior's apostles were completely oblivious to all of this. As faithful Pharisees, they had been trained during their youth to believe that the stupendous prophecy of Daniel must be fulfilled which said that after the rise of the fourth empire—the kingdom of iron—God would send his Messiah to set up his own kingdom that would crush the iron kingdom and restore the Jews to their rightful inheritance as the chosen people of the Almighty.[1]

If someone had told the apostles that God's kingdom of power seen by Daniel was still nearly 2,000 years in the future, they would have denounced it as rank heresy.

After all, their Messiah had arrived. Jesus was the Christ. The power of God was in him. Had he not healed thousands of afflicted people, provided miraculous food to feed thousands more? Had he not cast out devils, walked on the sea and raised the dead?

Of course, the rabbis had plainly taught that miracles were not positive proof that he was the Messiah. They said the real proof

---

[1] Daniel 2:44.

would come only when he called down fire and brimstone to destroy the Romans.[2]

But to the apostles, that was no problem. It was simply a matter of time.

Not only did they have a testimony that Jesus was that promised Messiah, but Peter, James and John had stood in the presence of the glorified Moses and Elijah on the Mount of Transfiguration and had already received the sacred keys for the ministry of God's kingdom under Christ's direction.[3]

THE APOSTLES PERCEIVED JESUS TO BE THE KING-MESSIAH NOT KNOWING THAT HE HAD TO COME FIRST AS THE REDEEMER-MESSIAH

As our story unfolds, we shall see what a shock it was to the apostles to learn that their beloved Jesus was not yet the King-Messiah. At this point he had come in the role of the Redeemer-Messiah who had to be crucified and resurrected before he could take his rightful place beside the Father as the glorious King-Messiah whom the apostles had prematurely assumed that he was.

But we have already seen that the apostles' mistaken identity of the Savior was all part of a divine plan to fulfill the righteous purposes of God.[4] It was not the Father's intention to illuminate the minds of the apostles and share with them the heavenly secret concerning the true identity of Jesus until after the resurrection.

As we have already noted in Volume One, Jesus had told the apostles about his crucifixion and resurrection, but Luke explains:

"They understood none of these things, and this saying was hid from them, neither knew they the things which were spoken."[5]

---

[2]See vol. I, p. 84.
[3]See vol. I, pp. 411-412.
[4]See vol. I, pp. 87-89.
[5]John 18:34.

What a glorious revelation it must have been when the Holy Ghost subsequently quickened their memories, so they could recall what Jesus had said.[6] Only then did they begin to fully understand the sublime meaning of all they had seen and heard.

THE SAVIOR'S QUIET INTERLUDE BETWEEN THE FEAST OF THE TABERNACLES AND THE FEAST OF DEDICATION

During the three months between the Feast of the Tabernacles, which ended early in October, and the Feast of Dedication in December, Jesus appears to have circulated through many of the tiny towns and villages which were in the immediate vicinity of Jerusalem.

It is entirely possible that Jesus made his headquarters during most of this time at the home of his beloved friends, Mary, Martha and Lazarus. We know that Jesus had gone to this home just before the Feast of the Tabernacles and probably stayed there throughout his visit.[7]

Bethany was a convenient hub from which Jesus could visit all the surrounding towns, and we presume that undoubtedly these three months provided the most peaceful and pleasant interlude of his entire ministry. The circumstances would indicate that he not only had his apostles with him but he enjoyed the companionship of his beloved friends, Mary, Martha and Lazarus.

THE SAVIOR'S TEACHINGS IN THE VICINITY OF JERUSALEM

None of the Gospel writers make a studied attempt to describe the Savior's activities in exact chronological order during this period. Instead, they focused on certain important themes we believe he emphasized in this final phase of his ministry around Jerusalem. These would have included the following teachings which deserve to be repeated even though some of them may have been mentioned in Volume One.

---

[6]John 14:26.
[7]See vol. I, p. 448.

FOLLOW THE SAVIOR

The foremost gospel rule is to follow in the Savior's footsteps. This requires that we commit ourselves to obeying the Father's commandments and controlling the appetites of the flesh. He wanted us to know that taking up his cross is not the burden that many have supposed, but the pathway to happiness. And the reward for the effort is eternal life. So Jesus said:

"Whosoever will come after me, let him deny himself, and take up his cross, and follow me."[8]

Walking in the footsteps of the Savior becomes easier as we develop a proper perspective on the priorities of life. He who selfishly makes his own life the center of the universe will not only lose the kind of life he is seeking, but he will also lose his eternal place in the universe which God has prepared for him. Jesus said:

"For whosoever will save his life shall lose it; but whosoever shall lose his life for my sake and the gospel's, the same shall save it."[9]

And just to emphasize the point, he added:

"For what shall it profit a man, if he shall gain the whole world, and lose his own soul?"[10]

The bottom line for each individual is the price a person is willing to pay to gratify certain aspirations. When people are focused on satisfying immediate physical gratifications, they may be paying a very high price for passing phantoms. God's goals for mankind are eternal and real. So every individual must answer this question:

"What shall a man give in exchange for his soul?"[11]

---

[8]Mark 8:34.
[9]Mark 8:35.
[10]Mark 9:36.
[11]Mark 8:37.

IS IT REALLY WORTH IT?

Jesus provided a warning which each of us should consider before answering this question. He said:

"Whosoever therefore shall be ashamed of me and of my words in this adulterous and sinful generation; of him also shall the Son of man be ashamed, when he cometh in the glory of his Father with the holy angels."[12]

We cannot help wondering what it means to be ashamed of Jesus.

The Savior knew that many would look at the Savior's plan of happiness and say: "It is just too much. It involves too many disciplines, too many meetings, too many calls to service, too many inconveniences, and too many restraints on the fun things of life." Then they add, "Maybe fun has its temptations, but we don't want to miss anything."

In the final analysis, it is a question of attitudes. Jesus knew that all mankind tend to get caught up in their own ambitions and aspirations. For some, their goals will be immediate creature comforts and the physical joys of an exciting, materialistic pattern of life. On the other hand, there are those who catch the larger vision of a heavenly lifestyle that leads to the fullness of joy in a celestial world.

THE LIFESTYLE OF THE SERVANTS OF GOD

Experience demonstrates that the lifestyle of the servants of Christ is the only genuine formula for joy and long-lasting happiness. It is also designed to accommodate the obligations of discipleship. There are many tasks to perform, services to be rendered, and missions to be filled.

It was so with the apostles in the days of Christ. It is equally true with the servants of God today. I once saw the schedule of a modern apostle who was old enough to have retired long ago, but when I

---

[12]Mark 8:38.

realized what he was expected to accomplish on a single trip, I asked the Lord to forgive me for feeling a little overburdened sometimes.

However, it might be said that in spite of our good intentions, there are moments of weariness that sometimes make the burdens of the Lord's lifestyle seem overwhelming. That is the time to turn to the Savior who said:

"Come unto me, all ye that labour and are heavy laden, and I will give you rest.

"Take my yoke upon you, and learn of me; for I am meek and lowly in heart: and ye shall find rest unto your souls.

"For my yoke is easy, and my burden is light."[13]

It was on this same theme that the Psalmist said:

"Cast thy burden upon the LORD, and he shall sustain thee: he shall never suffer the righteous to be moved."[14]

JESUS MOURNS OVER THOSE WHO REVEL IN EVIL RATHER THAN RIGHTEOUSNESS

In contrast to those who lean upon the Lord and ask him to help carry their burdens, there are those who don't carry any burdens at all. In fact, they revel in the snarls of evil.

As Jesus looked around at the great crowds of people who followed him, he observed that those who opposed his message seemed to gravitate together in identifiable groups and inflame one another against the Savior's teachings. Jesus therefore decided to take them on, one group at a time. He said:

"Woe unto you, Pharisees! for ye tithe mint and rue and all manner of herbs, and pass over judgment and the love of God: these ought ye to have done, and not to leave the other undone.

---

[13]Matthew 11:27-30.
[14]Psalms 55:22.

"Woe unto you, Pharisees! for ye love the uppermost seats in the synagogues, and greetings in the markets."[15]

Jesus wanted them to know that their "greatness" was, in reality, so infinitesimal that after they were gone, no one would even know they ever existed. He said:

"Woe unto you, scribes and Pharisees, hypocrites! for ye are as graves which appear not, and the men that walk over them are not aware of them."[16]

JESUS ADDRESSES HIMSELF TO THE LAWYERS

A lawyer listening to the Savior's indictment felt his reproach was spilling over onto his own profession. He said:

"Master, thus saying thou reproachest us also."[17]

Jesus assured him he had guessed correctly. He said:

"Woe unto you also, ye lawyers! for ye laden men with burdens grievous to be borne, and ye yourselves touch not the burdens with one of your fingers."[18]

Originally the law was quite simple, and everyone was required to know the laws and the statutes of the Lord.[19] In other words, everyone was supposed to be a lawyer or a careful student of God's law.

But gradually the learned men of Israel made the law complex and multi-faceted. They introduced a wide variety of interpretations and applications which required the scrutiny of Talmudic scholars to defend a person before the judges. Jesus said that by this means the lawyers had gradually "laden men with burdens grievous to be

---

[15]Luke 11:42-43.
[16]Luke 11:44.
[17]Luke 11:45.
[18]Luke 11:46.
[19]Exodus 18:20.

borne." Even worse, they gloried in all of this complexity, and did not raise a finger to untangle the knots they had tied in the law.

In the past, the prophets had come testifying against this corruption of the law, but these righteous men were stoned. Later, when their prophecies came true, the new leaders would praise them and build monuments to them, but at the same time they would build monuments to those who had killed the prophets. So Jesus said:

"Woe unto you! for ye build the sepulchres of the prophets, and your fathers killed them.

"Truly ye bear witness that ye allow [justify] the deeds of your fathers: for they indeed killed them, and ye build their sepulchres."[20]

Next came the most serious indictment of all. The Savior declared that this vicious cycle of honoring prophets after they were murdered and simultaneously honoring those who killed them was a deadly abscess in the culture of God's people. He wanted these lawyers to know that this cultural cancer might have been eliminated in their own day if they had repented and responded to the message of John the Baptist and the Savior. But they had rejected this opportunity, and therefore Jesus said:

"The blood of all the prophets, which was shed from the foundation of the world, may be required of this generation;

"From the blood of Abel unto the blood of Zacharias [the father of John the Baptist[21]] which perished between the altar and the temple: verily I say unto you, It shall be required of this generation."[22]

And as for the corrupting of the entire body of the original law, he said:

---

[20]Luke 11:47-48.

[21]Joseph Fielding Smith, *Teachings of the Prophet Joseph Smith*, Salt Lake City: Deseret Book, 1967, p. 261.

[22]Luke 11:50-51.

"Woe unto you, lawyers! for ye have taken away the key of knowledge: ye entered not in yourselves, and them that were entering in ye hindered."[23]

CONCERNING THE LAWYERS IN ANCIENT AMERICA

This same problem had arisen among God's people in America, and once again it was attributed to the lawyers. In their history we read:

"Now...those men who sought to destroy [two of God's servants, Alma and Amulek]...were lawyers, who were hired or appointed by the people to administer the law at their times of trials, or at the trials of the crimes of the people before the judges.

"And it came to pass that [as] they began to question Amulek....

"He perceived their thoughts, and he said unto them: 0 ye wicked and perverse generation, ye lawyers and hypocrites, for ye are laying the foundation of the devil; for ye are laying traps and snares to catch the holy ones of God....

"Behold, I say unto you, that the foundation of the destruction of this people is beginning to be laid by the unrighteousness of your lawyers and your judges."[24]

What Amulek had said about the lawyers in America was almost identical with the problem Jesus had encountered among the lawyers in Judah.

THE LAWYERS IN JERUSALEM TRY TO SILENCE JESUS BY MAKING HIM AN OFFENDER FOR A WORD

The shafts of criticism which Jesus shot into the minds of his critics had pricked their hearts, but not unto repentance. The lawyers, the scribes and the Pharisees all began to agitate against him in

---

[23]Luke 11:52.
[24]Alma 10:14-17,27, B. of M.

hopes he would say something incriminating and thereby discredit his testimony against them.

Luke says:

"And as he said these things unto them, the scribes and the Pharisees began to urge him vehemently, and to provoke him to speak of many things:

"Laying wait for him, and seeking to catch something out of his mouth, that they might accuse him."[25]

JESUS TURNS AWAY FROM HIS CRITICS
TO TEACH THE MULTITUDE

Having pronounced his judgment upon the Pharisees and scribes, Jesus turned away from those who were trying to make him an "offender for a word,"[26] and addressed the crowd of people who had gathered to hear the debate. It was a huge crowd, "insomuch that they trode one upon another."[27]

Even though he could not be heard by so vast a throng, at least he could take advantage of what had just transpired and make it a learning experience for his disciples. So he said to them:

"Beware of the leaven of the Pharisees, which is hypocrisy."[28]

Jesus wanted them to know that all these high-minded patrons of pretense and pomposity would one day be exposed for what they really were. All their plots and plans inspired by Satan would be laid bare for all to see. Jesus said:

"There is nothing covered that shall not be revealed, neither hid that shall not be known.

---

[25]Luke 11:53-54.
[26]Isaiah 29:21.
[27]Luke 12:1.
[28]Luke 12:1.

"Wherefore whatsoever ye have spoken in darkness shall be heard in the light; and that which ye have spoken in the ear in closets shall be proclaimed upon the housetops."[29]

LEARNING HOW TO PRAY

On another occasion, the disciples of the Savior came upon him while he was engaged in fervent prayer. Afterwards, one of his disciples said:

"Lord, teach us to pray, as John also taught his disciples."[30]

Jesus then recited to the disciples, and others who were listening, the Lord's prayer just as he had given it in his Sermon on the Mount.[31]

Then he told them a story about a man who had some friends who arrived late at night when he had no bread. Therefore, he went to his neighbor to borrow some bread. However, the neighbor said:

"Trouble me not: the door is now shut, and my children are with me in bed; I cannot rise and give thee."[32]

Jesus then made his point. He said that although the neighbor had replied that he did not want to get out of bed and get the bread, the man kept pleading with his neighbor, until he finally went to the trouble of providing the bread so he could get back to sleep. Jesus concluded by saying that this story illustrates the importance of being persistent in prayer.

HOW IMPORTANT IS IT?

There is a vast organization of God's servants beyond the veil who have the responsibility of executing God's purposes over there just as his servants carry out his will on this side of the veil. Nothing is done automatically. In each case, the petitioner must not only wish

---

[29]Luke 12:2-3.
[30]Luke 11:1.
[31]Matthew 6:9-13.
[32]Luke 11:7.

for something, but make it plain that the need is vital. This is done by fasting, persistent prayer, and righteous living.

Jesus said that when this rule of heaven is followed, "every one that asketh receiveth; and he that seeketh findeth; and to him that knocketh it shall be opened."[33]

But, as Paul pointed out, there "are principalities and powers" beyond the veil[34] that must be overcome before prayers are answered. These are Satan's minions who are the "accuser of the brethren day and night."[35]

The answers to prayers must be "justified" according to the laws of heaven before God's servants can overcome this opposition and demonstrate that the answer to the prayer is truly warranted.

A LESSON FROM DANIEL'S JOURNAL

Daniel describes how he fasted and prayed for three weeks before a messenger of the Lord came to him. This heavenly messenger said:

"From the first day that thou didst set thine heart to understand, and to chasten thyself before thy God, thy words were heard, and I am come for thy words.

"But the prince of the kingdom of [Satan] withstood me one and twenty days: but, lo, Michael, one of the chief princes, came to help me....

"Now I am come."[36]

The importance of persistent prayer was emphasized in a later parable where Jesus told about a widow who importuned an unjust judge until he finally grew weary of her constant petitioning and

---

[33]Luke 11:10.
[34]Ephesians 6:12.
[35]Revelation 12:10.
[36]Daniel 10:12-14.

"avenged" those who had wronged her, just so she wouldn't bother him any more. Jesus said the point he wanted to make was that "Men ought always to pray, and not to faint."[37]

A FUTURE VISION IN WHICH GOD WILL REVEAL ALL SECRETS

Whenever multitudes of the Savior's followers crowded around him to ask questions and hear his explanations, Jesus would often share some of his choicest teachings. These moments were not for the world, but for his most faithful disciples. The gems of spiritual wisdom he proclaimed on these occasions might be called excerpts from the Savior's "General Conference" talks.[38]

For example, he told them about a heavenly device by which everything which happens is recorded. No document, no speech, and no act, is lost. Whether for good or evil, all of these are on the heavenly record.

Of course, as far as individuals are concerned, the greatest blessing of the Savior's gospel program, is that private sins can be "blotted out" from this heavenly record.[39]

But all human offenses that are not blotted out through repentance, baptism, and the atoning sacrifice of the Savior will be shown in full color and three dimensions when the Lord reveals the history of the world the way the heavens recorded it.

In a modern revelation, the Lord reveals just how detailed and comprehensive this great revelation will be. It will be shown in a great millennial conference to all the hosts of mankind who have inhabited the earth since the days of Adam:

"And then shall the first angel again sound his trump in the ears of all living, and reveal the secret acts of men, and the mighty works of God in the first thousand years.

---

[37]Luke 18:1-7.
[38]Luke 12:1.
[39]Acts 3:19; Doctrine and Covenants 109:34; 98:44.

"And then shall the second angel sound his trump, and reveal the secret acts of men, and the thoughts and intents of their hearts, and the mighty works of God in the second thousand years—

"And so on, until the seventh angel shall sound his trump; and he shall stand forth upon the land and upon the sea, and swear in the name of him who sitteth upon the throne, that there shall be time no longer; and Satan shall be bound, that old serpent, who is called the devil, and shall not be loosed for the space of a thousand years."[40]

ONE SIN WHICH CANNOT BE FORGIVEN

From time to time, Jesus would mention one sin that cannot be forgiven. Let us review once more this teaching which Jesus wanted his disciples to thoroughly understand.

"And whosoever shall speak a word against the Son of man, it shall be forgiven him: but unto him that blasphemeth against the Holy Ghost it shall not be forgiven."[41]

This unpardonable sin against the Holy Ghost is explained in greater detail by the Lord in modern times. He said:

"Thus saith the Lord concerning all those who know my power, and have been made partakers thereof, and suffered themselves through the power of the devil to be overcome, and to deny the truth and defy my power—

"They are they who are the sons of perdition, of whom I say that it had been better for them never to have been born;

"For they are vessels of wrath, doomed to suffer the wrath of God, with the devil and his angels in eternity;

"Concerning whom I have said there is no forgiveness in this world nor in the world to come—

---

[40]Doctrine and Covenants, 88:108-110.
[41]Luke 12:10.

"Having denied the Holy Spirit after having received it, and having denied the Only Begotten Son of the Father, having crucified him unto themselves and put him to an open shame.

"These are they who shall go away into the lake of fire and brimstone, with the devil and his angels—

"And the only ones on whom the second death shall have any power;

"Yea, verily, the only ones who shall not be redeemed in the due time of the Lord, after the sufferings of his wrath."[42]

From this we learn five things:

1. The only individuals who can commit the "unpardonable sin" are those who have been quickened by the Holy Ghost so that they have been able to see the heavens opened and have a scientific knowledge of the reality of God's glory and power.

2. Having received this marvelous privilege, they then sin against this heavenly knowledge, or the things they have witnessed under the quickening influence of the Holy Ghost, and deny what they know to be true.

3. This involves coming out in open defiance against the power of God by denying the divinity of Jesus Christ, and putting him to open shame.

4. Such individuals are declared sons of perdition and are cast into outer darkness to suffer with Satan and his angels FOREVER.

5. All others who reject the Savior's atonement and die in their sins must also go into outer darkness, but they only remain long enough to suffer until they have paid for their sins. They are then brought forth to receive whatever degree of glory is appropriate for them.

---

[42]Doctrine and Covenants 76:31-38.

WHEN IS ENOUGH, ENOUGH?

Finally, we come to another theme, which Jesus repeated from time to time, concerning wealth. The subject came up when one of the Savior's "company" asked Jesus to settle a dispute between himself and his brother over their inheritance. The Savior refused, saying:

"Take heed, and beware of covetousness: for a man's life consisteth not in the abundance of the things which he possesseth."[43]

One cannot help but ask, of what SHOULD a man's life consist? When we think of those we consider truly great, it is always in terms of their capacity for service, the capacity to discover and share knowledge, the capacity to love, and the capacity to build that which will enrich and bless mankind.

The wealth of the earth is part of the human legacy from a loving Creator, but having the right attitude toward these bounties—whether from the mine or from the harvest—becomes an important part of the human stewardship.

In Volume One we quoted the prophet Jacob, one of the American prophets, who described what our attitude should be. He declared:

"But before ye seek for riches, seek ye for the kingdom of God.

"And *after* ye have obtained a hope in Christ ye shall obtain riches, *if* ye seek them; and ye will seek them for the intent to do good—to clothe the naked, and to feed the hungry, and to liberate the captive, and administer relief to the sick and the afflicted."[44]

Building industries, cultivating farms and structuring networks of distribution through business empires are a great blessing to the

---

[43]Luke 12:15.
[44]Jacob 2:18-19, B. of M. (emphasis added).

human family since they not only provide employment but life's necessities. Nevertheless, all those who begin to accumulate wealth and influence need to know when enough is enough."

We have a friend who is a billionaire, but he is far from blessed. He is on a money-making merry-go-round and can't get off. Under these circumstances, he says his wealth is a curse, a burden, and a continuous worry.

Jesus described such a man. He was obsessed with the passion to build bigger and better, get more, and always promised that some day he would take his "ease" and do all the good he had intended to do. But according to the parable, God said unto him:

"Thou fool, this night thy soul shall be required of thee: then whose shall those things be, which thou hast provided?

"So is he that layeth up treasure for himself, and is not rich toward God."[45]

The Lord is simply saying that in the world of enterprise, fame and fortune, the wise man will combine doing good with making money, and in the end will know when "enough is enough."

* * * *

TOPICS FOR REFLECTION AND DISCUSSION

1. Describe what you think it means to follow in the Savior's footsteps. What do you think Jesus meant when he said "to take up the cross"? What do you think it meant to lose one's life for the Savior's sake and thereby save one's life in eternal glory?

2. Have you ever thought what it would be like to have the Savior ashamed of you when he presents you to the Father? In what way would you say our burdens are lightened when we take them to the Lord? In what way is the Savior's "yoke" easy to bear?

---

[45]Luke 12:20-21.

3. The Savior had some rather harsh things to say about many of the lawyers of that day. What were some of his criticisms?

4. Did professional lawyers have some of these same proclivities among the Christians in America? Did the prophet who criticized them also include corrupt judges?

5. Do people need to be taught how to pray? Jesus taught his listeners something about prayer they may have never considered. What was it? Have you ever thought about how prayer sets in motion heavenly machinery?

6. Are God's servants organized on the other side of the veil the same way they are organized here? What do we learn from Daniel's experience in praying?

7. Is every human act—both good and bad—recorded in heaven? Will these be shown someday for all the world to see?

8. How can you blot out those things from your record that you do not want to have shown? Everybody makes mistakes, but can the Savior help us clean up our lives as we go along? What must we do to achieve it?

9. There is one sin which cannot be forgiven or blotted out. What is that? However, not everyone has seen enough or been honored by God sufficiently to be able to commit this offense. What must people have received through the Holy Ghost before they can commit the unpardonable sin? What do they do that makes their offense "unpardonable"?

10. Some people spend their lives seeking riches but never find happiness. In what way did the prophet Jacob say a person could have both? What is the first thing he said a person must do? How do you think a person can tell when "enough is enough"?

*   *   *   *

CHAPTER 27

JESUS ATTENDS THE FEAST OF DEDICATION AND USES A MIRACLE TO ESCAPE BEING STONED

By this time it was getting close to the winter season in Judea. Some years they even enjoyed the excitement of a little snow. Modern tourists buy picture post cards showing up to six inches of snow in Jerusalem.

And among the Jews, this was a season for a special celebration. It was to commemorate the glorious events of nearly two centuries earlier when the Jews had gained a season of independence and rededicated their temple. They therefore called this celebration the Feast of Dedication.

HOW THE JEWS ESCAPED FROM THE CRUEL CAPTIVITY OF ANTIOCHUS EPIPHANES

To go back in history, it will be recalled that Alexander the Great had conquered the massive Persian empire and ruled everything from Greece to western India. However, when he suddenly died in 323 B.C. at the age of only 33, his empire was divided among his generals.

Judea, along with Syria and the eastern Mediterranean states, fell under the rule of a Greek general named Seleucus. He established the Seleucid dynasty, and it was his descendant, Antiochus Epiphanes, who ruled from 175-164 B.C.[1] This cruel and oppressive

---

[1]Menahem Stern, *History of Israel*, Jerusalem: Keter Books, 1973, p. 103.

monarch decided to compel all the countries under his dominion to adopt the Greek gods and institute the Greek sacrifices.

King Antiochus sent agents to Jerusalem with specific instructions to annihilate Judaism. An image of Zeus was erected in the Holy of Holies of the temple, and a sow was sacrificed on the altar of the temple in honor of Zeus.[2]

These desecrations of the temple finally ignited a revolt among the Jews, which was led by the Hasmonean family. The five Hasmonean brothers called themselves the Maccabees—the hammers—who would hammer out freedom for the Jews.[3]

THE GREAT VICTORY

In 165 B.C., the Jews won an important battle and recaptured Jerusalem. Judas, one of the five Maccabean brothers, led the assault, and as soon as the Jews gained possession of the city, he had all of the heathen shrines demolished. The priests then cleansed and refurbished the temple so that it could be rededicated that year.[4]

Thus the great Jewish Feast of Dedication was born. It lasted eight days and was a time of great rejoicing. During the refurbishing of the temple, the priests had found a single jar of consecrated oil, still bearing the seal of the earlier high priest. This was only enough to illuminate the interior of the temple for one day and night, but a miracle occurred when the people watched the extension of this supply of oil for the full duration of the feast—eight days and nights.[5]

Thereafter, this miracle was commemorated during the Feast of Dedication by having the entire temple brilliantly lighted. In fact, it became known as the "Festival of Lights" or the Hanukkah (sometimes written "Chanukah").

---

[2]Josephus, *Antiquities of the Jews*, Book XII, ch. 5:3-4.
[3]Menahem Stern, *History of Israel*, pp. 105-107.
[4]Ibid., p. 105.
[5]Joan Camay, *The Temple of Jerusalem*, New York: Holt, Rinehart and Winston, 1975, p. 122.

Because this celebration coincides with the traditional season of Christmas, it is a time of celebration for both Jews and Christians.

JESUS AND HIS APOSTLES ATTEND
THE FEAST OF DEDICATION

Since the Savior's ministry had been in the vicinity of Jerusalem during the previous three months, it was more convenient than in the past for Jesus to assemble his apostles and attend the Feast of Dedication.[6]

For this particular feast, John becomes our principal informant. In fact, John begins reciting an important series of events in chapter 9 of his Gospel, and then reveals clear over in chapter 10 that he is talking about the Feast of Dedication. This enlightening passage suddenly appears as follows:

"And it was at Jerusalem the feast of dedication, and it was winter."[7]

We then go back to John, chapter 9, to find out what had been happening at this Feast of Dedication.

"WHO DID SIN, THIS MAN OR HIS PARENTS?"

Soon after Jesus and his disciples arrived at the temple, they happened to pass by a blind beggar on the sabbath day. As the disciples looked at the beggar they said to Jesus:

"Master, who did sin, this man, or his parents, that he was born blind?"[8]

These disciples were aware that in some instances the circumstances of life here on earth are related to actions that occurred in the pre-existence—our First Estate—where we were

---

[6]John 10:22.
[7]John 10:22.
[8]John 9:2.

tested before coming into this life.[9] It may be recalled that when Jeremiah tried to avoid serving as a prophet, the Lord told him:

"Before I formed thee...[in the womb] I knew thee; and before thou camest forth out of the womb I sanctified thee, and I ordained thee a prophet."[10]

The apostles were well aware of the doctrine that the Father's children come into this mortal life with "trailing clouds of glory"[11] from our pre-earth life. But what if a person had faltered during the pre-existence? In the case of this blind man, was it possible that he had been born blind as a result of his own actions in the spirit world before he was born? Or was it the fault of his parents who had sinned in this life? Jesus replied:

"Neither hath this man sinned, nor his parents: but that the works of God should be made manifest in him."[12]

Jesus then set about so that the "works of God" would be put into operation immediately. John says:

"When he had thus spoken, he spat on the ground, and made clay of the spittle, and he anointed the eyes of the blind man with the clay,

"And said unto him, Go, wash in the pool of Siloam, (which is by interpretation, Sent.) He went his way therefore, and washed, and came seeing."[13]

Jesus and his disciples went on their way, and when this former blind beggar was observed by the people they asked, "How were thine eyes opened?"[14]

---

[9]Abraham 3:25-26, P. of G. P.
[10]Jeremiah 1:5.
[11]William Wordsworth, "Ode to the Intimations of Immortality."
[12]John 9:3.
[13]John 9:6-7.
[14]John 9:10.

The man explained what had happened, and said Jesus had restored his sight. But Jesus was nowhere to be seen, so the people took the man to the Pharisees and had him relate what had happened. The Pharisees were highly indignant and said:

"This man is not of God, because he keepeth not the sabbath day. Others said, How can a man that is a sinner do such miracles? And there was a division among them.

"They say unto the blind man again, What sayest thou of him, that he hath opened thine eyes? He said, He is a prophet."[15]

Still refusing to believe the former blind man, the Pharisees questioned his parents. Was he really born blind? The parents assured them that he was. Then they asked them what made it possible for him to see. The parents perceived that the Pharisees were trying to snare them, and so they said:

"He is of age; ask him."[16]

The Pharisees were at a dead end. The man was born blind; Jesus put spittle and clay on his eyes and told him to go to the nearby pool of Siloam to wash it off. He did so, and immediately he could see for the first time in his life. It seemed quite wonderful, but it was done on the sabbath day, so that by their interpretation it had to be evil. Finally, they said to the man:

"Give God the praise: we know that this man is a sinner.

"He answered and said, Whether he be a sinner or no, I know not: one thing I know, that, whereas I was blind, now I see."[17]

This irrefutable fact demoralized the Pharisees, and because they could find no explanation they ended up reviling the man and then

---

[15]John 9:16-17.
[16]John 9:21.
[17]John 9:24-25.

endeavored to cover up their frustration by bearing their testimony concerning Moses. They said:

"We are Moses' disciples. We know that God spake unto Moses: as for this fellow [who had performed the healing], we know not from whence he is.

"The man answered and said unto them, Why herein is a marvelous thing, that ye know not from whence he is, and yet he hath opened mine eyes.

"Now we know that God heareth not sinners: but if any man be a worshipper of God, and doeth his will, him he heareth.

"Since the world began was it not heard that any man opened the eyes of one that was born blind. If this man were not of God, he could do nothing."[18]

JESUS IDENTIFIES HIMSELF TO THE FORMER BLIND MAN

A short time later Jesus learned that the Pharisees had excommunicated this man from his synagogue. The Savior therefore sought him out, and when he found him, he said:

"Dost thou believe on the Son of God?

"He answered and said, Who is he, Lord, that I might believe on him?

"And Jesus said unto him, Thou hast both seen him, and it is he that talketh with thee.

"And he said, Lord, I believe. And he worshipped him."[19]

---

[18]John 9:28-33.
[19]John 9:35-38.

Then a very interesting thing happened. Some of the Pharisees were still standing around and heard this rather amazing conversation. As they listened, Jesus said:

"I am come into this world, that they which see not might see; and that they which see might be made blind.

"And some of the Pharisees which were with him heard these words, and said unto him, Are we blind also?

"Jesus said unto them, If ye were blind, ye should have no sin: but now ye say, We see; therefore your sin remaineth."[20]

To the minds of the Pharisees, these words probably conjured up the possibilities of an intriguing mystery that they must discuss further. They seem to have wandered away completely oblivious to the manifestations of God's power that had been demonstrated so dramatically before their eyes that day.

THE GOOD SHEPHERD

When Jesus was alone with his disciples, he felt this was an appropriate time to stress the importance of distinguishing between a good shepherd and those thieves and robbers such as the Pharisees who would raid the flock.

He pointed out that the porter at the gate, or their Heavenly Father who has custody of the sheep, only opens the gate to the true shepherd who calls the sheep by name. Jesus said the Father's sheep would recognize the voice of the true shepherd and follow him.

Unless one has been to the Holy Land and watched the shepherds literally call out their sheep in this manner, one may not fully appreciate this symbolism. During the night, the sheep of several shepherds are herded together in a common enclosure. The following morning, each shepherd comes to call out his sheep. Only

---

[20]John 9:39-41.

those which belong to him respond to his call. The rest remain until they hear the familiar voice of their own shepherd.

These shepherds have a great affection for their sheep. They give each one a name and teach the sheep to follow their own shepherd from the time they are lambs. These sheep are not driven. They follow along behind their shepherds!

Knowing this gives realistic significance to the Savior's statement that:

"My sheep hear my voice, and I know them, and they follow me."[21]

THE APOSTLES FAIL TO ASK JESUS ABOUT HIS OTHER SHEEP

A short time before this, Jesus had been in prayer and conversed with his Father about the Israelites, or sheep of the Lord's flock in America. At that precise time, the majority of the American Israelites were much more apostate than the Jews, but Jesus knew that in about three months there would be such a widespread destruction and cleansing of the American Israelites that the remnant would sorely repent and, eventually, every person known to be on the American continent would become members of the Savior's church.[22]

So it is understandable why Jesus would want to tell his disciples in Jerusalem about these other sheep in America. However, the Father forbade him to do so unless his Jewish apostles asked about them. Therefore, Jesus was only allowed to say:

"Other sheep I have, which are not of this fold: them also I must bring, and they shall hear my voice; and there shall be one fold, and one shepherd."[23]

---

[21]John 10:27.
[22]4 Nephi 1:2, B. of M.
[23]John 10:16.

As we have mentioned earlier, Jesus waited expectantly for the slightest sign of intellectual curiosity or a direct response to the Spirit that would induce them to say, "What other sheep?"

But nothing happened. Therefore the Jewish disciples missed the opportunity of hearing about the American Christians and also about the Lost Ten Tribes whom Jesus was planning to visit after his resurrection.[24]

When Jesus visited his American saints, he described how frustrated he was when his apostles would not pick up on his words and ask him about his "other sheep." Here is what he later said to the Christians in America:

"And not at any time hath the Father given me commandment that I should tell it unto your brethren at Jerusalem [concerning you].

"Neither at any time hath the Father given me commandment that I should tell unto them concerning the other tribes of the house of Israel, whom the Father hath led away out of the land.

"This much did the Father command me, that I should tell unto them:

"That other sheep I have which are not of this fold; them also I must bring, and they shall hear my voice; and there shall be one fold, and one shepherd.

"And now, because of stiffneckedness and unbelief they understood not my word; therefore I was commanded to say no more of the Father concerning this thing unto them."[25]

---

[24]3 Nephi 16:1-4, B. of M.
[25]3 Nephi 15:14-18, B. of M.

JESUS DENOUNCES THE SCRIBES, PHARISEES, SADDUCEES, AND PRIESTS

Now Jesus had something to say about the Pharisees, the scribes, the priests and the Sadducees. He boldly identified them as "hirelings," and cowardly hirelings at that. Said he:

"He that is an hireling... seeth the wolf coming, and leaveth the sheep, and fleeth: and the wolf catcheth them, and scattereth the sheep. The hireling fleeth, because he is an hireling, and careth not for the sheep."[26]

Jesus wanted them to distinguish between the hireling and the good shepherd who loves his sheep. He said:

"I am the good shepherd, and know my sheep, and am known of mine. As the Father knoweth me, even so know I the Father: and I lay down my life for the sheep...."[27]

Now Jesus shares with us two precious passages of scripture that we will carefully consider when we come to the account of the crucifixion. He said:

"Therefore doth my Father love me, because I lay down my life, that I might take it again. No man taketh it from me, but I lay it down of myself. I have power to lay it down, and I have power to take it again."[28]

The most astounding thing about the crucifixion is that Jesus could have come down from that cross at any time during those six torturous hours. He had the power to do it, but he had promised the Father he would drink to the dregs this horrible ordeal.[29] And he did.

---

[26]John 10:12-13.
[27]John 10:14-15.
[28]John 10:17-18.
[29]Matthew 26:42.

At this juncture, the scripture says a great contention erupted among the people. Some said:

"He hath a devil, and is mad; why hear ye him?

"Others said, These are not the words of him that hath a devil. Can a devil open the eyes of the blind?"[30]

This last verse refers back to the healing of the blind man in John, chapter 9.

THE PLOT TO KILL JESUS AT
THE FEAST OF DEDICATION

As the Feast of Dedication came to a conclusion, Jesus prepared to close his ministry at Jerusalem until he would return for the climactic week of his life a little over three months later. But Jesus was prevented from leaving. John writes:

"Then came the Jews round about him, and said unto him, How long dost thou make us to doubt? If thou be the Christ, tell us plainly."[31]

The Pharisees and many others who hated Jesus wanted him to testify against himself. They wanted him to say, "I am the Christ," since that would be interpreted as blasphemy and give them an excuse to stone him. But instead, he always seemed to say words that meant the same thing but he did not articulate the precise phrase these legalistic Pharisees needed for a capital offense.

So when they asked him to tell them plainly if he were the Christ, he said:

"I told you, and ye believed not: the works that I do in my Father's name, they bear witness of me. But ye believe not, because ye are not of my sheep, as I said unto you.

---

[30]John 10:20-21.
[31]John 10:24.

"My sheep hear my voice, and I know them....My Father, which gave them me, is greater than all; and no man is able to pluck them out of my Father's hand.

"I and my Father are one."[32]

The Pharisees pricked up their ears. Had he blasphemed? Of course! He had not quite said the fatal words, "I am Christ," but they heard him say, "I and my Father are one." Was that close enough? The lawyers and Pharisees agreed that it was. Therefore, John says:

"The Jews took up stones again to stone him."[33]

"FOR WHICH OF THE WORKS DO YE STONE ME?"

Under the ancient law, when a person was stoned, the critical question was who would cast the first stone. This had to be one of the witnesses. When everybody picked up some rocks, there was usually a pause while they waited for someone to take the responsibility of casting the first stone.

This pause was a significant advantage to Jesus. It allowed him sufficient time to divert their attention. He did this by asking them if they were sure they knew why they were stoning him. In that highly critical moment the Savior said:

"Many good works have I shewed you from my Father; for which of those works do ye stone me?

"The Jews answered him, saying, For a good work we stone thee not; but for blasphemy; and because that thou, being a man, makest thyself God.

"Jesus answered them, Is it not written in your law, I said, Ye are gods?"[34]

32[John 10:25-30.](#)
33[John 10:31.](#)
34[John 10:32-34.](#)

Jesus was quoting Psalms 82:6 wherein the Psalmist declared, "I have said, YE ARE GODS; and ALL OF YOU ARE CHILDREN OF THE MOST HIGH." Paul later taught the same doctrine to the learned men of Athens when he talked about the one true God, and said, "FOR WE ARE ALSO HIS OFFSPRING."[35] Now these Pharisees were confronted with a scripture of monumental implications.

So Jesus reasoned with them, saying:

"If he called them gods, unto whom the word of God came, and the scripture cannot be broken;

"Say ye of him, whom the Father hath sanctified, and sent into the world, Thou blasphemest; because I said, I am the Son of God?"[36]

And, just to drive his point home he offered a pragmatic test to go along with the scripture, saying:

"If I do not the works of my Father, believe me not. But if I do, though ye believe not me, believe the works: that ye may know, and believe, that the Father is in me, and I in him.

"Therefore they sought again to take him: but he escaped out of their hand."[37]

This was rather amazing. There was a large crowd surrounding Jesus, but all of a sudden he was gone. This leads us to assume that he used the same device of last resort that he had used at the Feast of the Tabernacles.[38] He simply veiled their eyes and thus "escaped out of their hand."[39]

---

[35]Acts 17:28.
[36]John 10:35-36.
[37]John 10:37-39.
[38]John 8:59.
[39]John 10:39.

The apostles knew from experience that "now you see him, now you don't." But it would be interesting to know what the disciples did whenever this phenomenon occurred. No doubt they would realize what had happened as soon as he disappeared, so their task was to quietly retire to some secure place where Jesus could find them and safely join them again.

In this instance, the disciples no doubt rejoiced as he put in his appearance again, but they soon learned that Jesus was planning to take them completely away from Jerusalem.

*   *   *   *

TOPICS FOR REFLECTION AND DISCUSSION

1. Can you recite the circumstances which led to the establishment of the Feast of Dedication? Why is it sometimes called the "Festival of Lights"?

2. How did the Greeks happen to have dominion over the Jews at that time? Why did the five Hasmonean brothers call themselves the Maccabees? What did the name mean?

3. Is it fair to have some of our circumstances in this life determined by what happened in our premortal life? The blind man was told to wash the clay from his eyes in the Pool of Siloam before he could be healed. Was it the clay and the washing that did the healing?

4. What action did the rulers of the synagogue take against the man who had been healed of his blindness? When Jesus heard about it, what did he do to comfort the man?

5. Why do you think Jesus wanted the Jews to know about his "other sheep"? To whom was he referring? What prevented the Jewish apostles from learning about the other sheep at that time? How do we know this was very disappointing to Jesus?

6. How can you distinguish a "good shepherd" in the church? How did Jesus describe a "hireling" who might be assigned to tend the sheep? What does a hireling do when there is danger?

7. Why did the Pharisees want Jesus to come right out and say, "I am the Christ"? Had he said it in the past?

8. What did the Pharisees and scribes determine to do when Jesus said, "I and my Father are one?" On what grounds did they think they were justified? Why were the Jews taken aback when Jesus quoted Psalms 86:2, where it says, "Ye are gods?"

9. When the accusers of Jesus decided Jesus could be convicted before the Sanhedrin, what did they try to do? Apparently what did Jesus do in order to escape? Had Jesus done this before?

10. By what means do you think Jesus and his apostles managed to get together again? Did they stay around Jerusalem?

* * * *

CHAPTER 28

JESUS GOES BACK TO PEREA WHERE HIS MINISTRY BEGAN

After the Feast of Dedication was over, Jesus gathered his apostles together and prepared to leave the hostile precincts of Jerusalem. He led his followers eastward toward the place where the Savior had first met John the Baptist and began to select his disciples. We read that Jesus:

"Went away again beyond Jordan into the place [Bethabara] where John at first baptized; and there he abode.

"And many resorted unto him, and said, John did no miracle: but all things that John spake of this man were true.

"And many believed on him there."[1]

THE MINISTRY IN PEREA

Jesus was now in the area where John the Baptist had opened up his ministry and where Jesus had been baptized. Not far away was the wilderness where Jesus had fasted forty days and nights and lived in suspended animation as he communed with his Heavenly Father.[2] According to Mark, it was there that angels ministered unto him.[3]

This was also the place where John the Baptist had pointed to Jesus and testified that he was the Christ.[4]

---

[1]John 10:40-42.
[2]JST Matthew 4:2.
[3]Mark 1:13.
[4]John 1:36.

Now, after nearly three years, Jesus was back.

This region "beyond Jordan" was called Perea and was part of the domain of Herod Antipas. It was in Perea that John the Baptist had castigated Herod for his incestuous marriage to his brother's wife. It was here he was arrested and held in prison. It was not far from here that most authorities believe John was finally executed—at the fortress of Macherus overlooking the Dead Sea.

The Savior's return to Perea turned out to be very gratifying both for Jesus and the people of this region. Matthew says:

"Jesus... came into the coasts of Judaea beyond Jordan; And great multitudes followed him; and he healed them there."[5]

JESUS BLESSES THE CHILDREN

Crowds always attract children, and when the disciples saw their parents trying to squeeze through to get up front where Jesus could touch their little ones, and bless them, the disciples restrained them. According to the Inspired Version, the disciples told the parents:

"There is no need, for Jesus hath said, such shall be saved."[6]

Nevertheless, Jesus saw what was happening and said:

"Suffer little children, and forbid them not, to come unto me: for of such is the kingdom of heaven.

"And he laid his hands on them, and departed thence."[7]

THE SEVENTIES RETURN

It is not indicated how long the seventies were out on their special mission, but it is usually presumed to have been about three months.

---

[5]Matthew 19:1-2.
[6]JST Matthew 19:13.
[7]Matthew 19:14-15.

Since they were sent out just before Jesus left Capernaum, they should have been returning shortly after the Feast of Dedication. But by that time, Jesus had gone to Perea. Nevertheless, because of the Savior's status as a celebrity, they probably had little difficulty discovering where he was.

Like all missionaries, they were anxious to let the Savior know of their great success. They were excited that they were able to perform some of the miracles Jesus had performed. They were especially joyful to tell the Savior that "even the devils are subject unto us through thy name."[8]

It is understandable why these newly ordained ambassadors of the Lord would rejoice in the power that came with their calling. However, Jesus told them there was much more to animate their joy than casting out devils. He said:

"Rejoice that your names are written in heaven."[9]

Jesus knew that these humble servants, who appear to have been selected almost entirely from Galilee, were acting out in their daily lives the very things the ancient prophets had seen in vision or read about in scripture.

Those great men of the past, many of whom were required to labor under much more dangerous and difficult circumstances, wished most fervently that they could have come forth in the days of the blessed Messiah. No doubt Jesus said to the seventy what he had previously said to his apostles:[10]

"Blessed are the eyes which see the things that ye see: For I tell you, that many prophets and kings have desired to see those things which ye see, and have not seen them; and to hear those things which ye hear, and have not heard them."[11]

---

[8]Luke 10:17.
[9]Luke 10:20.
[10]Matthew 13:16-17.
[11]Luke 10:23-24.

Jesus simply wanted his disciples to appreciate that their calling was somewhat envied by God's great prophets who had seen their day in vision.

As we study the four Gospels concerning the ministry in Perea, we gain the impression that this was a pleasant interlude for the Savior. In spite of an occasional encounter with hostile Pharisees, Jesus appears to have been surrounded by friends and believers most of the time.

As a result, we enter into a period which literally blossoms with stories and parables relating to some of the more profound and definitive teachings of Jesus Christ.

THE APOSTLES HEAR DOCTRINES BEYOND THEIR COMPREHENSION

The Savior seems to have been fully aware that many of his teachings were beyond the immediate comprehension of the disciples. Nevertheless, as John states in chapter 14, verse 26, Jesus knew that after his resurrection, the Holy Ghost would reveal to the minds of his disciples the prophecies and important things he had said.

So the Savior's immediate task was to articulate the great truths that needed to be recorded on the heavenly record. When we go through the New Testament and observe how much his disciples did not understand, we can appreciate the importance of this heavenly frame of reference which the Holy Ghost would later provide for them after the resurrection.

THE SECOND COMING

In Perea, Jesus had the task of beginning to unfold the grand spectacle of the *Second* Coming even though his listeners did not yet understand the importance and necessity of the *First* Coming. What Jesus wished to emphasize was the need for the members of his kingdom to be ready when he came to reign in power and glory over the whole earth. He said:

"And ye yourselves [are] like unto men that wait for their lord, when he will return from the wedding; that when he cometh and knocketh, they may open unto him immediately.

"Blessed are those servants, whom the lord when he cometh shall find watching....

"And if he shall come in the second watch, or come in the third watch, and find them so, blessed are those servants."[12]

This is the first time the Savior had suggested that his coming in power and glory might be far in the future. From generation to generation, Jesus wanted every member of his church to assume that his Second Coming was nigh so they would feel motivated to be fully prepared for his glorious return. With this thought in mind, Jesus said:

"And this know, that if the goodman of the house had known what hour the thief would come, he would have watched, and not have suffered his house to be broken through.

"Be ye therefore ready also: for the Son of man cometh at an hour when ye think not."[13]

Peter then spoke up and provided us with clear evidence that the disciples had no idea what the Savior was talking about. Peter said:

"Lord, speakest thou this parable unto us, or even to all?"[14]

The Savior said he will hold ALL those who are made rulers over his kingdom, responsible for feeding each generation of Saints "their portion of meat" so that they will remain faithful and be anxiously awaiting the Savior's return.[15]

---

[12]Luke 12:36-38.
[13]Luke 12:39-40.
[14]Luke 12:41.
[15]Luke 12:42.

THE TASK OF GOD'S OFFICERS IN THE KINGDOM

Concerning these faithful bishops, stake presidents, and general authorities, the Lord said:

"Blessed is that servant, whom his lord when he cometh shall find so doing. Of a truth I say unto you, that he will make him ruler over all that he hath."[16]

Of course the greatest threat to the Lord's kingdom has always been those servants who become slothful in their duties, and have carelessly introduced certain elements of distortion or corruption into the administration of the church.

Jesus was anticipating the long, dark shadow of the great apostasy. He knew it would eventually drive the church into the wilderness. The apostle John, who heard these teachings in Perea, later received a panoramic vision of virtually overwhelming dimensions, in which he saw just how the Savior's church would be corrupted and changed by unworthy servants. However, that was far in the future. In Perea Jesus simply said:

"If that servant say in his heart, My lord delayeth his coming; and shall begin to beat the menservants and maidens, and to eat and drink, and to be drunken;

"The lord of that servant will come in a day when he looketh not for him, and at an hour when he is not aware, and will cut him in sunder, and will appoint him his portion with the unbelievers."[17]

The Savior said there would be a very severe punishment for those servants who deliberately apostatized and sinned against knowledge. A much lighter punishment would be given to those whom they deceived and who sinned without understanding the serious nature of their offenses. He said:

---

[16]Luke 12:43-44.
[17]Luke 12:45-46.

"And that servant, which knew his lord's will, and prepared not himself, neither did according to his will, shall be beaten with many stripes.

"But he that knew not, and [yet] did commit things worthy of stripes, shall be beaten with few stripes. For unto whomsoever much is given, of him shall be much required: and to whom men have committed much, of him they will ask the more."[18]

THE TRUTH DIVIDES

Jesus next attempted to prepare his servants for the season of strife and contention which always occurs when new truth is introduced. Among the righteous the truth unites, but truth threatens the adversary and therefore he stirs up every dark spirit in the earth to oppose it.

Jesus wanted his "rulers" to inform the saints that they must be prepared to see the gospel dividing families, and even causing nations to rise up against one another in war. He said:

"Suppose ye that I am come to give peace on earth? I tell you, Nay; but rather division:

"For from henceforth there shall be five in one house divided, three against two, and two against three.

"The father shall be divided against the son, and the son against the father; the mother against the daughter, and the daughter against the mother; the mother in law against her daughter in law, and the daughter in law against her mother in law."[19]

Jesus wanted his disciples to be prepared for this element of opposition and know how to handle it. In every possible way, they must avoid contention among themselves, and remember that "a soft word turneth away wrath." Nevertheless, when all else fails, they

---

[18]Luke 12:47-48.
[19]Luke 12:51-53.

must be willing to endure the accusations and slander of the evil one and all his imps, even unto death.

DO CALAMITIES ALWAYS SIGNIFY GOD'S PUNISHMENT OF EVIL?

During the ministry in Perea, the Savior discussed a number of topics which he had covered in the earlier part of his ministry. However, since we have already discussed those subjects in Volume One, they will not be repeated here.

One of the new topics brought up in Perea was when Jesus addressed the question of whether or not calamities are the direct results of "evil people getting their just deserts." Often people use this belief as an excuse for shunning the victims of calamities and not helping them with charity and kindness.

Obviously, some calamities, such as the great flood, came in consequence of wickedness. However, Jesus said the very nature of our earthly existence involves calamities from time to time, and his disciples were not to assume that the victims of these catastrophes were necessarily evil people whom God was punishing.

He gave two examples, the last of which was the collapse of a tower overlooking the pool of Siloam in Jerusalem. Concerning it he said:

"Those eighteen, upon whom the tower in Siloam fell, and slew them, think ye that they were sinners above all men that dwelt in Jerusalem?

"I tell you, Nay: but, except ye repent, ye shall all likewise perish."[20]

Jesus did not want his listeners to go away thinking that just because they hadn't been the victims of some calamity, they could jump to the conclusion that they were acceptable to God in their present sinful condition.

---

[20]Luke 13:4-5.

It was appropriate for Jesus to close this discussion with the warning that there is a punishment decreed for every evil act unless the sinner has taken advantage of the heavenly principles of repentance and baptism, so as to gain a forgiveness of sins through the atonement of the Messiah.[21]

ONE TIME WHEN THE SAVIOR'S CRITICS WERE ASHAMED

While in Perea, Jesus healed many sick and afflicted persons just as he had done elsewhere. Among those he healed was a woman with a crooked back who had been bent over for eighteen years. The ruler of the synagogue severely chastised Jesus because he had healed this woman on the sabbath.

Jesus turned on his adversary and said:

"Thou hypocrite, doth not each one of you on the sabbath loose his ox or his ass from the stall, and lead him away to watering?

"And ought not this woman, being a daughter of Abraham, whom Satan hath bound, lo, these eighteen years, be loosed from this bond on the sabbath day?

"And when he had said these things, all his adversaries were ashamed."[22]

As soon as the people saw that their local leaders had been humbled by the Savior's remarks, they felt free to express their true feelings. It says:

"And all the people rejoiced for all the glorious things that were done by him."[23]

---

[21]Luke 13:5.
[22]Luke 13:15-17.
[23]Luke 13:17.

WHY IT IS VITAL FOR MEMBERS OF THE
KINGDOM TO REMAIN VALIANT

At different times Jesus stressed the importance of remaining true and faithful in the kingdom. Some think that once they are baptized and confirmed they can always be treated as fully certified members no matter how far they may have strayed.

Jesus told two stories. one was to demonstrate how much a person loses by neglecting or abusing his standing in the kingdom. The second was to emphasize that there is great rejoicing when a person repents and turns back toward the kingdom, even though his sins may have cost him his original inheritance.

The first story was told when someone asked Jesus the following question, "Lord, are there few that be saved?"

Jesus replied, "Many...will seek to enter in, and shall not be able."[24]

Then he told the story of a man who had locked the door for the night, but there were those who knocked loudly and said:

"Lord, Lord, open unto us; and he shall answer and say unto you, I know you not whence ye are:

"Then shall ye begin to say, We have eaten and drunk in thy presence, and thou hast taught in our streets.

"But he shall say, I tell you, I know you not whence ye are; depart from me, all ye workers of iniquity."[25]

God is loving and forgiving, but all blessings are predicated upon obedience to certain sacred laws. As Jesus has declared in our own day:

---

[24]Luke 13:23-24.
[25]Luke 13:25-27.

"There is a law, irrevocably decreed in heaven before the foundations of this world, upon which all blessings are predicated—

"And when we obtain any blessing from God, it is by obedience to that law upon which it is predicated."[26]

Without obedience, the blessings do not come. In fact, the Lord emphasized that for all those who take their blessings for granted and do not obey the laws, there are heartbreaks awaiting them. He said:

"There shall be weeping and gnashing of teeth, when ye shall see Abraham, and Isaac, and Jacob, and all the prophets, in the kingdom of God, and you yourselves thrust out."[27]

Jesus also wanted to emphasize how many great ones of the earth would be the least in the kingdom of heaven. These are those who used tooth and claw to fight their way to power and notoriety. However, when they are ushered into the next world they find themselves very low on the totem pole. The people in charge of everything in the next life turn out to be those who spent their lives humbly seeking to obey God and serve their fellow men in righteousness. As Jesus explained it:

"And, behold, there are last which shall be first, and there are first which shall be last."[28]

Or, as Jesus said it in another place, according to the Inspired Version:

"But there are many who *make themselves* first, that shall be last, and the last first."[29]

---

[26]Doctrine and Covenants 130:20-21.

[27]Luke 13:28.

[28]Luke 13:30.

[29]JST Mark 10:30 (emphasis added).

THE PARABLE OF THE PRODIGAL SON

Next, Jesus told a different kind of story."[30]

Nearly everyone knows the essential elements of the parable of the prodigal son, but we will summarize the highlights so we can appreciate the important lesson Jesus was trying to teach at the conclusion of this parable.

First of all, Jesus said a younger son asked for his inheritance while his father was still alive. The father gave it to him, even though his request was premature.

The son, you will recall, went out and splurged his inheritance in every direction. Mischievous fellows pretended to be his friends so they could take advantage of his profligacy.

But suddenly this son discovered he was broke. His friends left him when he was reduced to poverty. To make matters worse, a terrible famine struck the land and the once-proud spendthrift was reduced to feeding swine just to survive. Then the scripture says:

"He fain would have filled his belly with the husks that the swine did eat: and no man gave unto him.

"And when he came to himself, he said, How many hired servants of my father's have bread enough and to spare, and I perish with hunger!

"I will arise and go to my father, and will say unto him, Father, I have sinned against heaven, and before thee,

"And am no more worthy to be called thy son: make me as one of thy hired servants."[31]

---

[30]Luke 15:11-32.
[31]Luke 15:16-19.

But Jesus said the profligate son had miscalculated the abundance of love in the heart of his father. His father saw him far down the road, and ran to meet him, rejoicing. Jesus related in considerable detail how the father had his servants kill a fatted calf, and had the prodigal bathed, and dressed in fine clothing. Then he invited the young people of the neighborhood to come and help celebrate his son's return.

Jesus had now made his first point—that the heavens rejoice when a lost sheep is found and returns to those who love him.

Jesus made his second point when he related how the older son returned and was disgusted when he saw all the fuss and excitement being made over this renegade, runaway brother.

This older son went to his father and reminded him how he had worked faithfully; he had honored his father, and performed his duties with fidelity. Yet there had never been any fine parties put on for him. There had been no fatted calf killed, nor any luxurious clothing provided, or even a fine ring.

The father patiently listened to his older son's complaints, and then said just two things. Let us consider them in reverse order. He said:

"It was meet that we should make merry, and be glad: for this thy brother was dead, and is alive again; and was lost, and is found."[32]

But, he had also said:

"Son, thou art ever with me, and *ALL THAT I HAVE* is thine."[33]

THE IMPORTANT HIDDEN LESSON IN THE PARABLE OF THE PRODIGAL SON

Jesus wanted his disciples to know that the Father will always welcome back, with great rejoicing, any member of his kingdom who

---

[32]Luke 15:32.
[33]Luke 15:31 (emphasis added).

has strayed, but when it comes to distributing inheritances, "ALL" that the father has belongs to those who were faithful and valiant.

His children who stray and then come back too late to cultivate the crop and bring in the harvest will receive a loving welcome and a marvelous blessing, but not ALL that the Father has.

This is why Amulek declared:

"For behold, this life is the time for men to prepare to meet God; yea, behold the day of this life is the day for men to perform their labors.

"And now, as I said unto you before, as ye have had so many witnesses, therefore, I beseech of you that ye do not procrastinate the day of your repentance until the end; for after this day of life, which is given us to prepare for eternity, behold, if we do not improve our time while in this life, then cometh the night of darkness wherein there can be no labor performed."[34]

In other words, when the harvest is over, and the opportunity for labor is past, the inheritance must go exclusively to those who produced the harvest. Nevertheless, our Heavenly Father has an abundance of love for all his children. Therefore, with an eye on some future, though lesser harvests, the Father continues to bestow appropriate blessings on his children whether they become full heirs to his kingdom or not.

JESUS IS CRITICIZED FOR MINGLING WITH THOSE CONSIDERED TO BE SINNERS

Before Jesus told the story of the prodigal son, he had responded to certain Pharisees who criticized him for mingling with tax collectors and "sinners." This was an old story with the Savior. He had endured this accusation for nearly two years in Galilee.

Here in Perea, as in Galilee, he had no apology for searching out and associating with people of all kinds, good and bad. Nevertheless,

---

[34]Alma 34:32-33, B. of M.

he did not want to be misunderstood, and therefore he did as he had done on an earlier occasion, he began telling stories. By this time, the apostles could almost anticipate which stories he would tell.

THE FAMOUS STORY OF THE LITTLE LOST SHEEP

The first story was about the man with a hundred sheep, but one became lost. The most strenuous efforts were made to find this stray sheep, and when it was found there was a joyous celebration.

Jesus said it was the same way with the Father's choice sheep. Every one is precious, and that means that whenever one is lost it is a heavenly tragedy. By the same token, when a stray sheep is found and brought back to the fold, it is like finding a treasure. This is so important in the economy of heaven, that Jesus said:

"I say unto you, that likewise joy shall be in heaven over one sinner that repenteth, more than over ninety and nine just persons, which need no repentance."[35]

In this story Jesus did not say that the one lost sheep was any more precious than any of the ninety and nine, but it is the very nature of both God and man to celebrate the recovery of that which was lost. When we stop to think about it, our Heavenly Father has invested aeons of time and careful training in each of us. Even losing a single one of the Father's children is such a monumental loss that recovering one of his lost sheep is a phenomenal achievement.

ONE SEARCH WHICH ATTRACTED THE ATTENTION OF THE WHOLE WORLD

A few years ago, a child fell down an abandoned well shaft. She was still alive when they discovered her whereabouts, and all of a sudden that little girl became the most famous and precious child in the whole world. Huge tunneling machinery was brought in. Mining engineers were assembled. Workers volunteered by the hundreds. People all over the civilized world remained virtually glued to their radio and TV sets in order to get the latest report on that little girl.

---

[35]Luke 15:7.

Finally, they got her out, and she was still alive. What shouts of rejoicing were heard everywhere! Prayers of thanksgiving went up by the millions to thank God she had been saved.

Jesus said everyone knows the joy of finding something they have lost. His second story was about a woman who had her entire security tied up in ten pieces of silver. When she lost one of these precious coins, it threw her into a panic. She lighted a candle and swept the house trying to find it. Suddenly she saw it, and her relief was beyond measure. Jesus said she called her friends and exclaimed:

"Rejoice with me; for I have found the piece which I had lost."[36]

JESUS RECEIVES ANOTHER DEATH THREAT

As we have noted in Volume One, when the fame of Jesus swept up and down the land, Herod Antipas began having nightmares. He had beheaded John the Baptist, and felt certain that Jesus was John's reincarnated spirit that had come back to avenge the Baptist's death.

This prompted a well-meaning person in one of his audiences to warn Jesus. He said:

"Get thee out, and depart hence: for Herod will kill thee."

But Jesus was not intimidated. He replied:

"Go ye, and tell that fox, Behold, I cast out devils, and I do cures to day and to morrow, and the third day I shall be perfected.

"Nevertheless I must walk to day, and to morrow, and the day following: for it cannot be that a prophet perish out of Jerusalem."[37]

When Jesus said, "today" and "tomorrow," he meant today and the immediate future. Jesus still had some work to do and neither Herod nor anyone else would prevent it. He was not yet in

---

[36]Luke 15:9.
[37]Luke 13:31-33.

Jerusalem, and he knew that nothing would happen to him until he came within the precincts of that great city where it was prophesied he would die.[38]

In passing, we note how unusual it was for Jesus to refer to Herod or any dignitary by an uncomplimentary epithet, but after the murder of John the Baptist, Herod was lucky to get by with the Savior merely calling him a "fox."

THE CHIEF OF THE PHARISEES
INVITES JESUS TO DINNER

In Luke, chapter 15, we learn that Jesus was invited to eat at the home of the chief of the Pharisees. It was no small affair because this ruler of the Pharisees in that area had invited many of his friends. And it was held on a sabbath day.

Given these circumstances, Jesus knew he was under the closest scrutiny. The scripture says these strict enforcers of the rabbinical law carefully "watched him."[39] We soon learn that the Savior had not been invited to this banquet as a gesture of kindness, but to beguile him.

It seems the festivities had not progressed very far when Jesus noticed a man nearby who was suffering from a dreadful disease. The scripture calls it "dropsy."[40]

This is a form of edema which is described as the massive accumulation of fluid in the tissues. It is usually in consequence of kidney failure, a congestive heart condition, or a disease of the liver. To relieve the excessive pressure of the liquid in the tissues, tiny incisions were sometimes made, thereby allowing the fluid to exude in small droplets—hence, the name, "dropsy."

---

[38]Luke 13:33; see also JST Luke 13:34.
[39]Luke 14:1.
[40]Luke 14:2.

After seeing the man trying to endure his misery, Jesus did an interesting thing. He turned to his host and the company of dignitaries, and asked:

"Is it lawful to heal on the sabbath day?"[41]

The scripture says, "They held their peace," which was almost like saying, "We dare you to try it." The Savior didn't hesitate. Luke says:

"And he took him, and healed him, and let him go."[42]

The statement that Jesus "let him go," would imply that the man had been brought to the dinner to test Jesus and was not one of the guests.

In any event, the healing was so spectacular that it seems to have left the Pharisee and his guests temporarily speechless. But Jesus knew there would be an outcry of protest at any moment. After all, he had suffered more persecution for healing the sick on the sabbath day than from any other cause. But before this audience could spawn enough indignation to speak out, Jesus anticipated what was in their hearts, and said:

"Which of you shall have an ass or an ox fallen into a pit, and will not straightway pull him out on the sabbath day?

"And they could not answer him again to these things."[43]

THREE UNIQUE STORIES

Jesus had learned long ago that when he had an audience of Pharisees, he could hold their attention with parables. On this particular occasion he took advantage of the situation by telling two more stories.

---

[41]Luke 14:3.
[42]Luke 14:4.
[43]Luke 14:5-6.

The first story was about themselves. Jesus said he had observed that when they were invited to a wedding or some auspicious occasion where the celebration might last several days, they were inclined to seek out the highest, nicest rooms. However, when someone of higher rank arrived, it was obviously very embarrassing to be asked to take one of the more modest rooms in order to make room for the new dignitary.

Jesus suggested that it would be much wiser to ask for a more modest room in the beginning, and then the host could compliment this person by saying, "Friend, go up higher." Jesus suggested that it was always wise to remember that in this life:

"Whosoever exalteth himself shall be abased; and he that humbleth himself shall be exalted."[44]

It is interesting how Jesus talked to these proud Pharisees as though he were a father talking to a teen-age son.

Then he brought up another situation.

He observed that when they had dinners and banquets, they usually invited relatives or well-to-do friends who would feel obligated to return the favor by inviting them to dinner at their houses later.

Jesus suggested that they could gain a great blessing by occasionally holding a dinner for the poor, the needy, and the crippled. He said if they did this, it would be noted in heaven. Furthermore, the very fact that none of these unfortunate people could return the favor, meant that a kindness shown to them would carry extra merit in the final judgment after the resurrection.

At this point, one of the more erudite Pharisees made a pious remark which was probably designed to attract attention to himself. He said:

---

[44]Luke 14:11.

"Blessed is he that shall eat bread in the kingdom of God."[45]

Jesus immediately picked up on this and began describing a situation very similar to the one which confronts the Father when he prepares a great gospel feast for the people. Jesus began by saying:

"A certain man made a great supper, and bade many."[46]

Then he related that even though the highest members of society were told that the dinner was ready, they all sent excuses—too busy, unexpected circumstances, family problems, and so forth.

Jesus said this made the host of the banquet very angry, and so he sent out his servants to gather in the poor, the maimed, the lame and the blind. When there was still room left he had his servants gather in strangers from the highways and byways, and they all partook of the feast.

Meanwhile, the host vowed that all of those proud and haughty friends who had refused his hospitality would never partake of the bounties of his table again.

Whether or not the Pharisees caught the full implication of this parable, we are not told. Nevertheless, Jesus always seemed to leave the Pharisees with a lot to talk about after he was gone.

Having finished his dinner, Jesus left the house of the Pharisee and went out where a great multitude was waiting for him.

*   *   *   *

TOPICS FOR REFLECTION AND DISCUSSION

1. When Jesus went over to Perea beyond Jordan, what are some of the important things the scripture says had happened there? Was he welcomed or rejected? Did he heal any sick? What happened when

---

[45]Luke 14:15.
[46]Luke 14:16.

the parents crowded in to have Jesus bless their children? Why did the apostles think it wasn't necessary for the children to be blessed?

2. When the seventies returned, Bible scholars think they had been gone for about how long? Had they been successful or did the opposition defeat them before they could accomplish their mission?

3. What did Jesus say was even more important than the success of their missionary work? What are the duties of a seventy, both then and now? In what way were the seventies fulfilling this function while they were on their mission?

4. Have you ever wished you might have lived when Jesus was on the earth? Why do you think many of the ancient prophets had this earnest desire? Do you think the apostles and seventies in the Savior's day fully appreciated what a great blessing it was to serve with the Savior, or do you think this realization came upon them later?

5. Why do you think Jesus felt compelled to teach his disciples some doctrines when they obviously could not comprehend them? In what way did Jesus hint that his Second Coming was far distant? Then why has he allowed each generation to think the second coming might be very soon?

6. What negative psychological impact did Jesus say would result from people thinking he had delayed his coming? Give three reasons why you think the preaching of the truth divides people when its ultimate purpose is to unite them.

7. In addition to the cleansing of the earth by the great flood, can you think of any other time when the people suffered destruction as a direct result of their wickedness? But are we to assume that every calamity is merely to punish the wicked?

8. Can you explain why there is more rejoicing over a lost sheep when it is found than the joy expressed over the ninety and nine that are safely in their fold? What does the rescue of the little girl trapped in the abandoned well demonstrate?

9. Why did Herod Antipas want to kill Jesus? Why did Jesus feel he was safe until he reached Jerusalem?

10. Why do you think Jesus took the trouble to suggest to the Pharisees that when they attend sumptuous banquets, they should ask for the more modest rooms rather than the best? Do you think any of these men responded to the Savior's suggestion that they invite the poor and afflicted to a banquet instead of the high and mighty? How does this suggestion apply to us today?

*   *   *   *

CHAPTER 29

JESUS RECEIVES AN EMERGENCY MESSAGE FROM BETHANY: LAZARUS IS DEATHLY ILL

As nearly as we can tell, it was about this time that Jesus received an emergency message from Bethany.

The messenger said he had been sent by Mary and Martha to tell Jesus that their brother, Lazarus, was deathly ill. The apostle John makes a significant comment about this family:

"Now Jesus loved Martha, and her sister, and Lazarus."[1]

We have no background on these three. There is no reference to their parents, and it appears the two sisters and Lazarus were living alone. Authorities tend to believe Martha was the eldest. Mary seems to be next, thereby making Lazarus the youngest.

All the apostles knew of the Savior's affection for this family and they felt reassured when Jesus said:

"This sickness is not unto death, but for the glory of God, that the Son of God might be glorified thereby."[2]

The disciples had a sacred respect for the Savior's commentary on any situation, because they knew he had a mental awareness of

---

[1]John 11:5.
[2]John 11:4.

things that always turned out to be as he described them, even when he was far away from the scene of action.

With the assurance that the situation was not as serious as the messengers had indicated, the disciples assumed that Jesus would continue making his final visit to the many towns and villages of Perea. And that is exactly what he did for two days.[3]

Then Jesus shocked his disciples by saying:

"Let us go into Judaea again."[4]

The disciples were wondering why the Master would deliberately take the risk of returning to the area where he knew there was an ongoing plot to take his life. And it seemed especially strange since Jesus had indicated that the illness of Lazarus was not critical. The disciples tried to dissuade him, saying:

"Master, the Jews of late sought to stone thee; and goest thou thither again?"[5]

THE GREAT RISK IN RETURNING TO BETHANY

At both the recent Feast of the Tabernacles and the Feast of Dedication, the Pharisees and leaders of the Sanhedrin had indeed tried to kill Jesus. At both feasts he was compelled to escape by veiling the eyes of his enemies so that he could pass safely "through the midst of them."[6]

Now the Savior was saying that he was going to Bethany which was practically a suburb of Jerusalem. Bethany was only two miles east of Jerusalem and the disciples had heard there were spies in every quarter waiting for Jesus to come near enough to be killed or arrested. As the disciples expressed their fears about going to Bethany, Jesus gave them a strange answer. He said:

---

[3]John 11:6.
[4]John 11:7.
[5]John 11:8.
[6]John 8:59; 10:39.

"Are there not twelve hours in the day? If any man walk in the day, he stumbleth not, because he seeth the light of this world.

"But if a man walk in the night, he stumbleth, because there is no light in him."[7]

In the Savior's typically subtle manner, he was saying, in effect, "As long as I am with you, you are traveling by my light. And there are twelve hours in the day which means as long as my light is scheduled to be with you, it will guide you, and you can trust in the light of my leadership so you will not stumble. Of course, after I am gone, it will be night, and you will have to depend more on your own judgment."

By this means, Jesus was trying to assure them that nothing untoward would happen to them as long as he was with them, and they followed his lead.

Jesus then told them why he must go to Bethany. He said:

"Our friend Lazarus sleepeth; but I go, that I may awake him out of sleep."[8]

It was traditional among the Jews to speak of "sleep" as referring either to a peaceful rest or to death. The disciples took the optimistic interpretation and assumed Lazarus was merely recuperating and enjoying a restful repose. The disciples were encouraged and said:

"Lord, if he sleep, he shall do well."[9]

But Jesus stopped them cold, when he stated:

"Lazarus is dead."[10]

---

[7]John 11:9-10.
[8]John 11:11.
[9]John 11:12.
[10]John 11:14.

Nevertheless, Jesus wanted them to know that everything had its purpose, and that this incident was designed to further strengthen their faith. So he added:

"I am glad for your sakes that I was not there, to the intent ye may believe...Let us go unto him."[11]

Poor Thomas Didymus, the twin, was despondent. He always seemed to take a dim view of things; and it is obvious from his next remark that he had completely missed the Savior's comment about the "light" of the Savior's guidance and the need to follow his leadership so long as he was with them. The thing which haunted Thomas was the memory of those mobs at the last two feasts threatening to kill the Savior. In a mood of the darkest depression, he mournfully said:

"Let us also go, that we may die with him."[12]

THE RETURN TO BETHANY

So they began their journey. We do not know where Jesus was preaching in Perea when the messengers came from Mary and Martha. What we do know is that after commencing the journey it took the Savior and his disciples two days to cross the River Jordan and travel the fifteen mile road that led three thousand feet upward toward Bethany.

Jesus appears to have stopped just outside of Bethany at a safe distance from the town. By making casual inquiry he was able to learn that Lazarus had been in the tomb four days.[13]

This meant that he had probably been dead for at least five days. It appears from John 11:39 that he had not been given the customary Jewish embalming, and this would mean that he had been buried the day after he died. Authorities say that this usually occurred when there was no embalming. When we add to this the time element of

---

[11]John 11:15.
[12]John 11:16.
[13]John 11:17.

four days the body had been in the tomb, it would mean Lazarus had been dead five or six days.

This appears to have been important to Jesus. We are told that there was a tradition among the Jews that the spirit of a deceased person lingered near the body for four days. Then it departed into paradise.[14]

This may account for the reason Jesus did not hasten to Bethany when he was first told about Lazarus. He may have wanted those who saw this marvelous miracle to understand that the spirit of Lazarus had long since departed from the vicinity of his body.

Through some trusted friend, Jesus secretly sent word to the grieving sisters that he had come. It would have been extremely dangerous for the Savior to enter the town himself. The moment he was recognized, news of his whereabouts would have sped to Jerusalem. He needed time to visit briefly with the two sisters, perform the great miracle, and then quickly depart. After that, it would not matter whether Jerusalem heard about it or not.

MARTHA HASTENS TO MEET JESUS

When the Savior's messenger entered the home of Martha and Mary, he found the place swarming with people from Jerusalem who had come to join in the mourning rituals. This always required several days, with groups of mourners working in relays.

Martha leaped with excitement the moment she knew Jesus was nearby, but not Mary. She was virtually numb with grief. She sat disconsolate in the house while Martha hurried out to find Jesus. When Martha saw the Savior, she ran to him and said:

"Lord, if thou hadst been here, my brother had not died."[15]

No doubt this beloved family of friends had been with Jesus on his visits to Jerusalem and had seen him heal hundreds of people.

---

[14]Talmage, *Jesus the Christ*, pp. 500-501.
[15]John 11:21.

They knew he could have healed Lazarus had he arrived there in time. But now there was the question of whether or not he might raise Lazarus from the dead—and after he had been in the tomb for several days.

We know of only two occasions when Jesus had previously raised the dead, but that was when he was up in Galilee. Nevertheless, the two sisters may have heard of it. There is a hint of this as Martha timidly ventured to say:

"But I know, that even now, whatsoever thou wilt ask of God, God will give it thee."[16]

Jesus then told her exactly what was going to happen. He said:

"Thy brother shall rise again.

"Martha saith unto him, I know that he shall rise again in the resurrection at the last day.

"Jesus said unto her, I am the resurrection, and the life: he that believeth in me, though he were dead, yet shall he live."[17]

As the conversation continued, Jesus asked Martha a simple question and received more than a simple reply. Martha magnified her answer with a glowing testimony of her belief in the Savior's divinity. Jesus said to Martha:

"Whosoever liveth and believeth in me shall never die. Believest thou this?

"She saith unto him, Yea, Lord: I believe that thou art the Christ, the Son of God, which should come into the world."[18]

---

[16]John 11:22.
[17]John 11:23-25.
[18]John 11:26-27.

That beautiful expression of adoring faith was all Jesus needed to hear from Martha. Now he needed to see Mary, so he requested Martha to go back to the house and ask Mary to come. Martha returned the short distance to their home and whispered to Mary:

"The Master is come, and calleth for thee.

"As soon as she heard that, she arose quickly, and came unto him.

"Now Jesus was not yet come into the town, but was in that place where Martha met him."[19]

MARY AND THE MOURNERS GO TO MEET JESUS

When Mary came to Jesus, she was not alone. The mourners had seen her hastily rise up to leave, and they thought she was going to the tomb of Lazarus to weep. These friends felt it was their duty to go with her. But she went beyond the tomb. Then the mourners saw Jesus and his company of the twelve. No doubt they immediately realized that this secret rendezvous was a dangerous situation, but they stayed to see what would happen.

The scripture says:

"Then when Mary was come where Jesus was, and saw him, she fell down at his feet, saying unto him, Lord, if thou hadst been here, my brother had not died.

"When Jesus therefore saw her weeping, and the Jews also weeping which came with her, he groaned in the spirit, and was troubled."[20]

As we shall see in a moment, we have reason to believe that it was at this moment that Jesus sent up his petition to heaven and pleaded with his Father to let him have this great privilege of raising

---

[19]John 11:28-30.
[20]John 11:33.

up his beloved friend. The next few verses tell one of the most beautiful stories in the New Testament. Jesus said:

"Where have ye laid him? They [Mary and Martha] said unto him, Lord, come and see.

"Jesus wept.

"Then said the Jews, Behold how he loved him!"[21]

Jesus did indeed love Lazarus, but he had no reason to weep for him. He knew that very shortly Lazarus would come forth radiant with life and healed of whatever had caused his death. No doubt the reason he had "groaned" and seemed "troubled" was from the distress he felt as he watched the desolating sorrow that had fallen like a shroud over these two wonderful sisters.

It seems that shortly after being "troubled," Jesus received a message from on high that came in answer to his fervent prayer. At the tomb, Jesus revealed what this message was, and it is my opinion that this gratifying communication from his Father was what caused him to weep tears of joy, not sorrow.

It was natural for the mourners and friends who had come out with Mary to think of the death of Lazarus as an unmitigated tragedy. If only Jesus had arrived in time! They reflected on this and then said to one another:

"Could not this man, which opened the eyes of the blind, have caused that even this man should not have died?"[22]

JESUS APPROACHES THE TOMB

The tomb of Lazarus was a cave located just a short distance from where they were standing. John says the opening was covered by "a stone."[23]

---

[21]John 11:34-36.
[22]John 11:37.
[23]John 11:38.

In my youth, I was always troubled by this passage. Having been raised in a family of highway contractors, I knew that a stone large enough to seal the opening to a burial cave would be impossible for a few Jewish mourners to remove.

However, on my first trip to the Holy Land, I made a discovery. We saw that in front of each cave-tomb, the owner had carved or constructed a trough or groove. Then a round stone, somewhat like a rough millstone, would be placed in the groove and rolled over the entrance without much difficulty. This immediately solved one of my childhood Bible problems.

As the small company came up to the tomb, Jesus said:

"Take ye away the stone."[24]

This order to open the tomb created some immediate consternation. When Martha first met the Savior she said that even though her brother was dead, she knew the Father would do whatever the Son asked of him. This certainly carried a hint of hope that the Savior might do for Lazarus what people said he had done for two dead people in Galilee. But when Martha was confronted with the actual opening of the tomb, she panicked. Quickly she said to Jesus:

"Lord, by this time he stinketh: for he hath been dead four days." [Actually in the tomb four days.][25]

To strengthen her faith, Jesus said to Martha:

"Said I not unto thee, that, if thou wouldest believe, thou shouldest see the glory of God?

"Then they took away the stone from the place where the dead was laid."[26]

---

[24]John 11:39.
[25]Ibid.
[26]John 11:40-41.

No doubt the stone was rolled back by some of the disciples.

WHY JESUS WEPT

Now we come to the passage that suggests why Jesus wept a short time earlier. It is believed he wept at that moment when the Father confirmed that Jesus could raise his beloved friend. As he stood at the opening of this tomb, the scripture describes how the Savior lifted his eyes heavenward, and said:

"Father, I thank thee that thou hast heard me.

"And I knew that thou hearest me always: but because of the people which stand by I said it, that they may believe that thou hast sent me.

"And when he thus had spoken, he cried with a loud voice, Lazarus, come forth!"[27]

What a traumatic moment that must have been. Those who have been in some of the tombs of Bethany know that nearly all of them have steps leading from the entrance down into the crypt itself. The interior is very dark except for the dim light filtering through the narrow opening at the top of the stairs.

THE RAISING OF LAZARUS FROM THE DEAD

Imagine the feelings of Lazarus as his spirit reentered his dead body. An amazing part of the miracle was having that body resume its normal functions. The blood began to flow, warmth returned to the cold tissues. The afflicted organs of his body that had caused his death were healed.

It is very likely that when Lazarus first awakened, he did not know where he was. How did he get here? Then he heard a loud voice saying, "Lazarus come forth!" What a sensation to awaken and suddenly discover yourself in a tomb. Whether Lazarus had any recollection of his stay in the spirit world we are not told.

---

[27]John 11:41-43.

But we do know that when he tried to move it would have seemed virtually impossible. He was so tightly wrapped and bound by the grave sheets that his first effort to move would have been extremely difficult. A napkin was wrapped firmly under his chin to prevent the lower jaw from falling open after the *rigor mortis* diminished, and the muscles began to completely relax.

Outside, everyone must have waited breathlessly to see if Lazarus would actually come forth. It probably took so long that some must have begun to wonder, or even have doubts.

When Lazarus tried to sit up with his hands and arms wrapped tightly in the grave sheets, he must have strained mightily. Getting his legs over the side of the stone bier would have been the most difficult of all. Once he was erect and standing on the stone floor, he must have felt it was truly an achievement. However, when he tried to walk, he would have probably come close to falling. At best, he would have only been able to hobble.

If this crypt had a stairway like most of the others, he was surely confronted with the greatest challenge of all as he approached the first step. But at least he would have seen the dim light coming down from the entrance.

Slowly, slowly, he must have struggled as he ascended one step after another. This could only have been done by shuffling, straining, and making soft noises with each step.

Finally, he was there. He stood white and ghost-like, framed in the entrance of the tomb. Jesus said:

"Loose him, and let him go."[28]

THE REALITY OF A MIRACLE

It is not difficult to imagine what would have happened next. As the grave sheets were unwound, leaving Lazarus in his plain white burial robe, who could have restrained Mary and Martha? We

---

[28]John 11:44.

know—without even being told—that they must have rushed forward with eager, affectionate embraces, sobbing, and kissing his cheeks, his lips, his brow.

When Lazarus came to a full realization of what had happened and where he had been, we can well imagine him falling at the Savior's feet and clinging to him with tears gushing down his cheeks as he sobbed in grateful appreciation. But soon a gentle hand must have lifted him up and held his arm as these two loving friends returned to the house together.

THE NEWS IS SPREAD

Now the inevitable happened. Any miracle as spectacular as this one was destined to send those who saw it in two different directions. The apostle John was there and writes:

"Then many of the Jews which came [with] Mary, and had seen the things which Jesus did, believed on him.

"But some of them went their ways to the Pharisees, and told them what things Jesus had done."[29]

JESUS IS CONDEMNED TO DIE WITHOUT A TRIAL

John later found out what happened in Jerusalem after the chief priests were told the amazing news. The scripture says:

"Then gathered the chief priests and the Pharisees a council, and said, What do we? for this man doeth many miracles.

"If we let him thus alone, all men will believe on him: and the Romans shall come and take away both our place and nation."[30]

It is very important to catch the significance of this statement.

---

[29]John 11:45-46.
[30]John 11:47-48.

With these Jewish leaders, the Romans were the gods of the land. Notice how the manifest power of Israel's God which was so dramatically demonstrated in the multitude of miracles Jesus performed meant nothing. They even had eye-witness reports that he raised a man from the grave after he had been in the tomb four days. To them, this was totally irrelevant. The important thing was that this, more than anything else, might convince the people he was indeed their Messiah and they would revolt against Rome to make him their new king.

Of course, to Caiaphas and the Sanhedrin, that would be fatal. They themselves would be dethroned. At all costs they must preserve the approbation of their royal Roman masters. To Caiaphas it was even worth killing an innocent man to ensure the best interests of the nation, and especially of himself. We read:

"And...Caiaphas, being the high priest that same year, said...it is expedient for us, that one man should die for the people, and that the whole nation perish not."[31]

CAIAPHAS SEEKS FOR A POLITICAL SOLUTION

Notice that this was specifically and exclusively a political solution. It had nothing to do with the Savior's atoning sacrifice. Caiaphas was thinking only of his own security as a Roman appointee to the office of high priest, and to the perpetuation of the Jewish nation as a tributary of Rome.

John could not help but comment on the irony of this whole situation with Caiaphas, the high priest, plotting to have Jesus killed in order to prevent a political crisis, and yet prophesying "that Jesus should die for the people."

John says Caiaphas "spoke not of himself,"[32] indicating that he had intended to say one thing but had uttered words which meant something entirely different. In a very real sense his words were literally fulfilled when Jesus died, not only for the Jewish nation, but

---

[31]John 11:49-50.
[32]John 11:51.

to "gather together in one the children of God that were scattered abroad."[33]

What was actually in the mind of Caiaphas is recorded by John in the next verse:

"Then from that day forth they took counsel together for to put him to death."[34]

JESUS TAKES HIS DISCIPLES INTO HIDING

Once the members of the Sanhedrin had made up their minds to kill Jesus, they would have considered it a distinct advantage to have their spies catch the Savior alone in some rural area where his death would be merely an unfortunate "incident." The killer could remain forever unknown.

On the other hand, if Jesus eluded the spies and came up to Jerusalem for the Feast of the Passover, then Caiaphas and the Sanhedrin would have to concoct some type of conspiracy, based on false witnesses who would testify that Jesus had committed some heinous offense that carried the death penalty.

Of course, this would be a monumental challenge since the Roman law did not allow the Jews to execute any person without the consent of the Roman authority. Therefore their plot would have to be carried out without arousing the suspicions of Pilate, the Roman governor.

The Savior was well aware of all of this, and therefore the raising of Lazarus was barely accomplished before he and his disciples disappeared from Bethany and hastened through the mountains toward a city close to the wilderness.

John closes this important episode by saying:

---

[33]John 11:52.
[34]John 11:53.

"Jesus therefore walked no more openly among the Jews; but went thence unto a country near to the wilderness, into a city called Ephraim, and there continued with his disciples."[35]

As we shall see later, there is strong scriptural evidence that when Jesus took his disciples into the wilderness, he invited Lazarus to go along with him. No doubt he knew that the plot to kill Jesus would eventually include a plan to kill Lazarus.[36]

* * * *

TOPICS FOR REFLECTION AND DISCUSSION

1. After hearing of the illness of Lazarus, how long did Jesus wait before announcing that he was going up to Bethany? Why were his disciples afraid to have him go? How far is Bethany from Jerusalem? What did Jesus mean when he said, "Are there not twelve hours in the day?"

2. What did Jesus say about Lazarus that made the disciples think he was merely asleep? Then what did Jesus say that shocked them? What did Thomas say which reflected his rather cynical, pessimistic personality?

3. How long did it take Jesus and his disciples to reach the vicinity of Bethany? Why did Jesus stay on the outskirts rather than go into town? How did Mary and Martha learn where Jesus was?

4. Who came out to meet the Savior first? What did she say? Was there any hint that she had a slight hope that somehow Jesus might raise Lazarus from the dead? What did Martha say which clearly reflected the depth of her testimony concerning the divinity of Jesus?

5. Whom did Jesus send to get Mary? When Mary came out, why did others follow her? We are told that Jesus "groaned" and was "troubled." What appears to have been the reason? What is the

---

[35]John 11:54.
[36]John 12:10.

shortest verse in the Bible? Why was Martha alarmed when Jesus told his disciples to open the tomb?

6. As Jesus stood at the entrance to the tomb, he addressed a few words to his Father. Was it a petition to raise Lazarus or an expression of gratitude? When Jesus looked down into the tomb, what did he say? Describe the difficulty which Lazarus would have had in responding to the Savior's command.

7. Those who saw this great miracle divided into two groups. What were they? What was the reaction of Caiaphas and the Sanhedrin when they heard the news? What did Caiaphas say?

8. Was Caiaphas thinking of a divine atonement or of committing murder to achieve a political solution?

9. What does the scripture mean when it says that Jesus "walked no more openly among the Jews"? Where did he first go into hiding?

*   *   *   *

CHAPTER 30

VISITING A FEW FAVORITE TOWNS FOR THE LAST TIME

When Jesus and his disciples left their temporary place of security in Ephraim, the scripture says Jesus "passed through Samaria and Galilee."[1] Of course, Jesus eventually intended to return to Perea, beyond Jordan, where his farewell ministry was interrupted when Lazarus became ill.

During this leisurely journey, the Savior delivered a whole series of parables and teachings that were highly instructive. However, these incidents are not identified with any particular place. We therefore assume that they just "occurred along the way" and the apostles recorded them without considering it important to specify the location.

WHY WOULD JESUS RETURN TO GALILEE?

Since the Savior's ministry had already been completed in Galilee, we cannot help wondering why he went on this journey which was so far out of his way.

A possible explanation is the fact that the Feast of the Passover was only a few weeks away, and it was extremely important to Jesus that certain women from Galilee attend this feast.

Foremost among these women would be his mother, and the members of her family. By this time Mary was around fifty. It would be important for Jesus to know whether his mother had been able to arrange her affairs so she could go up to the feast with his half-brothers and half-sisters and possibly her grandchildren.

---

[1] Luke 17:11.

He would also be anxious to make certain that some of the women who had been among his staunchest disciples would be preparing to go up to Jerusalem. While they didn't know it yet, they were each going to play an extremely important role in the fast moving drama that would be unfolding at this feast.

One of these special women was Mary Magdalene, who would be the first to see Jesus as a resurrected being. There was also Mary, the mother of the apostles James the less and Joses. And another important woman was the mother of James and John.[2] A previous verse also speaks of "many women" who were associated with the ones we have just named.[3]

THE SAVIOR'S FUTURE COMING IN GLORY

As Jesus came out of Galilee and continued his journey through Samaria and into Perea, he discussed both prophecy and gospel principles with his disciples.

We observe that every so often—when the burden of the present and immediate future seemed to virtually overwhelm his mind—Jesus would do just what Isaiah often did. He would project his thinking beyond the present and contemplate the time when the Son of God would come to the earth in power and glory. As they travelled along, he first spoke of the prelude of darkness that would precede his Second Coming. His disciples heard him say:

"The days will come, when ye shall desire to see one of the days of the Son of man, and ye shall not see it.

"And they shall say to you, See here; or, see there: go not after them, nor follow them."[4]

During the following generations, the Jews ignored this warning a dozen different times. Every time they thought a Messiah had appeared, they would rise up in rebellion against whatever nation

---

[2]Matthew 27:56.
[3]Matthew 27:55.
[4]Luke 17:22-23.

had them under subjugation. And each time they would be slaughtered by the thousands.

Jesus said that when he came in glory and power, there would be no question about the reality of his Second Coming. During the next few weeks he referred to some of the signs that would accompany his Second Advent, and in contemplation of that day of triumph, he said:

"For as the lightning, that lighteneth out of the one part under heaven, shineth unto the other part under heaven; so shall also the Son of man be in his day."[5]

Of course, before all of these glorious things could happen, there had to be the offering of the great atoning sacrifice. Therefore, he told his disciples that in their own day the Savior:

"must...suffer many things, and be rejected of this generation."[6]

AS IT WAS IN THE DAYS OF NOAH

Jesus quickly added that even in the latter days there would be an era of evil and darkness that would precede the Savior's coming in glory. In fact, he said that before the glorious appearance of the Lord with his angels in the clouds of heaven, there would be a time of the most hideous wickedness, comparable to the time when the whole earth had to be cleansed by the great flood. Jesus said:

"As it was in the days of Noe, so shall it be also in the days of the Son of man."[7]

To get some idea of what it was like in the days of Noah, we turn to the writings of Enoch. He lived two generations before Noah, but the Lord showed him a vision of what it would be like in Noah's day.

---

[5]Luke 17:24.
[6]Luke 17:25.
[7]Luke 17:26.

We get the impression that when Enoch began to see this vision of Noah's day, he was not too concerned. He probably saw all the beautiful cities, the chariots, and the well-dressed multitudes covering the earth. However, Enoch was shocked when he saw the Lord weeping because of the wickedness of these people. They apparently did not look too bad to Enoch—what with their beautiful cities, numerous chariots, signs of affluence and prosperity everywhere. Enoch therefore said to the Lord:

"How is it thou canst weep?

"The Lord said unto Enoch: Behold these thy brethren; they are the workmanship of mine own hands, and I gave unto them their knowledge...and...that they should love one another...but behold, they are without affection, and they hate their own blood....In my hot displeasure will I send in the floods upon them, for my fierce anger is kindled against them....

"*Among all the workmanship of mine hands there has not been so great wickedness as among thy brethren.*"[8]

Then the Lord showed Enoch the debauchery and degeneracy that was going on inside all those beautiful buildings. It was so terrible, Enoch exclaimed that they ought to be cleansed from the face of the earth.[9]

But as terrible as it was, Jesus wanted his disciples to know that when it came time for his return to the earth in glory, the human family would be just as wicked as they had been in the days of Noah.

The latter days would also be a time of great destruction on both sea and land. However, that would not come until the gospel had been restored and the righteous had been gathered out from every nation, kindred, tongue and people.

---

[8]Moses 7:31-36, P. of G. P. (emphasis added).
[9]Moses 7:41, P. of G. P.

It will be recalled that after the great flood, the Lord had promised Noah he would never destroy the human family again by water,[10] but in the small print the scripture says the next time it would be by fire.[11]

WHEN THE RIGHTEOUS SHALL BE CAUGHT UP

To save the righteous, the Lord will quicken or transfigure—and catch up into the heavens—every person who is worthy and marked for preservation.

Paul described this momentous occasion as follows:

"For the Lord himself shall descend from heaven with a shout, with the voice of the archangel, and with the trump of God: and the dead in Christ shall rise first:

"Then we which are alive and remain shall be caught up together with them in the clouds, to meet the Lord in the air: and so shall we ever be with the Lord."[12]

Modern revelation describes this great future event in very similar language.[13]

As for the rest of the world, when fire sweeps the earth it will be almost as devastating as when the earth was submerged in water. The warning voices of the prophets will be ignored just as the prophets were ignored in the days of Noah, and also in the days of Sodom and Gomorrah. Therefore Jesus said it will not only be as it was in the days of Noah, but:

"Likewise also as it was in the days of Lot; they did eat, they drank, they bought, they sold, they planted, they builded;

---

[10]Genesis 9:15.
[11]2 Nephi 6:15, B. of M.; Joel 2:3.
[12]1 Thessalonians 4:16-17.
[13]Doctrine and Covenants 27:18; 88:96.

"But the same day that Lot went out of Sodom it rained fire and brimstone from heaven, and destroyed them all.

"Even thus shall it be in the day when the Son of man is revealed."[14]

Of course, as Jesus walked along the way with his disciples on this journey into Perea, all of these events lay far in the future. At the moment, however, Jesus was required to deal with the question emanating from the Pharisees which was much more immediate.

WHAT ABOUT DIVORCE?

In the days of the Savior, the subject of divorce was highly controversial because the "putting away" of wives for trivial causes was widespread. Therefore, on this particular journey, a group of Pharisees tried to snare the Savior by saying:

"Is it lawful for a man to put away his wife for every [*any*] cause?"[15]

Jesus had been asked this question before. Possibly one of the purposes of the Pharisees on this occasion was to get Jesus to endorse the loose practices which then prevailed, or to firmly support the Lord's original commandment to Moses which was very strict and secretly unpopular. The Pharisees knew that taking a firm position in either direction would immediately antagonize many of his listeners who held to the opposite position. Therefore, either way, the Pharisees would consider it a gain.

WHAT ABOUT HEROD ANTIPAS?

There is also a more diabolical possibility, and that is the hope that they could get Jesus killed for the same reason John the Baptist had been killed. John had criticized the adulterous and incestuous marriage relationship between Herod Antipas and Herodias. Perhaps

---

[14]Luke 17:28-30.
[15]Matthew 19:3.

by clever questioning, they also could get Jesus to denounce this marriage and get him arrested.

We think this confrontation with the Pharisees may have taken place in Perea where Herod Antipas ruled. Herod would therefore have the authority to arrest Jesus if he stumbled into this trap.

But, whatever their motives, Jesus side-stepped their clever snare by going back to basics and quoting the scriptures. He said:

"Have ye not read, that he which made them at the beginning made them male and female,

"And said, For this cause shall a man leave father and mother, and shall cleave to his wife: and they twain shall be one flesh?

"Wherefore they are no more twain, but one flesh. What therefore God hath joined together, let not man put asunder."[16]

WHAT WOULD MOSES HAVE SAID?

But then the Pharisees tried to trap Jesus by quoting Moses against him. They said:

"Why did Moses then command to give a writing of divorcement, and to put her away?"[17]

Here is the Savior's reply:

"Moses, because of the hardness of your hearts, suffered you to put away your wives: but from the beginning it was not so."[18]

The "hardness of heart" which prevailed among the Jews later prevailed among many of the Christians, just as it does today. Throughout the world, it continues to be a major problem, and the

---

[16]Matthew 19:4-6.
[17]Matthew 19:7.
[18]Matthew 19:8.

fractionalizing of the family threatens the very foundation of civilization in some places.

FACING THE PROBLEM CLOSER TO HOME

Even Moses imposed strict limitations on divorce, and the leaders of God's kingdom today strive to avoid divorces except in the most deplorable situations. The primary message of the prophets in modern times is to carefully *build* the marriage relationship rather than look for excuses to tear it apart. Furthermore, the church goal is to build marriage for time and all eternity, not just "until death do you part."

The major causes of divorce in modern times have been listed as follows:

1. Infidelity.

2. Physical violence against a spouse and/or children.

3. Money problems.

4. Intoxication, narcotics, or both.

5. Fault-finding, quarreling, nagging.

6. Serious aberrations in normal sexuality, trying almost anything for that ultimate thrill.

7. One of the spouses deliberately falls in love with someone else.

8. Differences in religious values.

9. Differences in racial cultures.

10. Differences in methods of raising children.

11. Pathological impatience with minor inadequacies in the behavior of a spouse.

The tempo and demands of modern life are believed to have accentuated and aggravated many of these problems. Nevertheless, the advice of the Savior to patiently learn how to love, honor and serve one another, is still the most vital solution to nearly all marital problems, whether ancient or modern.

The anxiety of church leaders to stem the epidemic of divorce has been successful to a degree—especially divorces based on snap judgment—but not as successful as they would have liked. Nevertheless, national surveys show that no major group in the American culture has maintained a divorce rate as low as the members of the Church of Jesus Christ of Latter-day Saints who have tried to live righteous lives and have been married in the temple.

JESUS AND HIS DISCIPLES
LEAVE PEREA FOR JERICHO

In the days of the Savior, the Jordan River had two main crossings where the stream was wide and shallow. On this journey, it is likely that Jesus crossed from Samaria into Perea at the upper crossing, believed to have been at Zaratan. This would have permitted him to travel south from village to village for a considerable distance until he reached Bethabara, which means, "house of the ford."[19]

As Jesus and his apostles crossed the Jordan River they had about seven miles to walk before reaching the city of Jericho. Some 1,400 years earlier, Joshua had crossed the river with the armies of Israel. After they had marched around the fortified city of Jericho seven times, an amazing thing happened:

"Suddenly the great stacks of stone, mortar and dried mud which had been the pride of Jericho's defense, began to tremble and quake like teetering piles of collapsing building blocks. In one great thunderous debacle they came tumbling down upon themselves with

---

[19]*LDS Bible Dictionary* under "Bethabara."

soldiers, stones, mortar and bricks all grinding and crashing together in one mammoth avalanche of devastating destruction."[20]

It was toward this famous historic site that the Savior and his disciples now made their way.

JESUS DELIVERS A MESSAGE
HIS APOSTLES CANNOT HEAR

Luke tells us that on the way to Jericho, Jesus took the twelve apostles off by themselves and made a pronouncement which Jesus did not intend them to understand or remember until after his resurrection. As we have mentioned earlier, the Holy Ghost revealed to the minds of the Gospel writers many of the things the disciples did not remember or did not understand while they were laboring with the Savior during his ministry.

In order to place a certain prophecy on the heavenly record for future reference, Jesus said:

"Behold, we go up to Jerusalem, and all things that are written by the prophets concerning the Son of man shall be accomplished.

"For he shall be delivered unto the Gentiles, and shall be mocked, and spitefully entreated, and spitted on:

"And they shall scourge him, and put him to death: and the third day he shall rise again."[21]

Now we come to the verse which describes what might be called the Savior's *modus operandi*. It was a special method of planting certain thoughts in the minds of his disciples and then causing them to remain hidden until the Holy Ghost awakened the memories of the apostles after the resurrection. In spite of the clarity and plainness of the words Jesus had just spoken, Luke explains what happened in the minds of the apostles:

---

[20]W. Cleon Skousen, *The Fourth Thousand Years*, Salt Lake City: Bookcraft, 1966, p. 485.
[21]Luke 18:31-33.

"And they understood none of these things: and this saying was hid from them, neither knew they the things which were spoken."[22]

THE HEALING OF BARTIMAEUS, THE BLIND BEGGAR

After Jesus and his disciples had passed through Jericho, (although Luke says it was before[23]) Mark indicates that there was "a great number of people" who decided to accompany them on the steep, six-hour journey to Jerusalem.[24]

The noise of such a crowd passing along the road would inevitably attract beggars of every description; in fact, it still does today. On this occasion one of these beggars was Bartimaeus (Bar-tie-ME-us), who was blind. The fame of Jesus as a healer was widespread, so Mark says:

"When he heard that it was Jesus of Nazareth, he began to cry out, and say, Jesus, thou Son of David, have mercy on me."[25]

But the crowd was hurrying to get to Jerusalem for the feast, so the scripture says:

"And many charged him that he should hold his peace: but he cried the more a great deal, Thou Son of David, have mercy on me."[26]

It was the very nature of Jesus to respond to a plea for help, so the cry of Bartimaeus did not go unheeded. Mark says:

"And Jesus stood still, and commanded him to be called."[27]

---

[22]Luke 18:34.
[23]Luke 18:35.
[24]Mark 10:46.
[25]Mark 10:47.
[26]Mark 10:48.
[27]Mark 10:49.

Now everything changed. It is amazing how patronizing and caring people can become when some woebegone outcast attracts the attention of a famous person. Mark says:

"And they call the blind man, saying unto him, Be of good comfort, rise; he calleth thee."[28]

When Bartimaeus was brought before Jesus, the Savior asked:

"What wilt thou that I should do unto thee?

"The blind man said unto him, Lord, that I might receive my sight.

"And Jesus said unto him, Go thy way; thy faith hath made thee whole. And immediately he received his sight."[29]

But the grateful Bartimaeus did not go his way. He went the Savior's way. Mark says:

"He...followed Jesus in the way."[30]

As they moved on toward Jerusalem, one can well imagine this jubilant beggar moving among the crowd joyously demonstrating that at last he could actually see.

JESUS OFFERS SALVATION TO A TAX COLLECTOR

As Jesus and the large assembly slowly moved up the Jericho road, a strange little man was running up and down trying to get a glimpse of Jesus. Luke describes it:

"Behold, there was a man named Zacchaeus [Za-KEE-us], which was the chief among the publicans [tax collectors], and he was rich.

---

[28]Ibid..
[29]Mark 10:51-54.
[30]Mark 10:54.

"And he sought to see Jesus who he was; and could not for the press, because he was little of stature.

"And he ran before, and climbed up into a sycamore tree to see him: for he was to pass that way."[31]

It is interesting, that, during my travels throughout the Holy Land, I have never seen but one sycamore tree, and it is located just outside Jericho, on the road leading to Jerusalem. Obviously, it is not the same sycamore Zacchaeus climbed so many centuries ago, but it is rather amazing that one would be very near the same place.

Some wag suggested that it might have been planted there by the Israeli Department of Tourism just to please Christian visitors! Fortunately, the tree is far too old for that, but still not old enough to have been growing there during the Savior's time.

Luke continues:

"And when Jesus came to the place, he looked up, and saw him, and said unto him, Zacchaeus, make haste, and come down; for to day I must abide at thy house."[32]

Except for Bartimaeus, there was probably no one on the Jericho road that day as excited as Zacchaeus. The scripture says:

"And he made haste, and came down, and received him joyfully.

"And when they saw it, they all murmured, saying, That he was gone to be guest with a man that is a sinner."[33]

He may have very well been a sinner, because the scripture says he was rich, and sinning was the way most tax collectors

---

[31]Luke 19:2-4.
[32]Luke 19:5.
[33]Luke 19:6-7.

accumulated their wealth. Nevertheless, sinner or not, here is what the crowd heard this tax collector say:

"Behold, Lord, the half of my goods I give to the poor; and if I have taken any thing from any man by false accusation, I restore him fourfold."[34]

For a tax collector to offer to give half of his wealth to the poor and promise to repay any abused taxpayer fourfold is repentance without precedent in all holy writ. So Jesus said the following to those critics in the crowd who wondered why the Savior would stay at the house of Zacchaeus:

"This day is salvation come to this house, forsomuch [forasmuch] as he also is a son of Abraham.

"For the Son of man is come to seek and to save that which was lost."[35]

Although there may have still been several hours of daylight in which to finish the trip to Jerusalem, it may have been part of the intention of Jesus to stay overnight with Zacchaeus so that the crowd would return to their homes in Jericho.

As we shall see in the next chapter, Jesus needed to be alone with his apostles and more mature disciples as they continued their journey the following day. He needed to give them many important instructions concerning their worldwide ministry which would soon be conferred upon them.

*   *   *   *

TOPICS FOR REFLECTION AND DISCUSSION.

1. How many fords that cross the Jordan River have been identified? What does Bethabara mean? Where is it located?

---

[34]Luke 19:8.
[35]Luke 19:9-10.

2. Can you think of any reason why Jesus would want to return to Galilee after closing his ministry there?

3. What elements of wickedness today would you compare with the wickedness in the days of Noah? Why do the scriptures warn us that this is a dangerous trend?

4. Why do you think the Lord plans to take the righteous up from the earth for a period of time? Would this require that they be temporarily transfigured?

5. What seemed to be the motivations of the Pharisees in getting Jesus to take a position one way or the other on the issue of divorce? Can you name three of the principle causes of divorce today?

6. Which group of church members have the lowest divorce rate? In this group what is the main emphasis on marriage?

7. What, to you, was most significant about the healing of the blind beggar, Bartimaeus? Do you think he might have been in the throngs that welcomed Jesus into Jerusalem?

8. Why were publicans or tax collectors considered "sinners" in the days of Jesus? What was so unusual about the repentance of Zacchaeus?

9. Why do you think Jesus made a stop-over with Zacchaeus when he was only six hours from Jerusalem? What did Jesus plan to teach his apostles and more mature disciples the following day?

10. Was Jesus plain and outspoken when he described to his apostles what would happen to him at the Feast of the Passover? Did his apostles understand what he was telling them? How do we know?

*　*　*　*

CHAPTER 31

JESUS PREPARES HIS APOSTLES FOR THEIR MISSION TO THE WORLD

As Jesus and his disciples walked slowly up the road toward Bethany, the Savior had a special burden on his heart in addition to the prospect of enduring a terrifying experience on the cross.

He knew that his time was drawing to a close, and he wanted a very select and dedicated following to establish his kingdom throughout much of the world. He knew this would take sacrifice, and so he told them that only those who were willing to be separated from their families and give the spreading of the gospel their top priority would be ready to take up the cross and follow him.

But going on a mission requires many considerations. He invited them to carefully count the cost before they committed themselves. He said it was like a man who is planning to build a tower. It is extremely important that he study the plans, and measure the cost, or he may not be able to finish it.[1]

He said the same thing is true of a military leader planning the strategy for a battle.[2] Jesus wanted all of them to know that he was engaged in a great and terrible battle and that he needed their help, but, said he:

---

[1]Luke 14:28-30.
[2]Luke 14:31.

"Whosoever he be of you that forsaketh not all that he hath, he cannot be my disciples."[3]

This is the wringer through which every general authority, every mission president, every full-time missionary, every stake president and every bishop must pass. Perhaps to a somewhat lesser but equally strenuous degree, the same is true of ward and branch officers, teachers, or even good neighbors.

Lining up our priorities is supremely important in accomplishing the Lord's work. Once our priorities are set, then we must strategize to make certain we have the means and materials to successfully accomplish what we have been called to do.

THE APOSTLES DID NOT UNDERSTAND
THE SAVIOR'S MISSION EVEN WHEN
HE EXPLAINED IT TO THEM

Strange as it may seem to us today, when Jesus and his company began ascending the three-thousand-foot climb from the Jordan valley to Jerusalem, he was the only one in this entire company who seemed to realize he was marching toward his doom.

Of course, Jesus had told his disciples several times during the past several months, that he was coming toward the end of his life. In fact, just recently he had told them in the plainest possible language that he was going up to the Feast of the Passover where he would be "betrayed...condemned to death" and then delivered over to the "Gentiles to mock, and to scourge, and to crucify him."[4]

The Gospel writers all confess that the apostles never did comprehend the reality of what Jesus was saying. Even when they partially understood, they assured him they would never let it happen.

---

[3]Luke 14:33.
[4]Matthew 20:18-19.

Jesus was aware that "they thought the kingdom of God would immediately appear,"[5] and once again they completely missed his plain and vital message that God's kingdom would not come in power and glory until the Savior's *Second* Coming.

Meanwhile, his task was to alert them to the fact that he would soon be leaving them and that they would be left in charge of God's work on earth. This is how he happened to tell them the "Parable of the Pounds," which is very similar to the "Parable of the Talents."

THE PARABLE OF THE POUNDS

In the parable of the pounds, Jesus portrayed himself as a nobleman who had to go to a far country where he would be designated the ruler over this particular kingdom. Meanwhile he had to leave the affairs of the kingdom in the hands of his servants. Jesus said:

"And he called his ten servants, and delivered them ten pounds, and said unto them, Occupy till I come....

"And it came to pass, that when he was returned, having received the kingdom, then he commanded these servants to be called unto him, to whom he had given the money, that he might know how much every man had gained by trading."[6]

We soon learn that each of the servants had the responsibility for one pound, so they all started out on the same footing. But when the nobleman returned, there had to be an accounting. The parable continues:

"Then came the first, saying, Lord, thy pound hath gained ten pounds.

---

[5]Luke 19:11.
[6]Luke 19:13-15.

"And he said unto him, Well, thou good servant: because thou hast been faithful in a very little, have thou authority over ten cities."[7]

Notice that this servant is not being rewarded in pounds, but his skill in handling the money is used as a criterion to determine how much of the new kingdom the nobleman will put under his charge.

"And the second came, saying, Lord, thy pound hath gained five pounds.

"And he said likewise to him, Be thou also over five cities."[8]

This leaves eight more to give an accounting, but Jesus skips down to the one he wishes to cite as an example of slothfulness. He said:

"And another came, saying, Lord, behold, here is thy pound, which I have kept laid up in a napkin....

"And he saith unto him...thou wicked servant....

"And he said unto them that stood by, Take from him the pound, and give it to him that hath ten pounds.

"And they said unto him, Lord, he [already] *hath* ten pounds."[9]

It might appear to a bystander that this seemed most unfair to take the pound from the man who had hoarded it, and give it to the man who had built one pound into ten. But the new ruler was looking for stewardship talent, not a welfare system, so he said:

---

[7]Luke 19:16-17.
[8]Luke 19:19-19.
[9]Luke 19:20-25.

"I say unto you, That unto every one which hath [developed his stewardship] shall be given; and from him that hath not, even that he hath shall be taken away from him."[10]

THE LAW OF CONSECRATION

It is interesting that under the Lord's Law of Consecration these same principles apply. Excess capital or newly acquired resources are assigned by the bishops to the stewards with the best record of production. Because everyone who belongs to the order profits from the fruits of the most efficient stewards, the bishops have the responsibility of allocating new resources to those who will make the most of them.

It can be readily seen why this system will only work for a righteous people. In the parable of the pounds it can be instantly seen how jealousy and resentment could fester into a growing abscess if the participants did not all appreciate how each member of the order profits by having the more efficient stewards get the most resources assigned to them.

It also should be kept in mind that an efficient steward does not become personally wealthy by having new resources assigned to him. Each year he, like everyone else, turns in all the fruits of his labors except that which is required for the immediate needs of himself and his family.[11]

The only advantage the efficient steward gets from all his hard work is the honor of being considered a greater asset to the community than some of the others.

We recall that this was the Lord's own definition for greatness when he said:

"He that is greatest among you shall be your servant."[12]

---

[10]Luke 19:26.
[11]Doctrine and Covenants 70:7-9.
[12]Matthew 23:11.

And again:

"If any man desire to be first, the same shall be last of all, and servant of all."[13]

Amazingly, it was only a short time later that two of the apostles demonstrated that they had not understood what Jesus had said. Yet they were two of the Savior's most devoted followers.

JAMES AND JOHN LEARN A LESSON

It was during this part of Christ's ministry that Mark relates how Satan whispered to James and John that they should seek preference over the other ten members of the twelve.[14]

However, in the account given by Matthew, he states that it was the *mother* of James and John who made this request. Since Matthew was present and saw it happen, we will use his text:

"Then came to him the mother of Zebedee's children with her sons, worshipping him, and desiring a certain thing of him.

"And he said unto her, What wilt thou? She saith unto him, Grant that these my two sons may sit, the one on thy right hand, and the other on the left, in thy kingdom.

"But Jesus answered and said, Ye know not what ye ask."[15]

At this point, Jesus would no doubt appreciate why a mother might seek a little preference for her sons, but Jesus took advantage of the situation to turn to James and John and challenge them. He asked:

---

[13]Mark 9:35.
[14]Mark 10:35-41.
[15]Matthew 20:20-22.

"Are ye able to drink of the cup that I shall drink of, and to be baptized with the baptism that I am baptized with? They say unto him, We are able."[16]

Little did James realize that he would be the first apostle to be martyred. In 44 A.D. Herod Agrippa would have him executed by the sword.[17]

John also would drink of a cup that would be so traumatic that it would turn to bitterness in his stomach.[18] Jesus knew all this was coming, so he said:

"Ye shall drink indeed of my cup, and be baptized with the baptism that I am baptized with: but to sit on my right hand, and on my left, is not mine to give, but it shall be given to them for whom it is prepared of my Father."[19]

This entire scene was very distasteful to the rest of the twelve. Therefore the scripture says:

"And when the ten heard it, they were moved with indignation against the two brethren."[20]

Jesus decided to make one final point to emphasize a basic principle of righteous government in his new kingdom. He said:

"Ye know that the princes of the Gentiles exercise dominion over them, and they that are great exercise authority upon them.

"*But it shall not be so among you:* but whosoever will be great among you, let him be your minister;

---

[16]Matthew 20:22.
[17]Acts 12:1-2.
[18]Revelation 10:10.
[19]Matthew 20:23.
[20]Matthew 20:24.

"And whosoever will be chief among you, let him be your servant."[21]

THE GENIUS OF GOD'S ORDERLY GOVERNMENT

It is said that the first law of heaven is obedience and the second law is order.

The first law requires that all members of the kingdom serve enthusiastically wherever they are assigned, because that is where they are needed. Under this principle the keeper at the door of the temple is as important as the high priest. In God's government, everyone is important. This is why Paul later wrote what Jesus had wanted James and John to understand:

"If the whole body were an eye, where were the hearing? If the whole were hearing, where were the smelling?

"But now hath God set the members every one of them in the body, as it hath pleased him....

"And the eye cannot say unto the hand, I have no need of thee: nor again the head to the feet, I have no need of you.

"Nay, much more those members of the body, which seem to be more feeble, are necessary:

"And those members of the body, which we think to be less honourable, upon these we bestow more abundant honour; and our uncomely parts [unpleasant assignments or seemingly humble positions] have more abundant comeliness [beauty in God's sight when faithfully fulfilled]."[22]

There is a host of important lessons to be learned from these few verses.

---

[21]Matthew 20:25-27 (emphasis added).
[22]1 Corinthians 12:17-23.

We all know there cannot be order without organization, and this means arranging the Lord's servants in a hierarchy of authority according to the level of their responsibility. But there are no inheritable ranks in God's kingdom such as princes, lords, barons or counts. The Lord appoints people to positions according to ability and need, not according to status.

Each person who is given an executive or presiding position as a steward of the Lord must look upon himself or herself as one who has been made "first among equals." A humble person will recognize this.

Furthermore, one of the most unique aspects of God's government, is its flexibility. All offices are subject to change according to a prevailing need and in accordance with the inspiration given to those who must fill that need.

Recently when an outstanding religious leader was released from his important position, some people wondered how he would feel going back to his ward as "just a regular member." We soon found out.

The Sunday School superintendent asked the former stake president to teach a class of little girls. At the next testimony meeting this noble priesthood holder stood up and said he had never enjoyed an assignment so much as this new job of teaching those little girls.

At the time I could not help thinking, "And he will be blessed as abundantly for teaching those little girls as he was for presiding over five thousand members of the kingdom."

DIFFERENT ASSIGNMENTS CAN BRING THE SAME REWARD

On one occasion, while teaching at Brigham Young University, I asked a class to select a prophet or apostle whose place they would liked to have filled if they had been given the opportunity to choose their role in life.

To my amazement, I received practically no response. It turned out that they knew too much about the hardships of God's great leaders to covet their various roles in life. Several said they would take the assignment if the Lord gave it to them, but they would never volunteer for any of those roles.

Then I asked the class whether each of these great prophets and apostles should be rewarded according to the hardship of the assignment they fulfilled, or whether they should all receive the same reward because they answered the need of the Lord when he called.

Some said that to be fair, the reward should be equated with the length and difficulty of the assignment. Others pointed out that each prophet or apostle was given his assignment according to the needs and desires of the Lord. The individual did not choose it. All performed with equal faithfulness, therefore their reward should be equal. However, the first group protested. They said an equal reward for widely varied assignments was entirely out of harmony with modern wage-labor theories.

I then told the class to listen carefully as the Lord gave his own answer to this troublesome question. We then read together the parable of the laborers, in which Jesus said:

"The kingdom of heaven is like unto a man that is an householder, which went out early in the morning to hire labourers into his vineyard.

"And when he had agreed with the labourers for a penny a day, he sent them into his vineyard."[23]

Then an interesting thing happened. The householder went to the marketplace the third hour and when he found a group of men standing idle, he hired them and promised to pay them "whatsoever is right."[24]

---

[23]Matthew 20:1-2.
[24]Ibid.

This was repeated the sixth hour and the ninth hour. And toward the very end of the working day—the eleventh hour—he went out once more and hired those who were idle.

When these laborers came for their pay, he gave them each a full day's wages of one penny, whether they had worked one hour or many hours. Of course, there was murmuring among those who had worked all day, but he said:

"Friend, I do thee no wrong: didst not thou agree with me for a penny?

"Take that thine is, and go thy way: I will give unto this last, even as unto thee.

"Is it not lawful for me to do what I will with mine own?"[25]

Here the Lord emphasizes two principles of law. The first is that when two people make an agreement, they are both bound by its provisions. The second rests on the primary rule governing private property, and that is the power of the owner to do whatever he wishes to do with it, so long as it does not violate the law or public policy.

But Jesus also had a broader sense of justice and equity than this parable may at first suggest. What was important to the householder was the fact these men had all waited patiently throughout the day for someone to hire them. This was a great convenience to the householder because he could hire them as he needed them. Some had waited practically all day long, and if they had not, they would not have been available when he wanted them. Furthermore, the householder knew that all of them needed to make a living which was represented by the going wage of a penny a day. All had been faithful in waiting until they were called, and all had performed the work assigned to them when the call came.

---

[25]Matthew 20: 13-15.

Therefore, to the householder, they were all of equal value, and so he paid them an equal wage. To those who criticized the householder for trying to be just, he said:

"Is thine eye evil, because I am good?"[26]

WHAT IT MEANS TO BE EQUAL IN HEAVEN

This parable laid the foundation for a rather amazing principle that prevails in heaven. We have to reflect on it for a moment to recognize how just and generous the purposes of our Heavenly Father really are. Surprising as it may seem, he has made it possible for each of us to be equal with one another in our respective kingdoms to which we will be assigned.

As we know, there are three degrees of glory in heaven, and the assignment to each of these kingdoms is based on the principle of obedience. However, the Lord says that once a person is judged to be worthy of a particular kingdom, that person can go forward and progress until he or she receives a fullness of the glory in that kingdom. The Lord says:

"Ye who are quickened by a portion of the celestial glory shall then receive of the same, even a fullness.

"And they who are quickened by a portion of the terrestrial glory shall then receive of the same, even a fullness.

"And also they who are quickened by a portion of the telestial glory shall then receive of the same, even a fullness."[27]

This scripture clearly states that all those within a particular kingdom can work until they enjoy the "fullness" of its glory. This means that eventually everyone in that kingdom can become equal!

The prophet describes how marvelous this element of equality turns out to be in the highest of the kingdoms:

---

[26]Matthew 20:15.
[27]Doctrine and Covenants 88:29-31.

"And thus we saw the glory of the celestial, which excels in all things—where God, even the Father, reigns upon his throne forever and ever....

"They who dwell in his presence are the church of the Firstborn; and they see as they are seen, and know as they are known, having received of his fullness and of his grace;

"AND HE MAKES THEM EQUAL IN POWER, AND IN MIGHT, AND IN DOMINION."[28]

As James and John now know, when EVERYBODY has EVERYTHING that exists in a kingdom, there is neither preference nor inequality. This is God's way.

Then there is another thing to consider. When all of the Father's children are virtually overwhelmed with far more than they deserved or could have earned, there really isn't any basis for comparison or complaint as there might be in this life.

The Lord has assured us that this element of overwhelming blessings beyond all expectations is very real in the next life. Even in the very least of the kingdoms—the telestial—the prophet wrote:

"We saw, in the heavenly vision, the glory of the telestial, which SURPASSES ALL UNDERSTANDING;

"And no man knows it except him to whom God has revealed it."[29]

All of this adds up to just one thing: "Trust in God. Obey his commandments. For all who do, the future is equally glorious!"

---

[28]Doctrine and Covenants 76:92-95 (emphasis added).
[29]Doctrine and Covenants 76:89-90 (emphasis added).

THE NEED TO ENDURE

Under God's system of government, there needs to be the strength of character in each of the Lord's servants that generates the capacity to continue faithfully in an assignment even though it may be painful, tedious, or difficult to endure.

I often think of Isaiah.

This prophet's immediate mission was to a wicked and perverse generation of his own people at Jerusalem. He knew he wasn't converting any souls, and so he agonized in his complaint before the Lord:

"I have laboured in vain, I have spent my strength for nought."[30]

"I gave my back to the smiters, and my cheeks to them that plucked off the hair: I hid not my face from shame and spitting."[31]

But Isaiah was made of the stuff that produces great prophets. After a little meditation he said:

"The Lord God will help me...therefore have I set my face like a flint, and I know that I shall not be ashamed."[32]

I also think of President David O. McKay, a modern-day prophet who led the Church of Jesus Christ of Latter-day Saints during the 1950s and '60s.

I had occasion to visit with him briefly after one of the illnesses that persisted during the last ten years of his life. He was confined to his apartment in the Hotel Utah where he also had his desk.

As we shook hands, he apologized for not being able to stand. We visited briefly and I could not help but look around the room.

---

[30]Isaiah 49:4.
[31]Isaiah 50:6.
[32]Isaiah 50:7.

There were oxygen tanks, needles for emergency injections, and bottles of pills and medicine. His mind was sharp but his body was frail.

My thoughts turned to King Benjamin who, under similar circumstances, was instructed by the Lord to turn his work over to his son, Mosiah. The aged Benjamin then lived in comfortable retirement for three more years.

President McKay suddenly brought my reflections to a halt by saying:

"The Lord has never granted me the authority to follow the example of King Benjamin."

I was embarrassed. Had he read my thoughts? Or was he also thinking of King Benjamin?

Then he added, "But I am blessed with two fine counselors."

President McKay knew his assignment at this stage of his life was to *endure*. His illness extended through several more years until he finally went home to his Heavenly Father at the age of 96 on January 18, 1970. But as a prophet and president of the church, his last ten years were his best.

In spite of extended periods of intense illness during those last ten years of his life, here is what President McKay and his counselors accomplished in that one decade:

The membership of the church practically doubled.

Four temples were built and dedicated.

The number of missions all over the world increased from 58 to 92.

The wards and branches increased from 2,882 to 4,922.

The number of stakes increased from 319 to 537.

But even before these last ten brilliant years, President David O. McKay had been an outstanding leader. From the time he first became President of the church in 1951, he initiated or approved 3,750 church buildings. That was more than all the church construction of the previous 120 years. And that was typical of the progress of the church during his administration. But in spite of all his early successes, his greatest and final task was to *endure* faithfully to the end.

The arduous and often painful task of enduring to the end has been required of every prophet in the latter-day dispensation. And some amazing things have been accomplished by these inspired leaders who set their faces like flint and pressed forward, even after their ages had reached into the eighties and nineties.

THE MEANING OF TOTAL COMMITMENT

With the above examples in mind, we can better appreciate an event which took place as Jesus and the apostles were slowly making their way toward Jerusalem. Luke writes:

"And a certain ruler [presiding officer in a synagogue] asked him, saying, Good Master, what shall I do to inherit eternal life?

"Jesus said unto him...Thou knowest the commandments....

"And he said, All these have I kept from my youth up."[33]

One would have thought this declaration of righteous deeds would have satisfied the Savior. One might have expected him to say, "Very well. Follow me." But he did not. Instead, the Savior looked earnestly at the young ruler and said:

"Yet lackest thou one thing: sell all that thou hast, and distribute unto the poor, and thou shalt have treasure in heaven: and come, follow me."[34]

---

[33]Luke 18:18-21.
[34]Luke 18:22.

This was the basic commitment Jesus had expected of all his apostles, his seventies, and any others who wished to become full-time servants of the Lord.

But it was too much for this young ruler. Luke continues:

"When he heard this, he was very sorrowful: for he was very rich.

"And when Jesus saw that he was very sorrowful, he said, How hardly shall they that have riches enter into the kingdom of God!"[35]

Then the Savior added an editorial comment:

"It is easier for a camel to go through a needle's eye, than for a rich man to enter into the kingdom of God."[36]

This reference to "the eye of a needle" is thought to refer to the night gate at the main entrance to the city. After the main gate was closed at the end of the day, latecomers were required to go through a tiny security gate where no camel could pass without first having all of its baggage unloaded. This seemed like a perfect illustration of the point the Savior was trying to make.[37]

Wouldn't this young ruler have been amazed if he had known what Jesus had in mind for him if he had just passed the test?

He might have been the disciple chosen to replace Judas Iscariot. In that case he would have been made an apostle. Or he might have gone on a mission with Paul, Peter or some of the other illustrious and faithful servants of the Lord. Whatever the Lord had in mind for this man, it faded into oblivion as the rich young ruler sadly walked away.

In contrast to this, we cannot help but think of some of the greatest leaders in scripture who started out rich and wicked, but

---

[35] Luke 18:23-24.
[36] Luke 18:25.
[37] Talmage, *Jesus the Christ*, p. 485.

repented and humbly went forward in service and dedication to reach the highest levels of discipleship. Take for example, Amulek, or Alma the Younger, who tried to destroy the church over which his father presided; or King Lamoni, who had been cruel and killed his servants for trivial offenses.

All these were challenged to forsake all and serve the Lord. Through a humble response and a total commitment, they found their genuine destiny. Who knows what great callings awaited the rich young ruler if he had just passed the test.

SACRIFICES FOR THE KINGDOM WILL NOT GO UNREWARDED

The apostles were puzzled as they watched the "sorrowful" rich young ruler walk away. This young man had been obeying all of the commandments. He just didn't feel comfortable selling all he had, giving it to the poor, and becoming an itinerant disciple of Jesus. Among themselves, they murmured:

"Who then *can* be saved?"[38]

Jesus simply said:

"Things which are impossible with men are possible with God."[39]

This was like saying, "Don't worry about it. God will work it out."

But Peter was not satisfied. The young ruler had declined to "forsake all," and follow Jesus. But what about the apostles? Peter wanted to know where they stood. Therefore he said:

"Lo *we* have left all and followed thee."[40]

---

[38]Luke 18: 26.
[39]Luke 18:27.
[40]Luke 18:28 (emphasis added).

It is clear that he was seeking the Savior's confirmation that they had paid the price and were worthy to be saved. But it was equally clear that they were just like the rest of the Jews. They thought salvation could be "earned."

Their understanding of the beauty of Christ's atonement had to come later. Eventually they would understand that righteous living and good works can only "qualify" a person to receive the free gift of salvation through the atoning sacrifice of the Son of God. In other words, the disciples could earn the right to receive salvation, but they had no capacity whatever to create it. Only the Savior was in a position to do that. (At a later time we will discuss why this was so.[41])

Jesus wisely elected not to stir up their tender feelings by discussing the real genius of the atonement. At this time he felt it would be sufficient to assure them that their many sacrifices would not go unrewarded. So he said:

"Verily I say unto you, There is no man that hath left house, or brethren, or sisters, or father, or mother, or wife, or children, or lands, for my sake, and the gospel's, but he shall receive an hundredfold...and in the world to come eternal life."[42]

Well, that is all the apostles wanted to hear. To be rewarded a hundredfold and have eternal life besides—what more could one ask?

* * * *

TOPICS FOR REFLECTION AND DISCUSSION

1. As you watch the general authorities of the church perform their duties, what seems to be the order of their priorities?

---

[41]See Appendix F.
[42]Mark 10:29-30.

2. How would you grade the efficiency rating of the general authorities as a group? Does this strike you as remarkable in view of the age level that most of them have attained?

3. Make a list of your own priorities in terms of your responsibilities to the Lord, your family, your employer and your friends. In view of what the Savior taught, do you think it would be an advantage to give the Lord's work a somewhat higher priority?

4. What is the lesson Jesus taught in the parable of the pounds? In what way does this reflect the guidelines in the Lord's Law of Consecration?

5. Is there a human tendency to be tempted to seek preferences like James and John? Who was the first apostle to suffer martyrdom?

6. Can you explain how all of those assigned to a particular kingdom of glory can eventually be equal? Can you cite the scripture which teaches this doctrine?

7. In what way have the prophets of the latter days demonstrated a phenomenal capacity to endure? What kind of tribute do you think their counselors deserve when we consider the load they carry when the prophet is indisposed?

8. Can you name three tremendous things that happened during the last decade of President McKay's life when he was ill so much of the time? What do you think we can learn from this?

9. What did Jesus apparently mean when he said it is as difficult for a rich person to get into heaven as it is for a camel to go through the needle's eye?

10. Do "good works" allow us to earn our salvation or do they simply make us eligible to receive the blessings of salvation through the atonement?

*   *   *   *

CHAPTER 32

THE ROYAL PROCESSION OF THE UNCROWNED KING

After enjoying the overnight hospitality of Zacchaeus, the rich but repentant tax collector, Jesus and the apostles were probably no more than five or six hours away from Bethany. This meant Jesus probably arrived at the home of Mary and Martha during the early afternoon of Friday. John fixes the date of their arrival as "six days before the passover."[1]

The sabbath began at sunset on Friday, and no doubt Jesus and his apostles made the next twenty-four hours a sabbath of much needed rest.

Because Jesus was a fugitive from the diabolical plot of the Sanhedrin, it is not likely that he went to the synagogue on this particular sabbath day. As John tells us:

"Both the chief priests and the Pharisees had given a commandment, that, if any man knew where he were, he should show it, that they might take him."[2]

Furthermore, this was the Savior's last sabbath in mortality, and surely he must have had many things he wanted to share with Mary and Martha on this beautiful spring day in early April.

Meanwhile, in Jerusalem, there was great anxiety concerning Jesus. They wondered whether or not he would come to the feast. Many of them had undoubtedly brought their sick, their blind, and their crippled with them in hopes that Jesus, the marvelous healer, would come. John says:

---

[1] John 12:1.
[2] John 11:57.

"Then sought they for Jesus, and spake among themselves, as they stood in the temple, What think ye, that he will not come to the feast?"[3]

The chief priests and Pharisees were equally concerned lest the presence of Jesus on the feast day might cause some kind of commotion that would attract the attention of the Romans. As we have already mentioned, they had sent out the word that if Jesus were seen by any of their spies, they should report his whereabouts immediately so they could take Jesus out of circulation before there was an uproar.

THE ROYAL PROCESSION

The morning after the sabbath, Jesus told two of his disciples to go about a mile down the road to Bethphage (BETH-fa-gee). Just as Bethany means "house of dates," so Bethphage has a literal significance, meaning "house of figs."[4]

The two disciples were not sent to look for a man, but were told to look for a certain animal with a nearly full-grown colt.[5]

This animal is the ass of the Middle East which is a beautiful, fleet animal used by the rulers and upper classes. This animal was always used by the Jewish royalty and aristocracy. Here is what we read in one of the Bible dictionaries:

"The ass as found in eastern countries is a very different animal from what he is in western Europe. The most noble and honorable amongst the Jews were wont to be mounted on asses....In the east it is especially remarkable for its patience, gentleness, intelligence, meek submission and great power of endurance."[6]

This animal is not a hybrid, such as a mule, and it is not a donkey. Its description continues:

---

[3]John 11:56.
[4]Peloubet's *Bible Dictionary*, under "Bethphage."
[5]Luke 19:30.
[6]Peloubet's *Bible Dictionary*, p. 53.

"The color is usually a reddish brown, but there are white asses, which are much prized. The ass was the animal of peace, as the horse was the animal of war; hence the appropriateness of Christ in his triumphal entry riding on an ass."[7]

So that his disciples would not be accused of stealing, Jesus said:

"And if any man ask you, Why do ye loose him? thus shall ye say unto him, Because the Lord hath need of him.

"And they that were sent went their way, and found even as he had said unto them.

"And as they were loosing the colt, the owners thereof said unto them, Why loose ye the colt?

"And they said, The Lord hath need of him."[8]

Behind this dialogue there is an important human interest story, but the Bible does not disclose it. The man who owned these two animals was obviously a disciple of Jesus. We cannot help wondering whether Jesus had been in communication with him or whether the Savior knew by inspiration that he would respond positively when he was told "the Lord hath need of him." The complete answer will have to wait for further revelation.

The two disciples must have asked themselves these same questions. It was rather amazing that the man surrendered the nearly full grown colt so willingly. And it was interesting that Jesus even knew this colt had never been ridden.[9] No doubt the two disciples enjoyed a moment of special satisfaction as they brought this beautiful young animal to the Master. Luke says:

---

[7] Ibid..
[8] Luke 19:31-34.
[9] Luke 19:30.

"And they brought him to Jesus: and they cast their garments upon the colt, and they set Jesus thereon."[10]

In all of this, John saw the literal fulfillment of an ancient prophecy by Zechariah who wrote:

"Rejoice greatly, O daughter of Zion; shout, O daughter of Jerusalem: behold, thy King cometh unto thee: he is just, and having salvation; lowly, and riding upon an ass, and upon a colt the foal of an ass."[11]

We should mention in passing, that the King James translation of Matthew 21:2 indicates that the disciples brought "them," meaning both the mare and the colt. However, the Inspired Version says "it," meaning that they brought only the colt, thereby harmonizing this passage in Matthew with the accounts of the other three Gospel writers.

THE CROWDS ASSEMBLED ALL ALONG THE ROAD TO WELCOME JESUS TO JERUSALEM

It is not difficult to imagine the excitement of the people as the word spread throughout Jerusalem that Jesus was coming to the Feast. John writes that the great crowds of "...people that were come to the feast, when they heard that Jesus was coming to Jerusalem,

"Took branches of palm trees, and went forth to meet him, and cried, Hosanna: Blessed is the King of Israel that cometh in the name of the Lord."[12]

The record suggests that the composition of this huge crowd that came pouring down from Jerusalem was made up mostly of the Savior's own constituency. Here were the hundreds he had healed, along with their families, neighbors and friends. Here were men leaping for joy who had been lame all their lives until Jesus touched them. Here were the hunchbacks who now stood tall and straight.

---

[10]Luke 19:35.

[11]Zechariah 9:9; John 12:14-15.

[12]John 12:12-13.

Here were those who had been blind, deaf or suffering from an impediment of speech until they felt the healing power of Jesus.

Then there were people who came primarily on faith. They had heard the testimony of others and already half-believed. They had come to see for themselves. Among these were probably several hundred who had heard about Lazarus. This miracle was virtually unbelievable. John says:

"The people therefore that was with him when he called Lazarus out of his grave, and raised him from the dead, bare record.

"For this cause the people also met him, for that they heard that he had done this miracle."[13]

THE SURGING CROWD MEETS JESUS

The Roman road from Jericho to Jerusalem climbs past Bethany and then curves a little to the south toward Bethphage. After that it moves around the southern end of the Mount of Olives and descends gradually toward the Brook Kidron before climbing up to the eastern gate of Jerusalem.

The great crowds met Jesus and his apostles just as they were rounding the southern flank of the Mount of Olives. John says:

"And when he was come nigh, even now at the descent of the mount of Olives, the whole multitude of the disciples began to rejoice and praise God with a loud voice for all the mighty works that they had seen."[14]

From this verse it becomes obvious that most of these people were the Savior's disciples who had either been healed by Jesus or had personally witnessed his "mighty works."

Mark gives his version of what happened. He writes:

---

[13]John 12:17-18.
[14]Luke 19:37.

"And many spread their garments in the way: and others cut down branches off the trees, and strawed them in the way."[15]

Only kings and conquerors were greeted with such extraordinary manifestation of adoration and respect. In Rome, this was called "a triumph."

To welcome Jesus, this crowd marched in joyful acclaim both before and behind the Savior. Mark says:

"And they that went before, and they that followed, cried, saying, Hosanna; Blessed is he that cometh in the name of the Lord:

"Blessed be the kingdom of our father David, that cometh in the name of the Lord: Hosanna in the highest."[16]

The prophets of God had been anticipating this glorious moment for nearly four thousand years![17]

THE ANGRY FRUSTRATION OF
THE HIGH PRIESTS AND PHARISEES

When the members of the Sanhedrin and other leaders of the people saw the joyous excitement of the crowds pouring out of the city to meet Jesus, they exclaimed one to another:

"Perceive ye how ye prevail nothing? behold, the world is gone after him!"[18]

Some of the high priests and Pharisees could not stand it. They determined to hurry out and meet Jesus so they could see for themselves what was happening. However, when they heard such expressions as "Blessed be the King" and "Hosanna to the Son of David," they almost suffered an attack of apoplexy. Some of them got close enough to Jesus to speak to him, and said:

---

[15]Mark 11:8.
[16]Mark 11:9-10.
[17]Moses 7:45-46, P. of G. P.
[18]John 12:19.

"Master, rebuke thy disciples!

"And he answered and said unto them, I tell you that, if these should hold their peace, the stones would immediately cry out."[19]

There have been many attempts to explain what Jesus meant by the "stones" that would cry out if the Savior's entry into Jerusalem had gone unacknowledged. Some have assumed that he must have meant the gentiles or the Romans. However, there is clear scriptural evidence that Jesus was speaking literally of the stones, the very elements, the substance of the planet that Jesus, himself, had organized. They gloried in the Great Jehovah now come to earth as the Christ. They recognized him in this hour of triumph even if the high priests did not.

Within a few days these stones actually would cry out, but in anguish. They would grind and shake, causing a severe earthquake that would rumble through the crust of the earth in protest against the agony which the Savior would be suffering on the cross. Matthew later wrote about it, saying:

"And, behold, the veil of the temple was rent in twain from the top to the bottom; and the earth did quake, and the rocks rent."[20]

The stones indeed *COULD* cry out, and within a few days, when the intelligences in these elements had gone beyond the threshold of their endurance, they would roar out in anger. Enoch saw in vision how the earth was "pained" because of human wickedness[21] and beheld that when Jesus was crucified:

"All the creations of God mourned; and the earth groaned; and the rocks were rent."[22]

---

[19]Luke 19:39-40.

[20]Matthew 27:51.

[21]Moses 7:48, P. of G. P.

[22]Moses 7:56, P. of G. P.

JESUS STOPS THE PROCESSION TO WEEP

After descending the Roman road some distance, the Savior could look directly across the valley and see the city in full view. There was Mount Moriah crowned with the beautiful temple Herod had built. It was surrounded by large courtyards to accommodate the people, and beyond the temple, on another mount higher than Moriah, were the splendid palaces of Pilate and the aristocracy of the Jews. At this point, Luke says:

"And when he was come near, he beheld the city, and wept over it, Saying, If thou hadst known, even thou, at least in this thy day, the things which belong unto thy peace! but now they are hid from thine eyes.

"For the days shall come upon thee, that thine enemies shall cast a trench about thee, and compass thee round, and keep thee in on every side,

"And shall lay thee even with the ground, and thy children within thee; and they shall not leave in thee one stone upon another; because thou knewest not the time of thy visitation."[23]

All of this violent destruction would come upon Jerusalem in 70 A.D., with a horror never to be forgotten.

Now the road wound down across the valley of Kidron and upward toward the acropolis. In a surge of joyous exultation, the royal procession carried the uncrowned king up to Mount Moriah and entered the temple esplanade.

KING DAVID WOULD HAVE
REJOICED TO SEE THIS SIGHT

Except for the absence of trumpets and cymbals, this royal cortege would have done justice to any of the kings of ancient Israel. Jesus came riding on the same royal creature that was the popular mount for David and his sons. The crowds were acclaiming the

---

[23]Luke 19:41-44.

Savior as their Messiah, which was a higher tribute than any other king of Israel had ever received.

Matthew says some of the people who may have been from distant places were astonished when they saw what was happening. Matthew writes:

"And when he was come into Jerusalem, all the city was moved, saying, Who is this?

"And the multitude said, This is Jesus the prophet of Nazareth of Galilee."[24]

It is very likely that the most exuberant leaders of the crowd advancing immediately ahead of the Savior included a vast throng from his own region of Galilee. They would be quick to assure the strangers that this was not only the famous Jesus, but Jesus who hailed from Nazareth of Galilee!

As Jesus dismounted and went into the Court of the Gentiles, the crowd surged in with him, singing, dancing and shouting.

GREEK CONVERTS SEEK AN AUDIENCE WITH JESUS

Among the strangers who had come to the feast, none would be more thrilled and excited than the new converts to Judaism. This was like coming to their first General Conference. And when they learned that there was a celebrity in attendance, even the great Jewish Messiah, they desperately wanted to converse with him.

As is the case with most new conference visitors, their desires may not have been merely for their own sakes, but to be able to relate to the folks back home whom they had met and what they had seen. This is always an important part of "going to Conference."

With the Jews more or less monopolizing the space immediately around Jesus, the Greeks decided to ask one of the apostles to help

---

[24]Matthew 21:10-11.

them reach Jesus, perhaps even speak to him. So John says, they "... came therefore to Philip, which was of Bethsaida of Galilee, and desired him, saying, Sir, we would see Jesus.

"Philip cometh and telleth Andrew: and again Andrew and Philip tell Jesus."[25]

It is interesting how Jesus greeted these eager Greek converts. He knew that before this feast was over, they would have the shocking experience of witnessing the Savior's crucifixion, and he apparently wanted to prepare them for this traumatic experience. Almost immediately, he plunged into a discussion of the atoning sacrifice which was at the very core of the Jewish passover ritual. To these Greeks, he said:

"The hour is come, that the Son of man should be glorified."[26]

But how would he be glorified? Jesus had to tell them that it would come as a result of his being killed. What a shocking revelation of religious news this turned out to be. But there was a rationale behind it all. He said:

"Verily, verily, I say unto you, Except a corn of wheat fall into the ground and die, it abideth alone: but if it die, it bringeth forth much fruit."[27]

He wanted them to know that if a great harvest could be brought about by the sacrifice of his life, it was not to be counted as a great loss but the means for a heavenly harvest. As for himself, he wanted them to understand that one of the unique principles of heaven is this:

---

[25]John 12:21-22.
[26]John 12:23.
[27]John 12:24.

"He that loveth his life shall lose it; and he that hateth his life [or is willing to sacrifice his life for a good cause] in this world shall keep it unto life eternal."[28]

But these converts could not help but wonder where *they* were supposed to fit in. Jesus said:

"If any man serve me, let him follow me; and where I am, there shall also my servant be: if any man serve me, him will my Father honour."[29]

SUDDENLY JESUS FALTERS

What Jesus was talking about was not storybook fiction. It was terrible and real. Just talking about it suddenly overwhelmed his feelings. Almost as though he were in a state of sublimation, or engaging in a soliloquy and conversing with himself, these people heard him say:

"Now is my soul troubled; and what shall I say? Father, save me from this hour: but for this cause came I unto this hour."[30]

Then the Savior's very soul burst forth in a cry to his Heavenly Father. He pleaded:

"Father, glorify thy name!"[31]

Jesus was faltering. It would happen again at the Last Supper, and also in the Garden of Gethsemane. This was an anguish of haunting depression no other member of the human family would ever experience so deeply. The scripture says:

"Then came a voice from heaven, saying, I have both glorified it, and will glorify it again.

---

[28]John 12:25.
[29]John 12:26.
[30]John 12:27.
[31]John 12:28.

"The people therefore, that stood by, and heard it, said that it thundered: others said, An angel spake to him."[32]

The Father's reassurance was all the Savior needed in order to regain his composure. To those standing near him, he said:

"This voice came not because of me, but for your sakes."[33]

These people who witnessed the trembling of the very Son of God needed reassurance also.

And Jesus, having regained his strength, felt a surge of exhilaration pass through his being. He said:

"Now is the judgment of this world: now shall the prince of this world be cast out.

"And I, if I be lifted up from the earth, will draw all men unto me.

"This he said, signifying what death he should die."[34]

Once Jesus had heard his Father's voice he could talk about his death without having it drown him in apprehension. He could speak of being "lifted up" in a way that was immediately recognized by those around him as a prediction that he would die by crucifixion.

But by this time a crowd of traditional Jews appear to have joined the crowd. They were expecting a Messiah who would destroy their enemies and reign forever. What was this talk about being "lifted up"? They saw a great inconsistency between Jesus as the promised Messiah and Jesus who talked of being crucified. They said:

---

[32]John 12: 28-29.
[33]John 12:30.
[34]John 12:31-33.

"We have heard out of the law that Christ [the Anointed one, or the Messiah] abideth for ever: and how sayest thou, The Son of man must be lifted up? who is this Son of man?"[35]

These traditional Jews began to suspect that there must be a distinction between the Messiah who "abideth for ever," and this Son of man who is to be crucified.

It is interesting that Jesus did not answer their question directly. He simply spoke of himself as "the Light," and left them with a statement they would no doubt mull over in their minds long after he was gone. He said:

"Yet a little while is the light with you. Walk while ye have the light, lest darkness come upon you: for he that walketh in darkness knoweth not whither he goeth.

"While ye have light, believe in the light, that ye may be the children of light."[36]

HOW JESUS ESCAPED FROM THE ADORING CROWD

About this time Jesus was getting ready to depart, and so Mark says:

"When he had looked round about upon all things, and blessed his disciples, the eventide was come; and he went out unto Bethany with the twelve."[37]

However, when John was writing his account of the Savior's life he felt something important had been left out. If we stop to think about it, there is no way that Jesus could have simply excused himself and walked away from this great crowd of loving disciples and admirers. They would have followed him wherever he tried to go. This would have been particularly true of those who had brought their blind, their crippled and their sick to be blessed and healed.

---

[35] John 12:34.
[36] John 12:35-36.
[37] Mark 11:11.

Jesus was no doubt fully aware of their desires, but the healing of the sick and afflicted was something he was planning to take care of the next day.

Meanwhile, his present task was to disengage himself and escape from this adoring crowd without having them follow him. Jesus therefore did what he had done several times before. He performed that convenient miracle which we call the "veiling of the eyes." John says:

"Jesus...departed, and did hide himself from them."[38]

Apparently his apostles knew he would be going over the Mount of Olives and down the other side to Bethany. We assume that somewhere along the path where it was safe for Jesus to join them, Jesus made his reappearance.

We also assume that Jesus stayed with his beloved friends, Mary, Martha and Lazarus, and no doubt there were numerous friends in Bethany who felt honored to provide accommodations for the apostles.

* * * *

TOPICS FOR REFLECTION AND DISCUSSION

1. Why were the people so anxious to know whether Jesus was coming to the feast? Who would be particularly worried lest he not come?

2. Why were the chief priests and Pharisees so anxious to arrest Jesus and get him out of circulation before the beginning of the Feast of the Passover?

3. Why were the rulers of the Jews so fearful of the reaction of the Romans in case of an uprising? Who was the Roman governor in Jerusalem at this time?

---

[38]John 12:36.

4. Did the Savior's disciples bring both the mare and the colt from Bethphage for Jesus? Was it a donkey? Describe the kind of animal this colt really was. Why did this particular animal attract the fancy of kings?

5. When the people began spreading cloaks, flowers and palm fronds along the way, what did it indicate? What did the cheering and joyful people say that outraged the chief priests and Pharisees?

6. Do the scriptures indicate that the stones and other earthly elements could display an intelligent reaction to the mistreatment of the Savior?

7. Why did Jesus stop the procession when the city of Jerusalem came into full view? What did he say was going to happen to Jerusalem?

8. Describe the highlights of the Savior's conversation with the Greeks who were apparently new converts to Judaism. What happened during this conversation that suddenly caused Jesus to falter? What happened to help him regain his composure?

9. Would it have been readily feasible for Jesus to have excused himself and left the crowd at the temple? Who would have been particularly anxious to follow him?

10. What did Jesus do? Where is it believed he went for the night? About how far would he have to walk to get there?

*　*　*　*

CHAPTER 33

THE SAVIOR INTENSIFIES HIS ACTIVITIES AS HIS MINISTRY DRAWS NEAR TO THE END

On Monday morning, Jesus gathered up his disciples and began the two-mile walk from Bethany to the temple. It was an early start. None of them had eaten breakfast.

Apparently Jesus had intended to gather some of the early figs from a tree he had noticed the evening before. It was covered with rich foliage and should have provided an early-morning snack for all of them.

But when they reached the tree, there was no fruit on it.

Unlike most other trees, the fruit of the fig tree begins to develop before the foliage, so this tree was in full foliage, and should have been laden with figs. In many respects it was like the scribes and Pharisees, all foliage, no fruit.

Jesus was angry with this abnormal and dissolute tree, and said:

"No man eat fruit of thee hereafter for ever."[1]

It would not be until the following day that the apostles would realize what the words of the Savior had done to this tree.

---

[1] Mark 11:14.

JESUS CLEANSES THE TEMPLE
FOR THE SECOND TIME

As Jesus and his apostles entered the east gate and then climbed up to the temple mount, Jesus knew what he would see. He had noticed it the day before but had decided to wait until this second day to do something about it.

The large Court of the Gentiles, surrounding the temple, was like a bazaar. There were haggling money changers, bellowing calves, bleating sheep, and boisterous merchants standing in front of their booths and calling for people to see their wares.

Everything was just as it had been three years earlier when Jesus had denounced the people for making the temple a "house of merchandise" instead of a house for prayer.[2] Three years earlier he had even used an improvised whip made of small cords to clear out the whole motley crowd.

But now they were back, and so was Jesus. As the Savior came to his last Feast of the Passover, he saw that all around the temple precincts—even this early in the morning—the same money-mongering was taking place. There were the noisy money changers along with the outcries of the merchants selling doves, lambs, calves, herbs, vegetables, jewelry, and trinkets.

It was obvious to Jesus that his earlier warning had been arrogantly ignored, and as he surveyed the scene, a sense of righteous indignation rose in him. Suddenly, he strode into the midst of the clamor and declared in a loud voice:

"My house is the house of prayer: but ye have made it a den of thieves!"[3]

It is interesting that three years earlier he had said, "Make not my *FATHER'S* house an house of merchandise."[4] Now he was ready to

---

[2]John 2:16.
[3]Luke 19:46.
[4]John 2:16 (emphasis added).

assume his own jurisdiction over the kingdom his Father had given him. He therefore boldly spoke of the temple as "MY house" that had been desecrated by a "den of thieves."

His voice of indignation must have attracted some attention in the immediate vicinity, but when he began to express his feelings by taking direct action, it soon had everybody's attention. With his strong hands, he began turning over tables, opening dove cotes, releasing lambs and calves, and driving the frightened merchants in all directions as they clung frantically to their money bags.

The people saw Jesus in a completely different perspective than that which had existed three years earlier when he cleansed the temple. On that earlier occasion he only had with him his family and perhaps five of his future apostles. Nevertheless, he *had* successfully cleansed the temple.

But now in many ways, things were different. As Jesus came to his last Feast of the Passover, he was indeed a force to be reckoned with. This carpenter from Galilee had become one of the most famous personalities in all the land. In this multitude he was no doubt surrounded by thousands of faithful supporters who had been in the royal procession the day before.

No one tried to stop Jesus as he proceeded to clear the huge courtyard where most of this desecration was taking place. The trafficking of merchandise had turned the temple precincts into a common thoroughfare, but once the temple was cleared, Mark says Jesus "would not suffer that any man should carry any vessel through the temple."[5]

At the northwest corner of the temple esplanade was the Roman fortress called the Antonia. Soldiers were stationed there to put down any uprising among the people. However, this was no uprising. The soldiers probably stood on the parapet of the fortress, viewing with

---

[5]Mark 11:16.

the greatest amusement this one determined Jew driving crowds of other Jews before him like a flock of frightened birds.

JESUS HEALS THE LAME, BLIND, CRIPPLED AND SICK

Once the storm of indignation had passed, Jesus returned to the task of his gentle and compassionate ministry.

Just as he had done three years earlier, he moved among the beggars who were incapacitated and unable to flee. And there were the parents who also had remained with their loved ones who were blind, deaf, lame or sick. They had come to this feast hoping Jesus would heal them. And he did. Matthew says he healed every one.[6]

Not only was there great rejoicing among those who were healed, but the crowds of believers surged toward the Savior. They were elated to see Jesus performing the great works for which he had become famous. Even the children copied their elders by singing out their rapturous praise.

However, there was no such praise coming from the chief priests, scribes, and Pharisees. This acclamation of adoration aroused in them a spirit of horrified vituperation. They made their way to Jesus and said:

"Hearest thou what these say? And Jesus saith unto them, Yea; have ye never read, Out of the mouth of babes and sucklings thou hast perfected praise?"[7]

WERE THE RULERS OF THE JEWS BLINDED?

The apostle John left some interesting comments about the rulers of the Jews which illustrate a degree of sympathy for their situation since they did not understand what was happening. John, for example, knew that a mind touched by the Spirit of God is susceptible to responses which an unenlightened mentality would

---

[6]Matthew 21:14.
[7]Matthew 21:16.

never comprehend. Keeping this in mind, we note the following comment by John:

"Though he had done so many miracles before them, yet they believed not on him....

"They could not believe, because...[as] Esaias said...

"He hath blinded their eyes, and hardened their heart; that they should not see with their eyes, nor understand with their heart, and be converted, and I should heal them."[8]

Here is an interesting concept. John is suggesting that it was in the wisdom of God to withhold his light from the leaders of the Jews so that they *"could not"* believe and that, of course, left them with hardened hearts and eyes that could not see.

Isaiah said this was necessary lest they be converted and the Savior should heal them. We cannot help wondering whether John is suggesting that if they had been converted Jesus would not have been killed, and if he had not made his atoning sacrifice, the whole plan of salvation would have been defeated.

This implies that some of the Jews needed to be left in darkness so that the crucifixion would take place. It also implies that some of those who consented to the crucifixion of Jesus would be counted among those who sinned in ignorance, and would therefore be eligible for conversion when the apostles taught them the gospel after the resurrection.[9]

The words of both John and Isaiah trumpet a message declaring that mankind must be cautious in their judgments and condemnation of those whom God himself must be the final adjudicator. We human beings, restricted by the limited parameters of life's tunnel vision,

---

[8]John 12:37-40; Isaiah 53:1.
[9]Acts 3:17-18.

cannot understand all of God's judgments, or how things will eventually turn out. As the Lord said in a modern revelation:

"But remember that all my judgments are not given unto men."[10]

John makes another editorial comment which is interesting:

"Among the chief rulers also many believed on him; but because of the Pharisees they did not confess him, lest they should be put out of the synagogue:

"For they loved the praise of men more than the praise of God."[11]

As this story continues to unfold we will get a far deeper understanding of what John and Isaiah were talking about.

JESUS IDENTIFIES HIMSELF AS HIS FATHER'S MESSENGER

The Savior's mortal ministry was drawing to a close. We sense this in his renewed emphasis on the design of the Father to send Jesus as his messenger. His purpose was to get the Jews to accept him as the Father's ambassador since they claimed they truly believed in the Father. John describes how the Savior tried to appeal to the people on this basis. He wrote:

"Jesus cried and said, He that believeth on me, believeth not on me, but on him that sent me.

"And he that seeth me seeth him that sent me."[12]

This verse is very similar to the statement the Savior later made to Philip when he said:

---

[10]Doctrine and Covenants 29:30.
[11]John 12:42-43.
[12]John 12:44-45.

"He that hath seen me hath seen the Father."[13]

This statement clearly emphasizes what Paul would later say, that the Son is in "the express image of the Father."[14] This same phrase is used in describing the remarkable resemblance between Adam and Seth. Concerning Seth the scripture says:

"Seth...was in the express image of his father, Adam."[15]

But Jesus had more to say about his relationship with his Father beside their identical physical appearance. He asked Philip:

"Believest thou not that I am in the Father, and the Father in me? the words that I speak unto you I speak not of myself: but the Father that dwelleth in me, he doeth the works.

"Believe me that I am in the Father, and the Father in me: or else believe me for the very works' sake....

"And whatsoever ye shall ask in my name, that will I do, that the Father may be glorified in the Son."[16]

Jesus wanted his disciples, as well as the Jewish traditionalists who were listening, to know that not only he and his Father look alike, but they think alike, and they function alike. The Father completely honors the son by granting that which his disciples ask in the name of his Son.

Now Jesus moved to a different subject. He wanted them to know the risk that the people were taking if they knowingly rejected his message. His words take on deeper meaning if we fill in a little background.

---

[13]John 14:9.
[14]Hebrews 1:3.
[15]Doctrine and Covenants 138:40.
[16]John 14:10-13.

THE BASIS FOR GOD'S JUDGMENT

As we mentioned earlier, before the great last judgment there will be a panoramic vision in which every person who ever lived upon this earth will get to see "the secret acts of men, and the thoughts and intents of their hearts, and the mighty works of God" during the first thousand years of human history. Then they will see the second thousand years, the third, and so on until the seventh thousand years.[17]

Every person's life will be seen as he or she lived it. The only exception will be those acts and thoughts that were brought under the atonement and blotted out.[18]

The rest of each individual's acts, thoughts and words will remain on the record to be revealed to all mankind. So Jesus wanted his disciples to ask themselves the question: What will condemn a person at the great last judgment? Obviously, it will be those words, acts, and thoughts that remained on the record.

With this in mind, notice what Jesus had said a little earlier:

"I am come a light into the world, that whosoever believeth on me should not abide in darkness.

"If any man hear my words, and believe not, I judge him not: for I came not to judge [condemn] the world, but to save the world.

"He that rejecteth me, and receiveth not my words, hath one that judgeth him: the WORDS THAT I HAVE SPOKEN [that he or she rejected], the same shall judge him in the last day."[19]

So everyone will be condemned or judged by their own acts and if they knowingly rejected the Father's words or the gospel message, it will stand against them.

---

[17]Doctrine and Covenants 88:108-110.
[18]Acts 3:19.
[19]John 12:47-48.

Jesus closed his ministry on Monday by emphasizing that rejecting his words was not an affront to him, but to the Father. As he explained:

"I have not spoken of myself; but the Father which sent me, he gave me a commandment, what I should say, and what I should speak."[20]

With this, Jesus concluded his message to the Jews for that day. Since he had healed all their sick,[21] he apparently had no difficulty disengaging himself from either his critics or admirers. Matthew therefore simply says:

"He left them, and went out of the city into Bethany, and he lodged there."[22]

ON TUESDAY JESUS COMMENCED THE LAST DAY OF HIS PUBLIC MINISTRY

Early the next morning Jesus and his apostles commenced their two-mile journey back toward Jerusalem and the temple. This time they apparently partook of their breakfast before leaving. At least they did not depend on the fruitless fig tree.

However, the apostles were astonished when they came to the tree. It had withered to the roots as though it had been struck by a blight. Peter spoke up and said:

"Master, behold, the fig tree which thou cursedst is withered away."[23]

As Jesus had emphasized on other occasions, he wanted them to understand that the intelligences in all things will obey one who speaks with the power of sufficient faith. Therefore he said:

---

[20]John 12:49.
[21]Matthew 21:14.
[22]Matthew 21:17.
[23]Mark 11:21.

"Verily I say unto you, If ye have faith, and doubt not, ye shall not only do this which is done to the fig tree, but also if ye shall say unto this mountain, Be thou removed, and be thou cast into the sea; it shall be done.

"And all things, whatsoever ye shall ask in prayer, believing, ye shall receive."[24]

However, a righteous prayer requires a pure heart and a forgiving spirit. Therefore Mark mentions that Jesus also said:

"And when ye stand praying, forgive, if ye have ought against any: that your Father also which is in heaven may forgive you your trespasses.

"But if ye do not forgive, neither will your Father which is in heaven forgive your trespasses."[25]

THE RULERS CHALLENGE JESUS

We gain the impression that the reason Jesus was not challenged on the two occasions when he cleansed the temple was because the rulers were suffering from a guilty conscience and could not think of a basis for stopping the Savior from doing what they should have done themselves. But the day after the second cleansing, the leaders had a plan. Matthew says:

"The chief priests and the elders of the people came unto him as he was teaching, and said, By what authority doest thou these things? and who gave thee this authority?"[26]

Three years earlier, the priests had asked for a "sign" to provide proof that God had designated Jesus as his surrogate to cleanse the temple. However, with all the healings they had seen the day before, it would seem superfluous to ask him for a sign. So their tactic was to ask him by whose "authority" he had cleansed the temple. After

---

[24]Matthew 21:21-22.
[25]Mark 11:25-26.
[26]Matthew 21:23.

all, they were in charge, and certainly they had not given him any authority.

"And Jesus answered and said unto them, I also will ask you one thing, which if ye tell me, I in like wise will tell you by what authority I do these things.

"The baptism of John, whence was it? from heaven, or of men?"[27]

The chief priests and elders of the temple were old hands at tactical strategy, but Jesus had put them on the defensive. No doubt they could learn a lesson or two in polemics from this maddening fellow from Galilee. The scripture says:

"And they reasoned with themselves, saying, If we shall say, From heaven; he will say unto us, Why did ye not then believe him?

"But if we shall say, Of men; we fear the people; for all hold John as a prophet.

"And they answered Jesus, and said, We cannot tell." [28]

This was an admission of total defeat. It left the central question of the Savior's authority lying on the table. Jesus sidestepped the whole issue by saying:

"Neither tell I you by what authority I do these things."[29]

THE PARABLE OF THE TWO SONS

There was no doubt about it, in the eyes of the Pharisees this Galilean was a slippery fellow. He had outwitted them. Perhaps they should hold a private caucus and figure out a new tactic. But before they could leave, Jesus stopped them and said:

---

[27]Matthew 21:24-25.
[28]Matthew 21:25-27.
[29]Matthew 21:27.

"But what think ye? A certain man had two sons; and he came to the first, and said, Son, go work to day in my vineyard.

"He answered and said, I will not: but afterward he repented, and went."[30]

Obviously, they couldn't leave now. It was quite plain Jesus was setting them up in front of the listening crowd. What would he say next? Jesus continued:

"And he came to the second, and said likewise. And he answered and said, I go, sir: and went not."[31]

Now Jesus pointed the lance at them with this simple question:

"Whether of them twain did the will of his father?

"They say unto him, The first."[32]

This was the right answer, and it gave the Savior a weapon which they had launched out of their own mouths for a stunning blow.

"Jesus saith unto them, Verily I say unto you, That the publicans and the harlots go into the kingdom of God before you."[33]

The harlots and hated publicans (dishonest tax collectors) represented the first son. They made no pretense that they would obey the Father's law, but when they were taught the gospel, they repented and did what they had formerly thought they would never do.

And it followed, of course, that the second son must be the chief priests, scribes, Pharisees and elders who had made the most solemn and impressive promises that they would obey the Father's law. But

---

[30]Matthew 21:28-29.
[31]Matthew 21:30.
[32]Matthew 21:31.
[33]Ibid.

they had not. And Jesus did not want them to claim they didn't have a chance to repent and mend their ways. He said:

"For John came unto you in the way of righteousness, and ye believed him not: but the publicans and the harlots believed him: and ye, when ye had seen it, repented not afterward, that ye might believe him."[34]

At this point the chief priests and elders should have hurried away, but they lingered. They were too fascinated to leave. A moment later, it was too late. Jesus said: "Hear another parable."[35]

If they thought Jesus was laying on the lash in that previous parable, it was nothing compared to what they would hear now.

THE PARABLE OF THE WICKED HUSBANDMEN

Jesus said, "There was a certain householder, which planted a vineyard, and hedged it round about, and digged a winepress in it, and built a tower, and let it out to husbandmen, and went into a far country."[36]

It would not take the crowd long to figure out that the householder was the Father who had set up his kingdom on earth and returned to the far country of his heavenly home. Furthermore, that would mean that the husbandmen were the chief priests and elders who were left to tend the vineyard.

Jesus continued:

"And when the time of the fruit drew near, he sent his servants to the husbandmen, that they might receive the fruits of it.

"And the husbandmen took his servants, and beat one, and killed another, and stoned another."

---

[34]Matthew 21:32.
[35]Matthew 21:33.
[36]Ibid.

Clearly the servants were the prophets whom God had sent from time to time. They had not only been rejected, but persecuted, beaten, stoned, some even killed.

"Again, he sent other servants more than the first: and they did unto them likewise.

"But last of all he sent unto them his son, saying, They will reverence my son."[37]

The literal reality of this parable is so apparent, there was no way that any person within the range of the Savior's voice could miss his next point. He was about to prophesy that these chief priests, elders and rulers of the temple were going to have him slain. He confirmed this when he said:

"But when the husbandmen saw the son, they said among themselves, This is the heir; come, let us kill him, and let us seize on his inheritance.

"And they caught him, and cast him out of the vineyard, and slew him."[38]

What a terrible parable! Jesus was exposing what these chief priests and rulers had been plotting for over a year. But Jesus was not through. He had an ominous warning to address to these wolves in sheep's clothing. He said:

"When the lord therefore of the vineyard cometh, what will he do unto those husbandmen?"[39]

The crowd shouted:

---

[37]Matthew 21:36-37.
[38]Matthew 21:38-39.
[39]Matthew 21:40.

"He will miserably destroy those wicked men, and will let out his vineyard unto other husbandmen, which shall render him the fruits in their seasons."[40]

HAVING SPOKEN OF THE FATHER, JESUS THEN SPOKE OF HIMSELF

There was a famous prophecy in Psalms 118:22-24 which said:

"The stone which the builders refused is become the head stone of the corner.

"This is the LORD's doing; it is marvelous in our eyes.

"This is the day which the LORD hath made; we will rejoice and be glad in it."[41]

The Jews had practically memorized the psalms and they were familiar with this astonishing prophecy that God's cornerstone would be rejected by the builders, but that in the end it would become the great stabilizing anchor for God's whole kingdom.

The Savior wanted to remind this large gathering of the passage in Psalms, because on this very day they were witnesses that the builders had rejected him. Nevertheless, the prophecy said that one day he would become the very cornerstone of God's great kingdom. So he said:

"Did ye never read in the scriptures, The stone which the builders rejected, the same is become the head of the corner: this is the Lord's doing, and it is marvelous in our eyes?

"Therefore say I unto you, The kingdom of God shall be taken from you [the Jews], and given to a nation [the Gentiles] bringing forth the fruits thereof."[42]

---

[40]Matthew 21:41.
[41]Psalms 118:22-24.
[42]Matthew 21:42-43.

Jesus knew that in less than forty years, the Jews would cease to exist as a nation. They might kill their Messiah, but in consequence of their following a false Messiah four decades hence, the Romans would completely crush them and cause them to suffer a *diaspora* that would send them to the four corners of the earth. As Jesus put it:

"Whosoever shall fall on this stone shall be broken: but on whomsoever it shall fall, it will grind him to powder."[43]

By this time the fury of the chief priests and elders had reached a fever pitch. Had it not been for the security provided by this large, loyal crowd, Jesus might have been killed on the spot. Matthew says:

"When the chief priests and Pharisees had heard his parables, they perceived that he spake of them.

"But when they sought to lay hands on him, they feared the multitude, because they took him for a prophet."[44]

Under these favorable circumstances, Jesus could not resist telling the crowd one more story.

THE PARABLE OF THE KING'S SON

The Savior said:

"The kingdom of heaven is like unto a certain king, which made a marriage for his son."[45]

But when the king, representing the Father, invited all of his choicest friends to the wedding dinner, they ignored the invitation. So he sent out other servants to urge these friends to come. This time the king's servants were terribly mistreated as though the king were their enemy.

---

[43]Matthew 21:44.
[44]Matthew 21:45-46.
[45]Matthew 22:2.

Consequently, the king sent forth his armies and destroyed these people who were supposed to be his friends.

Meanwhile, the great wedding dinner had been prepared and everything was in order, but guests had to be provided. Therefore Jesus quoted the king as saying:

"They which were bidden were not worthy.

"Go ye therefore into the highways, and as many as ye shall find, bid to the marriage.

"So those servants went out into the highways, and gathered together all as many as they found, both bad and good: and the wedding was furnished with guests."[46]

Originally, it was intended that the choice seed of Israel would qualify as a kingdom of priests, "a royal priesthood, an holy nation, a peculiar people" that would "show forth the virtues of him who hath called you...."[47]

Unfortunately, that did not happen. Today Israel, through her stiffneckedness, is a scattered remnant of diverse peoples, and many of them are completely lost. Therefore, the Father has decreed that he will raise up the guests for the wedding out of every nation, kindred, tongue, and people. Furthermore, he will prepare them in his holy temples with their wedding garments, and their righteous lives will reflect the marvelous blessings God had planned from the beginning for all those who are invited to the wedding feast.

We are fortunate today, because we now know the world is being prepared at this very moment for the great wedding feast which will be celebrated at the Second Coming of the Father's Beloved Son.

---

[46]Matthew 22:8-10.
[47]1 Peter 2:9.

JESUS WARNS AGAINST IMPOSTORS
AT THE WEDDING

Jesus had one final point to make. Human nature being what it is, the Savior knew that some impostors would try to get into the wedding feast by deception. He wanted his listeners to know how dangerous such an escapade could be. He told about a man who got himself invited as a guest, but was not really qualified for a wedding garment which could only be secured through holy ordinances in the temple. When he arrived at the wedding and the Father saw that he was an impostor, here is what happened:

"He saith unto him, Friend, how camest thou in hither not having a wedding garment? And he was speechless.

"Then said the king to the servants, Bind him hand and foot, and take him away, and cast him into outer darkness; there shall be weeping and gnashing of teeth."[48]

The "outer darkness" referred to in this passage, is the place where individuals go to pay for their own sins because they had not prepared themselves to have their sins remitted by the atonement of the Savior.[49] They had their opportunity, but postponed their day of repentance until it was too late and they lost their legacy of salvation.[50]

The desire of the Father is to have as many as possible accept the gilt-edged invitation to come to his Son's wedding feast and partake. But like the king in the parable, The Father knows that:

"Many are called, but few are chosen."[51]

Nevertheless, those who do attend the feast have a glorious reward indeed. A modern revelation describes it:

---

[48]Matthew 22:12-13.
[49]Alma 40:13, B. of M.
[50]Alma 34:32-35, B. of M.
[51]Doctrine and Covenants 121:34; Matthew 22:14.

"They are they who are the church of the Firstborn.

"They are they into whose hands the Father has given all things—

"They...received of his fullness, and of his glory....

"Wherefore, all things are theirs, whether life or death, or things present, or things to come, all are theirs and they are Christ's, and Christ is God's."[52]

*　*　*　*

TOPICS FOR REFLECTION AND DISCUSSION

1. On Tuesday morning when the apostles saw the cursed fig tree, what had happened to it? In what way was the fig tree that Jesus cursed like unto the Sadducees and the Pharisees? See if you can describe the conditions which existed at the temple when Jesus arrived to cleanse it the second time.

2. Why did the chief priests challenge Jesus concerning his "authority"? How did he challenge them?

3. What did Jesus do immediately after he cleansed the temple? Had he done the same thing three years earlier? What were the children doing that aroused the anger of the chief priests?

4. John suggests that the Jews who consented to the crucifixion of Christ were "blinded." Why did Isaiah suggest that the Lord allowed many of the Jewish leaders to be blinded when the gospel was taught to them? How did this turn out to be an advantage to all mankind?

5. Did Peter indicate that since the Holy Ghost did not touch the hearts of those who crucified the Savior, they might, in due time, have an opportunity to receive the gospel and all its benefits? Can you explain his line of reasoning?

---

[52]Doctrine and Covenants 76:54-59.

6. Did John believe that a number of the Jewish leaders were convinced that Jesus was the Messiah? Then why did he say they did not support him openly?

7. In the parable of the two sons, whom did the first son represent? Whom did the second son represent?

8. Can you give the highlights of the parable of the wicked husbandmen? When Jesus asked what should be done to the wicked husbandmen, what did the crowd say?

9. In what way would you describe the Savior as the cornerstone of God's kingdom? Because the Jews would reject the "cornerstone," what did he say would happen to the Jewish nation? Was that fulfilled? But is there a promise that they would be gathered again in the latter days?

10. Recite the highlights of the parable of the king's son who was about to have a wedding dinner. What is your impression of the man who came to the king's wedding dinner, but did not have a wedding garment? How would that apply today?

*   *   *   *

CHAPTER 34

THE PUBLIC MINISTRY OF JESUS COMES TO AN END

In the previous chapter we considered the direct confrontation which took place on Tuesday morning between Jesus and the rulers of the temple in Jerusalem.

It is doubtful that anything could have been more distressing to these chief priests and leading Pharisees than the series of parables the Savior related that day. Each parable was like a succession of symbolic daggers hurled at the hearts of these men who had been plotting to kill Jesus.

It was fortunate that this exchange took place in the presence of a large crowd of supporters, or the chief priests and Pharisees might have assaulted the Savior then and there.[1]

However, the scripture tells us that in the midst of their frustrated fury, they finally decided it would be prudent to withdraw long enough to formulate a new strategy. Matthew says:

"Then went the Pharisees, and took counsel how they might entangle him in his talk.

"And they sent out unto him their disciples with the Herodians...."[2]

This is an interesting tactic. They had decided to divide themselves into teams, and each one would take turns trying to get Jesus to testify accidentally against himself.

---

[1]Matthew 21:46.
[2]Matthew 22:15-16.

THE HERODIANS SEEK TO ENSNARE JESUS

The first team was a group of politicians. They were the Herodians who belonged to the faction which favored harmonious relations between the house of Herod and the Roman rulers. This team had the assignment of making Jesus look like an insurrectionist against Rome by opposing the hated tax, or inducing him to come out in favor of the Roman tribute which would make him an enemy of the people. The Pharisees sent along some of their own "disciples" to make certain the Herodians followed instructions.[3]

Notice the patronizing and fawning servility with which they approached the Savior. The Herodians said:

"Master, we know that thou art true, and teachest the way of God in truth, neither carest thou for any man: for thou regardest not the person of men.

"Tell us therefore, What thinkest thou? Is it lawful to give tribute unto Caesar, or not?"[4]

What a clever trap. No matter how he answered, these politicians would have made Jesus either an enemy of Rome or an enemy of the people. Matthew says:

"But Jesus perceived their wickedness, and said, Why tempt ye me, ye hypocrites?

"Shew me the tribute money. And they brought unto him a penny.

"And he saith unto them, Whose is this image and superscription?

---

[3]Matthew 22:16.
[4]Matthew 22:16-17.

"They say unto him, Caesar's. Then saith he unto them, Render therefore unto Caesar the things which are Caesar's; and unto God the things that are God's."[5]

The Savior's reply was brilliant. It left the Herodians stunned. Their trap was so cleverly set, how could Jesus escape from it without even a stammer? Matthew says:

"When they had heard these words, they marvelled, and left him, and went their way."[6]

One can almost hear the Pharisees asking the returning Herodians, "Did you get him?" And all they could say would be, "No...too smart."[7]

THE SADDUCEES SEEK TO ENSNARE JESUS

The next team that the rulers sent to waylay Jesus were the Sadducees. These were the proud, wealthy, intellectual cynics of the temple aristocracy. They were in the habit of ridiculing the Pharisees for believing in the existence of human spirits, the possibility of human immortality or the reality of the resurrection.

They had a series of carefully prepared situational arguments ready to use against traditional believers, so they were all primed to use one of their favorite riddles on Jesus. In reality, it was a very complicated and fanciful story, but that is why the Sadducees liked it. They said:

"Master, Moses said, If a man die, having no children, his brother shall marry his wife, and raise up seed unto his brother."[8]

The Sadducees were referring to a passage in Deuteronomy which said:

---

[5]Matthew 22:18-21.
[6]Matthew 22:22.
[7]Matthew 22:22.
[8]Matthew 22:24.

"If brethren dwell together, and one of them die, and have no child, the wife of the dead shall not marry without unto a stranger: her husband's brother shall go in unto her, and take her to him to wife, and perform the duty of an husband's brother unto her.

"And it shall be, that the firstborn which she beareth shall succeed in the name of his brother which is dead, that his name be not put out of Israel."[9]

The Sadducees used this scripture on which to build a fanciful charade which they did not think Jesus could answer. They said:

"Now there were with us seven brethren: and the first, when he had married a wife, deceased, and, having no issue, left his wife unto his brother:

"Likewise the second also, and the third, unto the seventh.

"And last of all the woman died also.

"Therefore in the resurrection whose wife shall she be of the seven? for they all had her."[10]

JESUS USES A THIMBLE TO BAIL OUT
A BARREL OF QUESTIONS ON MARRIAGE

It was very apparent to Jesus what these shrewd Sadducees were trying to do. This carefully contrived story was not merely designed to ensnare Jesus, it was also intended to make the doctrine of the resurrection look ridiculous because of the practical problems it would create.

Jesus responded:

"Ye do err, not knowing the scriptures, nor the power of God.

---

[9] Deuteronomy 25:5-6.
[10] Matthew 22:25-28.

"For in the resurrection they neither marry, nor are given in marriage, but are as the angels of God in heaven."[11]

Luke gives the contents of this last verse in more detail. He says:

"The children of this world marry, and are given in marriage:

"But they which shall be accounted worthy to obtain that world, and the resurrection from the dead, neither marry, nor are given in marriage:

"Neither can they die any more: for they are equal unto the angels; and are the children of God, being the children of the resurrection."[12]

The Savior's answer probably left the Sadducees mumbling to themselves. They did not know whether he had answered them or not. What was worse, they wouldn't dare admit that they failed to get his point lest it expose their lack of scriptural comprehension.

Had they been worthy to receive a full answer, the Savior could have illuminated their minds along the lines of scriptures, both ancient and modern, which tell us the following:

The children of "this world" marry until death do them part. But those who attain "that world" where the Father resides are married for time and eternity. As Paul would later teach, "Neither is the man without the woman, neither the woman without the man, *in the Lord.*"[13]

And this relationship continues in "the resurrection," so that they will not "die any more," for they are eternal beings. They are "equal unto the angels" and are allowed to dwell in the presence of God forever.

---

[11]Matthew 22:29-30.
[12]Luke 20:34-36.
[13]1 Corinthians 11:11 (emphasis added).

Of course, it is understandable why Jesus did not consider it wise to go beyond the simple statement outlined by Matthew and Luke. To have gone further in those circumstances would have been somewhat like "casting pearls." Therefore we noted that he simply said:

"Ye do err, not knowing the scriptures, nor the power of God."

Nothing could deflate the egotistical arrogance of a Sadducee more effectively than to accuse him of not knowing the scriptures and not understanding the nature and power of God. After all, the Sadducees were in charge of the temple, and considered themselves the most erudite of all Jewish intellectuals.

JESUS TARGETS THE SADDUCEES
ON THE RESURRECTION

But Jesus was not finished with the Sadducees.

Before they could catch their breath or thoroughly digest what he had just said to them, the Savior fastened their attention on the issue of the resurrection. This was the main focus of their story, so he said:

"But as touching the resurrection of the dead, have ye not read that which was spoken unto you by God, saying,

"I am the God of Abraham, and the God of Isaac, and the God of Jacob? God is not the God of the dead, but of the living."[14]

The Sadducees liked to think of themselves as the masters of pure logic, equal to the most pedantic Greeks. So what did God say to Moses? He declared around 1,500 B.C.:

"I am the God of thy father, the God of Abraham, the God of Isaac, and the God of Jacob."[15]

---

[14]Matthew 22:31-32.
[15]Exodus 3:6.

God spoke these words to Moses at the time of the burning bush incident and at a time when Abraham, Isaac and Jacob had been dead for generations. Now if the Sadducees were right, and there is no immortality of the human spirit—and hence, no resurrection—then this passage is saying the Almighty is the God of men who are not only dead, but have ceased to exist. Is this logical? It is ridiculous!

The multitude who were crowding around to hear this debate caught on immediately—the Sadducees might try to play games with the scriptures, but they were no match for Jesus. Matthew says:

"And when the multitude heard this, they were astonished at his doctrine."[16]

This suggests that they were astonished with the manner in which Jesus could so deftly handle the scriptures to silence the Sadducees. This sentiment is reflected in the words of a scribe who cried out:

"Master thou hast well said!"[17]

And Luke adds:

"After that they durst not ask him any questions at all."[18]

THE PHARISEES SEND A LAWYER TO ENSNARE THE SAVIOR

One can well imagine the bitter disappointment of the chief priests and elders when the Sadducees returned. The scripture says:

"When the Pharisees had heard that he had put the Sadducees to silence, they were gathered together.

"Then one of them, which was a lawyer, asked him a question, tempting him, and saying,

---

[16]Matthew 22:23.
[17]Luke 20:39.
[18]Luke 20:40.

"Master, which is the great commandment in the law?"[19]

This was a trick question. Originally, God had given Moses ten commandments and approximately eighty fairly simple statutes to serve as guidelines in a godly society. However, the analytical rabbinical scholars had multiplied these laws into a total of 613.[20]

To identify any one of them as THE great commandment would probably produce a pandemonium of violent controversy by those favoring different laws. And that is what this question was designed to provoke.

But an interesting thing happened. According to Mark we read:

"Jesus answered him, The first of all the commandments is, Hear, O Israel; The Lord our God is one Lord: And thou shalt love the Lord thy God with all thy heart, and with all thy soul, and with all thy mind, and with all thy strength: this is the first commandment.

"And the second is like [unto it], namely this, Thou shalt love thy neighbour as thyself. There is none other commandment greater than these."[21]

The lawyer (whom Mark says was a scribe[22]) was astonished. Jesus had taken what he called the first great commandment from Deuteronomy 6:5, and then proceeded to turn clear back to Leviticus 19:18 for the second commandment. As the lawyer ruminated in his mind the broad ramification of these two commandments, he finally said:

"Well, Master, thou hast said the truth: for there is one God; and there is none other but he:

---

[19]Matthew 22:34-36.
[20]Talmage, *Jesus the Christ*, p. 565.
[21]Mark 12:29-31.
[22]Mark 12:38.

"And to love him with all the heart, and with all the understanding, and with all the soul, and with all the strength, and to love his neighbour as himself, is more than all whole burnt offerings and sacrifices."[23]

This was an amazing compliment for a lawyer to pay a common Galilean who was supposed to be an uneducated rustic. It was even more astonishing when the scripture specifically says the lawyer had asked Jesus the question to tempt him.[24]

We deduce two things from this account. The first is that the lawyer was supremely impressed by the Savior's astuteness, and secondly, he was humble enough to acknowledge that these two commandments encompassed the whole gamut of 613 laws dealing with "offerings and sacrifices." Mark then says:

"And when Jesus saw that he answered discreetly, he said unto him, Thou art not far from the kingdom of God."[25]

Coming from Jesus, this was a high compliment to the lawyer. It meant that Jesus saw in him sufficient humility and scriptural insight to make him susceptible to conversion. We wish we had the rest of the story so we would know how it all turned out.

JESUS ASKS THE PHARISEES A QUESTION

Matthew provides a final reference to the Savior's dialogue with the Pharisees. Since they had struggled so long trying to stump him with their questions, he decided to turn the tables and let them struggle with one of his own questions. Matthew says:

"While the Pharisees were gathered together, Jesus asked them,

"What think ye of Christ? whose son is he?"

---

[23]Mark 12:32-33.
[24]Matthew 22:35.
[25]Mark 12:34.

Jesus knew they did not accept him as the Christ, so he was not asking about himself *per se.* He was asking about the prophetic Messiah, the Anointed One, whom all the Jews were expecting. So, he asked, "whose son is he?" rather than "Whose son am I?" Matthew continues:

"They say unto him, The Son of David."[26]

There was no stronger or more gratifying doctrine taught among the Jews than the idea that the Messiah, when he came, would be a descendant of David. In fact, this was a promise the Lord had made to David himself.[27] Isaiah talked about the Messiah inheriting the throne of David.[28] Jeremiah talked about the great Messiah as a descendant of David.[29]

Once Jesus had secured a statement from the learned Pharisees that the Messiah was to be a descendant or a Son of David, he then handed them a scriptural problem that left them mentally dazed.

"He saith unto them, How then doth David in spirit call him Lord, saying,

"The LORD said unto my Lord, Sit thou on my right hand, till I make thine enemies thy footstool?

"If David then call him Lord, how is he his son?"[30]

Jesus was actually quoting from one of David's psalms.[31] The meaning of it was crystal clear to anyone who had a gospel background. It simply said:

"The Lord [the Father] said to my Lord, [David's Lord, Jehovah] Sit thou on my right hand, till I make thine enemies thy footstool."

---

[26]Matthew 22:42.

[27]1 Chronicles 17:12-14 with a discussion in *The Fourth Thousand Years,* by Skousen, p. 116.

[28]Isaiah 9:7.

[29]Jeremiah 23:5-6.

[30]Matthew 22:42-45.

[31]Psalms 110:1.

Once a person understood the true doctrine of the Godhead, it was easy to see how David's "Lord" (Jehovah) would one day be David's "son" or descendant when he came in the flesh.

But it was not clear to the learned Pharisees, nor to the Sadducees. They were completely befuddled. The scripture says:

"And no man was able to answer him a word, neither durst any man from that day forth ask him any more questions."[32]

JESUS PRESENTS HIS FINAL TEMPLE DISCOURSE

As soon as the Savior's antagonists had retired from the temple arena, Jesus gathered his disciples around him. It seems a vast multitude of the common people also gathered close enough to hear.

During the next hour or so, Jesus was going to bring his public ministry in mortality to a conclusion. He had spent three years traveling up and down the length of the country on foot. He had showered his love and compassion on the people under trying circumstances. On one occasion he had fed an estimated crowd of 15,000, including men, women and children. Shortly afterwards he had fed an estimated crowd of 12,000, including men, women and children.

He had cast out devils, blessed lifelong cripples so they could walk, cured the blind who had never seen the light of day since they were born, straightened those with crooked backs, given hearing to the deaf, cured leprosy, dropsy, and numerous other diseases. On at least three occasions, he had raised the dead. Jesus had ordained some to the priesthood. He had personally baptized many. He had prepared all who had repented and were baptized for the gift of the Holy Ghost. Now he would give them his last public discourse.

Jesus apparently felt at the beginning of his talk that those around him were not only his faithful disciples but also a multitude of sympathetic listeners. Therefore, he taught them accordingly, and said:

---

[32]Matthew 22:46.

"The scribes and the Pharisees sit in Moses' seat:

"All therefore whatsoever they bid you observe, that observe and do...."[33]

Jesus was always respectful of a man in his official capacity or high office, even though the personal life of the man may have been reprehensible. All the apostles seem to have followed this same example, especially Paul. They did not rail against wicked rulers. However, Jesus did not want them to follow in the footsteps of these high and mighty officials when they were wicked. He said:

"But do NOT ye after their works: for they say, and do not.

"They bind heavy burdens and grievous to be borne, and lay them on men's shoulders; but they themselves will not move them with one of their fingers.

"All their works they do for to be seen of men: they make broad their phylacteries [prayer ornaments], and enlarge the borders of their garments,

"And love the uppermost rooms at feasts, and the chief seats in the synagogues,

"And greetings in the markets, and to be called of men, Rabbi, Rabbi."[34]

At this point Jesus wanted to impress upon his apostles, and those who would become the more advanced leaders and scholars of the Gospel, that titles are worldly tributes and accolades that have no place in the kingdom of God. Therefore, he said to them:

"Be not ye called Rabbi [master]: for one is your Master, even Christ; and all ye are brethren.

---

[33]Matthew 23:2-3.
[34]Matthew 23:3-7.

"Call no man your father [as a salutation] upon the earth: for one is your Father, which is in heaven....

"But he that is greatest among you shall be your servant.

"And whosoever shall exalt himself shall be abased; and he that shall humble himself shall be exalted."[35]

It is in keeping with this instruction that general authorities of the Church of Jesus Christ of Latter-day Saints are not addressed as "Apostle," but simply as "Elder." The title "President" is appropriate when one is in the First Presidency or presiding over a temple or a stake. The object is to show love and respect, but not obeisance or servility.

THE SORROW OF JESUS FOR THE SCRIBES AND PHARISEES

Had we been present on this particular Tuesday afternoon, we might have noticed that while Jesus was talking, groups of scribes and Pharisees began sauntering back to join the crowd. This development is suggested by the fact that Jesus suddenly discontinued his instructions to his disciples and sympathizers in order to concentrate on those who counted themselves his enemies.

It is difficult to fully understand the depth of the Savior's feelings as he looked into the faces of these proud and sometimes haughty rulers who would bring down upon the heads of this whole people a plague of continuous calamities. These people had rejected John the Baptist. They had rejected the call to repentance. They had rejected the message of their long awaited Messiah. They had rejected the manifest power of God in the Savior's performance of hundreds of miracles.

As Jesus thought of the judgment that awaited them for their stiffneckedness and rebellion against their God who loved them, he felt moved to present a bill of particulars describing their sins. He said:

---

[35]Matthew 23:8-12.

"Woe unto you, scribes and Pharisees, hypocrites! for ye shut up the kingdom of heaven against men: for ye neither go in yourselves, neither suffer ye them that are entering to go in....

"Ye devour widows' houses, and for a pretence make long prayer: therefore ye shall receive the greater damnation....

"Ye compass sea and land to make one proselyte, and when he is made, ye make him twofold more the child of hell than yourselves.

"Woe unto you, ye blind guides, which say, Whosoever shall swear by the temple, it is nothing; but whosoever shall swear by the gold of the temple, he is a debtor!

"Ye fools and blind: for whether is greater, the gold, or the temple that sanctifieth the gold?"[36]

The rabbis had concocted a set of rules concerning oaths and vows which were ridiculous in the extreme. James E. Talmage summarizes this irrational set of regulations as follows:

"If a man swore by the temple, the House of Jehovah, he could obtain an indulgence for breaking his oath; but if he vowed by the gold and treasure of the Holy House, he was bound by the unbreakable bonds of priestly dictum. Though one should swear by the altar of God, his oath could be annulled; but if he vowed by the corban gift or by the gold upon the altar, his obligation was imperative."[37]

THE PHARISEES HAD CONFUSED THEIR PRIORITIES

Jesus continued denouncing several more ambiguities in their system of vows and oaths, and then he said:

"Woe unto you, scribes and Pharisees, hypocrites! for ye pay tithe of mint and anise and cummin, and have omitted the weightier

---

[36]Matthew 23:13-17.
[37]Talmage, *Jesus the Christ*, p. 556.

matters of the law, judgment, mercy, and faith: these ought ye to have done, and not to leave the other undone.

"Ye blind guides, which strain at a gnat, and swallow a camel....

"Ye make clean the outside of the cup and of the platter, but within they are full of extortion and excess.

"Thou blind Pharisee, cleanse first that which is within the cup and platter, that the outside of them may be clean also...."[38]

JESUS PORTRAYS THE PHARISEES AS WHITED SEPULCHRES

"Ye are like unto whited sepulchres, which indeed appear beautiful outward, but are within full of dead men's bones, and of all uncleanness.

"Even so ye also outwardly appear righteous unto men, but within ye are full of hypocrisy and iniquity....

"Because ye build the tombs of the prophets, and garnish the sepulchre of the prophets.

"Wherefore ye be witnesses unto yourselves, that ye are the children of them which killed the prophets. Fill ye up then the measure of your fathers.

"Ye serpents, ye generation of vipers, how can ye escape the damnation of hell?"[39]

JESUS SPEAKS AS JEHOVAH, GOD OF THE OLD TESTAMENT

At this point, Jesus could not help but reflect on his role as Jehovah during the Old Testament epoch. He said:

---

[38]Matthew 23:23-26.
[39]Matthew 23:27-33.

"Wherefore, behold, I send unto you prophets, and wise men, and scribes: and some of them ye shall kill and crucify; and some of them shall ye scourge in your synagogues, and persecute them from city to city:

"That upon you may come all the righteous blood shed upon the earth, from the blood of righteous Abel unto the blood of Zacharias son of Barachias, whom ye slew between the temple and the altar."[40]

As we pointed out in chapter 2, this passage is defective. The prophet Zacharias, son of Barachias, was not slain in the temple. However, another ancient prophet with almost the same name was slain between the temple and the altar, but he was the son of Jehoida.[41] Some ancient scribe thought Jesus was talking about the prophet whose writings appear in the Old Testament, and so he inserted "son of Barachias," without realizing how much confusion he was creating.

As mentioned in Volume One, it was revealed to Joseph Smith that the Zacharias Jesus was talking about was the father of John the Baptist, whom the Jews had slain three decades earlier. Joseph Smith wrote:

"When the father [Zacharias] refused to disclose his [John's] whereabouts, and being the officiating high priest at the temple that year, he was slain by Herod's order, between the porch and the altar, *as Jesus said*."[42]

This revelation was an original contribution to New Testament history, and it was later verified after the discovery of some ancient Christian writings.[43]

---

[40]Matthew 23:34-35.

[41]2 Chronicles 24:20-22.

[42]Smith, *Teachings of the Prophet Joseph Smith*, p. 261 (emphasis added).

[43]Robert Matthews, *A Burning Light*, Provo, Utah: Brigham Young University Press, 1972, p. 25.

Now Jesus wanted to emphasize the high price the Jews of that generation would pay for all of the blood of the prophets that had been spilt down through the years. Jesus said:

"Verily I say unto you, All these things shall come upon this generation."[44]

This did not mean that the Jewish leaders of that generation were the only ones being held accountable for those crimes. Jesus just wanted those who were listening to him to know that history had caught up with God's chosen people, and from then until the latter days, there would never be another sovereign Jewish nation anywhere on the face of the earth.

Speaking once more as Jehovah, Jesus said:

"O Jerusalem, Jerusalem, thou that killest the prophets, and stonest them which are sent unto thee, how often would I have gathered thy children together, even as a hen gathereth her chickens under her wings, and ye would not!

"Behold, your house is left unto you desolate!"[45]

Then, speaking for himself, Jesus said:

"For I say unto you, Ye shall not see me henceforth, till ye shall say, Blessed is he that cometh in the name of the Lord."[46]

THE WIDOW'S MITE

For all intents and purposes the public ministry of Jesus had come to an end. However, an interesting incident happened as Jesus and the apostles were leaving the temple. They passed by the treasury where many of the rich were making donations. Mark says:

---

[44]Matthew 23:36.
[45]Matthew 23:37-38.
[46]Matthew 23:39.

"There came a certain poor widow, and she threw in two mites, which make a farthing.

"And he called unto him his disciples, and saith unto them, Verily I say unto you, That this poor widow hath cast more in, than all they which have cast into the treasury:

"For all they did cast in of their abundance; but she of her want did cast in all that she had, even all her living."[47]

As Jesus and his disciples were leaving the temple esplanade, some of the disciples pointed out the massive bulk of many of the huge stones which had been quarried out of Mount Moriah to provide the foundation for the temple. Jesus said:

"Verily I say unto you, There shall not be left here, upon this temple, one stone upon another, that shall not be thrown down."[48]

The apostles wanted to know more. For example, how could this occur? And when would it happen? Very shortly they had an opportunity to ask him, and in the next chapter we will study what Jesus said would happen during the next two thousand years.

*   *   *   *

TOPICS FOR REFLECTION AND DISCUSSION

1. How would you describe the group of Jews who called themselves Herodians? Narrate the manner in which they tried to trick Jesus into making himself either an enemy of Rome or an enemy of the Jewish people. How did Jesus avoid the trap?

2. What were the unique characteristics of the group of Jewish leaders who called themselves Sadducees? What basic beliefs of the Jews did they refuse to accept? What complicated riddle did they present to Jesus to discredit him and the principle of the resurrection? How did Jesus refute and confuse them?

---

[47]Mark 12:42-44.
[48]JST Matthew 24:2.

3. When the Pharisees sent in a lawyer to snare Jesus, what question did he ask? Why was this a "trick" question? What did Jesus reply? Then what was the lawyer's response? Was Jesus impressed with this lawyer's prospects as a new disciple?

4. List five great things Jesus had done for the Jewish people during his ministry.

5. Jesus said the people were to listen to their leaders and do what? What were they NOT to do? Who did he say should be the greatest among them?

6. Not since Jesus closed his ministry in Galilee had he poured forth such a rhetorical volley of fire and brimstone on the scribes and Pharisees as he did on the last day of his ministry. Why do you think he did this? Did he mention one single act of righteousness they had performed?

7. Describe the set of rules for oaths and vows that Jesus denounced. What does it mean to strain at a gnat and swallow a camel? Do you see any of that happening today?

8. Explain why you think many different nations have worshipped the sepulchers of their dead prophets while trying to kill their living prophets.

9. In this final sermon, Jesus suddenly assumed his Old Testament role as Jehovah. What did he say he had done for Jerusalem down through the centuries? Now what did he say would happen to this great city?

10. As Jesus closed his mortal ministry to the Jews, he walked past the treasury where the rich were making contributions. Who made the greatest contribution of all? Explain why. How does that apply to God's people today?

*   *   *   *

CHAPTER 35

JESUS DESCRIBES THE HISTORICAL HIGHLIGHTS OF THE NEXT 2,000 YEARS

When Jesus had performed his last miraculous healing, narrated his last parable, and delivered his last sorrowful warning to those who wanted to kill him, he prepared to leave the temple.

However, as we pointed out in the last chapter, when they were departing, his disciples began to point out the massive temple stones that had been quarried out of the bowels of Mount Moriah. Deep down in the solid rock of this mountain are huge caverns where the master builders of Solomon and Herod carved out enormous monoliths of stone for the temple. As Jesus contemplated the remarkable workmanship of the temple, he said to his disciples:

"Verily I say unto you, There shall not be left here, upon this temple, one stone upon another, that shall not be thrown down."[1]

THE APOSTLES ASK JESUS THE BIG QUESTION

As they left the temple, Jesus walked ahead of the apostles, leaving them to contemplate these last words. They assumed he would cross the Brook Kidron and then take the shortcut over the top of the Mount of Olives to follow the well-travelled path that leads down toward Bethany. But Jesus did not go that far.

Part way up the hill, Jesus sat down to rest and waited for the apostles. Mark tells us:

---

[1] JST Matthew 24:2.

"And as he sat upon the mount of Olives over against [across the valley opposite] the temple, Peter and James and John and Andrew asked him privately...."[2]

The four things they wanted to know were later recorded by Matthew as follows:

"Tell us WHEN shall these things be which thou hast said concerning the destruction of the temple, and the Jews; and what is the sign of thy coming, and of the end of the world, or the destruction of the wicked, which is the end of the world?"[3]

It turns out that "WHEN?" is always the big question whenever people begin discussing prophecy.

WHY THE LORD DOES NOT PROVIDE A PROPHETIC TIMETABLE

No one could have asked a much bigger question than the one posed by these four apostles as they requested Jesus to give them a specific timetable for God's planned agenda during the next 2,000 years.

However, the Lord never gives us a timetable in connection with prophecies. He likes to describe the "times" and the "seasons" so we may recognize when the time is near, but he does not give us the specific dates.

THE SAVIOR'S PREDICTIONS ARE BELIEVED TO HAVE BEEN DICTATED TO THE GOSPEL WRITERS BY THE HOLY GHOST

As a direct result of the questions raised by the four apostles, Jesus gave his famous prophetic sermon describing the events that would highlight the next twenty centuries.

It would be safe to assume that none of these Galilean fishermen had an opportunity to write down what Jesus said at the time, and

---

[2]Mark 13:3.
[3]JST Matthew 24:4 (emphasis added).

we therefore conclude that the entire text of this sermon was subsequently dictated to the apostles by the Holy Ghost as indicated in the following passage:

"But the Comforter, which is the Holy Ghost, whom the Father will send in my name, he shall teach you all things, and bring all things to your remembrance, whatsoever I have said unto you."[4]

JESUS GIVES THEM THE "BAD NEWS" FIRST

Jesus said he first wanted to talk to them about "the beginning of sorrows" for the Jews.[5] He predicted that the worst holocaust in the entire history of the Jews would occur in the near future. It came in less than four decades when the Jews rose up in rebellion against Rome. Jesus said:

"For then shall be a great tribulation, such as was not since the beginning of the world to this time, no, NOR EVER SHALL BE."[6]

The fuse that set this off turned out to be a group of false prophets and false messiahs. That is why Jesus said to his apostles:

"Take heed that no man deceive you. For many shall come in my name, saying, I am Christ; and shall deceive many."[7]

"And many false prophets shall rise, and deceive many."[8]

Within fifteen years this would begin to happen.

A consortium of spurious Jewish messiahs and false Jewish prophets came up out of Egypt and began preaching that it was the will of God that the Jews should immediately prepare to liberate themselves from Rome.[9]

---

[4]John 14:26.
[5]Matthew 24:8.
[6]Matthew 24:21 (emphasis added).
[7]Matthew 24:4-5.
[8]Matthew 24:11.
[9]*Encyclopedia Judaica*, and *History Until 1880*, Jerusalem, Israel, Keter Publishing House, Ltd., 1973, pp. 123-126.

These fictitious holy men even claimed they had the divine power to blow down the Roman walls of Jerusalem with the breath of their mouths.[10]

By around 50 A.D., many zealots in Israel foolishly embraced these promises, and launched a campaign of widespread agitation for a massive revolt against Rome. At first there were only sporadic elements of rioting from time to time, but in 66 A.D. a full-fledged revolution burst into flame.[11]

THE ILLUSION OF AN EARLY VICTORY DISSOLVES INTO A HORRIBLE DEFEAT

At the beginning of the revolt, the Jews enjoyed the fruits of what appeared to be a glorious Messianic victory. The Roman garrison in Jerusalem was totally annihilated. Then the Roman army in Syria tried to intervene and was soundly defeated. The Jews were jubilant. After proclaiming their complete independence, the triumphant rebels set up their own provisional government.[12]

But the wrath of Rome soon descended on Israel like a tidal wave of molten lava. Jerusalem was put under siege and by 70 A.D., General Titus had forced the starving city of Jerusalem to capitulate. He tore down the walls, dismantled and burned the temple, and butchered thousands of the survivors. Other thousands were made slaves or used as bait for famished wild beasts at Roman festivals.[13]

The destruction of the temple was so complete that not one stone—from its foundation to its ramparts—was left in place. Josephus says many of these stones were 67 feet in length, over 7 feet in height and 9 feet wide.[14]

As for the Jews themselves, over a million lost their lives when Jerusalem fell, and millions more lost their lives during the ensuing

---

[10]Ibid.

[11]Ibid.

[12]Ibid.

[13]Ibid., pp. 127-129.

[14]*Josephus—Complete Works*, Grand Rapids, Michigan, Kregal Publications, 1963, pp. 334-336.

years. Jesus had already told his disciples that in all Jewish history, this particular holocaust or "abomination of desolation" would be the worst they would ever witness.[15] The Savior's apostles would live to see this prophecy fulfilled, and therefore Jesus warned them:

"When you, therefore, shall see the abomination of desolation, spoken of by Daniel the prophet, concerning the destruction of Jerusalem...

"Then let them who are in Judea flee into the mountains."[16]

In the centuries that followed, Jesus indicated that the Jews would be dispersed to the four corners of the earth[17] and suffer "great tribulations."[18] They would undergo bitter persecution, but Jesus said that "for the elect's sake," they would survive.[19]

One of the most amazing sagas of any people in any age is the story of the survival of the Jews during six monumental epochs of their history.

These six stages have been carefully chronicled by Jewish historians, and we have summarized each of these in Appendix A of this book.[20]

JESUS WARNED THE APOSTLES THAT THE
CHRISTIANS WOULD ALSO BE PERSECUTED

The next part of the Savior's prophetic sermon was addressed primarily to those whom Jesus described as being persecuted for "my name's sake," meaning the Christians. He said:

---

[15]Matthew 24:21.

[16]Matthew 24:15-16.

[17]1 Nephi 13:39, B. of M.

[18]Matthew 24:21.

[19]Matthew 24:22.

[20]See Appendix A: "The Savior's Advice to the Jews: Once the Cataclysm Begins, Do Not Look Back."

"Then shall they deliver you up to be afflicted, and shall kill you, and ye shall be hated of all nations, for my name's sake."[21]

Jesus knew that the immediate future of his followers who were then living upon the earth was exceedingly bleak. He could only encourage them to remember their covenants and gird up their loins so they would be prepared to live or die for his "name's sake." The Savior knew that in the immediate future, a whirlwind of catastrophe would engulf them. When Jesus had previously spoken of these coming tribulations, he had said:

"These things have I spoken unto you, that ye should not be offended."[22]

It would be natural for the apostles and the Jewish congregations of Christians to feel that the Savior had forsaken them if they saw themselves virtually overwhelmed with afflictions. He wanted them to know that these future hardships were all part of the unfolding of history which the Lord knew was coming. To assure them that they were part of God's foreknowledge, compassion and concern, Jesus told them in advance what they might expect:

"They shall put you out of the synagogues: yea, the time cometh, that whosoever killeth you will think that he doeth God service.

"And these things will they do unto you, because they have not known the Father, nor me.

"But these things have I told you, that when the time shall come, ye may remember that I told you of them. And these things I said not unto you at the beginning, because I was with you."[23]

---

[21]JST Matthew 24:7.
[22]John 16:1.
[23]John 16:2-4.

THE EARLY MARTYRS

As far as the record shows, the first Christian to die as a martyr was Stephen, one of the seven who had been set apart to minister to the poor. He was a very spiritual man who performed many miracles which attracted the attention of the jealous leaders of Jerusalem. The scripture says Stephen's face was illuminated like that of an angel as he stood before the council which condemned him to death. He died by stoning, based on the testimony of false witnesses.[24]

As we have mentioned earlier, the first of the twelve apostles to die as a martyr was James, the brother of John. This occurred about 14 years after the crucifixion. Herod Agrippa sought to gain favor with the Jews by killing James. The scripture says:

"Now about that time Herod the king stretched forth his hands to vex certain of the church. And he killed James the brother of John with the sword. And because he saw it pleased the Jews, he proceeded further to take Peter also."[25]

However, Peter escaped.

Tradition has it that eventually both Peter and Paul died as martyrs in Rome between 64 and 65 A.D. The lecherous Emperor Nero is alleged to have set the city on fire and then blamed this seditious conflagration on the Christians. He said it would be appropriate to punish these Christian arsonists with fire. Nero therefore ordered many of them to be dipped in tar, then suspended on poles and set afire.

According to early Christian writers, others of the apostles also died as martyrs.[26] The last of the apostles to survive was John the Beloved, who was translated, meaning that his mortal body was quickened so that he would not die as the others did.[27] He

---

[24]Acts 6:8,15; 7:59.
[25]Acts 12:1-3.
[26]See *LDS Dictionary* under each of the Apostles' names.
[27]John 21:23; Doctrine and Covenants, Section 7.

disappeared from history after being exiled to the Isle of Patmos. There is a tradition that the Roman Emperor attempted to have him killed by throwing him into a cauldron of boiling oil, but that he came forth unharmed.[28]

Miracles of a similar nature likewise occurred when there were attempts to kill three of the American disciples who had also been translated.[29]

THE BETRAYAL OF ONE ANOTHER

All of these events demonstrate how quickly and literally the prophecies of Jesus began to be fulfilled. One of the saddest prophecies he shared with the apostles was the one relating to the breakdown of the infrastructure within the church. Jesus said:

"And then shall many be offended, and shall betray one another, and shall hate one another."[30]

A morbid passage in the writings of Tacitus tells the story. As we have mentioned, Rome was set on fire in 64 A.D. and Nero blamed the Christians, but he needed to obtain confessions to prove his charges. Tacitus writes:

"At first several [Christians] were seized, who confessed [under torture, of course], and then by their discovery a great multitude of others were convicted and executed."[31]

This betrayal of brethren became a pattern during the eight different campaigns of persecution by the Romans which extended over a period of 300 years.

Part of the Savior's great burden of grief was knowing that this would happen to his beloved disciples and many other hapless victims. Nevertheless, he said:

---

[28]Hastings, *Dictionary of the Bible*, New York: Charles Scribner's Sons, 1936, vol. II, p. 681.

[29]3 Nephi 28:19-21, B. of M.

[30]Matthew 24:10.

[31]Clarke, *Commentary on the New Testament*, New York: Eaton and Mains, 1884, vol. v, p. 135.

"He that remaineth steadfast and is not overcome, the same shall be saved."[32]

It is interesting that right in the midst of all these horror prophecies, Jesus introduced God's great message of hope for the future.

THE GREAT RESTORATION OF THE GOSPEL IN THE LATTER DAYS

The disciples knew that after a long period of apostasy, persecution, and darkness, the light of Christ would eventually shine down upon the earth once again. In his prophetic sermon, Jesus said:

"And AGAIN [just as in the days of the apostles], this gospel of the Kingdom shall be preached in all the world, for a witness unto all nations...."[33]

Peter was referring to this great event in the latter days when he told the Jews that the Savior would not return again to minister among men "until the times of RESTITUTION OF ALL THINGS."[34] Peter said this great restoration of the gospel in the latter days was "spoken by the mouth of all his holy prophets since the world began."[35]

THIS GREAT RESTORATION OF THE GOSPEL BEGAN IN 1820

This glorious event which had been "spoken by the mouth of all his holy prophets since the world began," was initiated in 1820. As with previous dispensations, it began with an opening of the heavens, the ministering of angels and a divine revelation of both the Father and the Son.[36]

---

[32]JST Matthew 1:11, P. of G. P.
[33]JST Matthew 1:31, P. of G. P.; Matthew 24:14.
[34]Acts 3:21 (emphasis added).
[35]Ibid.
[36]Joseph Smith History, 1:17, P. of G. P.

This time, however, the gospel did not begin to unfold in Jerusalem. It happened in America. The Old Testament prophets had known about this great event, and they knew where it would occur.

The ancient prophets said this divine "restitution of all things" in the latter days was destined to occur in "Zion." Of course, Jerusalem was sometimes referred to as Zion, but the Old Testament prophets knew that the Zion of the latter days would be a great land separate from old Jerusalem.[37] They spoke of this latter-day Zion as being located among the islands of the sea.[38] It was perceived as a great land "beyond the rivers of Ethiopia," or Africa,[39] and inhabited by a people "scattered and peeled."[40]

As we now know, this turned out to be the western hemisphere.

It was of this "Zion" that Jesus spoke when he said, "This gospel of the kingdom shall be preached in all the world for a witness unto all nations; and then shall the end come."[41]

THE OUTPOURING OF DIVINE MANIFESTATIONS

Once the heavens were opened, the restoration of the original gospel descended on mankind like a flood. Within twenty-two years, the Savior had not only launched a new dispensation of the gospel—just as he had told his ancient apostles he would do—but he had personally revealed himself to his chosen prophet and his immediate associates. During these direct communications with the heavens, there had come a mighty outpouring of revelations and new scriptures.

In order to gain a partial appreciation of the speed with which the restoration of the gospel took place, let us itemize the great treasure of scripture, doctrines, principles, ordinances and

---

[37]Isaiah 2:3.
[38]2 Nephi 10:20, B. of M.
[39]Isaiah 18:1.
[40]Isaiah 18:2.
[41]Matthew 24:14.

ceremonies of the original Christian church which had been restored in all their beauty and power by 1842.

1. The Book of Joseph predicted by Ezekiel[42] had been translated and published as a companion to the Bible under the title of *The Book of Mormon*.

2. The Aaronic Priesthood had been restored.

3. The Melchizedek Priesthood had been restored.

4. The quorum of the First Presidency had been established.

5. A quorum of apostles had been set up.

6. A quorum of seventies had been set up.

7. The organization and purpose of high councils had been revealed.

8. The office of bishop had been correctly defined.

9. Ward and stake precincts had been defined.

10. The law of consecration had been revealed.

11. The law of tithing had been revealed.

12. The proselyting procedure had been initiated.

13. The preliminary ordinances of the temple had been revealed.

14. The doctrine of eternal marriage had been revealed.

15. The principle of vicarious work for the dead referred to by Paul[43] had been reinstituted for the first time since the days of the apostles.

---

[42]Ezekiel 37:16-19.
[43]1 Corinthians 15:29.

16. The correct ordinances for baptism, confirmation, and the blessing of the sacrament had been revealed.

17. A vision of the three heavenly degrees of glory in the resurrection (seen by Paul[44]) had been revealed.

18. Over one hundred carefully structured revelations had been published containing the correct doctrines, principles, and ordinances of the gospel.

JESUS CLOSES HIS SERMON WITH A PARABLE FOR THE MEMBERS OF HIS CHURCH IN THE LATTER DAYS

As Jesus sat on the Mount of Olives with his beloved apostles around him, he decided to bring his prophecies to a conclusion by relating a parable specifically addressed to the members of his church in the latter days.

Jesus had already told the apostles how wicked humanity would become just before his Second Coming. He had said:

"As the days of Noe were, so shall also the coming of the Son of man be. For as in the days that were before the flood they...knew not until the flood came and took them all away; so shall also the coming of the Son of man be."[45]

From this we conclude that as Jesus contemplated the modern age in which we live, he perceived that the debauchery and depravity of the people would be comparable in every way to the wickedness of humanity before the great flood. Jesus then went on to tell the following parable in which he indicated that under the pressure of the gross iniquity in our day, the casualty rate among his followers might be as high as fifty percent.

Here is the parable.

---

[44]1 Corinthians 15:40-42.
[45]Matthew 24:37-39.

THE PARABLE OF THE TEN VIRGINS

Jesus said:

"Then shall the kingdom of heaven be likened unto ten virgins, which took their lamps, and went forth to meet the bridegroom. And five of them were wise, and five were foolish."[46]

But the bridegroom delayed his coming. Five of the virgins ran out of oil, so their lamps were extinguished. It is interesting that the Lord has identified the oil in the parable as the "Holy Spirit" which gives light to those who are virtuous and perform the good works of godly service.[47]

Then we read:

"And at midnight there was a cry made, Behold, the bridegroom cometh; go ye out to meet him."[48]

Unfortunately, the five who let their lamps go out were no longer ready, and therefore they ran about trying to secure more oil. Then it says:

"And while they went to buy, the bridegroom came; and they that were ready went in with him to the marriage: and the door was shut."[49]

Now we come to the sad part, which Jesus undoubtedly wished was not part of the parable. He said:

"Afterward came also the other virgins, saying, Lord, Lord, open to us. But he answered and said, Verily I say unto you, *I know you*

---

[46]Matthew 25:1-2.
[47]Doctrine and Covenants 45:56-57.
[48]Matthew 25:6.
[49]Matthew 25:10.

not."[50]   The Inspired Version gives the more correct translation where it says: "I say unto you, *you* know me not."[51]

WHY WILL THERE BE MEMBERS OF THE CHURCH WHOM THE LORD WILL NOT ADMIT TO HIS KINGDOM?

Jesus might have enlarged on his statement and said, "Where were you when I needed leaders with the Spirit of the Lord? Where were you when I needed bishops, stake presidents, missionaries, Relief Society presidents, financial contributors, inspired teachers, and inspired parents? I am sorry, you never knew me and I cannot admit you."

This parable may seem rather harsh, because we know Jesus is a loving person, but he needed to illustrate what a just God must do when it comes to granting admission to his kingdom where his faithful followers receive the greatest of all blessings. Tragically, for some, he will have to say, "I am sorry, but I cannot admit you."

Just to make certain that the Saints of the latter days would know this parable was about them, the Savior referred to it in two modern revelations. He said:

"And at that day, when I shall come in my glory, shall the parable be fulfilled which I spake concerning the ten virgins. For they that are wise and have received the truth, and have taken the Holy Spirit for their guide, and have not been deceived...shall abide the day. And the earth shall be given unto them for an inheritance."[52]

JESUS WILL REQUIRE AN ACCOUNTING WHEN HE COMES

It is interesting that Jesus followed his parable of the ten virgins with his parable of the talents. The word "talents" can refer to either money or abilities, because the parable is applicable in both cases. This parable is almost identical with the parable of the pounds

---

[50]Matthew 25:11-12 (emphasis added).

[51]JST Matthew 25:11.

[52]Doctrine and Covenants 45:56-58; 63:54.

mentioned by Luke,[53] and which we have previously discussed in chapter 31.

In the parable of the talents, Matthew quotes the Savior as saying:

"For the kingdom of heaven is as a man travelling into a far country, who called his own servants, and delivered unto them his goods. And unto one he gave five talents, to another two, and to another one; to every man according to his several ability; and straightway took his journey.

"Then he that had received the five talents went and traded with the same, and made them other five talents. And likewise he that had received two, he also gained other two.

"But he that had received one went and digged in the earth, and hid his lord's money.

"After a long time the lord of those servants cometh, and reckoneth with them. And so he that had received five talents came and brought other five talents, saying, Lord, thou deliveredst unto me five talents: behold, I have gained beside them five talents more.

"His lord said unto him, Well done, thou good and faithful servant: thou hast been faithful over a few things, I will make thee ruler over many things: enter thou into the joy of thy lord. He also that had received two talents came and said, Lord, thou deliveredst unto me two talents: behold, I have gained two other talents beside them. His lord said unto him, Well done, good and faithful servant; thou hast been faithful over a few things, I will make thee ruler over many things: enter thou into the joy of thy lord.

"Then he which had received the one talent came and said, Lord...I was afraid, and went and hid thy talent in the earth: lo, there thou hast that is thine.

---

[53]Luke 19:12-27.

"His lord answered and said unto him, Thou wicked and slothful servant....Take therefore the talent from him, and give it unto him which hath ten talents. For unto every one that hath shall be given, and he shall have abundance: but from him that hath not shall be taken away even that which he hath."[54]

The Savior is a loving Master, but he wants his investments in each of us to be multiplied. As he said in a modern revelation concerning those to whom "stewardships" have been entrusted under the law of consecration:

"And you are to be equal...every man according to his wants and his needs, inasmuch as his wants are just—And all this for the benefit of the church of the living God, that every man may improve upon his talent, that every man may gain other talents, yea, even an hundred fold, to be cast into the Lord's storehouse, to become the common property of the whole church—Every man seeking the interest of his neighbor, and doing all things with an eye single to the glory of God."[55]

This spirit of brotherhood, love, self improvement, and mutual concern for the Father's extended family is identical with the spirit developed by the apostles when they set up the kingdom in the meridian of time,[56] and it is identical with the Christlike spirit displayed in the lives of the American Christians under the prophet, Nephi IV. The record says:

"And it came to pass that there was no contention in the land, because of the love of God which did dwell in the hearts of the people.

"And here were no envyings, nor strifes, nor tumults, nor whoredoms, nor lyings, nor murders, nor any manner of

---

[54]Matthew 25:14-29.

[55]Doctrine and Covenants 82:17-19.

[56]Acts 4:34-35.

lasciviousness; and surely there could not be a happier people among all the people who had been created by the hand of God."[57]

* * * *

TOPICS FOR REFLECTION AND DISCUSSION

1. Whenever the Savior or his prophets have begun to describe the future, what is the first thing everybody asks—just as the apostles did on the Mount of Olives?

2. Where does it appear that Matthew obtained the words of Christ given in his 24th chapter?

3. Did many of the people who lived in the days of Christ live to see the destruction of Jerusalem? About how many were killed when the Romans destroyed Jerusalem? What did Jesus identify as the worst holocaust the Jews would ever have to endure?

4. As far as the scripture shows, who was the first Christian martyr? Who was the second?

5. Under pressure of the Roman persecutions of the Christians, what tragic weakness did Jesus predict among some of the members of the church?

6. Jesus spoke of the gospel of the kingdom coming forth in the latter days and being taught worldwide. Did the ancient prophets know where this would occur? What name did Isaiah use for America? How did he describe its location? How did he describe its native inhabitants?

7. What are some of the things Christianity had lost that needed to be restored?

8. What conditions did Jesus say would exist among mankind during the latter days, just before his Second Coming?

---

[57] 4 Nephi 1:2-3 (emphasis added), B. of M.

9. What parable did Jesus tell his apostles that applies to the members of God's kingdom in the latter days? How would you define the "wise virgins" in this parable? How would describe the "foolish virgins?"

10. According to the parable of the ten virgins, approximately what did Jesus predict would be the casualty rate among members of the church at the time of his Second Coming? What did Jesus indicate he would be compelled to say to those who were not ready?

*   *   *   *

CHAPTER 36

EVENTS LEADING UP TO THE PASSOVER

After Jesus had finished his discourse to the apostles concerning the events of the future for both the Christians and the Jews, he took his companions up over the top of the Mount of Olives and down the other side to Bethany.

Somewhere in this vicinity there was a bounteous banquet being prepared for them. Both Matthew and Mark indicate that this reception and dinner took place two days before the "feast day."[1] According to the calculations which we shall discuss in a moment, this would put the banquet on Tuesday evening.

SIMON THE LEPER PROVIDES AN OPEN HOUSE AND A BANQUET

It is interesting that this festive occasion should have been held at the house of Simon the leper.[2]

We are not told whether Jesus had healed this Simon or whether his disease was in remission and he had been declared "clean" by the priest. One or the other had happened, or Simon would have been considered a source of contagion and his house pronounced a defiled habitation.

We should also mention that the name of Simon was so commonplace that a surname or some other identifying emblem was often attached to it. For example, Peter's supplemental name was Simon but he was called "Simon Bar-jona" (son of Jonah) in order to distinguish him from all the other Simons.

---

[1]Matthew 26:2; Mark 14:1. These verses correct a misconception growing out of John 12:1-2 which led some to think this banquet occurred several days earlier.
[2]Matthew 26:6.

In the case of Simon the leper, he may have been identified as a leper so long that he continued to have this designation even after he became liberated from the dread disease.

Concerning this special dinner, the apostle John tells us that "they" made the Savior and his company a supper, "but Martha served."[3] From this we assume that both Mary and Martha had prepared the dinner, but Martha assumed her usual role of seeing that everything was served in order and in quantity, suitable to the occasion.

LAZARUS ATTRACTS MANY SPECTATORS

John also tells us that as the guests were invited to assemble around the festive board, "Lazarus was one of them."[4]

We have previously mentioned that it is this verse which suggests the possibility, along with other scriptures and circumstances, that Lazarus had been with Jesus and his company ever since Jesus raised Lazarus from the dead.

John tells us that the word was already spreading in Jerusalem "among the Jews," (mostly followers of Jesus, it seems) that he had returned to Bethany. We are told that quite a number made the two-mile journey to see Jesus and more particularly, the living miracle—the man Lazarus. We read:

"Much people of the Jews therefore knew that he was there: and they came not for Jesus' sake only, but that they might see Lazarus also, whom he had raised from the dead."[5]

Apparently Simon the leper had a large house and the curious visitors from Jerusalem were allowed to circulate quietly past the dining area where they could see Jesus, Lazarus and the apostles. In fact, it may have been such a source of pride for Simon the leper to have these distinguished guests in his home that he personally

---

[3]John 12:2.
[4]Ibid.
[5]John 12:9.

supervised or at least encouraged the visitors to take this little sightseeing tour through his home.

MARY AND HER FAMOUS ANOINTING OF JESUS

Earlier in the Savior's ministry, he had been at the home of another Simon, a prominent Pharisee, who was amazed when a woman who was known in the community to be "a sinner" came in to anoint the feet of Jesus. Her tears washed away the dust from his feet, and she used her hair to wipe his feet and kissed them as she applied a perfumed ointment. The Pharisee was even more astonished when Jesus said to the woman, "Thy sins are forgiven ....Thy faith hath saved thee; go in peace."[6]

But on this night in Bethany, there was another anointing, this time by one of the two sisters whom "Jesus loved."[7] The scripture says:

"Then took Mary a pound of ointment of spikenard, very costly, and anointed the feet of Jesus, and wiped his feet with her hair: and the house was filled with the odour of the ointment."[8]

At this juncture, Matthew says that "when the disciples saw it, they had indignation."[9] However, John says the indignation came from just one disciple, namely Judas Iscariot, so we will let John tell the story. He says:

"Then saith one of his disciples, Judas Iscariot, Simon's son, which should betray him,

"Why was not this ointment sold for three hundred pence, and given to the poor?"[10]

---

[6]Luke 7:48, 50.
[7]John 11:5.
[8]John 12:3.
[9]Matthew 26:8.
[10]John 12:4-5.

To appreciate how precious the spikenard ointment was in the eyes of Judas Iscariot, we have his own estimate of its value. He said it was worth three hundred times the daily wage of the common laborer, and that was a penny a day. If we multiply the average wage of a worker today by 300 it will give us some idea of the comparative value of this ointment in the days of the Savior.

John gives his own feelings concerning this occasion. He says Judas Iscariot had his own agenda and was not sincerely concerned about the poor. John calls him a "thief" in the following verse, which actually suggests that Judas was skimming money from the apostolic treasury which he had in his custody. Here are John's words:

"This he [Judas Iscariot] said, not that he cared for the poor; but because he was a thief, and had the bag, and bare what was put therein."

THE SAVIOR'S PROPHECY CONCERNING MARY

We next learn that Jesus was not at all pleased with the effort of Judas to disparage what Mary was doing. He turned to Judas and said:

"Why trouble ye the woman? for she hath wrought a good work upon me.

"For ye have the poor always with you; but me ye have not always.

"For in that she hath poured this ointment on my body, she did it for my burial."[11]

This reference to the "burial," obviously meant nothing to the apostles at the moment. John later explains that "These things understood not his disciples at the first...."[12]

---

[11]Matthew 26:10-12.
[12]John 12:16.

Jesus then made a remarkable prophecy concerning Mary and this act of kindness she had performed for him. The Savior said:

"Verily I say unto you, Wheresoever this gospel shall be preached in the whole world, there shall also this, that this woman hath done, be told for a memorial of her."[13]

Thus this pleasant evening ended. And just as the world would remember Mary and her devotion to the Savior, so would Jesus.

THE CHIEF PRIESTS CONSPIRE
TO KILL BOTH JESUS AND LAZARUS

After the dinner was over, it turned out that Simon's generosity in allowing people to see both Jesus and Lazarus had resulted in some interesting developments. Those people who had visited Simon's house made their way back to Jerusalem and immediately began spreading their convictions that Jesus was indeed the very Messiah. With their very own eyes they had seen the famous Jesus and also Lazarus whom he had raised from the dead.

But even though this eye-witness report converted some, it caused a virtual state of hysteria among the high priests whose jealousy of Jesus stirred them into a murderous mania. John says:

"But the chief priests consulted that they might put Lazarus also to death;

"Because that by reason of him many of the Jews went away, and believed on Jesus."[14]

JUDAS ISCARIOT

The diabolical nature of Judas Iscariot now began to manifest itself. The fact that more people began to believe in Jesus was irrelevant to him. The main development for Judas was the

---

[13]Matthew 26:13.
[14]John 12:10-11.

whispered rumor that the high priests were now desperately anxious to have Jesus betrayed into their hands (and for a price, of course).

For reasons that the apostles never clearly specify, Judas had been lacerating his soul with a rising tide of internal anger for some time. It was as though he had been burning out the very essence of his spiritual roots with mental vitriolic acid. Perhaps the Savior's rebuke after Judas criticized Mary was enough to trigger a compulsive explosion in his mind. In any event, his seething emotions suddenly reached the psychopathic threshold where a murderous hate distilled itself into a plot to destroy his Master. The scripture says:

"Then one of the twelve, called Judas Iscariot, went unto the chief priests,

"And said unto them, What will ye give me, and I will deliver him unto you? And they covenanted with him for thirty pieces of silver.

"And from that time he sought opportunity to betray him."[15]

THE LAST WEEK IN THE LIFE OF THE SAVIOR— A SUGGESTED CALENDAR OF EVENTS

By this time Jesus was well into the last week of his mortal life. However, it becomes difficult to follow the events during these crucial seven days unless we know which day we are talking about.

Until fairly recent times, it was extremely difficult to fix the events in the last week of the Savior's life with reasonable assurance. As we have previously indicated, many of the dates selected for Christmas, the Last Supper and the Crucifixion were not officially adopted until several centuries after the events occurred.

However, selecting Friday as the day of the crucifixion raises a number of questions among Bible scholars.

---

[15]Matthew 26:14-16.

For example, if the Last Supper were on Thursday, why did the Gospel writers stop their narratives on Tuesday? Didn't anything happen on Wednesday? Or is it possible that the calculations are off one day, and the busy apostles actually prepared the Last Supper on Wednesday, with the Crucifixion taking place on Thursday?

JESUS ANSWERS THE QUESTION HIMSELF

Jesus made it clear that the time he was in the tomb was comparable to the time Jonah was in the belly of the whale.[16] He said:

"For as Jonas was three days and three NIGHTS in the whale's belly; so shall the Son of man be three days and three NIGHTS in the heart of the earth."[17]

Notice that a crucifixion on Friday would only allow for two nights. Jesus always made it clear that he would rise from the tomb on the third day,[18] and it turned out to be very early on the third day.[19]

Since we know the resurrection was on the first day of the week, we can count backwards and verify that the crucifixion would have had to occur on Thursday. This would mean that Jesus was placed in the tomb Thursday evening, at the beginning of the Feast which was considered a special sabbath that lasted until Friday.[20] After the Feast day on Friday, he lay in the tomb another day, which was the *regular* sabbath or Saturday, and then he rose on the third day, which was Sunday.

From this calculation we can conclude that the Last Supper would have been eaten Wednesday night, and the dinner at the house of Simon the leper would have taken place on Tuesday evening.

---

[16]Jonah 1:17.
[17]Matthew 12:40.
[18]Matthew 20:19; Luke 24:7.
[19]Matthew 28:1-6.
[20]John 19:31.

The following calendar for the last week of the Savior's life helps to illustrate these events.

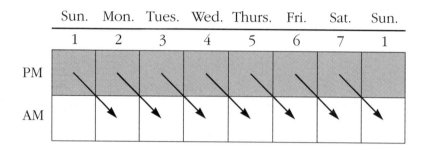

The Jews counted an "evening and a morning" as a day in accordance with Genesis 1:5.

So, from the Savior's own words we conclude that the crucifixion took place on Thursday, because this would allow for three full nights and three days in the tomb, with Jesus rising *early* on the third day as stated in the scripture.[21]

Fortunately, the Book of Mormon carefully chronicles the period beginning with the Savior's Crucifixion down to the time of the Resurrection. By counting backwards we are able to confirm each major event on the day we have indicated.

PREPARING THE FEAST OF THE
PASCHAL (PASSOVER) LAMB

For some 1,400 years, Israel had memorialized that terrifying night in Egypt when the life of the firstborn in each family was preserved while the firstborn of the Egyptians was slain.

In order for the angels of death to pass over a Hebrew home, it was necessary that the family, or a group of ten or more, take a lamb

---

[21]Matthew 28:19; Mark 9:31, 10:34; Luke 18:33, 24:7,46.

"without blemish, a male of the first year,"[22] and have it sacrificed without breaking any bones.[23]

On that fatal night in Egypt, the blood of the lamb was brushed over the lintel of the doorway, and along the two door posts, so that members of the priesthood from beyond the veil who had authority to call the spirits of the firstborn home would pass by those families with marked doors.[24]

THE PASSOVER MEAL

The passover meal itself was very simple, and more ceremonial than sumptuous. It was eaten with bitter herbs to remind them of the anguish the Israelites had suffered during their years of bondage. One or more goblets of red wine were on the table, reminding them of the blood of the lamb that was slain—the blood which was smeared on the lintel and the doorposts to save the lives of their firstborn. There were also cakes or wafers of unleavened bread to be eaten as part of the ceremony.

The preparations for the passover meal, which the Jews called the Seder, included the purchase and killing of an unblemished lamb that had been approved and consecrated by the priests at the temple. All of these preparations had to be accomplished on the first day of unleavened bread, which was the 13th day of the month of Nisin according to the Hebrew calendar.

However, because of the large number of lambs that had to be killed at Passover time, the priests at the temple could not handle them all in one day. By actual count at one of the Passover feasts, the Romans found that 256,500 lambs had been killed.[25]

Therefore, it became necessary, because of the congestion at the temple, to set aside TWO nights for the Passover meal, either of which could be chosen by the people for this purpose.[26]

It is interesting that Jesus chose the first night, whereas most of the people waited until the following night. It turned out that for all of these other Jews, the sacrifice of their lambs coincided exactly with the day when the Father's Beloved Son was sacrificed.

HOW THE TEMPLE ACCOMMODATED LARGE NUMBERS OF SACRIFICES

Ordinarily, sacrifices took place within the Court of the Priests, where the thirty-foot altar of sacrifice was located. However, the paschal lambs were brought to the larger Court of the Congregation.[27]

Because of the immense amount of butchering which took place at the Passover, it was extremely important that the disposal of the blood and refuse be immaculately arranged, and also that cleanliness be stringently enforced lest the temple area become so tainted that even the pleasant, pungent incense could not refresh the atmosphere. Dr. Alfred Edersheim gives us this description of the disposal facilities which had been structured below the temple esplanade:

"The system of drainage into chambers below and canals, all of which could be flushed at will, was perfect: the blood and refuse being swept down into Kidron and towards the royal gardens."[28]

This system required great quantities of water and a most elaborate network of cisterns. This was achieved by building an aqueduct that carried a substantial stream of water from Solomon's Pools, near Bethlehem, to fill the temple reservoirs.

Dr. Edersheim describes this water storage system as follows:

[26]Talmage, *Jesus the Christ*, op. cit., p. 618.
[27]For a detailed description of the temple, see Skousen, *The Fourth Thousand Years*, pp. 217-224.
[28]Alfred Edersheim, *The Temple*, London: William Clowestand Sons, p. 55.

"The cisterns appear to have been connected by a system of channels cut out of the rock; so that when one was full the surplus water ran into the next, and so on, till the final overflow was carried off by a channel into the Kidron. One of the cisterns—that is known as the Great Sea—would contain two million gallons; and the total number of gallons which could be stored [in all the cisterns] probably exceeded ten millions."[29]

THE SLAYING OF THE PASCHAL LAMB

Most of the sacrificial offerings at the temple were very elaborate. They often involved the opening of the animal, the removal of fat and kidneys to be burned on the altar, the disposal of the entrails, removal of the skin, and giving a portion of the animal to the priest.[30]

However, the slaying of the paschal lamb was rather simple. A member of the family or group that would eat the lamb came to the temple and placed his hand on the head of the lamb as the priest cut its throat and consecrated it. A small quantity of the blood was saved to sprinkle upon the altar, and the rest was washed down one of the numerous drains. The slain lamb was then said to have been "sacrificed," and was carried away to the residence or place where it was to be dressed, cooked and eaten.[31]

PETER AND JOHN ASSIGNED TO PREPARE
THE PASSOVER MEAL

In view of the above, it will be appreciated that the two apostles who were assigned to prepare the passover meal were in for a busy day. They had to select the place, purchase the lamb, and take it to the priest for consecration. Then it had to be killed and dressed. The herbs had to be purchased, and the meal prepared before sunset on Wednesday. Sunset would mark the beginning of the new day when the Passover meal must be eaten.

---

[29]Ibid., p. 56.
[30]See Skousen, *The Third Thousand Years*, Salt Lake City: Bookcraft, 1965, pp.339-341.
[31]Talmage, *Jesus the Christ*, p. 593.

According to our calculation, it was early Wednesday morning when the preparations began. The scripture says:

"And he sent Peter and John, saying, Go and prepare us the passover, that we may eat."[32]

IN WHOSE HOUSE WAS THE "UPPER ROOM?"

The first decision was selecting the place where the passover meal should be eaten. A number of places were available.

The night before, the Savior and his apostles had all attended a dinner at the house of Simon the leper, and no doubt he would have welcomed them back. Then there was the home of Mary, Martha and Lazarus, where Jesus had been staying. The Sanhedrin had ruled that both Bethany and Bethphage were considered part of Jerusalem, so legally speaking, the passover could have been prepared anywhere in the neighborhood.

However, Jesus chose a different place. When the disciples said, "Where wilt thou that we prepare?" Jesus answered:

"Behold, when ye are entered into the city, there shall a man meet you, bearing a pitcher of water; follow him into the house where he entereth in."[33]

Water was carried in jars from the Pool of Siloam located at the end of Hezekiah's tunnel, and on this day there would be many people fetching water. However, nearly all of them would be women. Jesus told Peter and John that when they saw a *man* carrying water, they should follow him to the house where the servant would lead them. Then Jesus said:

"Ye shall say unto the goodman of the house, The Master saith unto thee, Where is the guest chamber, where I shall eat the passover with my disciples?

---

[32]Luke 22:8.
[33]Luke 22:10.

"And he shall shew you a large upper room furnished: there make ready.

"And they went, and found as he had said unto them: and they made ready the passover."[34]

There is considerable speculation as to the identity of the man who owned this particular house. In the New Testament chronicle, this house is described as having "an upper room," and this figures very prominently in the story we are about to relate.

Obviously, the owner of the house would appear to be a disciple of Jesus, but which one? Subsequent circumstances point to the fact that it appears to have been the sumptuous home of the parents of young John Mark, who later wrote the Gospel of Mark.

The famous Bible scholar, Dr. Alfred Edersheim, provides the basis for this conclusion.

THE CIRCUMSTANTIAL EVIDENCE

Dr. Edersheim points out that in the book of Mark we read about a young boy who apparently was awakened at night by soldiers seeking Jesus to arrest him. The boy wrapped himself in a sheet and hurried to the Garden of Gethsemane to warn the Savior of the danger. However, he arrived too late, and Jesus was arrested. Some youths tried to seize this boy, but he left the sheet in their hands and fled into the darkness naked.[35]

But why had the soldiers gone to the home of this boy to find Jesus? Obviously, Judas had led them there. Judas had assumed that Jesus was still in the upper room where they had eaten the Last Supper. This suggests that the upper room was in the house where this boy lived and that is why he was awakened. Mark is the only Gospel writer who mentions this incident and it is presumed that Mark is the boy in the story.

---

[34]Luke 22:11-13.
[35]Mark 14:51-52.

In a later scripture Luke describes the home of Mark's parents. It was a large home surrounded by a wall with a locked gate. When Peter fled to this house he found many of the disciples there.[36] In fact, if this is indeed the house where the upper room was located, it is also the house where all of the apostles were staying after the Savior's resurrection.[37]

THE PASSOVER FEAST WAS OF SUPREME IMPORTANCE TO JESUS

As the twelve apostles extended themselves on the couches or cushions that customarily surrounded the table on which was spread the paschal (passover) meal, Jesus said:

"With *desire* I have desired to eat this passover with you before I suffer."[38]

Jesus had become intensely lonely, and to some degree, we think he may have already begun to feel the gradual withdrawal of his Father's Spirit. This process was part of the bitter cup that would come to such a terrible climax at the conclusion of the crucifixion.[39]

There had been symptoms of this for some time.

For example, just before Jesus took his apostles up to the Mount of Transfiguration, he seems to have sensed this growing breach gradually developing between himself and his Father. We noted the uncharacteristic way in which Jesus rebuked the apostle Peter when Jesus tried to discuss his coming ordeal and Peter had declared that the apostles would never let it happen.[40]

We also noted that when Moses and Elijah appeared on the Mount, they talked to Jesus about his death and resurrection and the

---

[36]Acts 12:12-14.
[37]Acts 1:13.
[38]Luke 22:15 (emphasis added).
[39]Matthew 27:46; Mark 15:14.
[40]Matthew 16:22-23; Mark 8:32-33.

great things he must accomplish in Jerusalem.[41] It was apparent they were trying to strengthen Jesus. Even the Father proclaimed his love and assurance on that occasion.[42]

But after Jesus came down from the mount, the haunting loneliness persisted. Only four days before the Last Supper, and just after Jesus had cleansed the temple for the second time, he suddenly sent up a plea to heaven with these words,

"Father, glorify thy name!"[43]

The Father immediately reassured him that all was well, and that his name would indeed be glorified. Thereafter, Jesus regained his composure.

But at the Last Supper the record is clear that the lonely gloom was increasing again. We think this is why Jesus told the apostles of his "DESIRE...to eat the Passover with you before I suffer."

Within another twenty-four hours the Father would be required to withdraw his Spirit from Jesus completely, and the anguish of it would cause Jesus to cry out as though the agony of being forsaken by the Father was more intense than the suffering on the cross.

THE FATHER'S ORDEAL WAS HAVING TO FORSAKE HIS SON

The events suggesting the gradual withdrawal of the Father's Spirit from his Son have been mentioned so that we might better appreciate the role of the Father in the redemptive sacrifice.

John tried to emphasize the point when he wrote:

---

[41]JST Luke 9:31.

[42]Matthew 17:5.

[43]John 12:28 (emphasis added).

"For God so loved the world, that he GAVE HIS ONLY BEGOTTEN SON, that whosoever believeth on him should not perish, but have everlasting life."[44]

The Father's ordeal was having to forsake his Son. The Savior's ordeal was having to endure it.

The Father's agony in having to surrender his Beloved Son to the rack of torture on the cross is seldom mentioned, but it seems the Father wanted at least one of his great servants to know—in a finite way—what it was like.

That servant was Abraham. As Jacob, the brother of Nephi, declared in one of his sermons:

"Abraham...offering up his son Isaac...is a similitude of God and his Only Begotten Son."[45]

Abraham's ordeal was the prospect of slaying his beloved Isaac with his own hand.[46] The Father's ordeal was deliberately forsaking his son, that others might slay him.

In the end, it had to be said that the Savior trod the wine press of the great last sacrifice alone.[47] That is why the gradual withdrawal of the Father's Spirit finally came to a climax when he withdrew his Spirit altogether just before Jesus died.[48]

Even the Savior did not anticipate how terrifying that would be.

* * * *

---

[44]John 3:16 (emphasis added).

[45]Jacob 4:5, B. of M.

[46]Genesis 22:10.

[47]Doctrine and Covenants 76:107; 133:50; Isaiah 63:3.

[48]Matthew 27:46.

TOPICS FOR REFLECTION AND DISCUSSION

1. What must have happened to Simon the leper before he could act as host for a community reception in the Savior's honor? Do we know how or when it happened?

2. Who were the two main attractions at the banquet? What provoked the rulers of the Sanhedrin right after the banquet that led them to devise a plan to kill both of these men?

3. Who appears to have prepared this important dinner? Who served it? Who anointed the Savior's feet on this occasion?

4. Why did Judas Iscariot say the anointing of Jesus was a waste of precious ointment? How much was the ointment worth? How did Judas say it should have been spent? What was his real reason for objecting?

5. Can you outline the major events in the last week of the Savior's life, and indicate on which day you think each event occurred?

6. Can you outline the scriptural events that led Dr. Alfred Edersheim to conclude that the "upper room" where the Last Supper took place was located in the rather sumptuous home of the parents of Mark?

7. Do we have any indication that this house became the headquarters of the apostles after the crucifixion?

8. What is the greatest evidence of the Father's love for his earthly children?

9. What was the Father's greatest ordeal as Jesus came to the close of his earthly mission?

10. Describe why you think the prophet Jacob would compare Abraham's willingness to sacrifice Isaac, with the Father's surrender of Jesus to the cross.

* * * *

CHAPTER 37

THE HIGHLIGHTS OF THE LAST SUPPER

Jesus knew his final feast of the passover would be an important historic event. It was the last quiet meal he would ever have with his beloved apostles in mortality. Shortly after his resurrection, he would partake of a little food to demonstrate to his apostles the nature of a resurrected being, but they would never have a full meal together until the Savior came again in power to usher in the millennium.

Therefore Jesus said:

"For I say unto you, I will not any more eat thereof, until it be fulfilled in the kingdom of God.

"And he took the cup, and gave thanks, and said, Take this, and divide it among yourselves:

"For I say unto you, I will not drink of the fruit of the vine, until the kingdom of God shall come."[1]

This was not the sacramental cup. That would come later. This was more like a blessing on the meal. The Savior's reference to the great future feast when "the kingdom of God shall come" anticipated a glorious future banquet after his Second Coming. On that occasion Jesus has said he will eat and drink with the whole congregation of his righteous servants from Adam on down. He describes it in a modern revelation:

"The hour cometh that I will drink of the fruit of the vine with you on the earth, and with Moroni...and also with Elias...and also John the son of Zacharias...and also Elijah...and also with Joseph and

---

[1] Luke 22:16-18.

Jacob, and Isaac, and Abraham, your fathers...and also with Michael, or Adam, the father of all...and also with Peter, and James, and John... and also with *all those whom my Father hath given me out of the world.*"[2]

Jesus wanted his faithful apostles to know that this victory banquet, some 2,000 years hence, would be especially joyous for them. At the Last Supper he told them:

"Ye are they which have continued with me in my temptations.

"And I appoint unto you a kingdom, as my Father hath appointed unto me;

"That ye may eat and drink at my table in MY KINGDOM, and SIT ON THRONES JUDGING THE TWELVE TRIBES OF ISRAEL."[3]

It seems especially significant that Jesus would talk about this marvelous banquet of the future, right at the time when he was partaking of a passover meal in the midst of gloom, darkness, and an impending betrayal by an apostle that would bring about his crucifixion.

But so it was.

JESUS INTRODUCES THE
ORDINANCE OF THE SACRAMENT

At some point during the Last Supper Jesus introduced an ordinance that would replace the blood sacrifices of the Old Testament. The scripture says:

"And as they were eating, Jesus took bread, and brake it, blessed it, and gave it to his disciples, and said, Take, eat; THIS IS IN REMEMBRANCE OF my body WHICH I GIVE A RANSOM FOR YOU.

---

[2]Doctrine and Covenants 27:5-14 (emphasis added).
[3]Luke 22:28-30 (emphasis added).

"And he took the cup, and gave thanks, and gave it to them, saying, Drink ye all of it;

"For this is IN REMEMBRANCE OF my blood of the new testament, which is shed for AS MANY AS SHALL BELIEVE ON MY NAME for the remission of THEIR sins."[4]

Notice that the blood sacrifices since the days of Adam had been in "ANTICIPATION" of the day when the Father's Son would be sacrificed. The sacrament of the Lord's Supper is in "REMEMBRANCE" of that sacrifice.

Once the Savior had been crucified as "the great last sacrifice,"[5] the Lord declared that blood sacrifices were to be discontinued. He said:

"And ye shall offer up unto me no more the shedding of blood; yea, your sacrifices and your burnt offerings shall be done away, for I will accept none of your sacrifices and your burnt offerings.

"And ye shall offer for a sacrifice unto me a broken heart and a contrite spirit. And whoso cometh unto me with a broken heart and a contrite spirit, him will I baptize with fire and with the Holy Ghost."[6]

WHAT ABOUT THE SONS OF LEVI?

The only exception to the Lord's mandate against blood sacrifices is the future requirement that the "Sons of Levi" or descendants of Levi who must offer an "offering unto the Lord in righteousness" after the temple is rebuilt in Jerusalem, shortly before the Second Coming.[7]

Malachi saw this day and said:

---

[4]JST Matthew 26:22-24, corrections in caps.
[5]Alma 34:10,13-14.
[6]3 Nephi 9:19-20.
[7]Ezekiel 43:21-27; 44:15.

"...he shall purify the sons of Levi, and purge them as gold and silver, that they may OFFER UNTO THE LORD AN OFFERING IN RIGHTEOUSNESS."[8]

This would lead us to assume that after this "offering in righteousness," the Levites will go on to receive the higher priesthood blessings.

This is suggested in a modern scripture as well. When the resurrected John the Baptist came to restore the Aaronic Priesthood, he said:

"...and this [Priesthood of Aaron] shall never be taken again from the earth, UNTIL the sons of Levi do offer again an offering unto the Lord in righteousness."[9]

WHO IS THE GREATEST?

One of the developments during the Last Supper that cast a dark shadow over the Savior was the apostles' discussion of their respective rights and special preferences based on their worthiness. This was a very sensitive point with the apostles who had been trained in the tradition of the Pharisees.

Preferential seating at a table or at a synagogue or in the Sanhedrin was a signal to the congregation and to other Pharisees of the recognized worthiness or "greatness" of an individual. To ignore this element of preference was interpreted as a chastisement or a deliberate "put down" of that person by the presiding host.

Only the week before, Jesus had tried to root out this false doctrine of the Pharisees when James and John had asked for an assurance that they would enjoy places of preference in Christ's kingdom.[10] Now Jesus patiently tried to proclaim the true doctrine again. He said:

---

[8]Malachi 3:3; 3 Nephi 24:3, B. of M. (emphasis added).
[9]Doctrine and Covenants, Section 13.
[10]Mark 10:35-41.

"The kings of the Gentiles exercise lordship over them; and they that exercise authority upon them are called benefactors.

"But ye shall not be so: but he that is greatest among you, let him be as the younger; and he that is chief, as he that doth serve.

"For whether is greater, he that sitteth at meat, or he that serveth?...I am among you as he that serveth."[11]

No greater compliment could come to a guest than to have his host serve him, and that is what Jesus had done for them.

THE ORDINANCE OF WASHING OF FEET

This was an excellent time for Jesus to demonstrate the role of a true leader. He prepared to wash the feet of all his apostles, including Judas.[12] Although Judas had already agreed to betray Jesus, he had not yet committed his rash act. Therefore, Jesus humbly washed the feet of this man whom, within an hour, he would refer to as "a son of perdition." The scripture says:

"He riseth from supper, and laid aside his garments; and took a towel, and girded himself.

"After that he poureth water into a basin, and began to wash the disciples' feet, and to wipe them with the towel wherewith he was girded."[13]

Now in the next verse we learn that Peter, who would later be named the chief of the apostles, had not presumed to sit next to Jesus. He was somewhere down the line. The scripture continues:

"Then cometh he to Simon Peter: and Peter saith unto him, Lord, dost thou wash my feet?

---

[11]Luke 22:25-27.
[12]This is apparent from John 13:10-11 and verses 26-30.
[13]John 13:4-5.

"Jesus answered and said unto him, What I do thou knowest not now; but thou shalt know hereafter.

"Peter saith unto him, Thou shalt never wash my feet!"[14]

Peter was speaking out of love and respect, not insubordination. He just could not visualize the very Son of God washing his feet. However, Jesus said:

"If I wash thee not, thou hast no part with me."[15]

Well, of course, if that which the Savior washed somehow became part of him, then so be it. Peter couldn't understand exactly what was happening, but then Jesus so often spoke in riddles, and certainly Peter had no desire to hinder the process. Therefore, Peter said:

"Lord, not my feet only, but also my hands and my head.

"Jesus saith to him, He that is washed needeth not save to wash his feet, but is clean every whit."[16]

Jesus was introducing a sacred priesthood ordinance and those who received it *worthily* were completely cleansed thereby. But there was one to whom this blessing did not apply even though he received the washing of his feet. It was Judas.

When Jesus had finished, he said:

"Ye are clean, but not all.

"For he knew who should betray him; therefore said he, Ye are not all clean.

---

[14]John 13:6-8.
[15]John 13:8.
[16]John 13:9-10.

"So after he had washed their feet, and had taken his garments, and was set down again, he said unto them, know ye what I have done to you?"[17]

Jesus used this ordinance to impress upon his disciples that they must love and serve one another. This was required especially of those in leadership positions. He did not want them to miss the point, and so he said:

"Ye call me Master and Lord: and ye say well; for so I am.

"If I then, your Lord and Master, have washed your feet; ye also ought to wash one another's feet.

"For I have given you an example, that ye should do as I have done to you....

"If ye know these things, happy are ye if ye do them."[18]

JESUS EXPOSES THE IDENTITY OF HIS BETRAYER

The sequence of events at the Last Supper is not always related in the same order by the Gospel writers, but it is the event itself, rather than the sequence, that is important. We think it was about this time that Jesus said:

"Verily, verily, I say unto you, that one of you shall betray me.

"Then the disciples looked one on another, doubting of whom he spake."[19]

This must have been extremely frightening to Judas, because if Jesus suspected that he had agreed with the high priests to cause the Savior's death, the whole plot would be undone. According to Matthew, Judas decided to settle the matter with a direct confrontation. He said to Jesus:

---

[17]John 13:10-12.
[18]John 13:13-17.
[19]John 13:21-22.

"Master, is it I?"[20]

Jesus looked at him and said:

"Thou hast said."[21]

This was like saying, "Affirmative." Just what was going on in the mind of Judas at this point is not revealed, but based on subsequent events, it can be assumed his mind was in a state of sudden panic. If Jesus knew of his duplicity, it was vital that Judas make his final move immediately.

Meanwhile, the apostles were burning with frantic curiosity. Who in their midst would betray their Master? John writes:

"Now there was leaning on Jesus' bosom one of his disciples, whom Jesus loved.

"Simon Peter therefore beckoned to him, that he should ask who it should be of whom he spake.

"He then lying on Jesus' breast saith unto him, Lord, who is it?

"Jesus answered, He it is, to whom I shall give a sop [of bitter herbs], when I have dipped it. And when he had dipped the sop, he gave it to Judas Iscariot, the son of Simon."[22]

Just a moment before, Jesus had said:

"Woe unto that man by whom the Son of man is betrayed! it had been good for that man if he had not been born."[23]

If Judas had not yet been born he would still be in the pre-mortal state and innocent of any offense. Now, however, he had doomed

---

[20]Matthew 26:25.
[21]Ibid.
[22]John 13:23-26.
[23]Matthew 26:24.

himself, and had sinned against knowledge and open revelation.[24] This sin cannot be forgiven either in this world or the world to come.[25]

If Judas had any doubt in his mind as to whether or not Jesus had found him out, that doubt should have been completely removed as Jesus handed Judas the sop of bitter herbs and then said:

"That thou doest, do quickly!"[26]

John then adds this comment:

"Now no man at the table knew for what intent he spake this unto him....

"He, [Judas Iscariot] then having received the sop went immediately out; and it was night."[27]

John continues his record by saying:

"When he [Judas] was gone out, Jesus said, Now is the Son of man glorified, and God is glorified in him....

"Little children, yet a little while I am with you. Ye shall seek me: and as I said unto the Jews, Whither I go, ye cannot come; so now I say to you."[28]

This last statement bothered the apostles just as it had the Jews. Where was he going? Why couldn't they follow him? Jesus knew what they were thinking, but went ahead to describe what he expected of them after he was gone. He said:

"A new commandment I give unto you, That ye love one another; as I have loved you, that ye also love one another.

---

[24]Doctrine and Covenants 76:31-35.
[25]Matthew 12:32.
[26]John 13:27.
[27]John 13:28-30.
[28]John 13:31-33.

"By this shall all men know that ye are my disciples, if ye have love one to another."[29]

JESUS REVEALS SOMETHING TO PETER HE CANNOT BELIEVE

It was obvious that the Savior was launching into a prolonged sermon, and Peter did not want him to proceed until Jesus had answered a question that was on everybody's mind. Peter therefore interrupted and asked:

"Lord, why cannot I follow thee now? I will lay down my life for thy sake."[30]

Luke inserts an important comment of the Savior which John did not include:

"And the Lord said, Simon, Simon, behold, Satan hath desired to have you, that he may sift you as wheat:

"But I have prayed for thee, that thy faith fail not: and when thou art converted, strengthen thy brethren."[31]

Of course, Peter thought he was already thoroughly converted. What he didn't know was that conversion is a process, not an event. He had a world of trials and extended maturing to go through before he was ready to take over his high office as president of the church. Not realizing this, Peter said:

"Lord, I am ready to go with thee, both into prison, and to death.

"And he said, I tell thee, Peter, the cock shall not crow this day, before that thou shalt thrice DENY THAT THOU KNOWEST ME."[32]

---

[29]John 13:34-35.
[30]John 13:37.
[31]Luke 22:31-32.
[32]Luke 22:33-34 (emphasis added).

Peter did not believe him. This becomes clear with the unfolding of subsequent events. Peter felt he knew his own strength. He would *never* deny the Christ. When it happened that very night, no one could have been more shocked, amazed, and disconcerted than Peter himself.

THE COMMAND TO CARRY A SWORD, PURSE AND SCRIP

Jesus now wanted his apostles to know that they were entering a whole new epoch of dangerous trials where they must protect their lives and have the means to travel and preach so that their ministry would not be impeded. He therefore said:

"When I sent you without purse, and scrip, and shoes, lacked ye any thing? And they said, Nothing.

"Then said he unto them, But now, he that hath a purse, let him take it, and likewise his scrip: and he that hath no sword, let him sell his garment, and buy one....

"And they said, Lord, behold, here are two swords. And he said unto them, It is enough."[33]

It was they who would need swords, not the Savior.

THE SAVIOR'S FINAL MORTAL INSTRUCTIONS TO HIS ELEVEN APOSTLES

Jesus now continued the sermon that Peter had interrupted. He said:

"Let not your heart be troubled: ye believe in God, believe also in me."[34]

---

[33]Luke 22:35-36,38.
[34]John 14:1.

This verse was not only for the apostles, but for the majority of mankind who say they believe in a "God," but refuse to believe in a plan of salvation through Jesus Christ, his Son.

Jesus then went on to say that there are many kingdoms or mansions in heaven, and a place is prepared for each one according to that which he or she deserves.[35]

Jesus said he would come again and receive them unto himself. Meanwhile he reminded them that he is "the way, the truth and the light." If they want to be with him, then follow him. There is no other way to get to the Father except through Jesus. Philip then said:

"Lord, shew us the Father, and it sufficeth us.

"Jesus saith unto him, Have I been so long time with you, and yet hast thou not known me, Philip? he that hath seen me hath seen the Father."[36]

As we mentioned in chapter 33, even the apostles could not quite grasp the astonishing degree of unity which exists between the Father and his Beloved Son. The Father and Son look alike, they think alike, and they act alike. Later Jesus would pray that his disciples might enjoy this same oneness that he and his Father enjoy—entirely united in purpose, even though they remain completely separate and distinct individuals.

Then Jesus introduced a new subject. He said:

"I will pray the Father, and he shall give you another Comforter, that he may abide with you for ever....

"But the Comforter, which is the Holy Ghost, whom the Father will send in my name, he shall teach you all things, and bring all things to your remembrance, whatsoever I have said unto you."[37]

---

[35]John 14:2.
[36]John 14:8-9.
[37]John 14:16,26.

Here is the key to the integrity of the Gospels and the validity of the Savior's words which later came to their memory through the ministry of the Holy Ghost. This is the underlying vindication of all prophecy and all scripture. As Peter said:

"For the prophecy came not in old time by the will of man: but holy men of God spake as they were moved by the Holy Ghost."[38]

A short time later, Jesus said:

"It is expedient for you that I go away: for if I go not away, the Comforter will not come unto you; but if I depart, I will send him unto you."[39]

Of course, the Holy Ghost was working behind the scenes all through the Savior's ministry.[40] However, as long as Jesus was with the disciples it was the Savior's prerogative to teach them and reveal the things they needed to know. After his departure, the Holy Ghost would reveal himself openly with spiritual gifts, revelations and prophecy.[41]

Jesus promised to return and visit his disciples from time to time, and even reveal the Father to them.[42] This is the Second Comforter.[43]

JESUS FINISHES HIS SERMON

The Savior wanted to stress the interdependence between the Father, the Son and those who serve in the ministry. This is the Savior's beautiful parable of the vine:

"I am the true vine, and my Father is the husbandman....I am the vine, ye are the branches: He that abideth in me, and I in him, the

---

[38] 2 Peter 1:21.

[39] John 16:7.

[40] for example, Luke 1:15; 1:41; 2:25-26; 4:1; 12:12.

[41] Acts 1:2; 2:1-7.

[42] John 14:23; Doctrine and Covenants 130:3.

[43] Smith, *Teachings of the Prophet Joseph Smith*, pp. 150-151.

same bringeth forth much fruit: for without me ye can do nothing. If a man abide not in me, he is cast forth as a branch, and...burned.

"If ye abide in me, and my words abide in you, ye shall ask what ye will, and it shall be done unto you. Herein is my Father glorified, that ye bear much fruit; so shall ye be my disciples."[44]

Jesus then stressed the consequences of sinning against knowledge by the people of that day. He said:

"If I had not done among them the works which none other man did, they had not had sin....

"But this cometh to pass, that the word might be fulfilled that is written in their law, They hated me without a cause."[45]

So everything that was about to happen to the Savior was foreknown, but the foreknowledge did not make it any easier for Jesus to endure it.

Here are a few more special nuggets from this final mortal sermon of Jesus. He said:

"Greater love hath no man than this, that a man lay down his life for his friends."[46]

"Ye are my friends, if ye do whatsoever I command you."[47]

"All things that I have heard of my Father I have made known unto you."[48]

"Ye have not chosen me, but I have chosen you, and ordained you."[49]

---

[44]John 15:1-8.
[45]John 15:24-25.
[46]John 15:13.
[47]John 15:14.
[48]John 15:15.
[49]John 15:16.

"When he, the Spirit of truth, is come, he will guide you into all truth."[50]

"Behold, the hour cometh, yea, is now come, that ye shall be scattered, every man to his own, and shall leave me alone."[51]

This last prophecy would be fulfilled that very night. Then Jesus concluded by saying:

"These things I have spoken unto you, that in me ye might have peace. In the world ye shall have tribulation: but be of good cheer; I have overcome the world."[52]

* * * *

TOPICS FOR REFLECTION AND DISCUSSION

1. At the Last Supper, Jesus talked about a great banquet he would hold after his Second Coming. Who will attend?

2. What were the blood sacrifices intended to memorialize? What did Jesus say they should present as a sacrifice to God when the blood sacrifices were done away?

3. What is the broken bread in the sacramental service designed to represent? What does the water or wine represent?

4. Will there be any blood sacrifices in Jerusalem after the new temple is built? Who must offer an offering unto the Lord in righteousness? Then what will happen to the Aaronic Priesthood?

5. Why was it customary for Pharisees to be sensitive about their place at a table or in the seating arrangement at the synagogue? Were the apostles raised as Pharisees?

---

[50]John 16:13.
[51]John 16:32.
[52]John 16:33.

6. What did Jesus demonstrate when he washed the apostles' feet? Was this simply for cleanliness or was it a ritual?

7. Do you think Judas realized that Jesus knew he was the betrayer? Based on your answer, what would you imagine his feelings were at this time?

8. What do you think it was like to preach without purse or scrip? In what way did Jesus suddenly change this procedure? What did he say about defending themselves from their enemies?

9. Why is it rather easy for millions of people to "believe in God," but very difficult to get them to believe in his Son, Jesus Christ? Who did Jesus say were his "friends"?

10. How were the apostles able to recall what Jesus had taught them? Why do you think Jesus said the Holy Ghost would not manifest his powers until Jesus had departed? Was the Holy Ghost working behind the scenes during the Savior's ministry?

*   *   *   *

CHAPTER 38

JESUS CONFRONTS THE GREATEST CRISIS OF HIS ENTIRE EXISTENCE

The greatest crisis Jesus would ever face probably began as he came to the conclusion of a prayer which he addressed to his Father toward the end of the Last Supper. This only appears in the Gospel of John and it comprises the entire seventeenth chapter.

In this prayer, Jesus addressed the Father as though he were entirely alone with him. It is a very intimate, personal prayer. The exact words in this prayer are so beautiful and profound that they were probably given to John by the Holy Ghost when the apostle undertook to write the highlights of the Savior's life in his Gospel story.[1]

THE SAVIOR REPORTS TO HIS FATHER

John introduces this prayer by saying:

"Jesus...lifted up his eyes to heaven, and said, Father, the hour is come; glorify thy Son, that thy Son also may glorify thee."[2]

From this passage it would appear that as of this moment, Jesus was filled with resolution and a strong commitment to fulfill his excruciating and indescribably painful assignment as the Messiah.

---

[1]John 14:26.
[2]John 17:1.

He told the Father he was grateful to have been given the power to provide eternal life for all those who were given to him by the Father. In these final hours of his ministry, Jesus felt he could say:

"I have glorified thee on the earth: I have finished the work which thou gavest me to do."[3]

Jesus then said he had searched out those special spirits the Father had given him, and taught them. They had accepted his teachings as coming from the Father, and now that he was about to leave the mortal world, he asked the Father to bless his disciples. Jesus acknowledged that these disciples were not really his but "ours." He said:

"All mine are thine, and thine are mine."[4]

Jesus reported to the Father that he had labored diligently to keep the disciples in the way of their duty. Then he added that "none of them is lost, but the son of perdition." Even the Psalmist knew that Judas would be a servant of Satan.[5]

A PRAYER FOR ONENESS

Jesus said his disciples would be hated as he sent them forth, but:

"I pray not that thou shouldest take them out of the world, but that thou shouldest keep them from the evil...

"Neither pray I for these alone, but for them also which shall believe on me through their word;

"That they all may be one; as thou, Father, art in me, and I in thee, that they also may be one in us: that the world may believe that thou hast sent me."[6]

---

[3]John 17:4.
[4]John 17:10.
[5]John 17:12; Psalms 109:7-8.
[6]John 17:15,20-21.

No passage in scripture captures the meaning of the "oneness" of the Father and the Son better than this one. The Father and Son enjoy a complete oneness in purpose and design—but not a oneness in personality, nor a uniting in bodily form so as to comprise a composite identity the way some have supposed as they wrote their creeds.

In 325 A.D. when the Roman emperor, Constantine, demanded that the Christian leaders describe the oneness of the Godhead, those learned theologians should have taken their creed from the Savior's teachings in these verses. Had they done so, the Nicene Creed would have come out quite differently.

The oneness of the Father and the Son was no different than the kind of oneness Jesus wanted his disciples to attain. He said:

"And the glory which thou gavest me I have given them; that they may be one, even as we are one:

"I in them, and thou in me, that they may be made perfect in one; and that the world may know that thou hast sent me."[7]

Jesus ended his prayer with these words:

"O righteous Father, the world hath not known thee: but I have known thee, and these have known that thou hast sent me. And I have declared unto them thy name, and will declare it: that the love wherewith thou hast loved me may be in them, and I in them."[8]

THE SAVIOR AND THE ELEVEN
DEPART FOR GETHSEMANE

At the conclusion of this prayer, Jesus and his disciples sang a hymn and then they departed out of the east gate, passed down the Kidron, and then crossed over to the Savior's favorite retreat prayer and meditation. This spot is sometimes referred to a garden. It was located among the vineyards and olive trees at t Oot

---

[7]John 17:22-23.
[8]John 17:25-26.

of the Mount of Olives, and the people called it "Gethsemane," meaning an "oil-press." This was where the pure oil of the olives was extracted at harvest time.

By the time Jesus had reached Gethsemane, the disciples had become alarmed as they perceived a drastic change coming over their Master.

It seemed as though a morbid depression had settled on his spirit, and this apparent collapse of their beloved Savior's morale was shocking to his apostles. He had always been so steadfast in his faith, so courageous, and so full of self-confidence. They had seen him defy storms, walk on the sea, raise the dead and cast out devils.

THE APOSTLES BEGIN TO SEE JESUS THROUGH DIFFERENT EYES

Suddenly these superhuman attributes seemed to be fading away. Before their very eyes he seemed to have become like ordinary mortals. They could see he was deeply depressed, as well as distressed, perhaps even frightened. Jesus himself said:

"My soul is exceeding sorrowful, even unto death."[9]

All of this had a very morbid impact on the apostles. They began to speak openly among themselves of something that was gradually creeping into their minds. In the Inspired Version, we read:

"The disciples began to be sore amazed, and to be very heavy and to complain in their hearts, *wondering if this be the Messiah.*"[10]

They knew how a King-Messiah was expected to conduct himself, and what they saw Jesus doing was completely out of character for a King-Messiah. The marked change in the Savior's behavior must have been intensely traumatic to have actually destabilized the apostles and shaken their faith.

---

[9] Matthew
[10] JST Mark   (emphasis added).

JESUS ENTERS THE GARDEN

No human being could have imagined the agonizing torment Jesus was experiencing at that very moment. Spiritually, physically and emotionally, he was encountering a force that was propelling him into a dungeon of darkness where he was being tempted to do what Enoch, Moses, Jonah and Jeremiah had all attempted to do—flee from a divine calling.

Near the entrance of the garden, Jesus stopped. The Inspired Version gives us some additional insights. Mark says:

"And Jesus *KNOWING THEIR HEARTS*, said to [eight of] his disciples, Sit ye here while I shall pray."[11]

Then Mark continues:

"And he taketh with him, Peter, and James, and John [back deeper into the grove], and REBUKED them, and said unto them, My soul is exceeding sorrowful, even unto death; tarry ye here and watch."[12]

Undoubtedly the rebuke was for the doubts that had entered their hearts and minds, and the disintegration of their faith.

THE PLEADING OF A FALTERING SAVIOR

As Jesus went off a short distance, these three principal apostles saw him fall upon the ground and begin to pray. But instead of being sympathetic and supportive with their own faith and prayers, the three apostles promptly fell asleep. It had been a very hard day for all of them, especially for Peter and John, who had prepared the passover feast.[13]

---

[11]JST Mark 14:32 (emphasis added).
[12]JST Mark 14:37-38 (emphasis added).
[13]Luke 22:8.

It is Mark who records the pathos of what really happened when Jesus went off by himself to pray. Mark was not present, but we assume the following was later given to him by the Holy Ghost.[14]

Mark says Jesus went a little distance from the three apostles, and "fell on the ground."[15] Matthew says he "fell on his face,"[16] suggesting that he literally collapsed and fell full length on the new spring grass beneath the trees.

However, during his subsequent prayers he may have knelt by a huge rock, as artists so often portray him. Luke speaks of him kneeling.[17]

From out of the labyrinth of the olive orchard came the cry of a tortured soul. In total anguish, Jesus pleaded:

"Father, all things are possible unto thee. *Take this cup from me!*"[18]

This was like saying, "Oh my Father, you are God. You are all-powerful. Somehow, you can achieve your eternal purposes without having me go through the agony of the cross. Please take this cup from me."

THE SAVIOR'S ONE TEMPTATION
THAT ALMOST OVERCAME HIM

Jesus was now in the process of confronting the horrible reality of his mission as the Messiah-Redeemer.

And at this very moment, he found himself suffering the humiliation of actually pleading to be released from the very mission for which he was consecrated and born.

---

[14]John 14:26.

[15]Mark 14:35.

[16]Matthew 26:39.

[17]Luke 22:41.

[18]Mark 14:36; Matthew 26:39 (emphasis added).

Mark indicates that even Jesus realized he might be making an impossible request, and therefore he humbly added:

"Nevertheless, not what I will, but what thou wilt."[19]

THE FATHER SENDS AN ANGEL

It is interesting that the Father did not speak from the heavens to comfort Jesus as he had done on several occasions in the past. We conclude from this that the Father's painful task of gradually "forsaking" his Son was already beginning to take place. However, the Father did not leave his Beloved Son entirely without comfort. Luke says:

"There appeared an angel unto him from heaven, strengthening him."[20]

Whom would the Father have selected for an errand as important as this one? We surmise it might have been Michael, whom we know as Adam.[21] After all, Michael was the Savior's valiant general in the war in heaven.[22] He had been the Savior's closest associate during the labors of the Creation. He was the one who initiated the Fall so that the Father's children might obtain temporal bodies and learn the difference between good and evil.

And now, since it was the Savior's supreme task to become the Divine Mediator, and his commitment was hanging in the balance, how completely appropriate it would have been to send Michael to bolster the Savior in this supreme crisis when he had to make the most important decision of his entire existence. But the scripture does not identify him.

No doubt this angelic being who came to Jesus explained to him that in the final analysis, he did not have to do it. Jesus still had his free agency. Nevertheless, the heavenly messenger would want him

---

[19]Ibid.

[20]Luke 22:43.

[21]Doctrine and Covenants 27:11; 107:54.

[22]Revelation 12:7-9.

to realize the devastating consequence that would follow if he did not fulfill this mission.

There is a clear indication in the scriptures that the Father's plan for the atonement did not provide any emergency backup device in case Jesus deserted his calling. The success of the entire project depended upon the courage, integrity and voluntary suffering of one person. As the scripture says:

"There is none other name given under heaven save it be this Jesus Christ, of which I have spoken, whereby man can be saved."[23]

"And moreover, I say unto you, that there shall be no other name given *nor any other way nor means whereby salvation can come unto the children of men,* only in and through the name of Christ, the Lord Omnipotent."[24]

WHAT IF JESUS HAD FAILED?

Had Jesus failed, there are prophetic writings indicating that everything the Savior had helped the Father organize in this round of creation would have been lost FOREVER.[25]

The Father would have been compelled to completely withdraw his Spirit, and all this vast array of magnificent structural design and beauty which the Savior had organized under the direction of the Father would have begun to disintegrate and eventually go back into its primal state of unorganized intelligences and unorganized matter. Paul calls it an "everlasting destruction from the presence of the Lord"[26] which, of course, means the total chaos of "outer darkness."[27]

---

[23] 2 Nephi 25:20, B. of M.

[24] Mosiah 3:17, B. of M. (emphasis added).

[25] 2 Thessalonians 1:9; Matthew 10:28; Mosiah 16:4, 3 Nephi 27:17, 2 Nephi 1:22, B. of M.; Doctrine and Covenants 93:35.

[26] 2 Thessalonians 1:9.

[27] Matthew 8:12; 22:13.

Even with the atonement, this fate overtakes those who sin against the Holy Ghost and place themselves beyond the Savior's power to save them. Their final fate is dissolution.[28]

THE THREAT OF POTENTIAL COSMIC DISASTER

As Jesus prayed in Gethsemane, this hazardous threat of potential cosmic disaster hung in the balance like a shroud of deadly darkness over the womb of eternity. Had Jesus failed in his mission, dissolution would have come upon everything.

There would have been no resurrection, no plan of salvation, no celestial kingdom, no terrestrial kingdom, not even a telestial kingdom. There would have been no family relationships, no husbands and wives united in eternal marriage, no further opportunity for eternal progression. This round of the Father's labors would have been virtually wasted with nothing left but "weeping, wailing, and gnashing of teeth."[29]

And what would have been the fate of Jesus? In an address dated July 31, 1864, President Brigham Young stated:

"Jesus was foreordained before the foundations of the world were built, and his mission was appointed him in eternity to be the Savior of the world, yet when he came in the flesh he was left free to choose or refuse to obey his Father.

"Had he refused to obey his Father, he would have become a son of perdition."[30]

Even for him, there would have been a devastating dissolution of his physical and spiritual embodiment if he had abandoned his mission in Gethsemane.[31]

---

[28]Brigham Young, *Journal of Discourses*, London: John Henry Smith, publisher, 1884, vol. 4, p. 54; vol. 8, p. 240; vol. 9, p. 149.

[29]Alma 40:13, B. of M.

[30]*Journal of Discourses*, vol. 10, p. 324.

[31]This process is referred to by Jesus in Matthew 10:28, and by Lehi in 2 Nephi 1:22, B. of M.

THE SINGULAR IMPORTANCE OF
THE ANGELIC VISITATION

It is interesting that only Luke tells about the heavenly messenger who was sent by the Father to strengthen Jesus. Matthew's account tells us that the Savior engaged in three separate prayer sessions, and that after each one Jesus would go back and find Peter, James, and John asleep.

Nevertheless, Matthew records one detail in connection with the Savior's second prayer which turns out to be very significant. He states that when Jesus went back the second time to pray, he seemed to be reconciled to the inescapable necessity of fulfilling his Messianic calling. Therefore, he said:

"Oh my Father, if this cup may not pass away from me, *EXCEPT I DRINK IT*, thy will be done."[32]

This would suggest that the angelic messenger had succeeded in fortifying the Savior sufficiently to arouse in him a firm resolution to forge ahead and perform the mission for which he was born.

WHAT CAUSED JESUS TO SWEAT
"GREAT DROPS OF BLOOD"?

Even so, the horrible contemplation of the suffering and agony of the cruel spikes of the Roman cross, and all of the flogging and sadistic abuse of the soldiers that went with it, flooded in upon the refined sensitivities of Jesus. What was even worse, as we shall see in a moment, the surge of terror was magnified a hundred times as the Savior found the Spirit of the Father withdrawing from him.

Luke says:

"And being in an agony, he prayed more earnestly; and his sweat was as it were great drops of blood falling down to the ground."[33]

---

[32]Matthew 26:42 (emphasis added).
[33]Luke 22:44.

As we have already mentioned, the withdrawal of the Father's Spirit had been in progress for some time. In the Garden of Gethsemane, the withdrawal began to be felt more severely. As we mentioned earlier, this was a prelude to the grim and terrifying moment toward the end of the crucifixion, when the Spirit of the Father would be withdrawn completely.[34]

But it was terrible, even in the Garden of Gethsemane. Brigham Young declared:

"The Father withdrew Himself, withdrew His Spirit, and cast a veil over him. That is what made him sweat blood. If he had had the power of God upon him, he would not have sweat blood...."[35]

JESUS AGREES TO BECOME THE MEDIATOR FOR EVERY REPENTANT SINNER

Another factor contributing to the sweat of blood was the Savior's commitment to overcome the demands of justice for every repentant sinner.[36] Jesus knew the price he would pay for this commitment and he verifies that the prospect of this ordeal, that he would be required to bear alone, caused:

"...myself, even God, the greatest of all, to tremble because of pain, and to bleed at every pore...and would that I might not drink the bitter cup, and shrink."[37]

THE DARK CLOUDS OF THE MOUNTING STORM

So, as Jesus concluded his three heavenly petitions and finally committed himself to the staggering burden of providing an infinite atonement for all things mortal, Jesus returned to his three sleeping apostles, and said:

---

[34]Matthew 27:46.
[35]*Journal of Discourses*, vol. 3, p. 206.
[36]Alma 34:15-16.
[37]Doctrine and Covenants 19:18.

"Sleep on now, and take your rest: behold, the hour is at hand, and the Son of man is betrayed into the hands of sinners."[38]

Suddenly Jesus stopped. In the darkness he could see, crossing the Kidron and coming toward them, "a band of men and officers from the chief priests and Pharisees...with lanterns and torches and weapons."[39]

Jesus shook the apostles awake and said:

"Rise! let us be going: behold, he is at hand that doth betray me."[40]

This was that critical moment of decision that must have sent echoes of hallelujahs along the corridors of heaven as the Son of God, *who could have cast a veil over their eyes and escaped*, boldly gathered his apostles around him and went to meet his enemy and his destiny.

FOR THE FIRST TIME IN HIS LIFE, JESUS ALLOWED HIMSELF TO BE ARRESTED

As Jesus strode toward the band of soldiers and the "multitude" who had come with them, there was a sudden confrontation.

In the darkness, with only dim torches to light the scene, the officers were unable to make out the Savior's identity, so Jesus said:

"Whom seek ye?

"They answered him, Jesus of Nazareth. Jesus saith unto them, I am he. And Judas also, which betrayed him, stood with them."[41]

The Savior's response seemed to send an electrifying shock wave through the multitude who had come with Judas. Suddenly they

---

[38]Matthew 26:45.
[39]John 18:3.
[40]Matthew 26:40-46.
[41]John 18:4-5.

were confronting the great healer, the man who single-handedly cleansed the temple, the one whom some people believed to be the actual King-Messiah. Eye witnesses had seen him raise the dead, heal cripples and control both wind and waves. These men had heard credible witnesses tell about such things. Therefore, the scripture says:

"As soon then as he had said unto them, I am he, they went backward, and fell to the ground."[42]

There was a moment of confusion and consternation, then Jesus said again:

"Whom seek ye? And they said, Jesus of Nazareth.

"Jesus answered, I have told you that I am he: if therefore ye seek me, let these go their way."[43]

At this point a bizarre thing happened. This whole episode was the work of Judas Iscariot. He therefore took the initiative to reassure the officers who had come with him by walking up to Jesus and kissing him. He had told the officers that by this means they would be sure they were arresting the right man.[44]

As Judas kissed Jesus, the fallen apostle said:

"Hail Master!"[45]

Jesus looked into the dark countenance of this benighted son of perdition and said:

"Judas, betrayest thou the Son of man with a kiss?"[46]

---

[42]John 18:6.
[43]John 18:5-8.
[44]Matthew 26:48.
[45]Matthew 26:49.
[46]Luke 22:48.

The officers, with weapons raised and ready, began to close in on Jesus. One of his disciples shouted, "Lord, shall we smite with the sword?"[47]

But Peter didn't wait for instructions. He was ready for war and drew out his sword. As the first officer came close, Peter struck a downward blow which would have split the man's skull if Peter had been an experienced fighter. Instead, the blade slipped down the side of the man's head and completely severed his ear. The man's name was Malchus, a servant and relative of the high priest.[48]

Peter's courageous action set the officers back a moment. It gave Jesus a chance to say:

"Peter, Put up thy sword into the sheath: the cup which my Father hath given me, shall I not drink it?"[49]

Then Jesus added:

"All they that take the sword shall perish with the sword.

"Thinkest thou that I cannot now pray to my Father, and he shall presently give me more than twelve legions of angels?"[50]

But Peter only did what he had promised he would do. Just prior to the Transfiguration, when Jesus first told Peter that the Pharisees would try to kill him, Peter had said he would never let the Pharisees do it. And Jesus told him at the time that if Peter ever tried to interfere and defend the Savior, he would be helping Satan.[51]

In any event, what was done was done. Jesus therefore touched the bleeding wound of the chief priest's servant, and he was instantly healed.[52] Malchus probably never knew what happened. He

---

[47]Luke 22:49.
[48]John 18:10.
[49]John 18:11.
[50]Matthew 26:52-53.
[51]Matthew 16:21-23.
[52]Luke 22:51.

probably screamed with pain when Peter first struck him, but after Jesus touched him on the side of the head and Malchus felt the ear in place, he probably said to himself, "Oh, I guess it wasn't as bad as I thought it was." Miracles are like that sometimes.

Jesus then turned to the multitude and said:

"Are ye come out as against a thief with swords and staves for to take me? I sat daily with you teaching in the temple, and ye laid no hold on me."[53]

That was the last thing Jesus had a chance to say. The soldiers closed in on him and the scripture says:

"Then all the disciples forsook him, and fled."[54]

But there was one who tarried. We have talked about him before. He was a teenager, wrapped in a sheet. The only explanation for his being there was the possibility, as suggested by Dr. Alfred Edersheim, that the "upper room" where the Last Supper had been served, was in his father's house, and when Judas had gone there with the officers looking for Jesus, the youth wrapped himself in a sheet and hastened to Gethsemane to warn Jesus. He had not arrived in time, but now he couldn't believe his eyes as he saw everyone deserting the Savior. As Jesus was bound and led away, the scripture says:

"And there followed him a certain young man, having a linen cloth cast about his naked body; and the young men laid hold on him: and he left the linen cloth, and fled from them naked."[55]

As we mentioned earlier, Mark is the only Gospel writer who records this incident, and it is believed by many Bible scholars that the young teenager was Mark, himself.[56]

* * * *

---

[53]Matthew 26:55.
[54]Matthew 26:56.
[55]Mark 14:51-52.
[56]Edersheim, *The Life and Times of Jesus,* vol. 2:485.

TOPICS FOR REFLECTION AND DISCUSSION

1. Up to the time of the Last Supper, Jesus said he had "finished the work" the Father had given him to do. What had he accomplished thus far?

2. After examining a copy of the Nicene Creed, compare it with the Savior's description of his "oneness" with the Father, and identify the differences.

3. What did the apostles see happening at the Last Supper which began to shake their faith in Jesus as the King-Messiah?

4. When Jesus asked the Father to "remove this cup from me," what is implied by the Savior's words, "all things are possible unto thee"?

5. Would it be accurate to say, "All things are possible unto the Father so long as he follows correct principles"? Read Alma, chapter 42, and write down what would happen to the Father if he did not follow correct principles.

6. Was the Savior the only means provided for an atoning sacrifice? What would have happened if he had failed? Do you think the Father had foreknowledge that he would not fail?

7. When the angel appeared to Jesus, how persuasive was he? After the heavenly messenger had left, what did Jesus say in his second prayer?

8. What are two of the factors which led Jesus to sweat great drops of blood?

9. Why did Judas kiss Jesus? As he did so, what did Jesus say? What kind of signal should this have sent to Judas?

10. Who was Malchus whose ear was clipped off by Peter's sword? Whom do Biblical scholars identify as the boy in the sheet who was the last to leave Jesus, and finally escaped by fleeing into the darkness naked?

*   *   *   *

CHAPTER 39

PETER'S VISION OF JESUS AS THE KING-MESSIAH BEGINS TO CRUMBLE

At the entrance to the garden of Gethsemane, the soldiers finally seized Jesus and bound him so he could not escape as they triumphantly led him away to the rulers of the Sanhedrin.

As for the apostles, the scripture says:

"And they all forsook him, and fled."[1]

But Peter only fled a short distance.[2] He had to stay and see what happened to the Savior.

PETER'S ORDEAL

So far, this had been a terrible night for Peter. So many strange and incomprehensible things had happened.

He and John had labored from early morning getting everything prepared for the feast,[3] and although everything had gone fairly well, Peter had embarrassed himself by first refusing to let Jesus wash his feet, and then by asking him to wash his feet, his head, and his hands.[4] The Savior's response had made him feel like a child.[5]

---

[1]Mark 14:50.
[2]Mark 14:54.
[3]Luke 22:8.
[4]John 13:6-10.
[5]John 13:10.

During the Last Supper, Peter had pledged to follow Jesus wherever he went,[6] but the Savior had talked to him as though he were not yet completely or permanently "converted."[7] Jesus had even predicted that before the night was over, Peter would deny that he even knew Jesus.[8] The Savior had also predicted that when his enemies engulfed him, all of the apostles would flee for their lives, leaving him alone.[9]

Later, as Peter had watched Jesus sink into the deepest despondency, and "sorrow even unto death,"[10] he and the apostles had allowed themselves to discuss the possibility that perhaps he was not the King-Messiah after all.[11]

Later, in the Garden of Gethsemane, Jesus had "rebuked" all three of the chief apostles, apparently for faltering in their faith.[12]

When Jesus had asked these three apostles to watch while he prayed, they had fallen asleep three different times.[13]

The climax had come when Judas Iscariot arrived with the soldiers, and Jesus made no attempt whatever to prevent the soldiers from taking him captive. Peter tried to intervene, but ended up being chastised for his effort.[14]

Finally, when the soldiers grappled to seize Jesus, Peter found himself running away like all the rest.[15]

Indeed, it had been a terrible night.

---

[6]Luke 22:33.
[7]Luke 22:31-32.
[8]Luke 22:34.
[9]John 16:32.
[10]Matthew 26:38.
[11]JST Mark 14:36.
[12]JST Mark 14:38.
[13]Mark 14:37, 40-41.
[14]John 18:10-11.
[15]Mark 14:50.

Then the scripture continues:

"And Peter followed him afar off, even into the palace of the high priest: and he sat with the servants, and warmed himself at the fire."[16]

However, John says that before Jesus was taken to the high priest, something else had happened.

JESUS IS HAULED UP BEFORE ANNAS

John tells us that the officers did not take Jesus directly to the house of Caiaphas, the high priest, who had ordered the Savior's arrest. Instead they took Jesus to the house of Annas, the father-in-law of Caiaphas.[17]

Annas had been a favorite of the Romans and was first appointed high priest in 7 A.D. He was replaced in 15 A.D., but three years later his son-in-law, Caiaphas, was made high priest, with Annas dominating the scenes from the background. This is supported by the fact that Annas was the first ruler of the Sanhedrin to see Jesus after his arrest. In fact, there is some indication that both men had been elevated by the Romans to the status of "high priests."[18]

Annas did not accuse Jesus of anything, but simply asked him about his followers and his doctrines. The object was to uncover any kind of secret conspiracy or smoldering embers of a planned insurrection. Jesus replied:

"I spake openly to the world; I ever taught in the synagogue, and in the temple, whither the Jews always resort; and in secret have I said nothing.

"Why askest thou me? ask them which heard me...they know what I said."[19]

---

[16]Mark 14:54.
[17]John 18:13.
[18]Ibid.
[19]John 18:20-21.

This interrogation was going nowhere. Jesus was putting Annas on the defensive, and for a prisoner to do this was sheer impudence. Therefore, it says:

"One of the officers which stood by struck Jesus with the palm of his hand, saying, Answerest thou the high priest so?

"Jesus answered him, If I have spoken evil, bear witness of the evil: but if well, why smitest thou me?"[20]

After the curiosity of Annas had been satisfied, Jesus was led "bound" to the house of Caiaphas.[21]

THE HOUSE OF CAIAPHAS

Archaeologists believe they may have actually found the remains of the rather palatial residence of Caiaphas. A set of weights and measures were found which was always kept in the house of the high priest. There are also escape-proof dungeons cut into the stone on which the foundation of the building once rested. These would have been required for prisoners of the Sanhedrin in the high priest's quarters.

The worn stone steps leading up to the building are of extremely ancient origin, and the custodians of a nearby church feel Jesus may have been forced to ascend these very steps when he was taken up to appear before Caiaphas.

CAIAPHAS SEEKS EVIDENCE THAT JESUS HAS COMMITTED A CAPITAL CRIME

With a major holy day coming upon the Jews in less than twenty-four hours, Caiaphas felt pressured to find some evidence that would warrant a death penalty so Jesus could be executed as soon as possible.

---

[20]John 18:22-23.
[21]John 18:24.

For the Savior, all of this was the beginning of a prolonged nightmare. Caiaphas had assembled the chief priests, the elders, and the scribes. It was immediately apparent what they wanted to do:

"The chief priests and all the council sought for witness against Jesus to put him to death; and found none.

"For many bare false witness against him, but their witness agreed not together."[22]

This ancient version of a kangaroo court went on into the night, but Jesus said nothing. Caiaphas was running out of time and patience. Finally, in total frustration he took over the prosecution himself. The scripture says:

"The high priest stood up in the midst, and asked Jesus, saying, Answerest thou nothing? what is it which these witness against thee?

"But he held his peace, and answered nothing. Again the high priest asked him, and said unto him, Art thou the Christ, the Son of the Blessed?

"And Jesus said, I am: and ye shall see the Son of man sitting on the right hand of power, and coming in the clouds of heaven."[23]

Oh, this was glorious! The accused was testifying against himself. And in open court. Now they were getting somewhere. For Caiaphas, this called for a demonstration of the most profound indignation. With his own sacred ears he had heard the accused commit blasphemy. The scripture says:

"Then the high priest rent his clothes, and saith, What need we any further witnesses? Ye have heard the blasphemy: what think ye? And they all condemned him to be guilty of death."[24]

---

[22] Mark 14:55-56.
[23] Mark 14:60-62
[24] Mark 14:63-64.

So the verdict was in. Jesus of Nazareth had committed blasphemy in open court and the Sanhedrin had condemned him to death. Of course, the trial was held in the middle of the night, so the whole proceeding was illegal, but they would remedy this technicality with another trial in the morning. Meanwhile, the accused was guilty and deserved to be treated as such. So it says:

"Some began to spit on him, and to cover his face, [blindfold him] and to buffet him, and to say unto him, Prophesy: and the servants did strike him with the palms of their hands."[25]

THE FALTERING FAITH OF THE CHIEF APOSTLE

All of this must have been frightening to Peter, a humble fisherman from Galilee who was a complete stranger to the corrupt operation of the most powerful life-and-death judicial body within the jurisdiction of the Jewish faith.

Most of the apostles were probably at somebody's house wondering what was going on, but Peter and John had followed "afar off" and saw Jesus taken to the "palace of the high priest."[26] As we have already indicated, this may have been to the house of Annas first, and then to the house of Caiaphas.

By this time the very soul of Peter was in convulsions. None of this should be happening. He had felt certain Jesus was the Christ, the anointed one, the King-Messiah who would redeem Israel and overthrow their enemies. Peter had so testified to thousands, to Jesus himself, and to the Jews. All of the disciples appear to have believed this.[27]

Furthermore, he had seen Jesus heal hundreds, perhaps thousands. He had seen him command the waves and the wind, and walk on the water. He had seen him feed thousands with a few loaves and fishes. He had seen him escape from multitudes who would have killed him on one occasion, and would have made him

---

[25]Mark 14:65.
[26]John 18:16.
[27]Luke 19:11, 24:21.

a king on another. He had seen him turn water into wine. He had even seen him raise the dead.

Of course, if Maimonides (1135-1204 A.D.), the famous authority on Judaism, was correct in summarizing the teachings of the rabbis concerning the Messiah, then Peter may have actually heard the Pharisees warning the people as follows:

"Do NOT think that Messiah needs to perform signs and miracles...revive the dead, and the like. It is not so....

"[But] if there arise a king of the house of David who...fights the battles of the Lord, then one may properly assume that he is the Messiah. If he is then successful in rebuilding the sanctuary on its site and in gathering the dispersed of Israel, then he has in fact proven himself to be the Messiah."[28]

Of course, Jesus had not qualified as the Messiah if these were the requirements. In fact, Peter must have been asking himself for over an hour, "What, in heaven's name, is Jesus doing in the house of Caiaphas, being tormented like a common criminal? How can this be?"

Where was the fire from heaven that would destroy the Romans? Where was his miraculous capacity to veil the eyes of his accusers and walk away as he had done several times before? What had happened to his power? It was a terrible thing to contemplate, but Peter was gradually persuading himself that whatever Jesus was, he was not the King-Messiah.

Peter felt a personal responsibility in all of this. People had trusted Peter when he had pointed to Jesus and said he was the Christ who would set up his kingdom in the immediate future.[29] They, too, had worshipped him and called him the King-Messiah. What would Peter say to them now?

---

[28]Gershom Scholem, *The Messianic Idea in Judaism*, New York: Schocken Books, 1971, p. 28.
[29]Luke 19:11.

HOW PETER GAINED ENTRANCE TO THE
HOUSE OF CAIAPHAS

Peter would have never made it past the guarded entrance at the house of the high priest if it had not been for John. John knew the high priest, and the woman at the door let him in while Peter stood outside. No doubt this woman knew John was also a disciple of Jesus, but because of his acquaintance with the high priest, she allowed him to enter.[30]

Then John used his good offices to get Peter admitted, but the woman challenged Peter, and a strange thing happened. The woman looked closely at Peter and asked him if he were a disciple of Jesus. Peter promptly replied:

"I am not!"[31]

This was not a coward speaking. This was a heartbroken, disillusioned apostle. Peter's response must have surprised John, but he apparently said nothing. Perhaps he recalled what had happened a short time earlier at the Last Supper. Peter had said to Jesus:

"I will lay down my life for thy sake. [But] Jesus answered him...the cock shall not crow till thou hast denied me thrice."[32]

Matthew describes the second denial as follows:

"And when he was gone out into the porch, another maid saw him, and said unto them that were there, This fellow was also with Jesus of Nazareth.

"And again he denied with an oath, I DO NOT KNOW THE MAN!"[33]

---

[30]John 18:15.
[31]John 18:17.
[32]John 13:37-38.
[33]Matthew 26:71-72 (emphasis added).

Notice how literally this statement fulfills the Savior's prophecy when he said:

"The cock shall not crow this day, before that thou shalt thrice deny that thou *knowest* me."[34]

After this second denial, the prophecy was yet to be fulfilled once more.

However, during each of these denials, the true state of Peter's mind would have probably been more accurately reflected if he had said, "I do not know *THAT* man!"

To this great apostle, Jesus was not turning out to be the King-Messiah Peter thought he was; but if he was not the King-Messiah, then WHO was he?

MALCHUS CHALLENGES PETER

Then came the third denial:

"And after a while came unto him they that stood by, and said to Peter, Surely thou also art one of them; for thy speech betrayeth thee."[35]

This challenger was referring to Peter's dialect as a Galilean, and, according to John, this final challenger was someone Peter would have preferred not to meet. It was Malchus, the man whose ear Peter had cut off a couple of hours earlier.[36] Perhaps this accounts for his exceptionally violent reaction when Malchus accused Peter. Matthew says:

"Then began he to curse and to swear, saying, *I know not the man.* And immediately the cock crew."[37]

---

[34]Luke 22:34 (emphasis added).
[35]Matthew 26:73.
[36]John 18:26-27.
[37]Matthew 26:74 (emphasis added).

That instant the Savior's prophecy came flooding back into Peter's mind, and just as Jesus was being taken out of the judgment chamber, the eyes of the apostle connected with those of his Master.[38] For a split second, it must have seemed as though time stood still. At that instant the whole internal strength of the courageous Peter completely collapsed. Matthew says,

"He went out and wept bitterly."[39]

We are led to believe that the "weeping" Peter was a much more complex human being than merely a guilt-stricken apostle weeping because he had denied Jesus three times. This apostle loved Jesus. He had followed him faithfully for three years. He had testified that he was the Christ. He had believed that he was the Christ. He would have died for him. But that night when Peter's eyes locked in with the eyes of Jesus, he saw the depth of his sorrow, and Peter knew something was terribly wrong. Everything Peter was witnessing seemed totally preposterous. It was irrational. The only soul-wrenching reality about the whole thing was Peter's bitter realization that Jesus was being maneuvered into a predicament where the only escape would be death. And worst of all, there was nothing the apostles could do about it.

Oh, if he had just been the real King-Messiah the way they thought he was. As one of the disciples would later say:

"We trusted that it had been he which should have redeemed Israel."[40]

And Luke wrote:

"They thought the kingdom of God should immediately appear."[41]

---

[38]Luke 22:61.
[39]Matthew 26:75.
[40]Luke 24:21.
[41]Luke 19:11.

Of course, if that had been the situation, they knew he could have called down fire from heaven and destroyed everybody from Caiaphas to the Roman legion in the Antonia. With a single shaft of light from his piercing eye, he could have incinerated the guards who held him. He could have called down twelve legions of angels to take over the government of the whole region.[42]

But it was not to be. Apparently Jesus was not the King-Messiah, and he was going to die. And it would be one of the most horrible of all deaths—being tortured on a Roman cross.

So Peter "went out and wept bitterly."[43]

PETER'S NEED FOR A RECONVERSION

Perhaps, four days later, Peter would suddenly remember something Jesus had said at the Last Supper. He had told Peter:

"I have prayed for thee, that thy faith fail not: and when thou art converted [actually RE-converted], strengthen thy brethren."[44]

At the time, Peter must have wondered why Jesus thought he would have to be converted any more than he already was. Now Peter was in the process of finding out.

JESUS PREPARES TO FACE HIS LAST DAY OF MORTALITY

It is believed Jesus was lowered into one of those escape-proof dungeons beneath the house of Caiaphas so he could await the holding of a "legal" trial at the first light of dawn. But in all likelihood, he did not have to wait long, because the night was far spent.

By morning Caiaphas and the Sanhedrin had recognized a new problem. The Sanhedrin had voted to kill Jesus for blasphemy, but that would not be a capital offense under Roman law. They must contrive some kind of new charge that would carry a death penalty under Pilate's code of law. They seemed to have been working out

---

[42]Matthew 26:53.
[43]Matthew 26:75.
[44]Luke 22:32.

the details of this new scheme right up to the time they took Jesus to Pilate.

Meanwhile, the Sanhedrin had to convene after brief snatches of sleep to make the charge of "blasphemy" legal, in case that became their last resort.

The Sanhedrin undoubtedly wanted this option available in case Pilate would not order Jesus to be crucified for violating the Roman law with which they were planning to charge him. In such an event, perhaps they could get Pilate to grant the Sanhedrin permission to kill Jesus by stoning him just as they would later stone Stephen.[45]

So the first step was to "legalize" the unlawful "blasphemy" trial they had held during the night. Luke tells us:

"And as soon as it was day, the elders of the people and the chief priests and the scribes came together, and led him into their council, saying, Art thou the Christ? tell us. And he said unto them, If I tell you, ye will not believe."[46]

Clearly, they were trying to get Jesus to testify against himself by committing blasphemy again. As we mentioned earlier, this was considered treason against God, and the penalty for this offense was stoning to death.[47] They therefore repeated the same tactics they had used a few hours earlier by asking him if he were the Christ. He said:

"And if I also ask you [whether I am the Christ], ye will not answer me, nor let me go."[48]

Jesus knew that the feelings of the people who had come to the feast were mixed, and if the Sanhedrin took a position either for or against Jesus it would have created an uproar. This is why the

---

[45]Acts 7:57-60.
[46]Luke 22:66-67.
[47]Leviticus 24:11, 23.
[48]Luke 22:68.

Sanhedrin wanted Pilate and his legions to pronounce judgment. Suddenly Jesus decided to bring the entire matter to a head by saying:

"Hereafter shall the Son of man sit on the right hand of the power of God.

"Then said they all, Art thou then the Son of God? And he said unto them, Ye say that I am.

"And they said, What need we any further witness? for we ourselves have heard of his own mouth."[49]

Jesus did not give them the same direct answer he had provided earlier, but under the rabbinical definition of "blasphemy," it was close enough to bring charges if need be. The scripture therefore says:

"And the whole multitude of them arose, and led him unto Pilate."[50]

* * * *

TOPICS FOR REFLECTION AND DISCUSSION

1. This particular Feast of the Passover had caused Peter a whole series of unhappy experiences. Can you name five of them?

2. At first, did Peter flee along with the other apostles? Then where did he go? Who was Annas?

3. As far as the record shows, when was the first time anyone struck Jesus? What did Jesus say to the man?

4. When Jesus was taken before Caiaphas, what was illegal about the session conducted by the Sanhedrin? What death-penalty crime did Caiaphas want Jesus to admit?

---

[49]Luke 22:69-71.
[50]Luke 23:1.

5. Did Jesus confess sufficiently to convince Caiaphas that he had proof of blasphemy? Then what did Caiaphas do?

6. How did Peter happen to get inside the palace of Caiaphas? When was his first denial? Why do we think this surprised John?

7. What was there about Peter's speech that aroused suspicion and caused the third challenge? Who was this person? What was Peter's reaction?

8. What happened immediately after Peter's third denial? Then what did Peter do? If Peter had been asked why he said, "I know not the man," what explanation do you think he would have given?

9. Did Jesus tell Peter he would have his faith shaken sufficiently to require a new conversion? One of the disciples described the role of the King-Messiah which they expected Jesus to fulfill. What did he say they expected Jesus to do? How soon?

10. Why did the Sanhedrin meet early in the morning to give Jesus a second trial? What did they try to get Jesus to say? What was the penalty for blasphemy? Since they planned to present a different charge when they took Jesus before Pilate, why did they think they also needed a conviction in the Sanhedrin for blasphemy?

*   *   *   *

CHAPTER 40

JESUS BEFORE PILATE

As Jerusalem awakened the next morning, the people would never have guessed what this day would bring. It would be the most important day in the history of the human race.

Scribes, lawyers, priests, and members of the Sanhedrin had worked frantically to prepare charges that would hold up under Roman law. Finally, they felt they were ready.

Jesus must have been physically exhausted. Nevertheless, with little sleep and apparently with no food since the Last Supper, he was forced to make the trek from the palace or home of Caiaphas to the palace of the Roman governor. It was called the *Praetorium.*

This elaborate structure was originally built by Herod the Great, but the Romans always expropriated the most luxurious facilities of any conquered nation for their own governors, who, in this case, was Pontius Pilate.

Pilate was appointed Roman governor or procurator of Judah in 26 A.D. by the emperor Tiberius. Ordinarily, he would have been at his military headquarters in Caesarea, but the Roman officials always came up to Jerusalem on special occasions such as the present Feast of the Passover.

Although most authorities feel that Pilate and his wife stayed at Herod's palace, it should be pointed out that the main military contingent was at the Antonia—a fortress at the northwest corner of the temple esplanade. The Romans had named this massive structure "Antonia," in honor of Mark Antony, and there is good reason to believe that Pilate and his wife may have taken up temporary quarters there. Both places had a hall of judgment, and "a judgment" was what the Sanhedrin was seeking from Pilate against Jesus.

JUDAS ISCARIOT PANICS

When the chief priests and a "multitude" of scribes and Pharisees left the palace of Caiaphas to charge Jesus before Pilate, it appears that neither Caiaphas nor Annas accompanied them. They would leave this dirty business of dealing with the Roman governor to lesser luminaries. But even more strangely, the Savior's principal enemy did not accompany them either. Something was happening to Judas Iscariot following the judgment of the Sanhedrin. The scripture says:

"Then Judas...when he saw that he [Jesus] was condemned, repented himself, and brought again the thirty pieces of silver to the chief priests and elders [who were probably at the temple],

"Saying, I have sinned in that I have betrayed the innocent blood. And they said, What is that to us? see thou to that."[1]

It is obvious that there is a lot more to the tragic story of Judas Iscariot than the scriptural record reveals. In a number of ways, Judas was a total enigma.

Judas was from Keriot (or Iscariot), a town of Judah south of Hebron.[2] Therefore he was the only apostle who was not a Galilean. We wonder why he was never converted to Jesus in spite of all the miracles he witnessed. And we wonder what motivated him to take the fatal step of betraying Jesus under circumstances which led the Savior to call him a son of perdition?[3] Even more important, what made Judas suddenly decide he had made a terrible mistake as he saw Jesus being led away to be condemned and crucified?

Only God knew the answers to these questions, but as for Judas, it says:

---

[1]Matthew 27:3-4.
[2]Hastings, *Dictionary of the Bible*, p. 796.
[3]John 17:12.

"And he cast down the pieces of silver in the temple, and departed, and went and hanged himself."[4]

However, the rope apparently broke. Luke later says:

"...falling headlong, he burst asunder in the midst, and all his bowels gushed out."[5]

THE RULERS OF THE SANHEDRIN SHIFT FROM RELIGIOUS TO POLITICAL CHARGES AGAINST JESUS

As the chief priests and the multitude arrived at the entrance to Pilate's judgment hall (which could have been either at the Antonia or the Praetorium), the accusers of Jesus stood outside "lest they be defiled," before the feast day.

It should be kept in mind that this was the 13th of Nisin, but the 14th would commence at sunset when the majority of the Jews would eat their passover meal. They would therefore consider Wednesday the 13th the day "before" the feast even though the "feast day" on the 14th would begin that same night. The Jewish calculation was based on Genesis 1:5 where it says, "the *evening* and the morning were the first day."

We recall that Jesus and his apostles had elected to eat the passover feast one day early. This was authorized by the Jewish authorities because the sacrifices had become so numerous the priests could not handle all of the sacrificial lambs in one day.[6] As we mentioned earlier, a Roman tally of the lambs which were sacrificed during one feast was 256,500.[7]

Now the tragic drama commenced which would end at Golgotha, the "Place of the Skull." The scripture says:

---

[4]Matthew 27:5.
[5]Acts 1:18.
[6]Talmage, *Jesus the Christ*, p. 618.
[7]Ibid.

"Pilate then went out unto them, and said, What accusation bring ye against this man?"[8]

The chief priests wanted to impress Pilate with the seriousness of the charges they were about to make against Jesus, therefore they said:

"If he were not a malefactor, we would not have delivered him up unto thee."[9]

Pilate was not impressed, but responded:

"Take ye him, and judge him according to your law."[10]

Just as the high priests had anticipated, Pilate was assuming that this clamor so early in the morning was just another incident of minor religious improprieties that were such a nuisance to the Roman administrators. However, the temple rulers really caught the attention of Pilate when they suddenly said:

"It is not lawful for us to put any man to death."[11]

Oh, a capital crime! That was quite different. Pilate would want to know about that. What had this Jesus done? Luke quotes the Savior's accusers as saying:

"We found this fellow perverting the nation, and forbidding to give tribute to Caesar, saying that he himself is Christ a King."[12]

This was amazing. There was no mention of blasphemy for which he had just been judged guilty by the Sanhedrin. Instead, Jesus was being charged with three felonious crimes against the state: treason, tax evasion, and being a pretender to the throne.

---

[8]John 18:29.
[9]John 18:30.
[10]John 18:31.
[11]Ibid.
[12]Luke 23:2.

PILATE INTERVIEWS JESUS

Pilate wheeled around and went back into the judgment hall. Then he sent for Jesus and asked him directly: "Art thou the King of the Jews?"[13]

Jesus answered with a question, "Sayest thou this thing of thyself, or did others [his accusers] tell it thee of me?"[14]

Pilate was not going to be put on the defensive. He shot back,

"Am I a Jew? Thine own nation and the chief priests have delivered thee unto me: what hast thou done?

"Jesus answered, My kingdom is not of this world: if my kingdom were of this world, then would my servants fight, that I should not be delivered to the Jews: but now is my kingdom not from hence.

"Pilate therefore said unto him, Art thou a king then? Jesus answered, Thou sayest that I am a king. To this end was I born, and for this cause came I into the world, that I should bear witness unto the truth. Every one that is of the truth heareth my voice."[15]

Now the Roman governor had his answer. This man was no threat. He was a philosopher, a dreamer with a kingdom in some other world. He closed the interview by cynically asking, "What is truth?" and then went out before the multitude and said to them:

"I find in him no fault at all."[16]

There was an uproar. The chief priests were outraged and shouted: "He stirreth up the people, teaching throughout all Jewry, beginning from Galilee to this place."[17]

---

[13]John 18:33.
[14]John 18:33-34.
[15]John 18:35-37.
[16]John 18:38.
[17]Luke 23:5.

Galilee? Pilate saw an opportunity to rid himself of the whole noisy multitude. He would send them with their prisoner to the nearby quarters of Herod Antipas, tetrarch of Galilee, who at that moment was in Jerusalem for the feast.

JESUS IS INTERVIEWED BY HEROD ANTIPAS

When Herod received word that Jesus was being sent to him, he was delighted. He had been anxious to see this miracle man for over a year. Perhaps he would entertain his court with some of his magic tricks. Up in Galilee, people of all sorts talked about his wonderful powers.

But when Jesus came in before Herod Antipas, there was nothing but grim silence. To Jesus this dissolute ruler was a depraved creature whose private passions had involved him in adultery, incest and murder—the latter having included the beheading of the Savior's beloved cousin, John the Baptist.[18] For Herod there would be no miracle, no pleading for mercy, not even a greeting to acknowledge his existence.

Herod tried to elicit something out of Jesus but to no avail. The scripture says:

"He questioned with him in many words; but he answered him nothing. And the chief priests and scribes stood and vehemently accused him. And Herod with his men of war set him at nought, and mocked him, and arrayed him in a gorgeous robe, and sent him again to Pilate."[19]

Then it concludes:

"And the same day Pilate and Herod were made friends together: for before they were at enmity between themselves."[20]

---

[18]Luke 1:36 indicates Jesus and John were second cousins.
[19]Luke 23:9-11.
[20]Luke 23:12.

PILATE ATTEMPTS TO RELEASE JESUS

So the ball was back in Pilate's court. The Roman governor thereupon declared to the chief priests and the "multitude:"

"Ye have brought this man unto me, as one that perverteth the people: and, behold, I, having examined him before you, have found no fault in this man touching those things whereof ye accuse him: No, nor yet Herod: for I sent you to him; and, lo, nothing worthy of death is done unto him. I will therefore chastise him, and release him."[21]

By this time, Pilate felt the private motives of the Sanhedrin rulers were completely evident to him. The scripture says:

"He knew the chief priests had delivered him for envy."[22]

Pilate therefore hit upon a scheme to get Jesus released. It was customary at a feast day to release some culprit whom the people felt was a political prisoner or "unjustly charged." Pilate therefore decided to tell the people that at this particular feast he intended to release Jesus. But to make it more palatable he decided to offer two names. One was the innocent Jesus, and the other was a man named Barabbas, a condemned insurrectionist who had even been convicted of murder.[23]

But after Pilate presented the two names, he was shocked when the crowd roared out, "Barabbas!"

So he asked them:

"What will ye then that I shall do unto him whom ye call the King of the Jews? And they cried out again, Crucify him.

---

[21]Luke 23:14-16.
[22]Mark 15:10.
[23]Luke 23:19.

"Then Pilate said unto them, Why, what evil hath he done? And they cried out the more exceedingly, Crucify him."[24]

Pilate was baffled. The whole situation was further complicated by the fact that sometime earlier his wife had come to him and said:

"Have thou nothing to do with that just man: for I have suffered many things this day in a dream because of him."[25]

PILATE BEGINS TO EQUIVOCATE

At this point Pilate found himself trying to cope with pressures coming down upon him from four different directions.

First, there was the haunting mandate of Emperor Tiberius who abhorred insurrections and had told Pilate to see that none occurred among the Jews. Second, there was the clamor from this mob of accusers who were thirsting for the Savior's blood. Third, there was the warning of Pilate's wife who told him to have nothing to do with this terrible affair. And finally, there was the gnawing pressure from Pilate's own conscience which told him both loud and clear that Jesus was an innocent man.

Trapped by these various pressures rising from within and without, Pilate did what public officials have done from time immemorial: he compromised. In some respects it was even worse than a compromise. He virtually capitulated. It was the old political ploy of sacrificing principle and personal convictions for expediency.

What Pilate did in the next two or three minutes would haunt him the rest of his life. His plan was to let Jesus be crucified, but make the Jewish leaders take the responsibility for it. In the midst of the tumult, and with the rulers crying out "Crucify him, Crucify him," Pilate made his decision.

---

[24]Mark 15:12-13.
[25]Matthew 27:19.

"He took water and washed his hands before the multitude, saying, I am innocent of the blood of this just person: see ye to it."[26]

This is what a modern newspaper reporter would have called a "cop out." Pilate had a moral and legal responsibility to protect the innocent, but the pressure was too great. Nevertheless, the words which immediately arose from the clamoring crowd were even worse. The scripture says:

"Then answered all the people, and said, *His blood be on us, and on our children.*"[27]

What a horrible legacy that generation imposed upon the heads of their posterity for hundreds of years to come.

JESUS AND THE JEWS

A week earlier, as Jesus had looked upon Jerusalem from across the valley, he had stopped the great procession to weep because he knew what would happen to the Jewish people in that generation. In a little over three decades, several million of these people would be slaughtered, many others enslaved, and the rest would be scattered to the four corners of the earth. [28]

On this fateful day the very calamity which the rulers had invoked on themselves and their children was poised on the horizon ready to be literally fulfilled. It would bring such a disaster to this people that never again would the Jews be united as a nation until the latter days. Never again would they be gathered together in freedom, peace and prosperity until they had drunk the very last dregs of their bitter cup.

Nevertheless, these were the Savior's people. He loved them. It was no accident that the heavens had woven together a complex tapestry of circumstances that made it possible for the Savior's own people to help him get through his cruel yet necessary assignment of

---

[26]Matthew 27:24.
[27]Matthew 27:25 (emphasis added).
[28]Isaiah 11:12.

suffering on the cross, but do it without robbing them of their opportunity for salvation.[29]

So Pilate proceeded with his plan. The scripture says:

"Then released he Barabbas [the insurrectionist, traitor, and murderer] unto them: and when he had scourged Jesus, he delivered him to be crucified."[30]

Such was the beginning of Pilate's sin against conscience which, many years later, contributed to the mental deterioration that caused him to take his own life.[31]

THE SCOURGING

A scourging, administered by a rough, sadistic, platoon of Roman legionnaires, was truly a taste of the bitterness of death itself. Only a Roman crucifixion was any worse.

The scourge was a whip carefully structured to punish a malefactor. It consisted of a strong handle, long enough to accommodate both hands, and with numerous strands of leather or rope to which were attached bits of sharp metal or cracked bone. These were specifically designed to cut into the soft flesh of the offender.

The scourge was considered a deadly weapon, because it could strip the rib cage of the offender down to the bone, and therefore offenders were sometimes literally scourged to death.

With Roman soldiers, hardened and accustomed to the horrors of the battle field, a scourging assignment was a diversion. The scripture accurately describes how degenerate and desolate of human compassion a scourging could become. Matthew says:

---

[29]Acts 3:17-19.
[30]Matthew 27:26.
[31]Eusebius, *Church History*, Book II, chapter 7.

"Then the soldiers of the governor took Jesus into the common hall, and gathered unto him [Jesus] the whole band of soldiers. And they stripped him...."[32]

It was at this point that they put the offender through the scourging, often by one soldier whipping from one side, while another soldier administered alternate lashes from the other.

And then they "put on him a scarlet robe. And when they had platted a crown of thorns, they put it upon his head, and a reed in his right hand: and they bowed the knee before him, and mocked him, saying, Hail, King of the Jews! And they spit upon him, and took the reed, and smote him on the head [forcing the thorns down against his skull].

"And after that they had mocked him, they took the robe off from him, and put his own raiment on him, and led him away to crucify him."[33]

But as Jesus was being brought out of the common hall in front of the multitude, Pilate stopped the soldiers.

PILATE MAKES ONE FINAL ATTEMPT TO PREVENT JESUS FROM BEING CRUCIFIED

All the time Jesus was in the common hall being scourged, abused and tortured, Pilate sat wrestling with the torment of his own conscience. He knew exactly what Jesus was being forced to endure. And as Jesus was brought out before the crowd, the sight of this terribly brutalized human being was a pitiful sight to behold.

As Pilate looked at Jesus with blood running down his face from the thorns in his crown, and the red blood stains seeping through his clothes from the scourging, it was obvious the Nazarene was about to collapse from exhaustion.

Pilate stood before the multitude and cried out:

---

[32]Matthew 27:27-28.
[33]Matthew 27:28-31.

"Ecce homo—behold the man!"[34]

If the condition of Jesus could arouse pity in the heart of a calloused Roman pagan, could not the Jews—who called themselves the chosen people of God—feel a small degree of compassion for this tortured fellow countryman? To Pilate's utter astonishment and disappointment, the multitude shouted again:

"Crucify him! Crucify him!"[35]

Then the chief priests said something that startled Pilate. Speaking in a pompous, pontifical tone, they said:

"We have a law, and by our law he ought to die, because he made himself the Son of God."[36]

So! This was a religious persecution after all. When this last statement made Pilate aware that he was putting the imperial seal on the religious persecution of an innocent man, it made him even "more afraid."[37] Obviously, the chief priests were using him and his imperial office to prosecute a religious dissenter.

Pilate strode into the judgment hall away from the crowd. He must talk to Jesus further. When Jesus had been brought before him, he said:

"Whence art thou? But Jesus gave him no answer.

"Then saith Pilate unto him, Speakest thou not unto me? knowest thou not that I have power to crucify thee, and have power to release thee?

---

[34]John 19:5.
[35]John 19:6.
[36]John 19:7.
[37]John 19:8.

"Jesus answered, Thou couldest have no power at all against me, except it were given thee from above: therefore he that delivered me unto thee hath the greater sin."[38]

Pilate didn't have time to debate the point with Jesus; he would rather debate with the chief priests. So John says:

"And from thenceforth Pilate sought to release him."[39]

But when Pilate came out before the crowd, he didn't know that the chief priests had concocted a strategy that would drive a permanent wedge between Jesus and himself. They cried out:

"If thou let this man go, thou art not Caesar's friend: whosoever maketh himself a king speaketh against Caesar."[40]

A moment before Pilate had been prepared to save Jesus and satisfy his conscience, but now the leaders of the Sanhedrin had played their trump card, and won. Pilate wanted to save Jesus from the religious persecution of his own people, but not at the risk of losing his own throne as the Roman governor of Judah. John continues:

"When Pilate therefore heard that saying, he brought Jesus forth, and sat down in the judgment seat in a place that is called the Pavement....[where final judgment was pronounced]

"And it was...about the sixth hour [noontime]: and he saith unto the Jews, Behold your King! But they cried out, Away with him, away with him, crucify him. Pilate saith unto them, Shall I crucify your King? The chief priest answered, We have no king but Caesar.

"Then delivered he him therefore unto them to be crucified."[41]

* * * *

---

[38]John 19:9-11.
[39]John 19:12.
[40]Ibid.
[41]John 19:13-16.

TOPICS FOR REFLECTION AND DISCUSSION

1. What were the three political charges the chief priests brought against Jesus? What was the offense for which he had been sentenced to death by the Sanhedrin?

2. Why would Pilate have resented the majority of complaints which were brought before him by the chief priests? After interviewing Jesus, what conclusion did he reach? What was the reaction of his accusers when Pilate told them he thought Jesus was innocent?

3. What was the name of the criminal who was known to be guilty of all the crimes attributed to Jesus? Whom did the people want released according to the custom of the feast day? What did they want to do to Jesus?

4. How did Pilate happen to send Jesus over to Herod Antipas, tetrarch of Galilee? What did Herod hope Jesus might do for him? What did Jesus actually do? Then where did Herod send Jesus?

5. What did Pilate's wife say about Jesus? What other pressures were on Pilate? What ceremony did Pilate go through to try to get out of any responsibility for the Savior's crucifixion?

6. What did the Savior's accusers say to assure Pilate they would take complete responsibility for the crucifixion? Did they include anyone besides themselves? What were some of the terrible consequences of this during the following centuries?

7. Nevertheless, in what ways did the Jewish people prove themselves to be a great blessing to the rest of the Father's children?

8. Why was scourging called a "deadly weapon"? Describe the various ways in which the soldiers taunted and tortured Jesus. Why did Pilate think this would arouse the sympathies of his accusers? When they saw the tortured Jesus, what did the chief priests say?

9. What else did the chief priests say that alerted Pilate to the fact that this was a religious persecution?

10. After interviewing Jesus again, what did Pilate resolve to do? What did the chief priests say to Pilate that drove a permanent wedge between Pilate and Jesus?

*   *   *   *

CHAPTER 41

ON THE WAY TO GOLGOTHA—THE PLACE OF THE SKULL

It was a triumphant crowd of passover pilgrims who joined with the high priests and their entourage of supporters to take the long walk from Pilate's Judgment Hall to Golgotha, where the crucifixion was to take place.

The Roman custom was to have the convicted felon carry his own cross to the place of execution. However, the timbers of the cross were very heavy, and very often the upright or "tree" of the cross was already at the site. In that case, Jesus would have been required to carry only the cross bar.

Even so, one of these might weigh from seventy-five to a hundred pounds, and in the Savior's weakened condition the soldiers thought he would collapse if he tried to carry it.

SIMON OF CYRENE CARRIES THE SAVIOR'S CROSS

Therefore, when the soldiers saw a robust passover pilgrim along the way, they commandeered him to carry the cross (or cross bar) for Jesus as they trudged slowly toward the place of execution outside the city wall. This Simon was a man from Cyrene, a city of north Africa, located between Carthage and Egypt.[1]

In one sense, this situation was ironical. Jesus had said to his disciples:

---

[1] Luke 23:26.

"And whosoever doth not bear his cross, and come after me, cannot be my disciple."[2]

However, in the case of this Simon, he reversed the arrangement and under compulsion of the Romans carried the Savior's cross. He may not have been a disciple before, but he certainly might have qualified as a disciple afterwards.

A great crowd followed behind Jesus as the Roman soldiers led him toward Golgotha. Among them were many of the Savior's followers. No doubt there were many whom he had healed, and mothers of children he had healed. Scarcely a week before, they had been in the procession that had welcomed Jesus into Jerusalem as an uncrowned king. Now they had to walk along the procession taking Jesus to the "place of the skull." It was outrageous. It was obscene.

As the women pressed forward to touch Jesus or express their anguish for this terrible and insane turn of events, Luke says:

"And there followed him a great company of people, and of women, which also bewailed and lamented him. But Jesus turning unto them said, Daughters of Jerusalem, weep not for me, but weep for yourselves, and for your children."[3]

Jesus was thinking of the Roman "abomination of desolation" which would sweep down on Jerusalem in that generation. Concerning it, Jesus had told his disciples a few days earlier:

"Then shall be great tribulation, such as was not since the beginning of the world to this time, no, NOR EVER SHALL BE. And except those days should be shortened, there should no [Jewish] flesh be saved: but for the elect's sake those days shall be shortened."[4]

---

[2]Luke 14:27.
[3]Luke 23:27-28.
[4]Matthew 24:21-22 (emphasis added).

In the latter days there would be another abomination of desolation at the battle of Armageddon, a siege that would destroy half of Jerusalem. Nevertheless, Jesus had prophesied that their greatest destruction would occur in 70 A.D. when Jerusalem would suffer virtual extinction.

Besides all these who followed after Jesus, there were two forlorn creatures who must have been judged habitual criminals. They, too, were destined for crucifixion. Matthew says:

"Then were there two thieves crucified with him, one on the right hand, and another on the left."[5]

THE PLACE OF THE SKULL

Precisely when the crucifixion took place is still uncertain. Mark says:

"And it was the third hour and they crucified him."[6]

According to Jewish customs, this would mean about 9 A.M. However, John says it was the sixth hour, or about noon, when Jesus was hauled away from the place where Pilate pronounced his judgment.[7] In view of the many events which took place that morning, it seems likely that the crucifixion probably began closer to noon than 9 A.M.

The location of Golgotha, the Place of the Skull—which in the Latin was called Calvary—was "without the gate,"[8] but "nigh to the city."[9] Two traditional sites have been suggested for the place of the crucifixion and the nearby garden where he was entombed, although the exact location is not positively known.

---

[5]Matthew 27:38.
[6]Mark 15:25.
[7]John 19:14-16.
[8]Hebrews 13:12.
[9]John 19:20.

When Christianity became an officially approved religion by Rome around 313 years after the time of Christ, Constantine was most anxious to know where Jesus had been buried during the three days and nights before his resurrection. Church leaders of the early Christian era pointed to a little chapel that was supposed to mark the spot. During political upheavals that chapel, and subsequent sacred buildings erected there, were destroyed. The Church of the Holy Sepulchre which marks this spot in Jerusalem today was built around the 12th century by the Crusaders. The tomb area was completely reconstructed and has been considered a most sacred shrine by members of the Latin church ever since.

More recently, a British General, Charles G. Gordon, who had spent many years in Africa trying to suppress the slave trade, took off a year (about 1882) to carefully study various Bible sites around Jerusalem. He came to the conclusion that the Holy Sepulchre could not be the right location, but where could it be? While workers were clearing away a hill just outside the city wall, General Gordon saw where the face of an exposed cliff seemed to have the shape of a skull with small caves suggesting the features of the eye sockets, nose and mouth.

Gordon knew from John 19:41, that if he had found the original Golgotha, there should be a garden nearby, and in the garden there should be a tomb. A garden was not discovered adjacent to the hill until several years after General Gordon was killed at the Sudan battle of Khartoum in 1885. However, not only was a garden found, but in it was a tomb as John had indicated.

Today, most Protestant churches consider the so-called "Garden Tomb" to have been the more likely place for the Savior's sepulchre. It is further felt that the nearby hill—that bears some resemblance to a skull—might very well be the original Golgotha. However, visitors are told that the actual crucifixion must have taken place down by the road, not on the hill, because it was the custom of the Romans to crucify criminals near a major thoroughfare where it could be an object lesson to the people.

THE SKILL REQUIRED BY THOSE
ADMINISTERING THE CRUCIFIXION

It is generally thought that Jesus and the two thieves were nailed to their respective crosses while these "trees" were lying on the ground, and that after the gruesome task was properly accomplished the crosses were "lifted up" as Jesus mentioned in John 12:32.

It is reported that the Roman soldiers who performed this task were required to have special skills.

For example, the nails in the palms of the hand needed to be directed between the tendons of the two middle fingers. Then, to make sure the weight of the body did not tear through the nails in the hands, spikes were driven through the wrists, which Isaiah calls the "nail in a sure place."[10]

The nails driven through the wrists required very special skill. The spikes were seven inches long and had to be driven between the radial artery and the ulnar artery. If the spike punctured either of these main blood channels there would be immediate hemorrhaging so that the life of the offender would quickly ebb away and the Romans would be robbed of the prolonged suffering which the crucifixion was intended to impose.

The soldier who had the task of fixing the nail in the right place performed his task by deftly feeling for the soft depression which identified the spot where the spike should be driven.

The Savior's feet, like those of the two thieves, had to be nailed to the main beam so that the long spikes passed between the metatarsals of the second and third toe. This provided the bone structure of the arch to support the Savior as he lifted the weight of his upper body so he could exhale after the chest muscles began to cramp.

---

[10]Isaiah 22:23-25.

The feet were nailed so that the knees were somewhat flexed to permit this respiration process. Later, when the legs of the two thieves were broken below the knee, they died almost immediately from self-asphyxiation.

THE CRUCIFIXION

Two Gospel writers mention that just before the soldiers were about to drive the first spikes into the hands and wrists of Jesus, someone offered him some sour wine or vinegar mingled with an aromatic but bitter herb, called myrrh. In those days it was thought to be a mild sedative against pain, but Jesus refused it.[11]

As the Savior was nailed securely to the cross and hoisted into position, he looked toward heaven and prayed:

"Father, forgive them; for they know not what they do. And they parted his raiment, and cast lots."[12]

This prayer is usually believed to have referred only to the Roman soldiers, who were simply following orders and did not know that Jesus was the very Son of God, the Messiah of the world. However, Peter later points out that this prayer was also applicable to the Jews who thought Jesus was an impostor and therefore assented to his crucifixion in ignorance.[13]

At this point in the narrative, John provides a few more details concerning the Savior's clothing and says:

"Then the soldiers, when they had crucified Jesus, took his garments, and made four parts, to every soldier a part; and also his coat: now the coat was without seam, woven from the top throughout.

"They said therefore among themselves, Let us not rend it, but cast lots for it, whose it shall be: that the scripture might be fulfilled,

---

[11]Matthew 27:34; Mark 15:23.
[12]Luke 23:34.
[13]Acts 3:17.

which saith, They parted my raiment among them, and for my vesture they did cast lots. These things therefore the soldiers did."[14]

THE TAUNTING OF THOSE
WHO PASSED ALONG THE WAY

The Romans always looked upon a crucifixion as an object lesson for the rest of the population. The place of execution was therefore set up along the side of some well traveled thoroughfare. Of course, the crucifixion of Jesus was so widely publicized that no doubt many came out from the city just to satisfy their morbid curiosity. Matthew says:

"And they that passed by reviled him, wagging their heads, and saying, Thou that destroyest the temple, and buildest it in three days, save thyself. If thou be the Son of God, come down from the cross. Likewise also the chief priests mocking him, with the scribes and elders, said, He saved others; himself he cannot save."[15]

These sophisticated rabbinical scholars then continued:

"*If* he be the King of Israel, let him now come down from the cross, and we will believe him. He trusted in God; let him deliver him now, if he will have him: for he said, I am the Son of God. The thieves also, which were crucified with him, cast the same in his teeth."[16]

THE DILEMMA OF THE APOSTLES

The amazing thing about this whole tragic scenario is the fact that eleven of the apostles were no doubt witnesses to this ghastly Roman execution and could scarcely believe what they were seeing. It contradicted everything they had been led to believe. Jesus had positively given them that marvelous promise at the Last Supper when he said:

---

[14]John 19:23-24; Psalms 22:18.
[15]Matthew 27:39-42.
[16]Matthew 27:42-44 (emphasis added).

"I appoint unto you a kingdom, as my Father hath appointed unto me; that ye may eat and drink at my table in my kingdom, and sit on thrones judging the twelve tribes of Israel."[17]

Now, just a few hours later, it was so tragically obvious that he was not going to have any kingdom, and there weren't going to be any thrones from which the apostles could govern in righteousness or judge the twelve tribes of Israel. And to think how they had trusted him because he had always been so dependable and truthful!

Probably no one in the whole world was suffering as great a state of perplexity and discouragement as the eleven apostles who watched their hopes for a glorious kingdom slowly expiring on that gruesome Roman cross.

THE KING OF THE JEWS

Suddenly a Roman soldier strode through the crowd. He was carrying a sign and climbed up where he could nail it over the Savior's head. It read: "JESUS OF NAZARETH THE KING OF THE JEWS." Then the scripture says:

"This title then read many of the Jews: for the place where Jesus was crucified was nigh to the city: and it was written in Hebrew, and Greek, and Latin [that it might be universally understood].

"Then said the chief priests of the Jews to Pilate, Write not, The King of the Jews; but that he *said*, I am King of the Jews. Pilate answered, What I have written I have written."[18]

ONE OF THE THIEVES DECIDES JESUS MIGHT BE THE GREAT MESSIAH AFTER ALL

In spite of all the wrangling going on, one of the thieves on a nearby cross began looking at the suffering Jesus through new eyes. It occurred to him that this might be the king of the Jews after all.

---

[17]Luke 22:29-30.
[18]John 19:20-22.

Perhaps his kingdom was in heaven. He might even be the promised Messiah whom the Jews had failed to recognize.

It seems apparent that the "light of Christ"—which "lighteth every man that cometh into the world"[19]—was working on this thief. But it was not working on the other malefactor. We read:

"And one of the malefactors which were hanged railed on him, saying, If thou be Christ, save thyself and us. But the other answering rebuked him, saying, Dost not thou fear God, seeing thou art in the same condemnation? And we indeed justly; for we receive the due reward of our deeds: but this man hath done nothing amiss.

"And he said unto Jesus, Lord, remember me when thou comest into thy kingdom. And Jesus said unto him, Verily I say unto thee, To day shalt thou be with me in paradise."[20]

THE SIGNIFICANCE OF THIS DIALOGUE

It is difficult to know the full extent of the understanding of this man hanging on a cross beside the Savior, but several things seem quite apparent.

First of all, he considered Jesus innocent of the crime for which he was being crucified. Second, he addressed the Savior as "Lord." Third, he expected Jesus to take over his rightful place at the head of a kingdom when he passed into the next sphere of existence. Fourth, he wanted Jesus to remember him when he came into his kingdom in the spirit world. This suggests that he hoped the Savior might intercede for him in spite of his criminal background.

We now know that the word, "paradise" should have been translated "world of spirits," where all spirits go as they pass from this life.[21] The fact that Jesus said they would both be there was designed by the Savior to give comfort to the thief, since the Savior wanted him to know he would have a friend.

---

[19]Doctrine and Covenants 93:2.
[20]Luke 23:39-43.
[21]Smith, *Teachings of the Prophet Joseph Smith*, op. cit., p. 309.

Nevertheless, the thief would not enter into an immediate state of bliss as many have supposed. He would have many things to learn, and furthermore—as we shall see in the next chapter—he would be given the opportunity to be trained and to prepare himself for a higher level of existence.

WHAT IT MEANS TO "CONFESS CHRIST"

The scripture would indicate that the thief had confessed Jesus as "Lord" and wanted to accept him as the Messiah. But as Jesus had taught in the Sermon on the Mount, to "confess Christ" is NOT an automatic assurance of salvation nor a passport into "paradise." But it is the first important step.

As we have mentioned before, Jesus taught that salvation is a "process," not an event.

The first and most important step in this process is to believe in God and "come unto Christ," as we discussed in the Sermon on the Mount.

The second step is to repent and turn away from a lifestyle that violates the commandments of God.

The third step is to enter into a covenant with God to follow his Son and obey the commandments of the Father. This is done through the ordinance of baptism by immersion at the hands of someone such as John the Baptist, the Savior, the apostles, or someone who has the priesthood authority to administer this covenant-making ceremony.

The fourth step is to receive continuous light and knowledge through the reception of the Holy Ghost, thus progressing throughout life and "enduring to the end."[22]

From this point on, life is a prolonged course that ascends upward along the straight and narrow path until it reaches the tree of life or the fountain of living water where one enjoys the blessing of

---

[22]1 Nephi 22:31, B. of M.

being in the presence of Jesus Christ and enjoying the glory of the Father.[23]

When Jesus told the thief, "Today shalt thou be with me in paradise,"[24] it was like saying, "We will both be in the world of spirits, and I will teach you." This was no doubt a great comfort to the repentant vagrant, just as Jesus intended it should be.

However, to those who might have thought they could throw the whole burden of their sins on Jesus by merely confessing his name, the Savior had previously said:

"Not every one that saith unto me, Lord, Lord, shall enter into the kingdom of heaven; but he that doeth the will of my Father which is in heaven."[25]

THE THREE HOURS OF DARKNESS

As we noted at the beginning of this chapter, the crucifixion began sometime during the morning hours. The scripture says:

"And it was about the sixth hour [noon], and there was a darkness over all the earth until the ninth hour."[26]

During these three hours from noon until 3 P.M., there was an exceptionally dark overcast, and toward the end there was a rumbling in the earth, followed by a severe earthquake. After that, however, everything seemed to settle back into place and tranquility was restored.

But in America there was a completely different story.

During the entire period of the Savior's last three hours of suffering, the American continent was in a state of violent upheaval. It was as though the very rocks were crying out in violent protest

---

[23]1 Nephi, ch. 8 and its interpretation in ch. 15, B. of M.

[24]Luke 23:43.

[25]Matthew 7:21.

[26]Luke 23:44.

against the torture and suffering of the earth's Creator and the Father's Beloved Son. The rumbling ranges of mountains were crying out. The huge tidal waves of the sea were crying out. The vast network of intelligences throughout the universe were crying out.[27]

ENOCH KNEW THIS WOULD HAPPEN

The scriptures indicate that the highly integrated system of intelligences throughout the Father's creations are extremely sensitive, and they exist in a sympathetic and affectionate harmony with the Savior, who is the Father's general manager.

This was impressed upon Enoch around 3,000 B.C., when he was shown a vision of the future history of the world. As he witnessed the degradation and wickedness just before the great flood, Enoch became so outraged that the scripture says:

"...his heart swelled wide as eternity...and ALL ETERNITY SHOOK."[28]

This seems to be the only prophet of record who has been allowed to look out into the eternities and perceive the Savior's network of intelligences reacting to the forces of wickedness and evil.

Then Enoch was allowed to see how these intelligences would react in the elements of the earth at the time of Christ's crucifixion. The scripture says:

"The Lord said unto Enoch: Look, and he looked and beheld the Son of man lifted upon the cross after the manner of men;

"And he heard a loud voice; and the heavens were veiled; and ALL the creations of God MOURNED; and the earth GROANED; and the rocks were RENT...."[29]

---

[27]3 Nephi, chapter 8, B. of M.
[28]Moses 7:41, P. of G. P. (emphasis added).
[29]Moses 7:55-56, P. of G. P. (emphasis added).

The American scripture says that after three hours of almost universal destruction, a most oppressive vapor of darkness settled down over the land, and it lasted three days.[30]

Meanwhile, at Golgotha, the last three hours of the Savior's suffering dragged wearily on.

THE WOMEN WHO HAD MINISTERED TO JESUS WATCHED THE CRUCIFIXION

All during the time Jesus hung on the cross, those who loved him the most watched in agonized wonderment. This included his mother and her close companions, who felt a sense of total devastation as they saw what was happening. Concerning these women, the scripture says:

"And many women were there beholding afar off, which followed Jesus from Galilee, ministering unto him: Among which was Mary Magdalene, and Mary the mother of James and Joses, and the mother of Zebedee's children [James and John]."[31]

In a number of important respects, these women differed from the apostles in their feelings and perspective. Even though it was apparent that Jesus was not going to fulfill the role of a King-Messiah, the important thing to these women was the simple reality of their deep and abiding love for Jesus as a person, as an individual. This feeling of devotion extended beyond his calling, his office, title, fame or even his Messiahship.

These women loved Jesus in this special way although sometimes they couldn't understand him, nor comprehend why these terrible things were happening to him. Nevertheless, when he was dead, they would stay to see that he was decently buried. Then they would return the first day of the week to demonstrate their last measure of unconditional love and devotion. This was the quality of feeling which these women had for Jesus.

---

[30]3 Nephi 8:20-23, B. of M.
[31]Matthew 27:55-56.

THE SAVIOR'S MOTHER SADLY LEAVES
THE SCENE OF THE CRUCIFIXION

As Jesus approached his final hour, some of the women drew near and gathered around the foot of the cross. Jesus looked down upon these choice women, one of whom was his mother. The scripture says:

"Now there stood by the cross of Jesus his mother, and his mother's sister, Mary the wife of Cleophas, and Mary Magdalene.

"When Jesus therefore saw his mother, and [John] the disciple standing by, whom he loved, he saith unto his mother, Woman, behold thy son! [No doubt nodding toward John.]

"Then saith he to the disciple, Behold thy mother! And from that hour that disciple took her unto his own home."[32]

This implies that the weeping, miserable, exhausted mother of the Savior was tenderly led away to the home of John the Beloved. Since Mary is later described as living with the apostles at the house with the "upper room,"[33] we assume this is where he took her.

This compassionate gesture performed by both the Savior and John allowed his mother to escape the worst of the Savior's ordeal which was about to occur.

However, let us add a brief footnote to this incident. We know that when Jesus spoke to John and his mother, it could only be done with the most desperate physical effort. After all these hours on the cross, the whole muscular system of the Savior's upper body was virtually paralyzed. As with all of us, Jesus could only speak while exhaling, and, to do this, he had to lift himself on those cruel, nerve-shattering spikes in his feet in order to exhale the air and say these few precious words.

---

[32]John 19:25-27.
[33]Acts 1:13-14.

Now the end was getting very close.

THE FATHER'S ULTIMATE ORDEAL—
COMPLETELY FORSAKING HIS SON

As the ninth hour drew near, Elohim faced the most bitter, soul-wrenching aspect of Godhood. He had to impose on his Beloved Son the last ounce of affliction so that the universal demands of justice imposed by the hosts of intelligences throughout the Father's kingdom would be satisfied, and it could be said that Jesus had indeed "trod the winepress alone."[34]

This meant that the gradual withdrawal of the Spirit of the Father, which appears to have caused Jesus such manifest distress in recent months, must now come to a traumatic finale as the Father's sustaining spirit was withdrawn altogether.

This would leave the soul of the Father's Beloved Son suspended in the outer darkness of a region which is known in scripture as the place of the second death.[35] It is where there is nothing but darkness. The Spirit of the Holy Ghost is not there. The Spirit of the Father is not there.[36]

It is in that outer region where the Lord says there is nothing but "weeping, wailing and gnashing of teeth."[37] It is the place where the wicked who reject the Gospel of Jesus Christ must go to suffer "their part" of God's "wrath" until they have paid the uttermost farthing.[38]

The complete withdrawal of the Father's Spirit, which encompassed Jesus in total darkness, apparently caught him completely by surprise. His physical suffering on the cross had been desolating, but this new devastation which now overwhelmed him was so terrible it caused him to suddenly cry out in the most extreme anguish. The scripture says:

---

[34]Isaiah 63:3; Doctrine and Covenants 76:107; 88:106.

[35]Doctrine and Covenants 63:17; 76:36-39; 101:90-91; 133:73.

[36]Citing Joseph Smith, *Journal of Discourses*, vol. 4, p. 266.

[37]Doctrine and Covenants 133:73.

[38]Doctrine and Covenants 76:38-39; 63:17.

"And at the ninth hour Jesus cried with a loud voice, saying, Eloi, Eloi, lama sabachthani? which is, being interpreted, My God, my God, why hast thou *forsaken* me?"[39]

The words of Jesus were misunderstood by those standing near the cross. When he cried out, "Eloi, Eloi," some thought he was calling for water. Others thought he was calling for Elias to come and save him.[40]

We do not know how long Jesus was left suspended in that agonizing region of outer darkness, but it was probably not very long—certainly no longer than was absolutely necessary to satisfy the stringent requirements for his role as the Messiah-Redeemer. When the Father's Spirit finally came surging back to sustain him, Jesus knew it was over. He had done it. The Father's Beloved Son had drunk the bitter cup to the very dregs.

And equally important, the Father's ordeal was also over. It could now be declared with resounding trumpets and heavenly choirs:

"For God so loved the world, that he gave his only begotten Son, that whosoever believeth in him should not perish, but have everlasting life.

"For God sent not his Son into the world to condemn the world; but that the world through him might be saved."[41]

Jesus now had only minutes to live. To slake his thirst, and to fulfill a prophecy, he said: "I thirst." John writes:

"There was set a vessel full of vinegar: and they filled a sponge with vinegar [diluted wine], and put it upon hyssop, and put it to his mouth.

---

[39]Mark 15:34.
[40]Matthew 27:47-49.
[41]John 3:16-17.

"When Jesus therefore had received the vinegar, he said, *It is finished!*"[42]

Jesus had the power within himself to retain his life until he was willing to surrender it.[43] When he said, "It is finished," it meant he knew he had fulfilled his manifest destiny.

His last words were, "Father, into thy hands I commend my spirit."[44]

Then he died. At that moment, Jesus became the Christ, the great Messiah-Redeemer.

SUDDENLY THINGS BEGAN TO HAPPEN IN QUICK SUCCESSION

Matthew says:

"The veil of the temple was rent in twain from the top to the bottom; and the earth did quake, and the rocks rent."[45]

The Roman centurion and the soldiers with him became very frightened and exclaimed:

"Truly this was the Son of God!"[46]

When the veil of the temple was ripped open it exposed the Holy of Holies as though the Father were declaring that the old order had passed away, and the new Christian era had begun.[47]

However, the old order would not pass away easily. One of the most ironic things which happened that day was the fact that while the Father's Only Begotten Son was being sacrificed on the cross, the

---

[42]John 19:29-30 (emphasis added); Psalms 69:21.

[43]John 10:18.

[44]Luke 23:46.

[45]Matthew 27:51.

[46]Matthew 27:54.

[47]Talmage, *Jesus the Christ*, p. 662.

Jews were in the process of slaying thousands of lambs after the pattern which God initiated with Adam to memorialize the infinite sacrifice of the Son of God.[48]

So, during the time the Jews were busily taking their "lambs without blemish" to the priests for sacrifice, they never suspected that the great, supreme, final sacrifice of the Father's lamb had just been made at Golgotha.

And because the old order would now pass away, the slaying of all these lambs at Passover would never be required by God again.[49]

But the people of Jerusalem were oblivious to all of this. They were too preoccupied with their preparations for the Feast of the Passover which would begin with the commencement of the new day just after sundown.[50]

This left scarcely a couple of hours to remove the victims from the three crosses so they would not desecrate the holy feast day. To accelerate the death process of the three victims, the soldiers were ordered to break the legs of the three so they would die in minutes from asphyxiation.

The smashing of the lower legs of the two thieves took place, but when the soldiers came to Jesus, they were surprised to find he was already dead. There was no need to break his legs, just as the bones were not to be broken in preparing or eating the paschal lamb.[51] Nevertheless, a heavy spear was thrust into the side of the upper body of the Savior, and when it was withdrawn, blood and water gushed out.[52]

This suggests that Jesus literally died of a broken heart, since the rupture of the heart causes the blood to accumulate in the

---

[48]Moses 5:5-7.
[49]3 Nephi 9:19, B.of M.
[50]John 19:14,31.
[51]Exodus 12:46.
[52]John 19:34.

pericardium where the corpuscles separate from the almost colorless, water serum.[53]

THE BODY OF JESUS IS PLACED IN A NEW TOMB

Joseph of Arimathaea, who was a rich man of influence in Jerusalem, asked for permission to dispose of the Savior's body. After Pilate verified through the Roman centurion that he was indeed dead, permission was granted. The body was carefully removed from its Roman torture rack and wrapped in fresh linen.[54]

The scripture says:

"And the women also, which came with him from Galilee, followed after, and beheld the sepulchre, and how his body was laid."[55]

Amazingly, Nicodemus from the Sanhedrin suddenly appeared on the scene with a hundred pounds of fragrant myrrh and aloes to wrap with the fresh linen around the body.[56]

Joseph had a private garden near the place of Golgotha. In it was a newly hewn tomb. The body of Jesus was placed carefully in the crypt, and after the mill-wheel shaped stone was rolled over the entrance, they all departed.[57]

There is just one somber note to add to this sacred story and that is the fact that the eleven apostles are never mentioned toward the end. It appears that they did not come forward to help remove the body, nor did they go with the women to the tomb.

Their mental state was a mixture of tragedy and chaos. What they had watched was the collapse of their hopes, their aspiration, even

---

[53]Talmage, *Jesus the Christ*, p. 669.

[54]Mark 15:43-46.

[55]Luke 23:55.

[56]John 19:39.

[57]Mark 15:46.

their testimonies. As of that dark, morbid moment, they could each echo Peter's words to Malchus:

"I DO NOT KNOW THE MAN!"[58]

*   *   *   *

TOPICS FOR REFLECTION AND DISCUSSION

1. Who carried the cross for Jesus? Name three of the different kinds of people who would be in the procession to Golgotha. Why did Jesus say the people of Jerusalem should weep for themselves rather than for him?

2. What is the story behind the Church of the Holy Sepulchre in Jerusalem? What is the story behind the Garden Tomb?

3. Before Jesus was actually crucified, can you name three important events that transpired during those early morning hours?

4. Why did those who supervised the crucifixion need to have a particular skill? Why were the nails driven into the wrists? Why were the feet nailed so the knees would be slightly flexed?

5. What did Jesus say to the Father concerning those who were responsible for his crucifixion? What were some of the things the enemies of Jesus said to Jesus while he was on the cross? When one of the thieves asked Jesus to remember him in the next world, describe what Jesus meant when he answered, "Today thou shalt be with me in paradise."

6. Does it appear that Mary was taken away before the Savior's death? What time did darkness settle over the land? But what was happening in America during these three hours? How long did the darkness last in America?

7. Toward the end, what was the Father's greatest ordeal? What did Jesus say when it happened? What is so terrible about the "outer

---

[58]Matthew 26:72.

darkness" mentioned in the scripture? What did Jesus say as soon as the Father's Spirit returned? And what did he say last of all?

8. Why were the legs of the two thieves broken? Why weren't the Savior's legs broken? Who lowered the body of Jesus from the cross and placed it in a new tomb? Who brought a hundred pounds of myrrh and aloes to wrap with the linen cloth about his body?

9. Does the scripture indicate there were any apostles present? Were some of the women present? In what way is it suggested that the perspective of the women was somewhat different than that of the apostles?

10. When Jesus died, what happened to the temple? What did the Roman centurion say? At that moment what were many of the Jews doing in Jerusalem? Will Christians offer any more blood sacrifices? (However we know the Levites will temporarily offer blood sacrifices when they build their new temple in Jerusalem.)[59]

*   *   *   *

---

[59]Malachi 3:3; Doctrine and Covenants, Section 13.

CHAPTER 42

WHAT HAPPENED TO THE SPIRIT OF JESUS CHRIST AFTER THE CRUCIFIXION?

When the spirit of the Savior slipped away from the dead body on the cross, there was great rejoicing in the spirit world. Millions had been waiting for this moment. His suffering was over. His victory was won. Now he was no longer the expected Messiah. When his suffering lips said, "It is finished!" he had become the Messiah-Redeemer in a very complete and literal sense.

The Savior's spirit did not go very far away. A modern prophet, who had been allowed to visit that sphere on several occasions, said:

"Where is the spirit world? It is right here....Do they [who die] go beyond the boundaries of this earth? No, they do not."[1]

Joseph Smith said the spirits of the departed are very close to us here on earth.[2]

NOW THERE WAS A GREAT NEW WORK TO BE DONE

The apostle Peter somehow learned what happened to Jesus when he died. Here is what he said the Savior did during the three days and nights while his body was in the tomb:

"For Christ...went and preached unto the spirits in prison; Which sometime were disobedient...."[3]

---

[1]Brigham Young, *Journal of Discourses*, 3:368.
[2]*Teachings of Joseph Smith*, p. 326.
[3]1 Peter 3:19-20.

Paul also knew that the gospel was taught to those in the spirit world, and he knew that those who accepted the gospel in the spirit world could have their temporal ordinances performed for them by those on earth.[4]

HOW JESUS TAUGHT THE GOSPEL TO TENS OF MILLIONS IN THE SPIRIT WORLD

It was not until modern times that a servant of the Lord was allowed to see and record a vision of the mammoth missionary work that was launched when Jesus visited the spirit world right after his crucifixion.

President Joseph F. Smith said:

"The eyes of my understanding were opened, and the Spirit of the Lord rested upon me, and I saw the hosts of the dead, both small and great."[5]

He saw that the first huge crowd that stood ready to welcome Jesus was a great conference of the righteous Saints who had lived on the earth since the days of Adam. This was the group that within three days would begin to be resurrected. The scripture says:

"For the dead had looked upon the long absence of their spirits from their bodies as a bondage."[6]

No doubt it is absolutely impossible for us to appreciate the jubilation of these people as they contemplated the blessings they were about to receive. It says:

"They were filled with joy and gladness, and were rejoicing together because the day of their deliverance was at hand. They were assembled awaiting the advent of the Son of God into the spirit world, to declare their redemption from the bands of death."[7]

---

[4]1 Corinthians 15:29.
[5]Doctrine and Covenants, 138:11.
[6]Doctrine and Covenants 138:50-51.
[7]Doctrine and Covenants 138:15-16.

But there was a much larger mass of spirits who would not get to see Jesus at this time. These were the multitudes who had never accepted the gospel. Nevertheless, he now extended a gesture of love and a deepest concern for them that they had not extended to him. He set up a vast priesthood organization so the gospel could be taught to them. Although he did not minister to them personally, the prophet says:

"From among the righteous, he organized his forces and appointed messengers, clothed with power and authority, and commissioned them to go forth and carry the light of the Gospel to them that were in darkness, even to all the spirits of men; and thus was the gospel preached to the dead....

"These were taught faith in God, repentance from sin, *vicarious* baptism for the remission of sins, the gift of the Holy Ghost by the laying on of hands,

"And all other principles of the Gospel that were necessary for them to know in order to qualify themselves that they might be judged according to men in the flesh, but live according to God in the spirit."[8]

So while the body of the Savior was in the tomb, this enormous and elaborately organized missionary enterprise was being launched in the spirit world.

But a lot of additional things were happening during these three special days.

THE SAVIOR'S TOMB IS SEALED
AND PLACED UNDER GUARD

After the crucifixion of the Savior, the chief priests and Pharisees were not entirely relieved or satisfied. They were masters of many devious and deceptive practices themselves, and they feared that the followers of Jesus might try to move the Savior's body and make the

---

[8]Doctrine and Covenants 138:30-34 (emphasis added).

people *think* he had risen from the dead. Fearful of such a possibility, the scripture says:

"Now the next day, that followed the day of the preparation, the chief priests and Pharisees came together unto Pilate."[9]

As we have already indicated, the "day of preparation" began Wednesday at sunset and ended Thursday at sunset. Therefore we assume it would be the "the next day," or Friday, when these officials visited Pilate. Because Friday was a feast day, John calls it "that sabbath day [which was] an high day," thereby distinguishing it from the regular sabbath which came on Saturday.[10]

"Saying, Sir, we remember that deceiver said, while he was yet alive, After three days I will rise again.

"Command therefore that the sepulchre be made sure until the third day, lest his disciples come by night, and steal him away, and say unto the people, He is risen from the dead: so the last error shall be worse than the first.

"Pilate said unto them, Ye have a watch: go your way, make it as sure as ye can.

"So they went, and made the sepulchre sure, sealing the stone, and setting a watch."[11]

The ironic part of this is the fact that *none* of the Savior's followers were expecting Jesus to be resurrected, or even claiming he would be resurrected.[12]

Nevertheless, Caiaphas and the rulers of the Sanhedrin knew that Jesus had talked about rising the third day, and while Caiaphas did not believe it would happen, he thought the disciples might steal the

---

[9]Matthew 27:62.
[10]John 19:31.
[11]Matthew 27:62-66.
[12]John 20:9.

body and then pretend that Jesus had been resurrected. Hence, all these precautions to guard the tomb.

MEANWHILE AMERICA HAD SUFFERED THE WORST CATASTROPHE SINCE THE GREAT FLOOD

It was also while Jesus was in the spirit world that he had to play a role in explaining to the inhabitants of America why they had just suffered the most devastating disaster since the time of the Great Flood.

It all began about 4 A.M. in America. That calculates to be about the same as noon in Jerusalem. Matthew says it was about the sixth hour, or noontime, when a strange darkness settled over that land.[13]

But in America it was 4 A.M and still dark. Anyone who happened to be up was waiting for the dawn. But then it happened.

What came to the western hemisphere was a sudden avalanche of total disaster. The huge tectonic plates on which the continent rested began to grind together as though they were writhing in utter agony. As in nearly all massive earthquakes, the people probably heard the noise from the bowels of the earth before they felt the first tremors. What followed could not be better described than the way Mormon recorded it. He said:

"There arose a great storm, such an one as never had been known in all the land. And there was also a great and terrible tempest; and there was terrible thunder, insomuch that it did shake the whole earth as if it was about to divide asunder.

"And there were exceedingly sharp lightnings, such as never had been known in all the land.

"And the city of Zarahemla did take fire. And the city of Moroni did sink into the depths of the sea, and the inhabitants thereof were drowned.

---

[13]Matthew 27:45.

"And the earth was carried up upon the city of Moronihah that in the place of the city there became a great mountain."[14]

These cities were major capitals in the land southward. The people learned that it was even worse in the land northward. Mormon writes:

"But behold, there was a more great and terrible destruction in the land northward; for behold, the whole face of the land was changed, because of the tempest and the whirlwinds and the thunderings and the lightnings, and the exceedingly great quaking of the whole earth;

"And the highways were broken up, and the level roads were spoiled, and many smooth places became rough."[15]

The tidal wave of death and destruction was everywhere. He continues:

"And many great and notable cities were sunk, and many were burned, and many were shaken till the buildings thereof had fallen to the earth, and the inhabitants thereof were slain, and the places were left desolate. And there were some cities which remained; but the damage thereof was exceedingly great, and there were many of them who were slain.

"And there were some who were carried away in the whirlwind; and whither they went no man knoweth, save they know that they were carried away. And thus the face of the whole earth became deformed, because of the tempests, and the thunderings, and the lightnings, and the quaking of the earth."[16]

These convulsions of the western hemisphere lasted "for the space of three hours." [17] This would be from around 4 to 7 A.M. in

---

[14]3 Nephi 8:5-10, B. of M.
[15]3 Nephi 8:12-13, B. of M.
[16]3 Nephi 8:14-17, B. of M.
[17]3 Nephi 8:19, B. of M.

America, but from about noon until 3 P.M. in Jerusalem. Even in Jerusalem the darkness that had settled over the land was punctuated with a sudden shuddering of a sharp quake which ripped the veil of the temple from top to bottom.[18]

AMERICA SHROUDED IN DARKNESS THREE DAYS AND NIGHTS

No doubt the terrified survivors in America were desperately anxious for daylight to come so they could find loved ones, assess the damages and see what must be done. But there was no daylight. Barely had the quakes and roaring thunders subsided when the most oppressive, damp darkness descended on the land like a shroud.

This was like the darkness that engulfed Egypt some 1,400 years earlier when:

"There was a thick darkness in all the land of Egypt three days. They saw not one another, neither rose any from his place for three days."[19]

In America, the scripture says the darkness could be "felt," and the vapor was so thick and soggy that no candle or torch could be lit, neither could a fire be kindled.[20] In many places the fumes from the bowels of the earth smothered whole multitudes.[21]

All during these three horror-filled days and nights the people cried out in mourning and terror. The people did not know it, but at the end of their ordeal they were going to hear the voice of an unseen person who would say: "I am Jesus Christ, the Son of God."[22] Later, he would appear among them.[23]

---

[18]Matthew 27:51.

[19]Exodus 10:22-23.

[20]3 Nephi 8:22, B. of M.

[21]3 Nephi 10:13 so indicates, B. of M.

[22]3 Nephi 9:15, B. of M.

[23]3 Nephi 11:8-10, B. of M.

PREPARATIONS FOR THE RESURRECTION

In the spirit world the righteous had anxiously waited for the moment when the resurrection process would begin. Anyone who has read the first chapter of Ezekiel may get the impression that people are resurrected *en masse*, but we learn that this sacred event comes to each person as a special ordinance.

A modern prophet describes this ordinance as follows:

"We have not, neither can we receive here, the ordinance and the keys of the resurrection. They will be given to those who have passed off this stage of action and have received their bodies again, as many have already done, and many more will.

"They will be ordained, by those who hold the keys of the resurrection, to go forth and resurrect the Saints, just as we receive the ordinance of baptism, then the keys to baptize others for the remission of their sins."[24]

So we learn that the resurrection is a sacred ordinance administered to individuals one at a time. Jesus was the first one to rise, and therefore he is called "the first begotten of the dead,"[25] or the "firstfruits of them that slept."[26]

Nowhere in scripture do we have a description of that sacred and historic moment when the spirit of Jesus re-entered his renewed, glorified, celestial body.

However, we can readily visualize what it must have been like when it happened and the Saints and prophets of the Old Testament surrounded him in love and adoration.

---

[24]Brigham Young, *Journal of Discourses*, vol. 15, p. 137.
[25]Revelations 1:5.
[26]1 Corinthians 15:20.

JESUS ORDAINS OTHERS TO LAUNCH
THE RESURRECTION PROCESS

The scriptures tell us that the resurrection of the Savior opened the flood gates to provide this same blessing for others, beginning with some of the foremost leaders of Old Testament times.

Among some of the first to receive this ordinance that brought about their resurrection were Moses and Elijah who appeared on the mount of Transfiguration.[27] Of course, up to this moment neither Moses nor Elijah had suffered death. Each of them had been translated at the end of their earthly missions so they could continue serving the Lord. Now, however, they would have to pass through the death process in "the twinkling of an eye,"[28] and then receive the ordinance of resurrection.

We know this happened because the unfolding of the resurrection drama is described as including:

"Noah also, and they who were before him; and Moses also, and they who were before him; And from Moses to Elijah, and from Elijah to John, who were with Christ in his resurrection."[29]

But all this had to be done according to the order of heaven. As a preliminary step, Jesus no doubt conferred the keys to perform this ordinance of resurrection upon these valiant leaders including John the Baptist.[30] As more were resurrected, they would be given similar keys, and the great chain of priesthood blessings could then be expanded outward in great waves of divine administrations. It is believed that this means literally millions of the faithful saints of the past received their glorified, resurrected bodies at this time.

---

[27]Doctrine and Covenants 133:55.

[28]3 Nephi 28:8, B. of M.

[29]Doctrine and Covenants 133:54-55.

[30]Doctrine and Covenants 133:55.

THE SURVIVORS IN AMERICA RECEIVE
A SPECIAL MESSAGE FROM THE RESURRECTED CHRIST

It must have been almost immediately after Jesus was resurrected that he gave the first of two messages to the descendants of Lehi who had survived the ordeal of the past three days and nights in America. No doubt the people had been crawling about in a state of panic and despair, not knowing what to expect next. The scripture says a group of men who were huddled together were heard to cry out:

"O that we had repented before this great and terrible day, and had not killed and stoned the prophets, and cast them out; then would our mothers and our fair daughters, and our children have been spared, and not have been buried up in that great city Moronihah. And thus were the howlings of the people great and terrible."[31]

It is important to keep in mind that the people who were still alive had probably gone without food and with very little sleep for about 72 hours. It was in this setting that the scripture tells us:

"And it came to pass that there was a voice heard among all the inhabitants...upon all the face of this land, crying:

"Wo, wo, wo unto this people; wo unto the inhabitants of the whole earth except they shall repent; for the devil laugheth, and his angels rejoice, because of the slain of the fair sons and daughters of my people; and it is because of their iniquity and abominations that they are fallen!"[32]

At this point the people had no idea how extensive this disastrous earthquake, storm, and terrestrial upheaval had been. Now the voice of the unseen stranger began to give them a partial idea. He named the principal cities up and down the length of the continent that had slid into the sea, been buried under mountains, swallowed

---

[31]3 Nephi 8:25, B. of M.
[32]3 Nephi 9:2, B. of M.

up in gaping cracks in the crust of the earth, burned with fire, or shaken down to their foundations.

He concluded by saying:

"And many great destructions have I caused to come upon this land, and upon this people, because of their wickedness and their abominations."[33]

THE AMERICAN SURVIVORS LEARN WHO IS SPEAKING

Some of the people may have already suspected who was speaking, but no doubt the multitudes were astonished when they unexpectedly heard the voice say:

"Behold, I am Jesus Christ the Son of God. I created the heavens and the earth, and all things that in them are. I was with the Father from the beginning. I am in the Father, and the Father in me; and in me hath the Father glorified his name."[34]

Every person who heard this voice knew that many prophets had been stoned because they tried to convince the people to believe in the coming of this Jesus Christ. A few had believed, but most had not. Then the voice took on the attributes of a loving Savior as he said:

"O all ye that are spared because ye were more righteous than they, will ye not now return unto me, and repent of your sins, and be converted, that I may heal you?

"Yea, verily I say unto you, if ye will come unto me ye shall have eternal life. Behold, mine arm of mercy is extended towards you, and whosoever will come, him will I receive; and blessed are those who come unto me."[35]

---

[33] 3 Nephi 9:1-12, B. of M.
[34] 3 Nephi 9:15-16, B. of M.
[35] 3 Nephi 9:13-14, B. of M.

JESUS REVEALS THAT HE IS ALREADY RESURRECTED

Tucked away in this message of the Savior is a passage which reveals that Jesus had already been resurrected before he began speaking to the survivors in America. He said:

"I have laid down my life, and have taken it up again; therefore repent, and come unto me ye ends of the earth, and be saved."[36]

This meant that what the prophets had said about the Savior had already happened. They had said he would be crucified by his own people and then rise from the dead on the third day. Jesus verified that this had happened. He said;

"I came unto my own, and my own received me not. And the scriptures concerning my coming are fulfilled."[37]

And because he was the Son whom the Father had surrendered and allowed to be sacrificed for the salvation of mankind, the law of sacrifice was fulfilled. Therefore he told these people in America what he had told his apostles:

"Ye shall offer up unto me no more the shedding of blood; yea, your sacrifices and your burnt offerings shall be done away, for I will accept none of your sacrifices and your burnt offerings.

"And ye shall offer for a sacrifice unto me a broken heart and a contrite spirit. And whoso cometh unto me with a broken heart and a contrite spirit, him will I baptize with fire and with the Holy Ghost."[38]

AFTER A SILENCE OF SEVERAL HOURS
THE SAVIOR LEAVES A FINAL MESSAGE

The scripture leaves no doubt as to the powerful impact which the message of the Savior had on the hearts of the people. It says:

---

[36] 3 Nephi 9:22, B. of M.

[37] 3 Nephi 9:16, B. of M.

[38] 3 Nephi 9:19-20, B. of M.

"So great was the astonishment of the people that they did cease lamenting and howling for the loss of their kindred which had been slain; therefore there was silence in all the land for the space of many hours."[39]

Then the Savior gave them his final message. It was an ultimatum. He said they must either repent and allow him to set up his kingdom among them, or this land would remain desolate "until the time of the fulfilling of the covenant to your fathers,"[40] which would be the latter days, some eighteen centuries hence.

The Savior's impact on these people was astonishing. Within two or three years, the entire population would enter the waters of baptism and become members of the church.[41]

Furthermore, they established the Holy Order of God, which remained strong and free of apostasy for approximately 288 years! Among the Savior's own people in the Holy Land, it lasted barely one generation.

THE DARKNESS IS LIFTED

Shortly after this second message, the 72 hours of darkness in America that the prophets had predicted was finally terminated, and the sunshine finally broke through. But what a scene of desolation extended in every direction. It would take many years of arduous labor to rebuild the cities and highways before they could restore the most basic rudiments of their once flourishing civilization.

The Savior had now completed everything he intended to do for the survivors in America. He would now leave them to ponder what had happened during the last 72 hours, and allow his beloved prophet, Nephi III and other priesthood leaders to prepare the people for the appearance of the resurrected Christ on the American continent many months later—toward the latter part of that year.[42]

---

[39] 3 Nephi 10:2, B. of M.
[40] 3 Nephi 10:7, B. of M.
[41] 4 Nephi 1:2, B. of M.
[42] 3 Nephi 10:18, B. of M.

THE DAWNING OF THE THIRD DAY IN JERUSALEM

Much of what we have described concerning the resurrection of the Savior, the distribution of the keys to administer the ordinance of the resurrection, and the two messages to the survivors in America, had all occurred in the early morning hours of the third day while Jerusalem was asleep.

None of the apostles, nor the women who had planned to finish the burial preparations for the Savior's body, would have guessed, in their wildest imagination, what was about to happen on this, "the third day."

* * * *

TOPICS FOR REFLECTION AND DISCUSSION

1. Is the spirit world upon another planet? Which of the apostles knew much of what Jesus would be doing while his body was in the tomb? What was the name of the modern prophet who saw a vision of what Jesus did in the spirit world?

2. Which of the spirits did Jesus administer to in person? Which group did not get to see him? Nevertheless, what did Jesus do so that they could hear the plan of salvation? What were these spirits taught in the place of baptism?

3. At about what hour did a terrible disaster strike the entire western hemisphere? What time was it in Jerusalem when this occurred? Something also happened in Jerusalem, but how was it different from what happened in America?

4. Briefly describe the principal events connected with the catastrophe in America. How many hours did the earthquakes and storm last? Where was the greatest damage done?. Zarahemla was the national capital in the land southward. What happened to it?

5. What happened to the city of Moroni? What happened to Moronihah?

6. Describe the smothering darkness that descended on the land. Could it be physically felt? Had something like this ever happened before? About how long did it last? Did any die from the fumes and gases escaping from the depths of the earth?

7. Does the resurrection require that an individual receive a special ordinance by a member of the Priesthood? How could this be made available to millions of righteous spirits who were waiting for their resurrection?

8. When the survivors in America heard the voice of the Savior, was it before or after his resurrection? What was the first thing he told them? Did Jesus ever reveal who was speaking to them? Then what did he invite them to do?

9. When Jesus gave his second message a few hours later, what was the ultimatum he presented to them? Did they take it seriously? How long was it before all of the people in America were converted?

10. How long did the Holy Order of God continue in America before it became severely tainted by apostasy?

*   *   *   *

CHAPTER 43

THE STORY OF THE FIRST EASTER

It will be recalled that the Savior's tomb was sealed and guarded by Roman soldiers. The third night in the tomb began at sunset on Saturday evening. Midnight would mark the end of the third night. The third "day" would begin at midnight, and sometime during the next few hours of this third day the time came for the Savior to rise from the dead.

As the time drew nigh, a remarkable event took place at the tomb of the Savior. The scripture says:

"And, behold, there was a great earthquake: for the angel of the Lord descended from heaven, and came and rolled back the stone from the door, and sat upon it.

"His countenance was like lightning, and his raiment white as snow: And for fear of him the keepers did shake, and became as dead men."[1]

But their paralysis did not last very long. As they gained control of their senses, the scripture says:

"Some of the watch came into the city, and shewed unto the chief priests all the things that were done."[2]

Nothing illustrates the hypocrisy of the chief priests more than the device they now employed to keep the people from finding out about the angel at the tomb and the testimony of the soldiers that the body of Jesus was no longer there. The scripture says:

---

[1]Matthew 28:2-4.
[2]Matthew 28:11.

"And when they were assembled with the elders, and had taken counsel, they gave large money unto the soldiers, saying, Say ye, His disciples came by night, and stole him away while we slept. And if this come to the governor's ears, we will persuade him, and secure you.

"So they took the money, and did as they were taught: and this saying is commonly reported among the Jews until this day.[3]

THE WOMEN RETURN TO THE TOMB

Meanwhile, the women—who were among the last to leave the tomb with Joseph of Arimathaea three days earlier—were the first to return to the tomb now that both the sabbath of the feast's "high day"[4] as well as the regular sabbath had passed. At last they could take care of their dead, and they had brought with them spices and ointments.[5]

We know that among these women who are specifically mentioned—either at the crucifixion or later at the tomb—were Mary Magdalene; Joanna, the wife of Herod's steward; Salome, who is not otherwise identified; Mary, sometimes called, "the other Mary," who was the mother of James the lesser and Joses; and Mary, the mother of James and John.[6]

But it also says there were "others" with them.[7] We wish their names had been mentioned. Our special interest is in knowing whether Mary and Martha, the sisters of Lazarus, were present. Jesus seems to have been closer to these sisters and their brother Lazarus than any other people outside of the apostles and his own family.

However, it is probable that if they had been present, one of the Gospel writers would have mentioned them. But their names are not there. Historically speaking, Mary, Martha and Lazarus now

---

[3]Matthew 28:12-15.
[4]John 19:31.
[5]Luke 23:56.
[6]Matthew 27:56,61; Mark 16:1; Luke 24:1, 10; John 19:25.
[7]Luke 24:1.

completely disappear from the annals of the New Testament narrative.

DID THE SAVIOR'S FOLLOWERS
EXPECT HIS RESURRECTION?

A most significant aspect of the pilgrimage of these women to the tomb was the fact that none of them expected Jesus to be resurrected "on the third day."

As we mentioned before, the Savior had told his apostles on several occasions that he would rise the third day, but it did not register with any of his disciples. Luke says the meaning of his words were "hid" from them,[8] and Mark says, "They understood not that saying, and were afraid to ask him."[9]

To the apostles as well as these women, the stark, ugly reality was the terrible fact that Jesus was dead. They had actually witnessed this wonderful friend suffer the excruciating pains of the crucifixion and then finally die. It seemed impossible that this could have happened. As one of the disciples would later say:

"We trusted it would be he which should have redeemed Israel."[10]

But he was dead. After all their glorious expectations of a great Davidic kingdom with twelve thrones and the apostles judging Israel, the vision had faded and died. He was not the great King-Messiah after all. The apostles had been too shocked and despondent even to help in disposing of the body so as to ensure a decent burial. Only the women had helped.

---

[8]Luke 18:34.
[9]Mark 9:32.
[10]Luke 24:31.

THE ANGUISH OF WAITING AND WONDERING

Without any comprehension of what to expect next, the apostles had undoubtedly spent most of the past sixty hours in the deepest meditation and discussion. The task was to sort it all out. Where had they been misled? After all the godly power they had seen manifest by Jesus, how could he be crucified? It was baffling. It defied understanding. It seemed insane.

Meanwhile, the women had spent the "high" sabbath of the passover (Thursday evening and Friday),[11] and the regular sabbath that followed (Friday evening and Saturday), in abject sorrow and unrestrained mourning. It was as though the light of the universe had suddenly been extinguished. Being too distressed to eat and with scarcely any sleep, they waited anxiously for the first day of the week when the law allowed them to minister to their dead.

THE WOMEN ENCOUNTER AN UNEXPECTED SHOCK

As dawn approached, the great city of Jerusalem was still asleep. Only the first glimmer of early morning light was becoming discernible in the eastern sky as the memorable events of this day began to take place.

Swiftly and silently the sandaled feet of these women felt their way along the narrow, empty cobblestone streets west of the temple. When they reached the tiny night gate of the towering city wall, they quickly slipped through the low aperture. Then they were immediately swallowed up in the labyrinth of darkness beyond.

As they approached the garden where they had seen Joseph of Arimathaea and Nicodemus place the body of Jesus in a new tomb, they suddenly remembered something. How would they manage to roll away the great wheel-like stone that covered the entrance to the tomb?

Only when they drew near were they able to perceive in the dim light that someone had been there before them. The stone was

---

[11]John 19:31.

already rolled away! A dark, gaping hole exposed the entrance that the stone had previously covered.

Had the grave been robbed? Frantically the women crowded into the sepulchre. The tomb was dark, but suddenly the interior was illuminated by the presence of two glorious personages in "shining garments."[12] Mark says they saw "a young man sitting on the right side, clothed in a long white garment."[13] The women were so frightened they bowed down to the earth trembling and panic-stricken. Then they heard the words:

"Why seek ye the living among the dead? He is not here, but is risen: remember how he spake unto you when he was yet in Galilee, saying, The Son of man must be delivered into the hands of sinful men, and be crucified, and the third day rise again. And they remembered his words, and returned from the sepulchre, and told all these things unto the eleven, and to all the rest."[14]

WHAT DID THE ANGELS REALLY SAY?

At this juncture Mark and John report a slightly different sequence of events. Nevertheless, they both agree that even though the heavenly messenger clearly enunciated what had happened—that he had risen—the women failed to comprehend it. Their minds were not conditioned in the slightest degree to receive a resurrection message. Mark says the women not only failed to get the whole message, but:

"...fled from the sepulchre; for they trembled and were amazed: *neither said they anything to any man*; for they were afraid."[15]

This would suggest that right after this occurred, they did not tell anyone. They probably found a quiet place to regain their composure and go over in their minds what had happened.

---

[12]Luke 24:4.
[13]Mark 16:5.
[14]Luke 24:5-9.
[15]Mark 16:8 (emphasis added).

But meanwhile, John says Mary Magdalene, who had been with these women,[16] did not wait for the others. She hastened away at top speed to tell the apostles what she thought the heavenly messengers had said. She exclaimed:

"They have taken away the Lord out of the sepulchre, and we know not where they have laid him."[17]

But what about the rest of the message that "he is risen?" Notice that Mary Magdalene didn't understand the last part of the message from the angels any more than the other women had.

Although John indicates that Mary Magdalene was the first to deliver this message to the apostles, Luke says the other women finally arrived and confirmed what Mary had said.[18]

But this story about angels appearing to the women was not very impressive to the apostles. Luke says:

"And their words seemed to them as idle tales, and they believed them not."[19]

THE REACTION OF THE APOSTLES

The report of the women that the tomb of the Savior had been raided by the chief priests or the Romans or some nefarious grave robbers should have been shocking to all eleven of the apostles. One would have thought they would have gone in a body to investigate. But not so. This is one of the clearest indications of how disillusioned and despondent they were when Jesus did not turn out to be the King-Messiah. Nine of the eleven did not move.

Nevertheless, it aroused the great apostle Peter and John "whom Jesus loved." Both Peter and John "ran" toward the garden which was outside the city wall and probably quite some distance from the

---

[16]Mark 16:1.
[17]John 20:2.
[18]Luke 24:9-10.
[19]Luke 24:11.

house of the "upper room" where the apostles were staying.[20] The scripture says:

"So they [Peter and John] ran both together: and the other disciple did outrun Peter, and came first to the sepulchre. And he stooping down, and looking in, saw the linen clothes lying; yet went he not in.

"Then cometh Simon Peter following him, and went into the sepulchre, and seeth the linen clothes lie, and the napkin, that was about his head, not lying with the linen clothes, but wrapped together in a place by itself."[21]

It was incomprehensible that *anyone* would steal the body of the crucified Jesus. John had respectfully waited until Peter had made the initial inspection, but after a few moments, the scripture says:

"Then went in also that other disciple, [John] which came first to the sepulchre, and he saw, and *believed*."[22]

WHAT DID THE APOSTLE JOHN BELIEVE?

John "believed" that the body of Jesus had, in reality, been stolen. It did not enter the heads of either of these apostles that a resurrection might have taken place. The scripture plainly states:

"For as yet they knew not the scripture, that he must rise again from the dead."[23]

It seemed things were getting worse by the moment—first the crucifixion, and now the robbing of the tomb. In total despondency, Peter and John trudged slowly and solemnly back to their quarters.

---

[20]Acts 1:13.
[21]John 20:4-7.
[22]John 20:8 (emphasis added).
[23]John 20:9.

MARY MAGDALENE HAD THE HONOR OF BEING
THE FIRST WITNESS TO THE RESURRECTION

Now the scene was set for one of the most glorious events in New Testament history. It seems that Mary Magdalene had returned to the garden as fast as she could with Peter and John. But now they were gone. They didn't even go into the city to make a formal complaint.

John, who had just left the scene, later learned what happened. He says:

"But Mary stood without at the sepulchre weeping."[24]

Then, for some reason, she felt constrained, even while weeping, to look once again into the tomb. She did not enter but merely peered through the entrance. Suddenly she saw two personages just as she and the other women had seen them when they first came. They spoke to her and said:

"Woman, why weepest thou?

"Because," she replied, "they have taken away my Lord, and I know not where they have laid him."[25]

Her answer disclosed that even in the presence of angelic messengers she had completely missed their earlier message.

They could have said more, but they did not. Someone else had come into the garden. The newcomer was standing behind Mary. At this point we notice that the women had previously recognized the angels as heavenly beings because they had come in glory with "shining garments,"[26] but this newcomer looked like an ordinary person. After his resurrection, Jesus consistently withheld his glory whenever he showed himself. His only badge of identification were the marks in his hands and feet and his side. So it did not seem to be

---

[24]John 20:11.
[25]John 20:13.
[26]Luke 24:4.

a heavenly personage who appeared to Mary, but an ordinary looking person who said:

"Woman, why weepest thou? Whom seekest thou?"[27]

As she turned away from the entrance to the tomb toward the person speaking to her, she dimly perceived him through her flood of tears. Almost automatically, she assumed he must be the gardener. She hopefully thought he might have opened the tomb and removed the body. Perhaps he would know where she could find it.

"Sir," she said, "if thou have borne him hence, tell me where thou hast laid him, and I will take him away."[28]

The tall personage looked down at the grief-stricken figure and spoke just one word. The soft tone of his voice carried a message of tenderness and love, as he said:

"Mary."[29]

Startled by the shock of suddenly recognizing the voice, she cried out: "Rabboni!" which means "my master!"[30]

Instinctively she rushed toward him, but he restrained her and said gently:

"Touch me not [in the Greek "Cease clinging to me"]; for I am not yet ascended to my Father: but go to my brethren, and say unto them, I ascend unto my Father, and your Father; and to my God, and your God."[31]

Then he was gone. It was unbelievable! Mary frantically ran in search of the other women to tell them the great news.

---

[27]John 20:15.
[28]Ibid.
[29]John 20:16.
[30]Ibid.
[31]John 20:17.

JESUS REPORTS BRIEFLY TO HIS FATHER
AND THEN RETURNS TO THE SCENE OF HIS MINISTRY

In a cosmos where travel appears to be accomplished with the speed of thought, Jesus ascended to the mansions of his Father and made his brief report. What a scintillating and brilliant moment in eternity that must have been as these two glorious resurrected beings embraced one another.

For the first time in a little over thirty-three years, Elohim, the Father, could hold in his arms this wonderful Jehovah, his Beloved Son. In their long and hazardous travail, they had won. They could have failed, but as Jesus would later say: "Glory be to the Father...I partook and finished my preparations unto the children of men!"[32]

It was as though he were saying from the depth of his very soul, "I did it! I did it! I did it!"

Then Jesus returned to the scene of his ministry. While he was away an interesting development had occurred at the sepulchre.

MARY MAGDALENE BREAKS THE NEWS
TO THE OTHER WOMEN

Mark tells us that when Mary Magdalene finally found the women they were gathered together mourning and weeping.[33] What a thrilling gratification it must have been as she joyfully announced the sensational news that she had seen the Master. He was alive!

But Mary was astonished at their reaction. As she watched their faces, the inspired animation in her countenance must have wilted. She could tell from their expressions that they "believed not."[34]

Nevertheless, Matthew says they agreed to go with Mary Magdalene to tell the apostles. As they were leaving the garden to go back into the city, a great scriptural event occurred.

---

[32]Doctrine and Covenants 19:19.
[33]Mark 16:10.
[34]Mark 16:11.

To the Savior, this seemed to be an ideal moment to reward these wonderful mothers of his apostles and others who had been so faithful during the years of his ministry. As the women were slowly making their way back to the city with Mary Magdalene, Jesus suddenly appeared before them, and said:

"All Hail!"[35]

No doubt they were alarmed and deeply frightened at first, but as their senses confirmed the reality of what they were seeing, the women must have been overjoyed with the glorious evidence of his living presence. Jesus allowed them to come close to him and touch him. Having been to the Father he could now receive their expression of affection. The scripture says:

"And they came and held him by the feet, and worshipped him."[36]

Even so, it was almost too much to believe, and Jesus could see the wonderment and astonishment in their faces. Therefore, he said to them:

"Be not afraid: go tell my brethren that they go into Galilee, and there shall they see me."[37]

Apparently the women then went joyfully to the place where the apostles were staying to deliver this jubilant message.

*   *   *   *

TOPICS FOR REFLECTION AND DISCUSSION

1. What frightened the Roman soldiers who were guarding the Savior's tomb? Why do you think they were willing to accept a bribe and deny something they had seen with their own eyes?

---

[35]Matthew 28:9.
[36]Ibid.
[37]Matthew 28:10.

2. What does this reveal concerning the high priests who had concocted the plot and paid the bribe? Do you think they believed the soldiers, or merely concluded that it was their superstitious imagination?

3. While the women were on the way to the tomb, what suddenly caused them deep concern? When they reached the tomb, what surprised them?

4. Were they expecting Jesus to be resurrected? When the angels told the women Jesus had risen, did they realize what they meant?

5. Were the apostles expecting Jesus to be resurrected on the "third day"? How do you account for this mental block when Jesus had predicted it so many times?

6. Why had the faith of the apostles been severely shaken? What were they expecting Jesus to do that he had not done? After Mary Magdalene told the apostles that the tomb had been robbed, how many apostles went to check on her story?

7. What happened when Peter and John reached the tomb? Was John convinced the tomb had been robbed? Did they see any angels?

8. Describe the circumstances when Jesus appeared to Mary Magdalene. Why did he restrain her from clinging to him?

9. Why was the Savior's report to his Father such a marvelous experience for both of them? When Mary told the other women she had seen the Savior alive, how would you explain why they wouldn't believe her?

10. When Jesus appeared to the women, why did he let them touch him, while Mary Magdalene was forbidden? After the Savior disappeared, what did the women resolve to do?

*   *   *   *

CHAPTER 44

THE RECONVERSION OF
THE APOSTLE PETER

At the Last Supper, it will be recalled that Jesus said something to Peter that puzzled him. Let us review the dialogue recorded by the Gospel writers in order to better appreciate some of the events that would now begin to transpire. The Savior had said to the apostles:

"Whither I go, ye cannot come....

"Simon Peter said unto him, Lord, whither goest thou? Jesus answered him, Whither I go, thou canst not follow me now; but thou shalt follow me afterwards.

"Peter said unto him, Lord why cannot I follow thee now? I will lay down my life for thy sake."[1]

Luke then inserts an important passage which John did not include. Luke writes:

"And the Lord said, Simon, Simon, behold, Satan hath desired to have you, that he may sift you as wheat.

"But I have prayed for thee, that thy faith fail not: AND WHEN THOU ART CONVERTED, strengthen thy brethren."[2]

As we mentioned earlier, the chief apostle considered himself the most converted of all his brethren, so he said:

---

[1]John 13:36-37.
[2]Luke 22:31-32 (emphasis added).

"Lord, I am ready to go with thee, both into prison, and to death."[3]

No disciple could have made a stronger commitment to Jesus than this, but the Savior looked at him and said:

"Peter, the cock shall not crow this day before that thou shalt thrice deny that thou knowest me."[4]

PETER'S FALTERING FAITH

And this is precisely what happened.

Because of the unexpected chain of events after the Last Supper, it is not too difficult to understand or at least sympathize with the mental and spiritual metamorphosis in the thinking of Peter that changed the whole perspective of the chief apostle during the next few hours.

When one idolizes a hero with all of the superlative qualities that Peter attributed to Jesus as the King-Messiah, and then suddenly realizes that he is not fulfilling his expected role, it shatters the Godly image.

On the night Jesus was arrested and hauled before the high priest, the apostle Peter saw things happening that would never have happened to the King-Messiah. Under the impact of this sudden realization that Jesus was not what Peter had thought, he refused to be identified with Jesus and even began to deny his discipleship. On the third challenge, the big, confused, but totally honest Galilean burst out:

"I know not this man!"[5]

Peter knew Jesus the healer, the man who cast out devils, liberated lepers from their terrible affliction, who fed thousands with

---

[3]Luke 22:33.
[4]Luke 22:34.
[5]Mark 14:71.

virtually nothing, who walked on the water and who even raised the dead, but this forlorn creature fettered and abused in the Court of the Sanhedrin had to be something else. Suddenly Peter realized he actually did not know him.

And when he heard the cock crow he remembered what his beloved friend had said at the Last Supper. In a way it was terrifying. Suddenly Peter went out into the night with his mind and spirit tortured by a convulsion of realities he could scarcely endure. Out there in the darkness, the scripture says, "He wept."[6]

THREE NIGHTS OF ANGUISH

Only Peter could describe what the apostles went through during the next three nights. None of them could explain what went wrong. All they knew for certain was that their dreams and hopes for God's new kingdom were lying buried in a borrowed tomb.

As the apostles rose from their beds on the first day of the week, Peter was still trying to regain his mental equilibrium. It had been a time of reconciliation—not reconciliation with the Lord, but coming to grips with a terrible reality. Jesus was dead. There wasn't going to be a divine kingdom. The Romans were not going to be wiped out with fire and brimstone. The apostles were not going to sit on twelve thrones to govern Israel in righteousness. Without the Holy Ghost to illuminate his understanding, Peter pondered the shambles of his faith.

The apostles were barely awake when Mary Magdalene arrived to breathlessly announce that she and the women had found the tomb open, the body of Jesus gone, and that two brilliant heavenly beings assured them he was not there. The other women came shortly afterwards and confirmed what Mary had said.

The apostles attributed the story of angels to the distraught minds of these women who were so devoted to Jesus.

As Luke later wrote:

---

[6]Luke 22:62.

"Mary Magdalene and...other women...told these things unto the apostles. And their words seemed to them as idle tales, and they believed them not."[7]

THE MOST EXCITING EVENT IN
THE LIFE OF THE APOSTLE PETER

However, sometime during this historic day, Peter was apparently off by himself and undergoing a season of lonely meditation when the most exciting event in his entire life occurred.

Suddenly, there was the Lord. No Gospel writer has attempted to describe that fantastic meeting. It was enough to shatter a man's mind. Peter had barely reconciled himself to the fact that Jesus was dead—as well as the fact that his tomb had been desecrated and the body stolen—when suddenly, in broad daylight, there he stood, alive.

The meeting was probably brief, as it had been with all the others, but when it was over Peter was totally reconverted. He made his way back to the upper room and announced to his brethren the unbelievable. We can well imagine the big fisherman exclaiming:

"Jesus is alive!"[8]

THE SAVIOR TAKES AN EXCURSION INTO THE COUNTRY

It is interesting that the angels who had appeared at the sepulchre appeared in a brilliant glory, but, as we have already mentioned, when Jesus began appearing among his disciples he seems to have always withheld his glory. In his resurrected perfection, his appearance may have been altered somewhat. In fact, when he appeared without his glory some of his own disciples could not recognize him. This was the case as Jesus came upon two of his close associates traveling along the four-mile road to Emmaus.

---

[7]Luke 24:9-10.
[8]Luke 24:34.

One of these disciples was named Cleopas[9], but the other remains unidentified. Both of them were forlorn and sorrowful. Jesus came alongside them, and said:

"What manner of communications are these that ye have one to another, as ye walk, and are sad?

"And the one of them, whose name was Cleopas, answering said unto him, Art thou only a stranger in Jerusalem, and hast not known the things which are come to pass therein these days?

"And he said unto them, What things?"[10]

We later learn these two men were closely associated with the apostles and had known Jesus well, but as of the moment the scripture says:

"Their eyes were holden [veiled] that they should not know him....

"And they said unto him, Concerning Jesus of Nazareth, which was a prophet mighty in deed and word before God and all the people: and how the chief priests and our rulers delivered him to be condemned to death, and have crucified him."[11]

THE DISCIPLES EXPRESS THEIR FEELINGS OF DESPAIR

Cleopas expressed the most tragic aspect of this whole affair. The Savior's followers were devastated by the realization that Jesus was not the King-Messiah after all. They said:

"We trusted that it had been he which should have redeemed Israel!"[12]

---

[9]Luke 24:18.
[10]Luke 24:17-19.
[11]Luke 24:16,19-20.
[12]Luke 24:21.

Next comes the passage that tells us that these two disciples were part of the company that was intimately associated with the apostles. They said:

"Certain women, also of our company, made us astonished, which were early at the sepulchre; And when they found not his body, they came, saying, that they had also seen a vision of angels, which said that he was alive.

"And certain of them which were with us went to the sepulchre, and found it even so as the women had said: but him they saw not."[13]

Obviously, these two disciples were among those who did not believe the women.[14]

THE RESURRECTED CHRIST TURNS TEACHER

Now Jesus had to do what he had tried to do for Nicodemus. He had to get these followers, who had probably been trained as Pharisees, to believe the scriptures they had studied all their lives.

He did not tell them who he was, but he began to rebuke them for being "slow of heart" and too dull "to believe all that the prophets have spoken."[15]

Then he shocked them intellectually by explaining that the prophets had predicted that their Messiah would be rejected, crucified, and die like an ordinary man.[16]

Jesus did not need a copy of the scriptures to give these disciples a lesson on the Messianic prophecies. He did just what he would later do for the apostles, and even later that year for his disciples in America. He began reciting a panorama of scriptures from the

---

[13]Luke 24:22-24.
[14]Luke 24:11.
[15]Luke 24:25.
[16]Luke 24:26.

writings of the prophets which, with the refreshing of their memories, they clearly remembered, but had never understood.

He began with their favorite prophet, Moses, and then expounded from "all the prophets"[17] what those inspired men had said about the life and death of their great Messiah. He pointed out that what the ancient prophets had predicted was precisely what had happened to Jesus.

THE EYES OF THE DISCIPLES ARE OPENED

The two disciples had conversed with their strange traveling companion for quite a distance. When they reached Emmaus, they urged the stranger to stop over with them, and he consented. During the meal, the stranger took bread, and broke it into pieces, and blessed it. Then he gave it to them. Both of the disciples had sensed a burning in the bosom and felt the strangest feelings while Jesus was talking to them.[18]

Then something wonderful happened.

"Their eyes were opened, and they knew him, and he vanished out of their sight."[19]

These disciples were only an hour away from Jerusalem, and neither darkness nor distance delayed them from hastening back to the apostles. Oh, did they have *great* news? It turned out that the apostles also had some great news for them.

IT IS NOT ALWAYS EASY TO SHARE GOOD NEWS

However, the scripture indicated that the first people the two disciples met were not the apostles, but the "residue." We assume these were the regular disciples, other than the apostles, who, like themselves, had taken up quarters near the house where the eleven apostles were staying. Mark indicates that when the two disciples

---

[17]Luke 24:27.
[18]Luke 24:32.
[19]Luke 24:31.

excitedly explained to the "residue" what they had experienced, their skeptical friends did not believe them.[20]

But when they got in to see the apostles—that was a different story. Luke says the apostles received their report with rejoicing:

"The Lord is risen indeed, and hath appeared to Simon."[21]

Then Cleopas and his companion "told what things were done in the way, and how he was known of them in breaking of bread."[22]

THE RESURRECTED CHRIST APPEARS
TO MOST OF HIS APOSTLES

At this point the apostles must have wondered what astonishing things might happen next. Already it was unbelievable. The dead Jesus was not dead. He was appearing to people, talking to people. Perhaps they might even see him. Then it says:

"And as they thus spake, Jesus himself stood in the midst of them, and saith unto them, Peace be unto you. But they were terrified and affrighted, and supposed that they had seen a spirit."[23]

It is one thing to have people describe how they have seen angels and even beheld the resurrected Christ, but to have this man who died three days ago suddenly standing alive in the midst of them—it was enough to shake their sanity and the very fiber of their beings. Luke says:

"And he said unto them, Why are ye troubled? and why do thoughts arise in your hearts? Behold my hands and my feet, that it is I myself: handle me, and see; for a spirit hath not flesh and bones, as ye see me have.

---

[20]Mark 16:13.
[21]Luke 24:34.
[22]Luke 24:35.
[23]Luke 24:36-37.

"And when he had thus spoken, he shewed them his hands and his feet."[24]

If ever a body of skeptics had tangible, irrefutable, scientific proof of the reality of the resurrection, it was this frightened group of men standing in that room. The unbelievable had finally become believable. This was their Savior. This was Jesus who had been crucified and placed in a tomb. Here he was alive, with the sacred tokens of the wounds in his hands and his feet to prove the reality of his identity.

And just to let them know that a person with a resurrected body can enjoy the bounties of life, he said:

"Have ye here any meat? And they gave him a piece of a broiled fish, and of an honeycomb. And he took it, and did eat before them."[25]

CHRIST TEACHES HIS APOSTLES
AN ENRICHED VERSION OF THE GOSPEL

As this body of men sat together in sacred communion, Jesus began to teach them a greatly enriched version of the gospel. As he had done with the disciples on the way to Emmaus, he now repeated, with those disciples present, the great message of the prophets concerning the First Coming of the Messiah. The scripture says:

"And he said unto them, These are the words which I spake unto you, while I was yet with you, that all things must be fulfilled, which were written in the law of Moses, and in the prophets, and in the psalms, concerning me."[26]

Jesus then began to "open the scriptures," which means to point out passages from the prophets in which God had revealed many details concerning the First Coming of Christ that they had

---

[24]Luke 24:38-40.
[25]Luke 24:41-43.
[26]Luke 24:44.

completely missed. These are the mysteries in the scriptures concerning which the Lord says:

"If thou wilt inquire, thou shalt know *mysteries* which are great and marvelous...that thou mayest bring many to the knowledge of the truth, yea, convince them of the error of their ways."[27]

And again:

"Unto him that keepeth my commandments I will give the *mysteries* of my kingdom, and the same shall be in him a well of living water, springing up unto everlasting life."[28]

And finally:

"Seek not for riches but for wisdom; and, behold, the *mysteries* of God shall be unfolded unto you, and then shall you be made rich."[29]

So Jesus commenced to reveal to the future leaders of his kingdom the scriptures which most certainly had been mysteries to them before this time. He exclaimed:

"Thus it is written, and thus it behoved Christ to suffer, and to rise from the dead the third day: And that repentance and remission of sins should be preached in his name among all nations, beginning at Jerusalem. And ye are witnesses of these things."[30]

THE APOSTLES RECEIVE A PROMISE
OF THE BAPTISM OF FIRE

As Jesus came to the close of this sacred hour, he said:

"Peace be unto you: as my Father hath sent me, even so send I you.

---

[27]Doctrine and Covenants 6:11 (emphasis added).
[28]Doctrine and Covenants 63:23 (emphasis added).
[29]Doctrine and Covenants 11:7 (emphasis added).
[30]Luke 24:46-48.

"And when he had said this, he breathed on them, and saith unto them, Receive ye the Holy Ghost:

"Whose soever sins ye remit, they are remitted unto them; and whose soever sins ye retain, they are retained."[31]

No greater compliment could come to a body of priesthood holders than this, and no greater expression of confidence could be expressed than to have the Savior trust them to listen to the whispering of the Spirit, in order to know who had repented and could be forgiven of their sins, and who could not.

With this, the Savior took his leave, and disappeared from among them as suddenly as he had come.

CONCERNING ONE SKEPTIC WHO WASN'T THERE

Now we come to a dramatic incident in scripture that John tells better than anyone:

"But Thomas, one of the twelve, called Didymus, was not with them when Jesus came. The other disciples therefore said unto him, We have seen the Lord.

"But he said unto them, Except I shall see in his hands the print of the nails, and put my finger into the print of the nails, and thrust my hand into his side, I will not believe.

"And after eight days again his disciples were within, and Thomas with them: then came Jesus, the doors being shut, and stood in the midst, and said, Peace be unto you."[32]

It is probably impossible for us to comprehend the feelings of Thomas at that moment. After he had convinced himself that the apostles, the women, and the disciples, had deceived themselves with wishful thinking, he found the living Jesus standing directly in front of him. How had the Master entered the room with the doors

---

[31]John 20:21-23.
[32]John 20:24-26.

shut? For Thomas this was the most awkward moment of his whole life. But Jesus spoke to him in a gentle voice and said:

"Thomas, reach hither thy finger, and behold my hands; and reach thither thy hand, and thrust it into my side: and be not faithless, but believing.

"And Thomas answered and said unto him, My Lord and my God."[33]

It is interesting that from what has been written, Thomas did not feel the Savior's hands and feet, nor even thrust his hand into his side. Just seeing was believing. He simply collapsed at his feet, exclaiming, "My Lord, My God!"

"Jesus saith unto him, Thomas, because thou has seen me, thou hast believed: blessed are they that have not seen, and yet have believed."[34]

Jesus was referring to the thousands of souls who would hear the testimonies of the apostles and be converted even though they had never seen Jesus. At the Last Supper he had said a special prayer for these future converts with these words:

"Neither pray I for these alone [the apostles], but for them also which shall believe on me through their word; That they all may be one; as thou, Father, art in me, and I in thee, that they also may be one in us: that the world may believe that thou hast sent me."[35]

The next time the apostles would see the Savior would be on the shores of the sea of Galilee. Thereafter, they would undergo more than a month of intensive training so they could learn how to establish the kingdom of God on earth.

*   *   *   *

---

[33]John 20:27-28.
[34]John 20:29.
[35]John 17:20-21.

TOPICS FOR REFLECTION AND DISCUSSION

1. Describe the circumstances when Jesus implied that Peter would falter in his faith and have to be reconverted. In one passage, did Peter say almost the exact words Jesus had predicted? What were they?

2. Why did Peter lose his faith in Jesus? Describe the Jesus Peter knew. Now describe the Jesus Peter expected him to become.

3. Why do you think Peter went out into the night and wept? Do you feel a sense of compassion for him under these circumstances?

4. Why didn't the apostles believe the women when they said they had seen two angels in the tomb? Did they know Jesus would unlock the keys to the resurrection? Did they know he would be resurrected the third day? Why not?

5. When the resurrected Savior appeared to Peter the first time, was he alone or with the other apostles?

6. Describe how you think Peter must have felt when the Savior stood before him.

7. How would you describe Peter's reconversion? Did he ever falter again? Did he give his life for his new testimony?

8. When Jesus joined the two disciples on the road to Emmaus, why did they say they were sad? Did these disciples know anything about the First Coming? When did they first recognize Jesus?

9. To appreciate what it did for the Savior's disciples as he went through the scriptures, read the 22nd Psalm and see how many verses apply to the First Coming of the Savior. Now read the 53rd chapter of Isaiah and see how many verses apply to the known events in the life of Jesus.

10. When Jesus appeared to his apostles, did he appear in glory or as an ordinary person? Why didn't Thomas believe his fellow apostles when they said they had seen the Savior alive? What did Thomas say when he actually saw the Savior? Whom did Jesus say would be more blessed than Thomas?

*   *   *   *

CHAPTER 45

THE APOSTLES ARE TRAINED TO SET UP THE KINGDOM OF GOD ON EARTH

When the apostles made their way back to their homes in Galilee, they had no idea what to expect next. Jesus had promised he would meet them there, but there was no indication as to the date, the place, or the purpose of their meeting.[1]

Little would they have guessed what lay just ahead.

THE FISHERMEN RETURN TO THEIR NETS

Their first task was getting back to making a living. Their families had been compelled to manage as best they could during the past three years, and no doubt the apostles recognized the need to get back to their fishing business as soon as they arrived home.

The apostle John tells us that seven of them were standing near the wharves contemplating what they should do when Peter said, "I go a fishing." The other six immediately chimed in and said, "We also go."[2]

John was one of the seven and the others are identified as being Peter, Thomas, Nathanael, John's brother James, and two other disciples who are not named.[3]

---

[1]Mark 14:28; 16:7.
[2]John 21:3.
[3]John 21:2.

Fishing with nets was hard work, and much of the time, some of them had to strip off their clothes and work the nets in the water. After a full night of strenuous effort, the seven men were very discouraged. They had caught nothing.

Shortly after daybreak they were coming back toward shore when they noticed a lone figure of a man standing on the beach. He shouted to them:

"Children, have ye any meat?"[4]

They replied in the negative, whereupon he shouted back:

"Cast the net on the right side of the ship, and ye shall find."[5]

So the apostles followed the suggestion and hefted the huge net across to the other side. As it settled to the bottom a whole school of fish came by and as the apostles struggled to draw it up they found they had caught more than they could handle.

JOHN BEGINS TO FEEL A SENSE OF "DEJA VU"

To the apostle John, it suddenly seemed that there was something very familiar about this scenario. Nearly three years before, Peter, Andrew, James and John had fished all night and come home empty. Then Jesus had told them to cast their net on the other side, and the next thing they knew, the quantity of fish almost capsized their boat.[6] No doubt this was in John's mind as he took one more look at the tall figure on the shore and then said to Peter:

"It is the Lord!

"When Simon Peter heard that...he girt his fisher's coat unto him, (for he was naked,) and did cast himself into the sea."[7]

---

[4]John 21:5.
[5]John 21:6.
[6]Luke:5:4-6.
[7]John 21:7.

And while Peter was swimming toward the shore, the other six got into a smaller boat or dinghy and gradually worked the net, filled with fish, toward the beach.[8]

As Peter came up out of the water, there was a slight impasse, a sort of stand off. Jesus was quietly waiting beside a small fire on which both fish and bread were cooking. Peter did not know exactly what to do or say, so the Savior relieved the tension by saying: "Bring of the fish which ye have now caught."[9]

Peter immediately went back to help the others with the net and sort out the catch. Altogether there were 153 large fish and the apostles were all astonished that the net had not broken.[10]

The scripture then says:

"Jesus saith unto them, Come and dine. And none of the disciples durst ask him, Who art thou? knowing that it was the Lord.

"Jesus then cometh, and taketh bread, and giveth them, and fish likewise."[11]

And so they began to eat. But what a quiet, solemn breakfast it was. No one dared say a word. This was the third time they had been in the presence of the resurrected Christ. It was awesome. This was not like the old days when Jesus was just one of them. They were now dealing with the very Son of God in his resurrected state, a Supreme Being who appeared in rooms when the doors were shut, who disappeared at will, and now appeared suddenly on the sandy shore of the Galilee, looking like any ordinary rustic mortal, cooking their breakfast.

---

[8]John 21:8.
[9]John 21:10.
[10]John 21:11.
[11]John 21:12-13.

"FEED MY SHEEP"

After they had finished eating, Jesus broke the uncomfortable silence by saying:

"Simon, son of Jonas, lovest thou me more than these?"[12]

Jesus was referring to Peter's fellow men. Peter hastily replied:

"Yea, Lord, thou knowest that I love thee."[13]

We visualize the Savior looking deeply into Peter's eyes as he said, "Feed my sheep."[14]

The formal atmosphere and solemnity of the occasion was further accentuated as Jesus proceeded to ask Peter this same direct question two more times. Each time Peter assured the Savior that he loved him, and each time the Savior said, "Feed my sheep." It was almost as though Jesus wanted Peter to bear his testimony three times to make up for the three denials at the palace of Caiaphas. No doubt he wanted Peter to "strengthen thy brethren" as he had told Peter at the Last Supper.

In all of this the Savior wanted to bolster Peter for the rugged road ahead as this apostle became the president, prophet, seer and revelator over the Savior's new church. The ramifications of Peter's new calling—with the very real possibility of martyrdom at the end—was vividly implied by the Savior's next statement. Jesus said:

"Verily, verily, I say unto thee, When thou wast young, thou girdest thyself, and walked whither thou wouldest: but when thou shalt be old, thou shalt stretch forth thy hands, and another shall gird thee, and carry thee whither thou wouldest not."[15]

---

[12]John 21:15.
[13]Ibid.
[14]Ibid.
[15]John 21:18.

John explains in his text that Jesus was "signifying by what death he should glorify God."[16] We cannot help but wonder if the prophetic eye of the Savior was actually looking down the corridor of the future and seeing Peter being crucified upside down on a cross in Rome? Tradition tells us this is what eventually happened.[17]

"And when he had spoken this, he saith unto him, Follow me."[18]

This was not the casual comment of a carpenter from Nazareth, nor the off-hand remark of a former beloved missionary companion with whom they had been intimately associated during the past three hectic years. A new sense of awe-inspiring majesty was gradually emerging in the minds of Peter and his companions as they looked upon this tall figure standing before them. The true relationship between themselves and this glorious being was beginning to blossom into a blazing white light of a stark reality. They were dealing with the Firstborn, the Only Begotten Son of Elohim, the Lamb slain from before the foundations of the world. This was not just Jesus. This was Jehovah!

And he had said, "Follow me."[19]

Thus the meeting was concluded, and we assume he disappeared just as he had on previous occasions.[20]

THE APOSTLES ARE INSTRUCTED TO MEET JESUS IN A CERTAIN MOUNTAIN

Matthew was not present at this preliminary meeting between the Savior and seven of his apostles, but in his Gospel writings Matthew says they were finally told to go into "a mountain where Jesus had appointed them."[21]

---

[16]John 21:19.
[17]Peloubet's *Bible Dictionary*, under "Peter," pp. 503-504.
[18]John 21:19.
[19]Ibid.
[20]Luke 24:31.
[21]Matthew 28:16.

There was one mountain which was already very sacred to the apostles and that was the Mount of Transfiguration. Both the scriptures and the circumstances indicate that this was clearly Mount Hermon and not Mount Tabor as modern tourists are often told when they go to the Holy Land. Mount Hermon looms into the sky 9,166 feet and is the highest and most majestic mountain in all northern Palestine. Lying in its lower foothills was the beautiful resort community of Caesarea-Philippi where the disciples had stayed at the time of the transfiguration.[22]

Since the apostles apparently had to be given a course of rigorous spiritual training during the next few weeks, it would have been convenient to reside in the town at night and then climb into the secluded, quiet precincts of the mountain for their heavenly instructions during the daytime.

It is entirely clear from the manner in which the apostles pursued the establishment of the church just a few weeks later that their concentrated indoctrination during this brief period was both penetrating and comprehensive.

Up to this time, they had simply been trained in the most elementary aspects of the gospel and its initiatory ordinances. Their past training, either in the schools of the Pharisees as young Galileans or as traveling missionaries with Jesus, would not have prepared them for the burdens that were about to fall upon them immediately after the ascension.

THE APOSTOLIC "SCHOOL OF THE PROPHETS" BEGINS

A major leap in the education of the apostles had taken place only a few days earlier when the apostles had learned that their Beloved Master was the Messiah after all. However, his First Coming had to be in his role as the Redeemer-Messiah to provide redemption for the world. Later he would come as the King-Messiah to rule the world. Intellectually, the apostles had to get all of this in its proper perspective.

---

[22]Matthew 16:13.

When they did, the apostles had the key to an understanding of the fifty-third chapter of Isaiah, which describes the First Coming of the Messiah. What a spiritual and intellectual shock this new knowledge must have brought to them. It began to open the minds of the apostles to a brilliant new vista of understanding. At last they could appreciate why the Savior's earthly mission had been completely opposite from the Davidic Kingship which they had felt certain he would establish.

Based on what the apostles taught and did after the Savior had placed the kingdom in their hands, we can conclude that the training the apostles received during the forty days between the resurrection and the ascension included the following:

THE NEW OFFICERS OF THE CHURCH

FIRST, they learned that the priesthood offices of the new church were quite different from those with which they were familiar in the synagogues and rabbinical schools. As Paul would later explain:

"And he gave some, apostles; and some, prophets; and some, evangelists; and some, pastors and teachers;

"For the perfecting of the saints, for the work of the ministry, for the edifying of the body of Christ:

"Till we all come in the unity of the faith, and of the knowledge of the Son of God, unto a perfect man, unto the measure of the stature of the fullness of Christ."[23]

THE SETTING UP OF CHRISTIAN COMMUNITIES AS "WARDS"

SECOND, they learned that the basic community of Saints would not be a synagogue, but a "ward,"[24] or, as the Bible uses it, an "oversight" or watched-over place.[25]

---

[23]Ephesians 4:11-13.
[24]1 Chronicles 25:8, Nehemiah 12:45.
[25]Hastings, *Dictionary of the Bible*, vol. IV, p. 896.

We should mention that the concept of a "ward" has continued in modern times as a community comprised of around one hundred families.[26]

The ward was greatly admired by the early American Founders as an ideal structure for efficient self-government. Thomas Jefferson wrote:

"These wards...are the vital principle of their governments, [in New England] and have proved themselves the wisest invention ever devised by the wit of man for the perfect exercise of self-government and for its preservation."[27]

The fact that the Lord adopted the word "ward" to describe his modern congregations of approximately one hundred families is further evidence that this is the traditional name for divine community grouping under the Mosaic code. Moses divided the people into family groups of tens, fifties, hundreds, thousands, and so forth.[28] Family groups of tens and fifties were sub-divisions of the community group of a hundred families, or a ward.

EACH WARD WAS TO BE
PRESIDED OVER BY A BISHOP

THIRD. Each community or congregation of the saints was to be presided over by a single bishop, not a ruler with a council of elders as was the case with the synagogues. The word "bishop" comes from the Greek meaning "overseer." Under the apostles, the qualifications for this office were of the highest order. As Paul later wrote:

"A bishop then must be blameless, the husband of one wife, vigilant, sober, of good behaviour, given to hospitality, apt to teach; Not given to wine, no striker [assault and battery], not greedy of filthy lucre; but patient, not a brawler, not covetous; One that ruleth well his own house, having his children in subjection with all gravity; (For if a man know not how to rule his own house, how shall he take care

---

[26] *Enc. Britannica,* 11th ed. under "ward."
[27] *Letters of Thomas Jefferson,* 1399:2.
[28] Deuteronomy 1:15.

of the church of God?) Not a novice, lest being lifted up with pride he fall into the condemnation of the devil. Moreover he must have a good report of them which are without; lest he fall into reproach and the snare of the devil."[29]

With bishops to preside over them, the members of the new church would now have an officer in charge of each Christian community who carried the title taken from the ancient order of the Aaronic priesthood.[30]

THE TWO ORDERS OF PRIESTHOOD ESTABLISHED

FOURTH. The Jews were only acquainted with one order of the priesthood, and that was after the Order of Aaron, with a subdivision called the Levitical Priesthood.[31]

The apostles were now introduced to the higher order, which was named after the great high priest Melchizedek of Old Testament times. This higher order was identified with Christ himself.[32]

The apostles learned that the higher order with its high priests, seventies and elders, was to minister the spiritual affairs of the church,[33] whereas the lower order, the Aaronic Priesthood—with its support quorums of Priests, Teachers, and Deacons—was to minister the temporal affairs of the church.

Any traditional Jew would immediately recognize that the apostles were getting a whole new order of things.

SETTING UP A ZION SOCIETY

FIFTH. Now we come to the hard part. The apostles were carefully tutored on how to set up a Zion society, where everyone not only looked upon his temporal possessions as a heavenly

---

[29]1 Timothy 3:2-7; Titus 1:7-9.

[30]Doctrine and Covenants 107:76. Where no descendant of Aaron is available, a high priest of the Melchizedek Priesthood is called to preside. (Doctrine and Covenants 107:69-71).

[31]See *LDS Dictionary*, under "Levites".

[32]Hebrews 7:15-17.

[33]Doctrine and Covenants 107:18; Hebrews 5:1

stewardship to take care of himself and his family, but also as a means of fulfilling his responsibilities in helping to take care of the needs of others as his circumstances permitted. The ultimate goal was to have "no poor among them."

The best description of how this system worked is found in the book of Acts where it says:

"And the multitude of them that believed were of one heart and of one soul: neither said any of them that ought of the things which he possessed was his own; but they had all things common."[34]

To a modern mind, this last phrase may be misleading. The disciples did not have their property in common. Rather, they had their *problems* in common, and tried to help one another solve them. In the fifth chapter of Acts, Peter explains that each person treated his property as a stewardship for which he was accountable to God. However, each person maintained legal title to his own property. The goal was to develop one's property in accordance with the parable of the talents, and thereby multiply their capacity to help one another.[35]

By pooling the excess property that went beyond their own immediate needs, it was not long before the apostles could say, "Neither was there any among them that lacked."[36]

We will have more to say about this in the next chapter.

BUILDING CHRISTIAN TEMPLES FOR ENDOWMENTS AND OTHER TEMPLE ORDINANCES

SIXTH. The apostles were instructed in the erection of Christian temples where the beautiful endowments and temple ceremonies, which had been lost among the Jews, could be performed.

---

[34]Acts 4:32.
[35]Acts 5:3-4
[36]Acts 4:34.

The conclusion that the apostles provided holy places and received these higher blessings is clearly suggested in a modern revelation. The Lord states that these ordinances and endowments are sacred rites which belong to "my holy house which *my people are ALWAYS commanded to build unto my holy name.*"[37]

Early Christians, after the days of the apostles, stated that the apostles had administered certain sacred rites that had been lost after these men passed away. Several of the early Christian writers refer to these esoteric rites, including Clement, Basil, Cyril, Ambrose, and Chrysostom.[38]

In Dr. John Laurence Von Mosheim's famous *Ecclesiastical History*, he states:

"That many tell us, that the earlier Christians had some sort of secret discipline, that is, [that they] did not communicate to all the same instructions, may be admitted as true....Unquestionably those whom they would bring to Christ were not introduced at once to the high mysteries of religion...but were first only taught such doctrines as mere reason readily admits, till they were able to bear those that are more sublime and difficult."[39]

Professor Yoram Tsafrir, famous archaeologist from the Hebrew University—who played a leading role in the Masada excavations and also supervised the construction of a model city of Jerusalem as it existed at the time of Herod, told this writer that one of his highest priorities is to find the site of a Christian temple. He told me in 1984:

"There is no doubt but that the Christians constructed holy places quite different from those of the Jewish temple builders. When we find a Christian temple, it will be an archaeological treasure."

---

[37]Doctrine and Covenants 124:39 (emphasis added).

[38]Dr. Stephen E. Robinson, *Are Mormons Christians*, Salt Lake City: Bookcraft, 1991, pp. 99-103.

[39]John Laurence Von Mosheim, *Institutes of Ecclesiastical History*, London: Longman, Brown, and Green and Longman, 1841, vol. 1, p. 105.

VICARIOUS ORDINANCES FOR THE DEAD

SEVENTH. The apostles had to be carefully instructed in the rites for loved ones who had passed on without an opportunity to hear the gospel. Undoubtedly, the entire doctrine of vicarious work for the dead was completely new to them. Nevertheless, the scripture verifies that they later saw the beauty of this labor of love for the dead and initiated its practice.

Paul used the ordinances for the dead as an argument for the reality of the resurrection. He said:

"Else what shall they do which are baptized for the dead, if the dead rise not at all? why are they then baptized for the dead?"[40]

Those who argue that these rites do not have to be performed for those who died without the gospel are perplexed by the Savior's words to Nicodemus when he said:

"Verily, verily, I say unto thee, Except a man be born of water and of the Spirit, he cannot enter into the kingdom of God."[41]

God would not be just, if he had not provided a program of vicarious ordinances for those who had never had an opportunity to accept the gospel during mortality.

Furthermore, another scripture says, "The work of justice could not be destroyed; if so, God would cease to be God."[42]

The apostles learned how a just God deals with this problem of their unredeemed dead—those who lived when there was no opportunity while on earth to hear or understand the gospel.

---

[40]1 Corinthians 15:29.
[41]John 3:5.
[42]Alma 42:13,22,25, B. of M.

A GREAT FALLING AWAY WILL OCCUR

EIGHTH. The apostles also had to be told that they were only the caretakers of the church for a short time. They were probably not told just how long it would last, but it turned out that the Church of Jesus Christ did not survive in its purity for even a century.

To a large extent, this contamination was due to the protracted campaign of bitter and vehement persecution by the Roman emperors. Historically, it was strangely ironic that in the fourth century when the emperor Constantine finally decided to reverse the policy of persecution and make Christianity one of the legally recognized religions of Rome, only fragments of the original faith remained. Nevertheless, the Roman Christian church carefully preserved what was left of the sacred scriptures, and these became a great boon to the work of the Lord when the restoration of the gospel commenced in the latter days.

It was a constant hope among the early Christians that the Second Coming would occur in their day. The apostles had to continually invoke the need for patience and tell them:

"Let no man deceive you by any means: for that day shall not come, except there come a falling away first."[43]

And again:

"The Spirit speaketh expressly, that in the latter times some shall depart from the faith, giving heed to seducing spirits, and doctrines of devils."[44]

BUT THERE WOULD BE A GREAT RESTORATION IN THE LATTER DAYS

NINTH. Nevertheless, the apostles were told that there would be a great restitution of all things in the latter days.[45] They knew that

---

[43] 2 Thessalonians 2:3.
[44] 1 Timothy 4:1.
[45] Acts 3:21.

the gospel of the kingdom would be preached to every nation, kindred, tongue, and people before the end came. Jesus had emphasized this prophecy during the early part of his ministry.[46]

It was also important for the apostles to retain in their minds not only the promise of a great restoration in the latter days, but also the prospects of a glorious millennium when Christ would reign for a thousand years. To galvanize these great hopes for the future in the minds of the apostles, we are told that Peter, James and John were allowed to see a vision of the great millennial day while they were on the Mount of Transfiguration with the Savior.[47]

THE APOSTLES RETURN TO JERUSALEM

None of the Gospel writers provides us with a convenient chronology of events during the forty days between Christ's resurrection and the time of ascension. However, we do know that after the weeks of intensive instruction on "the mountain," the apostles returned to Jerusalem, and were told to remain there until they had been endowed with the Holy Ghost.[48]

We are also told that the entire remaining quorum of eleven apostles took up their residence in a large, well-to-do home where the "upper room" was located.[49] And as we have already pointed out, the scripture and attending circumstances seem to indicate very strongly that this was the home of young Mark's parents.[50]

THE APOSTLES ARE INVITED
TO MAKE A FINAL REQUEST

We now know that while Jesus was conferring with his apostles at one of his last meetings, he apparently invited each of them to make a final request before he left them. We know he did this with his disciples in America as well,[51] and we now have a document

---

[46]Matthew 24:14.

[47]Doctrine and Covenants 63:21.

[48]Acts 1:4-5.

[49]Acts 1:13.

[50]Edersheim, *The Life and Times of Jesus the Messiah*, vol. I, p. 545.

[51]3 Nephi, ch. 28., B. of M.

which states that something similar happened with the apostles in Jerusalem.

As we mentioned in Volume One, this document, written by John, indicates that Peter expressed a desire to come speedily to the Savior as soon as his mission was completed.[52] An identical wish was expressed by nine of the disciples in America.[53]

However, during the conference with the apostles in Jerusalem, John the Beloved said:

"Lord, give unto me power over death, that I may live and bring souls unto thee.

"And the Lord said unto me: Verily, verily, I say unto thee, because thou desirest this thou shalt tarry until I come in my glory, and shalt prophesy before nations, kindreds, tongues and people."[54]

Now we have the explanation for a strange passage in the book of John. The apostle says that when Jesus saw that Peter was perturbed by John's request to have power over death and continue in the ministry, the Savior said to Peter:

"If I will that he tarry till I come, what is that to thee? follow thou me.

"Then went this saying abroad among the brethren, that that disciple should not die: yet Jesus said not unto him, He shall not die; but, If I will that he tarry till I come, what is that to thee?"[55]

Actually John, and all individuals who are translated—such as the people of Enoch, the three Nephites, and the people of Melchizedek—must go through the "death" process in order to be transformed into resurrected beings, but when that happens it takes

---

[52]Doctrine and Covenants 7:4.
[53]3 Nephi 28:2, B. of M.
[54]Doctrine and Covenants 7:2-3.
[55]John 21:22-23.

place in the "twinkling of an eye." As Jesus said to the three Nephites who had made the same request as John:

"Ye shall never endure the pains of death; but when I shall come in my glory ye shall be changed in the twinkling of an eye from mortality to immortality; and then shall ye be blessed in the kingdom of my Father.

"And again, ye shall not have pain while ye shall dwell in the flesh, neither sorrow save it be for the sins of the world; and all this will I do because of the thing which ye have desired of me, for ye have desired that ye might bring the souls of men unto me, while the world shall stand."[56]

THE APOSTLES ASK JESUS AN AMAZING QUESTION

On a certain day, the Savior had the apostles meet him on the summit of the Mount of Olives, and then he led them down a short distance toward Bethany.[57]

There is no indication that the apostles had any idea what was about to happen. However, they took advantage of this occasion to ask the Savior a rather astonishing question. They said:

"Lord, wilt thou at *THIS TIME* restore again the kingdom to Israel?"[58]

This is amazing. After all the teaching on the mountain, with the warnings of apostasy, and the promised "restitution of all things" in the latter days, the apostles still hadn't grasped the broad dimensions of God's time line. They still had anxieties to see the glorious kingdom of God immediately established which was spoken of by Daniel.[59] They could hardly wait to see the political kingdoms of the wicked swept away and God's great government established forever. Best of all, there was the Savior's promise that twelve thrones would

---

[56]3 Nephi 28:8-9, B. of M.
[57]Luke 24:50.
[58]Acts 1:6 (emphasis added).
[59]Daniel 2:44.

be provided from which the apostles would judge and govern the twelve tribes of Israel.[60]

So the question the apostles were asking on the mount of ascension was simply, "Is all of that going to happen NOW?"

Jesus did not give them a direct response to their question. Time after time he had tried to describe the signs of the times and the unfolding of the great events of the future, but, like many of us, they longed for an exact time table when all these good things would happen. But this was the one thing Jesus was not allowed to give them. Therefore, he merely said:

"It is not for you to know the times or the seasons, which the Father hath put in his own power."[61]

No doubt they were disappointed, but Jesus comforted them by saying that they would soon have the Holy Ghost to guide them,[62] and he promised it would teach them "all things."[63]

THE APOSTLES RECEIVE THEIR FINAL COMMISSION

Now the Savior was required to leave his beloved friends and disciples. They had a big assignment, but the Savior's task was far more monumental. He had the immediate assignment of introducing the fullness of the gospel to "the other sheep." This included visiting the Israelites in America and making a personal appearance among the famous lost Ten Tribes who as yet had not seen the Savior.[64]

So it was time that the Savior must be about his Father's business. He therefore lifted up his hands and blessed the apostles, after which he said:

---

[60]Matthew 19:28.

[61]Acts 1:7.

[62]Acts 1:8.

[63]John 15:26.

[64]3 Nephi 16:1-2; 17:4, B. of M.

"Go ye into all the world and preach the gospel to every creature. He that believeth and is baptized shall be saved; but he that believeth not shall be damned.

"And these signs shall follow them that believe; In my name shall they cast out devils; they shall speak with new tongues; They shall take up serpents; and if they drink any deadly thing, it shall not hurt them; they shall lay hands on the sick, and they shall recover."[65]

THE ASCENSION

Then a spectacular thing happened:

"And when he had spoken these things, while they beheld, he was taken up; and a cloud received him out of their sight. And while they looked steadfastly toward heaven as he went up, behold, two men stood by them in white apparel; Which also said, Ye men of Galilee, why stand ye gazing up into heaven? this same Jesus, which is taken up from you into heaven, shall so come in like manner as ye have seen him go into heaven."[66]

So there they stood. The great prophetic epoch of the First Coming of Christ was over, and a great new epoch was looming before them. They had their testimonies, they had their training, they had been endowed with divine authority, and they had their great worldwide commission.

As Luke continues their story in the book of Acts, it becomes vividly clear that a great change came over the apostles after they received the outpouring of the Holy Ghost. They went forth like humble young spiritual giants—to set up a Zion society, convert thousands, heal the sick, and even raise the dead.

Everything Jesus had promised them was about to come to pass.

*   *   *   *

---

[65]Mark 16:15-18.
[66]Acts 1:9-11.

TOPICS FOR REFLECTION AND DISCUSSION

1. When the apostles returned from a night of fishing and saw a lone figure on the shore, who was the first apostle to suspect it was Jesus? Why? What did Jesus tell Peter three times?

2. By this time, what new relationship was developing between Jesus and his apostles? Was Jesus encouraging this new appreciation of his exalted status for their benefit or for his own? Where does Matthew say the apostles received their new course of advanced training?

3. Give your definition for each of the officers of the church listed by Paul. Had you ever wondered where the word "ward" came from? About how many families did a "ward" represent? Is that about the same general number we use today?

4. Why was it new to the apostles to have a "bishop" preside over a ward? List five qualities of a bishop mentioned by Paul. Why don't people apply for the job of bishop? Why do you think the general authorities of the church say the office of the bishop is the greatest strength of the church?

5. Has there ever been a time when God's people were able to eliminate poverty? What quality of people does it take to build a Zion society? Under a Zion society do the people have their property "in common" or their problems "in common"? What is the difference?

6. What makes some of the archaeologists at the Hebrew University think the Christians had temples? How do the modern scriptures hint that this was true? Name three ways in which temples would strengthen a Zion society.

7. Did the Lord wait until after the resurrection of Christ to start vicarious ordinances for the dead? In what way would the plan of salvation be "unjust" if it did not provide for vicarious work for the dead?

8. Did the apostles in Christ's day know there was going to be a great falling away? By the time the Roman empire accepted Christianity as an authorized religion, what had happened to the church? What great

contribution did the Roman church make which greatly facilitated the restoration of the gospel in modern times?

9. When Jesus invited his apostles to make a final request, what did Peter say? How many of the Nephite disciples made the same choice? What did John the Beloved say? How many Nephites made the same choice as John? Do translated beings have to go through the "death process" prior to the resurrection? How long will it take?

10. When the apostles returned to Jerusalem, where does the Bible say they stayed? Did they all stay together? When the apostles met Jesus on the Mount of Olives, what question were they still asking? Why is this surprising? What did Jesus commission them to do? After he ascended, what did the two angels say?

* * * *

CHAPTER 46

THE APOSTLES LAUNCH
THE GOSPEL PROGRAM INTO
FULL OPERATION

After the Savior's ascension, the apostles anxiously returned to the home of John Mark's family where they were all staying.[1]

Not only was this house the residence for the apostles, but it also provided accommodation for the Savior's mother and his "brethren," who had now been converted.[2] The capacity of this house is indicated by the fact that on one occasion there were 120 of the Savior's disciples gathered there.[3]

This assembly was an official meeting of the church, and it seems to have been a select gathering of disciples who had some important duties to perform. So Peter stood up and said:

"Men and brethren, this scripture must needs have been fulfilled, which the Holy Ghost by the mouth of David spake before concerning Judas, which was guide to them that took Jesus.

"For he was numbered with us, and had obtained part of this ministry.

"Now this man purchased a field with the reward of iniquity; and falling headlong, he burst asunder in the midst, and all his bowels gushed out...."[4]

---

[1]Acts 1:13; Edersheim, op cit., pp. 484-485.
[2]Acts 1:13-14.
[3]Acts 1:15.
[4]Acts 1:15-18.

Peter then pointed out that David had been inspired by the power of the Holy Ghost, to predict in Psalms, 41:9, that just as David had been betrayed, so would the Savior suffer betrayal. He further stated in Psalms 109:8 that because of this wicked act, the office or bishopric of the traitor must be given to another. This now became the next order of business.

WHO COULD QUALIFY TO REPLACE JUDAS ISCARIOT?

Peter emphasized that they must be extremely careful in selecting a worthy person to replace Judas Iscariot. He said:

"Wherefore of these men which have companied with us all the time that the Lord Jesus went in and out among us, beginning from the baptism of John, unto that same day that he was taken up from us, must one be ordained to be a witness with us of his resurrection."[5]

At this point the names of those who could qualify as special witnesses were considered by the apostles, and they nominated two names to present before the Lord for the final selection. These two men were "Joseph, called Barsabas, who was surnamed Justus, and Matthias."[6]

Now notice how they sought God's guidance in making the final selection. The scripture says:

"And they prayed, and said, Thou, Lord, which knowest the hearts of all men, shew whether of these two thou hast chosen, that he may take part of this ministry and apostleship, from which Judas by transgression fell, that he might go to his own place.

"And they gave forth their lots; and the lot fell upon Matthias; and he was numbered with the eleven apostles."[7]

---

[5]Acts 1:21-22.
[6]Acts 1:23.
[7]Acts 1:25-26.

So now there was a full Quorum of the Twelve once more, and all of these apostles could personally testify concerning the Savior's ministry—beginning with the days of John the Baptist, right up to the day when Jesus "was taken up from us."[8]

This would imply that when the eleven apostles went up to the Mount of Ascension with Jesus, there were a number of other disciples present, including Matthias. Having witnessed all these things, Matthias could now testify boldly of his own personal knowledge right along with the other apostles.

THE DAY OF PENTECOST

It was just ten days after the Savior's ascension that an event transpired in Jerusalem which Christians have been celebrating ever since. It is called the Day of Pentecost.

Actually, the word "pentecost" means the fiftieth day after the Feast of the Passover, and it was a Jewish holiday set aside to celebrate the harvest which came toward the last of May in this region. For the Jews, this was a time of rejoicing and thanksgiving to God for the fruits of the orchard, the vineyard and the field.[9]

The ritual at the temple began with the "presentation of the two loaves," made from the first fruits of the wheat harvest. There was also an offering of two lambs, and these, with the loaves, were "waved" toward the altar as a peace offering to God, and then given to the priests. Sacrifices or burnt offerings were also placed on the altar. These consisted of a young bullock, two rams, and seven lambs, together with a meal (ground grain) and a drink offering, and a young goat for a sin offering.[10]

Because this was a harvest festival, great throngs assembled in Jerusalem to celebrate the harvest, participate in the religious rites and enjoy the social merriment that always accompanied this event.

---

[8]Acts 1:22.
[9]Peloubet's *Bible Dictionary*, under "Pentecost".
[10]Leviticus 23:17-19.

THE APOSTLES RECEIVE THEIR BAPTISM OF FIRE

Luke says that on the Day of Pentecost, the apostles and their immediate followers (previously described as about 120 disciples),[11] were gathered in "one place" and were in "one accord" which was previously described as meaning they were engaged in "prayer and supplication."[12] We later learn that this was about the third hour, or 9 A.M. in the morning.[13]

Then the scripture says:

"And suddenly there came a sound from heaven as of a rushing mighty wind, and it filled all the house where they were sitting.

"And there appeared unto them cloven tongues like as of fire, and it sat upon each of them. And they were all filled with the Holy Ghost, and began to speak with other tongues, as the Spirit gave them utterance."[14]

This same phenomenon occurred at the dedication of the Kirtland Temple in 1836. The record says:

"A noise was heard like the sound of a rushing mighty wind, which filled the temple, and all the congregation simultaneously arose, being moved upon by an invisible power; many began to speak in tongues and prophesy; others saw glorious visions....The people of the neighborhood came running together (hearing the unusual sound within, and seeing a bright light like a pillar of fire resting upon the temple), and were astonished at what was taking place. This continued until the meeting closed at eleven p.m."[15]

On the Day of Pentecost, we do not know where the apostles were meeting, but the place was soon surrounded by a multitude

---

[11]Acts 1:15

[12]Acts 1:14.

[13]Acts 2:15.

[14]Acts 2:2-4.

[15]*History of the Church*, of the Church of Jesus Christ of Latter-day Saints, Salt Lake City: Deseret News, 1904, vol. 2, p. 428.

who came running. We have already mentioned that the Feast of the Harvest always attracted huge throngs of people from all of the Jewish communities throughout the Mediterranean area. Therefore, at this time the scripture says:

"There were dwelling at Jerusalem Jews, devout men, out of every nation under heaven."[16]

Apparently the sound of the mighty wind and perhaps some phenomenon of fire similar to that which would be seen at Kirtland immediately attracted a large throng. So the scripture says:

"The multitude came together, and were confounded, because that every man heard them speak in his own language. And they were all amazed and marvelled, saying one to another, Behold, are not all these which speak Galileans? And how hear we every man in our own tongue, wherein we were born?"[17]

We gain a deeper appreciation of the conglomerate of nations represented in this crowd when we read that this throng included:

"Parthians, and Medes, and Elamites, and the dwellers in Mesopotamia, and in Judaea, and Cappadocia, in Pontus, and Asia, Phrygia, and Pamphylia, in Egypt, and in the parts of Libya about Cyrene, and strangers of Rome, Jews and proselytes, Cretes and Arabians."[18]

These people exclaimed, "we do hear them speak in our tongues the wonderful works of God."[19]

This would suggest that as the crowd began to assemble, the apostles, and perhaps other disciples, went out among the people and began to tell them about the Savior and the gospel. And each man heard the gospel in his own tongue. This could have occurred

---

[16]Acts 2:5.
[17]Acts 2:6-8.
[18]Acts 2:9-11.
[19]Acts 2:11.

through the gift of tongues given to the disciples by the Holy Ghost, or it could have happened through the interpretation of tongues, in which case the disciples would have spoken in Hebrew, but the listeners would have heard it in their own language as the Holy Ghost interpreted it for them in their minds.

The scripture says "all were amazed," but not all were impressed. When some of them heard all this incomprehensible jabbering in foreign tongues, they mocked the Savior's followers and said, "These men are full of new wine."[20]

But the apostle Peter was not going to take that. He situated himself in some prominent place where he could be readily heard and cried out:

"Ye men of Judaea, and all ye that dwell at Jerusalem, be this known unto you, and hearken to my words: For these are not drunken, as ye suppose, seeing it is but the third hour of the day. But this is that which was spoken by the prophet Joel;[21]

"And it shall come to pass in the last days, saith God, I will pour out of my Spirit upon all flesh: and your sons and your daughters shall prophesy, and your young men shall see visions, and your old men shall dream dreams...And I will shew wonders in heaven above, and signs in the earth beneath; blood, and fire, and vapour of smoke."[22]

PETER EXPLAINS WHY THE JEWS
WERE CHOSEN TO CRUCIFY CHRIST

With this as an introduction, Peter felt he had quoted enough scripture to prove that what they were seeing and hearing was a legitimate fulfillment of the words of the prophets. Now Peter had some words of his own to say:

---

[20]Acts 2:13.
[21]Joel 2:28-30.
[22]Acts 2:14-19.

"Ye men of Israel, hear these words; Jesus of Nazareth, a man approved of God among you by miracles and wonders and signs, which God did by him in the midst of you, as ye yourselves also know:

"Him, being delivered by the determinate counsel and foreknowledge of God, ye have taken, and by wicked hands have crucified and slain."[23]

Notice Peter's implication that the crucifixion of Christ was no accident. It was done by the "determinate counsel and foreknowledge of God."

Notice also that Peter was portraying these people as somewhat like Paul, who later stood by and watched as Stephen was stoned. In this same sense, Peter's listeners consented to the crucifixion of the Savior even after they had seen him perform marvelous miracles, wonders and signs.

However, there was one redeeming feature in it all, and that was the fact that they did not know they were consenting to the crucifixion of their Messiah. As Paul later said:

"For had they known it, they would not have crucified the Lord of glory."[24]

This part of Peter's sermon was designed to arouse a sense of guilt in the hearts of these people. Of course, they had thought the crucifixion was a just punishment for blasphemy committed by a man who had falsely claimed he was the Son of God. That is why they had felt justified in doing what they did. But now they were told that Jesus really was the Son of God. He was their Messiah, and they consented to his death.

---

[23]Acts 2:22-23.
[24]1 Corinthians 2:8.

Nevertheless, Peter wanted them to know that their misguided zeal did not destroy the Messiah because God had already raised him up again. Peter said:

"This Jesus hath God raised up, whereof we all are witnesses. Therefore being by the right hand of God exalted, and having received of the Father the promise of the Holy Ghost, he hath shed forth this, which ye now see and hear."[25]

Peter wanted to emphasize that God's confirmation of what he was saying was demonstrated in the heavenly things they had been allowed to "see and hear." There had been a mighty wind, with cloven tongues of fire, and every man had heard the disciples preaching the gospel in their own tongue. This truly had been amazing, and Peter did not want them to miss its significance.

With this as a preface, Peter then told the people what they had just done. He cried out:

"Let all the house of Israel know assuredly, that God hath made that same Jesus, WHOM YE HAVE CRUCIFIED, both Lord and Christ."[26]

This was Peter's first great missionary sermon since the resurrection of the Savior. It must have been accompanied by a powerful endowment of the Holy Spirit for the mind and spirit of every man and woman in this crowd suddenly felt a surge of guilt and remorse. The scripture says:

"When they heard this, they were pricked in their heart, and said unto Peter and to the rest of the apostles, Men and brethren, what shall we do?"[27]

These were the wonderful words Peter wanted to hear. Had he told them what to do without their asking, it would have been too

---

[25]Acts 2:32-33.
[26]Acts 2:36 (emphasis added).
[27]Acts 2:37.

early to be effective. However, they were now begging for an answer, and therefore this great apostolic missionary declared:

"Repent, and be baptized every one of you in the name of Jesus Christ for the remission of sins, and ye shall receive the gift of the Holy Ghost. For the promise is unto you, and to your children, and to all that are afar off, even as many as the Lord our God shall call....

"Save yourselves from this untoward generation."[28]

The impact of this sermon was phenomenal. In that crowd there were no doubt many who had spread palm fronds, cloaks, and flowers in the Savior's path and hailed him as a king just a few weeks earlier as he headed the royal procession from Bethphage to Jerusalem. Later, they had turned against him when he did not fulfill their expectations as a King-Messiah. He not only failed to overthrow the Romans, but he let the Romans crucify him. The word "impostor!" fell from the lips of thousands as they passed up and down the streets of Jerusalem.

Furthermore, in that crowd there may have been many who had shouted at Pilate, "Crucify him! Crucify him!" Indeed, if he was an impostor, he had committed blasphemy, and deserved to die.

However, in spite of all this, Peter was now saying that their misjudgment in consenting to his death had been anticipated by the "determinate counsel and foreknowledge of God." It served the purposes of God to have it happen. And Peter was saying that now they could be forgiven for their part in consenting to the Savior's death if they would sincerely beg God's forgiveness and be baptized.

The response was tremendous. It is rather amazing how quickly the vast throng caught on to the reality of what had happened and how they had inadvertently served the purposes of God in their ignorance. The scripture says:

---

[28]Acts 2:38-40.

"They that gladly received his word were baptized: and the *same day* there were added unto them about three thousand souls."[29]

It is no easy task to baptize three thousand souls in one day, especially with the small body of priesthood holders such as the apostles had available in the beginning. But they did it.

PETER AND JOHN PERFORM A MIRACLE AT THE TEMPLE

Shortly after this great harvest of souls on the Day of Pentecost, Peter and John went up to the temple one morning to pray. It was about 9 A.M.[30]

At that early hour, the crippled beggars were being carried to their various stations along the walls and at the gates to ask for alms. One cripple who was about 40 years old, and a well-known beggar, was being carried to his place near the Gate Beautiful. When he saw Peter and John, he decided to invite the apostles to be his first contributors. So he asked for alms.

"Peter, fastening his eye upon him with John, said, Look on us. And he gave heed unto them, expecting to receive something of them.

"Then Peter said, silver and gold have I none; but such as I have, give I thee: In the name of Jesus Christ of Nazareth rise up and walk.

"And he took him by the right hand, and lifted him up: and immediately his feet and ankle bones received strength."[31]

The feelings of this crippled beggar would be difficult to describe as he stood on his feet and felt the urge to run, skip and jump. And that is exactly what he did. The scripture says:

---

[29]Acts 2:41 (emphasis added).
[30]Acts 3:1.
[31]Acts 3:4-7.

"And he leaping up stood, and walked, and entered with them into the temple, walking and leaping, and praising God."[32]

Of course, they did not enter into the temple proper, but passed through the Gate Beautiful onto the temple esplanade. They would have come immediately into the largest court of the entire temple area. It was referred to as the Court of the Gentiles because anyone could approach the temple within the confines of this outer area.

At the end of the Court of the Gentiles was a beautifully pillared portico extending the full length of the wall on that side. It was called Solomon's porch. As Peter took the healed cripple to this portico, the news rippled through the large crowd circulating around the courtyard that a miracle had been performed.

As the crowd hurried toward them, Peter saw a marvelous opportunity for a powerful missionary sermon.

THE MOST SUCCESSFUL MISSIONARY SERMON IN HISTORY

Peter pointed to the man who had been healed of his crippled condition and said:

"Ye men of Israel, why marvel ye at this? or why look ye so earnestly on us, as though by our power or holiness we had made this man to walk?

"The God of Abraham, and of Isaac, and of Jacob, the God of our fathers, hath glorified his Son Jesus; whom ye delivered up, and denied him in the presence of Pilate, when he was determined to let him go."[33]

Peter was determined to drive spikes into the souls of these listeners so as to prepare them for his message of repentance which would come later. He castigated his listeners in the most severe language saying:

---

[32]Acts 3:8.
[33]Acts 3:12-13.

"Ye denied the Holy One and the Just, and desired a murderer to be granted unto you [Barabbas]; and killed the Prince of life, whom God hath raised from the dead; whereof we are witnesses."[34]

Now he was ready to tell them by what power they had healed the cripple. Peter said:

"Through faith in his [the Savior's] name [God] hath made this man strong, whom ye see and know; yea, the faith which is by him hath given him this perfect soundness in the presence of you all."[35]

The people could not deny that a cripple whom they had all known for many years was strong and well. And then, having made his point, Peter softened his tone to explain why the Father would forgive them if they repented. He said:

"Now brethren, I wot [know] that through ignorance ye did it, as did also your rulers."[36]

The Jews were well aware that God had always made allowances for those who have killed another in ignorance.[37] Peter had just accused them of delivering Jesus to Pilate and allowing a notorious murderer, Barabbas, to go free. He had also accused them of killing Jesus on the assumption that he was a spurious blasphemer, claiming to be the Son of God. Peter had not only pronounced them in error but he had borne witness that Jesus was actually the Son of God and Prince of Life whom the Father had now resurrected in spite of the fact that these Jews had consented to his death.

In his previous speech—the one that converted 3,000—Peter had told the Jews that the slaying of Jesus was by the "determinate counsel and foreknowledge of God." In other words it was required for God's purposes to have his Son become a redemptive sacrifice. Now that it had been accomplished, the Jews could be forgiven for

---

[34]Acts 3:14-15.
[35]Acts 3:16.
[36]Acts 3:17.
[37]Exodus 21:13; Numbers 35:22-25; Deuteronomy 19:4-5.

their part in bringing it about because they had not realized that they were killing their own Messiah.

Peter now launched into that same theme with this great throng at the temple. He said the proof that God needed this atoning sacrifice as part of his divine plan was demonstrated by the fact that:

"God before had shewed by the mouth of all his prophets, that Christ should suffer...."

Then he solemnly added that NOW:

"He hath so fulfilled."[38]

Of course, the rabbinical scholars had considered these prophetic writings to be a myth because they were convinced that the Jews would never kill their own Messiah. Such an idea seemed ridiculous. This is why they had done their best to purge the scriptures of all such prophecies. Consequently, by the time Jesus actually began his ministry, "no man" among the Jews knew about his First Coming, nor about the Savior's role as a sacrificial Redeemer.[39]

As we have mentioned earlier, they didn't even know a redeemer was necessary. They had thought Jesus was claiming to be the King-Messiah who would set up the kingdom promised by Daniel,[40] and when he failed to fulfill this role, they killed him as an impostor.

But Peter wanted them to know that everything God had wanted accomplished was now done, and that a plan had been provided by which they could gain forgiveness for that which they did in ignorance. In fact, he said:

---

[38]Acts 3:18.
[39]Doctrine and Covenants 133:66.
[40]Daniel 2:44.

"Ye are the children of the prophets, and of the covenant which God made with our fathers, saying unto Abraham, And in thy seed shall all the kindreds of the earth be blessed."[41]

This had reference to the redemption that would be wrought by the Savior who was of the seed of Abraham through David.[42]

Peter then emphasized how blessed they were because:

"Unto you *first,* God having raised up his Son Jesus, sent him to bless you, in turning away every one of you from his iniquities."[43]

Never in all scriptural history has a missionary sermon had a greater impact on a crowd than this one. Luke says:

"Many of them which heard the word believed; and the number of the MEN was about *five thousand.*"[44]

These, with their families, probably added to the church a total of twelve to fifteen thousand. And there were already 3,000 baptized the week before who, with their wives and children, probably constituted at least 10,000. So altogether, this would mean that the congregation of Christian Jews in Jerusalem had suddenly grown into a total of twenty to twenty-five thousand within a few weeks after the Savior's resurrection!

LAYING THE FOUNDATION FOR A ZION SOCIETY

It would appear that while Jesus was instructing his apostles during the forty days following the resurrection, he taught them the fundamental requirements for the setting up of a Zion society. This is indicated by the fact that as soon as the apostles had a substantial body of converts, they immediately began teaching them the precepts and practices designed to eliminate both poverty and crime.

---

[41]Acts 3:25.

[42]Matthew 1:1.

[43]Acts 3:26 (emphasis added).

[44]Acts 4:4 (emphasis added).

But there were major challenges.

The Jews, by nature, have strong personalities. However, they also have an inborn sense of loyalty and brotherhood when they are united in a cause.

Among the vast throng of new Jewish converts these two features congealed together to form a harmonious balance which the apostles gradually molded into the foundation for a whole new type of society. The Jewish competitive spirit turned into a cooperative spirit. The passion for possessions turned into a penchant for sharing. Pride and independence melted into a rich mixture of compassion, brotherly love, and concern.

Luke tells us:

"They continued steadfastly in the apostles' doctrine and fellowship....And all that believed were together, and had all things common."[45]

As a prophet in America told his people much earlier:

"And after ye have obtained a hope in Christ, ye shall obtain riches, if ye seek them; and ye will seek them for the intent to do good—to clothe the naked, and to feed the hungry, and to liberate the captive, and administer relief to the sick and the afflicted."[46]

This is the basic formula for a Zion culture under the principle of "stewardships" as God designed it. Luke continues to describe its development among the Jews:

"And they sold their [excess] possessions and goods, and parted them to all men, as every man had need. And they continued daily with one accord in the temple...praising God and having favour with

---

[45]Acts 2:42-44.
[46]Jacob 2:19, B. of M.

all the people. And the Lord added to the church daily such as should be saved."[47]

This remarkable community of the "pure in heart"[48] soon produced some phenomenal results. Luke describes their supreme achievement in setting up a society in which poverty had been eliminated, and, from all appearances, crime as well. He says:

"Neither was there ANY AMONG THEM THAT LACKED: for as many [as] were possessors of lands or houses sold them, and brought the prices of the things that were sold...and distribution was made unto every man according as he had need."[49]

Of course, each person was expected to maintain his own stewardship "as he had need," so it is assumed that those houses and lands that were sold were in the form of accumulated wealth that could be liquidated for the sake of the poor.

This system worked as long as the people were righteous and were allowed to live together as peaceful communities, but when the Christians began to be driven and persecuted by the Romans, it became impossible to maintain its original design.

A SIMILAR SYSTEM IS SET UP AMONG THE CHRISTIANS IN AMERICA

The Savior set up a similar system among the righteous Israelites in America a short time later, and it continued in its purity for several generations. After that it continued among the American natives, either in partial practice or as a beautiful memory of an earlier "golden age" or "mother culture" clear down to the time when the Spaniards arrived in 1492.[50]

Here is a description of the Zion society in early America:

---

[47]Acts 2:45-47.
[48]Doctrine and Covenants 97:21.
[49]Acts 4:34-35 (emphasis added).
[50] Milton R. Hunter, *Christ in America*, Salt Lake City: Deseret Book Company, 1959, vol. 2, p. 88.

"There was no contention in the land, because of the love of God which did dwell in the hearts of the people. And there were no envyings, nor strifes, nor tumults, nor whoredoms, nor lyings, nor murders, nor any manner of lasciviousness; and surely there could not be a happier people among all the people who had been created by the hand of God. There were no robbers, nor murderers, neither were there Lamanites, nor any manner of ites; but they were in one, the children of Christ, and heirs to the kingdom of God."[51]

Most of the major tribes in Central and South America—even in Hawaii—cherished the tradition of a great golden age under the bearded "fair god," who was known among the Aztecs and Toltecs as Quetzalcoatl.[52] According to the tradition, the "fair god" was supposed to return some day. This is why the Spanish were mistaken for Quetzalcoatl and his entourage when they first invaded Mexico and South America.[53]

This greatly facilitated the conquest of what is now called Latin America. The Hawaiians who had originated from the American mainland were also expecting the return of the fair god whom they called "Lono," and mistook Captain James Cook for their long-awaited "Lono" when he discovered the Hawaiian Islands in 1778.[54]

In summation, we might mention that the scriptures speak of six different societies which succeeded in making this marvelous system of brotherhood function successfully—politically, socially and economically.

The first one was Enoch.[55] The second was the City of Salem under Melchizedek.[56] And then came the order set up by the

---

[51]4 Nephi 1:15-17, B. of M.

[52]Hunter, *Christ in America*, p. 17 ff.

[53]Milton R. Hunter, et al., *Ancient America and the Book of Mormon*, Oakland, California: Kolob Book Company, 1950, pp. 195-222.

[54]Rex and Thea Rienits, *The Voyages of Captain Cook*, London: The Hamlyin Publishing Group, 1968, pp. 137-139.

[55]Moses 7:18, P. of G. P.

[56]JST or Inspired Version Genesis 14:33-36.

apostles of Christ.[57] There were also three Zion societies in America—the first under King Benjamin,[58] the second under Alma,[59] and the third under the prophet Nephi IV.[60]

THE SAVIOR'S PERCEPTION OF THE JEWS

By this time Peter's maturity in the gospel undoubtedly allowed him to appreciate how Jesus perceived this remnant of Israel, called the Jews.

It is apparent that Jesus loved the Jews. They were his own people. They were among his most loyal supporters during the war in heaven, and were among those referred to as "Israel" or "soldiers of God."[61] They were called "the Lord's portion."[62] Jesus selected them in the pre-earth life to be the ones who would be set up so they could help him get through the ordeal of the crucifixion without jeopardizing their own salvation.[63]

As this great human drama unfolds, we see the Jews through the Savior's eyes. The Jews were chosen to lay the foundation for Christianity in the meridian of time. All of the original twelve apostles were Jews, as were the seventy. The first massive conversion to the Church of Christ were Jews. The first Christian program to eliminate poverty and crime was set up among the Jews. The first messengers who went forth to the world-wide field of missionary labor to spread the message of Christian salvation were Jews.

And the first Christian martyrs were Jews.[64]

Peter could now see that the Jewish people had a glorious opportunity lying directly before them. They could recognize the

---

[57]Acts 4:32.
[58]Mosiah 2:13-14, 4:13-16, B. of M.
[59]Alma 1:26-31, B. of M.
[60]4 Nephi 1:2-3, B. of M.
[61]Deuteronomy 32:7-8; Revelations 12:11.
[62]Deuteronomy 32:7.
[63]Acts 3:17.
[64]Acts: 7:58-59; Acts 12:2.

mistake they had made, and accept the Savior's invitation to repent and be baptized so they could be forgiven.

It is astonishing how quickly several thousand Jews, as they heard Peter's sermon, recognized Jesus as THEIR Messiah and saw where they had played a part in helping Jesus get through his terrible ordeal of providing a redemptive sacrifice for all mankind.

PETER AND JOHN ARE ARRESTED

The same day that Peter's great sermon converted 5,000 men, the high priests and rulers feverishly gathered together to see how they might halt this sudden expansion of those who believed in Jesus. These rulers were Sadducees, and they were soon joined by many of their immediate kindred. It says they were:

"...grieved that they [Peter and John] taught the people, and preached through Jesus the resurrection of the dead."[65]

The idea of the resurrection was very offensive to the Sadducees, who were the most apostate of all the Jews. Not only did they denounce the possibility of the resurrection, but neither did they believe in spirits, angels, or immortality.[66]

These rulers arrested Peter and John just as the chief of the apostles was finishing his great speech. The two apostles were then put "in hold" until the next day because it was then "eventide."[67]

If all the facts were known, we might learn that while the two apostles were being held, all of their brethren were busy throughout the night baptizing as quickly as possible the five thousand men who had been converted by Peter's sermon. The wives and children over eight could be baptized later.[68]

---

[65]Acts 4:2.
[66]Hastings *Bible Dictionary*, vol. 4, p. 351.
[67]Acts 4:3.
[68]Doctrine and Covenants 68:27; JST Genesis 17:11.

THE PRINCIPAL CONSPIRATORS WHO HAD JESUS SLAIN NOW GET TO HEAR THE TESTIMONY OF PETER AND JOHN

When Peter and John were hauled in before the rulers the next morning, the high priests could not have asked Peter a more gratifying question than the one they immediately hurled at him. They said:

"By what power, or by what name, have ye done this?"[69]

These proud rulers of the Sanhedrin considered these two fishermen from Galilee as little more than rustic nobodies. Therefore their question was designed to humble and embarrass them. But Peter was suddenly endowed by the power of the Holy Ghost and he therefore spoke up boldly as one having authority. He said:

"If we this day be examined [for] the good deed done to the impotent man, [and as to the] means he was made whole, be it known unto you all, and to all the people of Israel, that by the name of Jesus Christ of Nazareth, whom ye crucified, whom God raised from the dead, even by him doth this man stand here before you whole."[70]

We immediately realize that these high priests and rulers must have brought in the beggar whom the apostles were said to have healed. For the rulers, this turned out to be a serious strategical error. The healed cripple became the number one exhibit for the apostles.

We also note that in a single sentence, Peter had made out a bill of particulars against Annas, Caiaphas, and all their proud relatives. He had accused them directly of arranging to have Jesus crucified, and now flung into their teeth the bold declaration that God had raised Jesus from the dead, and that it was by his power, and in his name, that the crippled man who stood before them had been healed.

---

[69]Acts 4:7.
[70]Acts 4:9-10.

Then he undermined their case further with a passage of scripture that made them look like perfidious traitors to the whole tribe of Judah. Peter said that this Jesus, whom they had crucified:

"...is the stone [mentioned in Psalms 118:22] which was set at naught of YOU BUILDERS, which is become the head of the corner."[71]

What is even more important, Peter said:

"Neither is there salvation in any other: for there is none other name under heaven given among men, whereby we must be saved."[72]

These rulers thought their troubles were over when they crucified Jesus, but now he was more threatening to them than he had been before. What was even worse, here was this former cripple standing before them as an irrefutable testimony that these men had some kind of power. So they gathered by themselves and said:

"What shall we do to these men? for that indeed a notable miracle hath been done by them is manifest to all them that dwell in Jerusalem, and we cannot deny it."[73]

They finally decided to warn Peter and John that they must never mention the name of Jesus again or they would be punished. Peter replied:

"Whether it be right in the sight of God to hearken unto you more than unto God, judge ye. For we cannot but speak the things which we have seen and heard."[74]

The Sadducee rulers were totally baffled. All they could do was reiterate their warning and turn them loose.

---

[71]Acts 4:11 (emphasis added).

[72]Acts 4:12.

[73]Acts 4:16.

[74]Acts 4:19-20.

When the apostles reported back to the members of the church who were anxiously waiting for them, there was joyful acclamation toward heaven like a Hosannah shout. They all united in a prayer of thanksgiving and petitioned the Father to bless them in their determination to now go forth and preach the gospel to every nation, kindred, tongue and people.

Suddenly, there was a rumbling in the bowels of the earth and the whole land seemed to shake. It was as though the voice of God was in that terrestrial manifestation, saying:

"Well done, my good and faithful servants. Well done!"[75]

*   *   *   *

TOPICS FOR REFLECTION AND DISCUSSION

1. Where were the apostles residing after the ascension of Jesus? Who was there with Mary? What had apparently happened to the Savior's "brethren"? Who was selected by the apostles to replace Judas Iscariot?

2. What was the Jewish Feast of the Pentecost? How long was it after the Feast of the Passover? Why were there so many Jews from foreign countries present? Describe what it was like when the apostles received their baptism of fire. What gifts did they receive?

3. What did Peter mean when he said that Jesus had been delivered into the hands of the Jews to be crucified by the "determinate counsel and foreknowledge of God"? Did Jesus choose to be slain by his own people or was that accidental? Did this exclude the Jews from later being baptized and gaining a remission of their sins?

4. Why could the Jews be forgiven even though they had consented to the Savior's death? As a result of this sermon by Peter, how many

---

[75]Acts 4:31.

were baptized "that day"? What well-known person did Peter and John heal at the temple? What was the reaction of the people? Why did Peter think this was an excellent time to deliver another missionary sermon? In what way was it similar to his first missionary sermon?

5. How many were converted? Did this get Peter and John into trouble with Annas and Caiaphas and their immediate relatives? To which sect did these rulers belong? What were their basic beliefs? What message was Peter preaching that offended them? When did Jesus indicate that Peter would falter in his faith and have to be reconverted? What did Jesus say Peter should do after his reconversion?[76]

6. When do we think the apostles were first told about a Zion Society, and how to set one up? About how soon after Christ's ascension did they undertake to prepare the church for this new type of society? What elements of the Jewish personality had to be molded to accommodate this new formula for happy living?

7. What is the principle of "stewardships"? Why did Jacob, an American prophet, encourage the acquisition of riches? But what did he say should be done first? Under the stewardship principle, did the members sell all their property or just their excess property beyond what they needed to support themselves?

8. Did the stewardship principle eliminate poverty? Did it tend to eliminate crime?

9. At the trial of Peter and John, whom did the rulers bring into the hearing who turned out to be a witness in favor of Peter and John? At the end of the hearing, why did the rulers admit there was nothing they could do to Peter and John?

---

[76]Luke 22:32.

10. What did Peter and John say when the rulers threatened to punish them if they ever mentioned the name of Jesus again? What was the response of the members of the church when Peter and John came back to report? When they all joined in a great prayer, what did they seek from the Lord? What seemed to confirm their petition in a very affirmative, positive manner?

*   *   *   *

THE PAST PORTENDS THE FUTURE

History now requires that we pause at this juncture of the New Testament record.

All that directly relates to the days of the living Christ has now been told.

After Jesus completed his ministry and surrendered himself to provide the redemptive sacrifice for all mankind, we see that he established a truly Messianic kingdom among the Jews.

The apostles were able to set up a Zion society similar to that of Enoch,[1] and they demonstrated that if the people were not persecuted or molested they could eliminate poverty and provide a righteous people with happiness, prosperity and peace.

Of course, by that time Jesus had ministered to the Nephite Christians in America, and had set up a kingdom identical with that which had been established among the Jews.[2] He had also visited the Lost Ten Tribes of Israel, and ministered the Gospel to them.[3]

As for the apostles, they launched forth to preach the gospel to all the nations of the world. Almost immediately they were performing marvelous miracles. Peter was able to raise a venerable and much loved woman from the dead.[4] Then he received a vision

---

[1]Acts 2:44-45; 4:32.
[2]4 Nephi 1:2-3, B. of M.
[3]3 Nephi 17:4, B. of M.
[4]Acts 9:36-41.

which directed him to open the ministry for the preaching of the gospel to the Gentiles.[5]

So there are hundreds of interesting and sometimes amazing events belonging to the remainder of the New Testament account and the centuries that followed.

There was the ministry and martyrdom of Stephen.

Then there was the ministry and martyrdom of Peter, head of the apostles.

There was the conversion, ministry and martyrdom of Paul the great apostle to the Gentiles.

And there were also many exciting events in the life of John the Beloved who asked to continue in the Savior's ministry and was therefore translated so he could do so.

The early apostolic era was immediately followed by three hundred years of deadly persecution of the Christians by the Romans.

Then the Romans adopted Christianity as their own official religion.

Thus the wheel of history turned. All of these events were highlights in the human drama that might be called, "The Fifth Thousand Years."

But it was only a prelude for the birth of the reformation and the opening scenes of what Peter called "the times of restitution of all things."

The apostles knew that in the latter days the heavens would be opened as they were in the days of Jesus and there would be a flood of new revelations from God. They also knew that great spiritual leaders would be raised up to prepare the world for the second

---

[5]Acts 10:15, 34-35.

coming of Christ. They knew it would be an hour of triumph for the Lord and the beginning of a great Millennial hope for all mankind.

When Jesus was on the Mount of Olives, he unfolded to his apostles the highlights of history leading up to the time when the Gospel of the Kingdom would be restored and preached to every nation, kindred, tongue and people. Matthew recorded the more important things the Savior described and put them in the 24th chapter of his gospel writings.

The most animating and impelling reality in all of this is the fact that right at this moment we are in the midst of seeing those predicted events transpire.

APPENDIX A

THE SAVIOR'S ADVICE TO THE JEWS: ONCE THE CATACLYSM BEGINS—DO NOT LOOK BACK

Jesus knew that once the terrible destruction began in Israel, there would be no hope for the Jews in Palestine until the latter days. He had spoken of the holocaust that would descend on their beloved promised land in 70 A.D. He knew it would disperse the Jewish people to the four corners of the earth. His advice to them was to look ahead and build something anew. There was no hope in what had been, and when it was the will of the Lord to have them return to their homeland, they would build something entirely different.

Jesus had these events in mind as he spoke to his apostles on the Mount of Olives. Since these tragic events would begin to transpire within the lifetime of that generation of Jews, the Savior said:

"When you, therefore, shall see the abomination of desolation, spoken of by Daniel the prophet, concerning the destruction of Jerusalem, then you shall stand in the holy place; whoso readeth let him understand."[1]

The "holy place" would be wherever God's leaders told the people to assemble. He knew the apostles would be able to tell the believers where their holy place would be.

---

[1] JST Matthew 24:12.

"Then let them who are in Judea flee into the mountains; Let him who is on the housetop flee, and not return to take anything out of his house; neither let him who is in the field return back to take his clothes."[2]

Jesus gave the Jews the same advice the angel gave to Lot and his family when they were fleeing from Sodom and Gomorrah. The Lord's messenger had said:

"Escape for thy life; look not behind thee, neither stay thou in all the plain; escape to the mountain, lest thou be consumed."[3]

As Lot and his family were fleeing from these wicked cities, there was a sudden sound of thunderous explosions, followed by the shaking of the earth and the roar of the consuming conflagration. The scripture says:

"The Lord rained upon Sodom and Gomorrah brimstone and fire...and he overthrew those cities...and all the inhabitants of the cities, and that which grew upon the ground."[4]

It spite of the warning of the angel, it is readily understood why Lot's wife looked back. This had been her home, and she had left everything behind. In sorrow she turned for one last look. But she paid a high price. The scripture says:

"His wife looked back from behind him, and she became a pillar of salt."[5]

If ever a people had been given a historical example of why they should obey the Lord when he said, "Do not look back," it was the Jews.

---

[2]JST Matthew 24:13-15.
[3]Genesis 19:17.
[4]Genesis 19:24-25.
[5]Genesis 19:26.

Jesus described to his apostles how terrible the coming devastation of the Jews would be. He said:

"In those days, shall be great tribulation on the Jews, and upon the inhabitants of Jerusalem, such as was not before sent upon Israel, of God, since the beginning of their kingdom until this time; no, nor ever shall be sent again upon Israel."[6]

We are now so far removed from the cataclysm and loss of life connected with the fall of Jerusalem that it is difficult to realize that there never was and never will be an affliction of the Jews as terrible as that one. That was their worst holocaust.

As we have already pointed out, the destruction of Jerusalem came about as a result of the people believing in false prophets and false Christs who said it was time to overthrow the Romans.

But even after the catastrophe in 70 A.D., the Jewish people could not resist looking back. Jesus predicted what would happen when they did. He said:

"And again, after the tribulation of those days which shall come upon Jerusalem, if any man shall say unto you, Lo, here is Christ, or there, believe him not; for in those days [after the fall of Jerusalem] there shall also arise false Christs, and false prophets, and shall show great signs and wonders, insomuch, that, if possible, they shall deceive the very elect, who are the elect according to the covenant."[7]

SIMON BAR KOKHBA—THE FALSE MESSIAH WHO LOOKED LIKE THE REAL THING

The most destructive and deceptive of all these false Messiahs was one which came along about sixty years after the fall of Jerusalem.

---

[6]JST Matthew 24:18.
[7]JST Matthew 24:22-23.

His name was Simeon bar Kosiba who became known in history as Simon Bar Kokhba (son of the star). At first, he looked like the real thing. By fomenting agitation and acts of sabotage, a tidal wave of support swept over the Jewish people throughout the western world. Even R. Akiba or Akiva, the highest rabbinical authority in the land, sent out the message: "This is the King Messiah!"[8]

Historians point out that the Jews had become extremely vulnerable to the claims of these religious charlatans because their rabbinical schools had abandoned the idea of the coming of a divine Messiah, and were teaching that when their Messiah came, he would be a great political, military leader—a great warrior—who would overthrow the enemies of the Jews.[9]

AT FIRST, SIMON BAR KOKHBA WAS AMAZINGLY SUCCESSFUL

If the Jews wanted a King Messiah, Simon Bar Kokhba seemed to have the credentials. In short order he drove the Romans completely out of Israel and set up a new provisional government. The 22nd Roman Legion was sent up from Egypt, but it was annihilated. All the legions from Syria were defeated. Finally, twelve legions were mobilized from all over the Roman empire. One of these even came down from far-away Britain.

As the legions pressed forward step by step, hundreds of thousands of Jews were slain and other thousands were captured. As had happened earlier under Titus, these captive Jews were consigned to the mines, became slaves—chained to the galleys—or were slain by famished wild beasts or the gladiators in the Roman circuses. By 135 A.D. the Jewish rebellion had collapsed, and one of the last to die was Simon Bar Kokhba.[10]

As Jesus had warned, "Don't look back!" It would be many centuries before the Jews would occupy their homeland again.

---

[8]Shmuel Safrai, *Israel History Until 1880*, Jerusalem: 1973, Keter Publishing House, 1972, p.147.
[9]Based on the writer's conversation with Rabbi Shlomo Goren, Chief Rabbi of Israel.
[10]Ibid. p. 148.

WARS AND RUMORS OF WARS

Jesus knew the task of the Jews for the next several centuries would be to simply survive, and survive in a world devastated by the convulsions of war. It was to be an endurance contest stretched out over nearly 2,000 years. Nevertheless, there was to be a reward. In the end, they would be among God's choicest people, and have the genius and compassion to bless the Father's children around the globe.

Meanwhile, Isaiah must be their model of endurance. He said "I will set my face like a flint, and I know that I shall not be ashamed."[11] To help gird up the strength of the Jews for the long haul, Jesus spoke of their early tribulations, and said:

"All these are the *beginning* of sorrows!"[12]

During the following centuries of tribulations, the Jews found that often the only relief would come through flight. As a result, strong Jewish colonies gradually developed in Babylon, India, the ghettos of Europe, and even in faraway China. When Marco Polo went with his father to eastern China in 1274 A.D., he was astonished to find Jews among the Chinese.

THE SIX GREAT EPOCHS OF JEWISH HISTORY

In tracing the writings of Jewish scholars, we find that the Jews have passed through at least six distinct historical periods, but with the best one yet to come.

Although some of these elements of the Jewish chronicle have already been mentioned, it is helpful to see a summary of the Jewish narrative through the eyes of their own historians.

---

[11]Isaiah 50:7.

[12]Matthew 24:8 (emphasis added).

These six great epochs are skillfully described by Dr. Bezalel Porten, Menahem Stern, and Haim Hirschberg in the *History of Israel Until 1880*.[13]

The following sketches summarize their description of each period:

I. THE ROMAN PERIOD OF 63 B.C. TO 633 A.D.

The famous Roman general named Pompey conquered Palestine in 63 B.C. and, after killing 5,000 Jews at Jerusalem, firmly planted the Roman Eagles on Mount Zion.

When Jesus was born, King Herod was on the throne by the grace of Rome, and when Jesus died, Pilate was the Roman governor.

As we have already seen, the era immediately following the ministry of the Savior was highlighted by the destruction of Jerusalem (including Herod's beautiful temple) in 70 A.D., and this was followed by a period of continuous persecution which led to the *Diaspora*, or dispersion of the Jews to many different parts of the world.

II. THE ARAB PERIOD OF 634 TO 1099 A.D.

One of the most influential personalities in all human history was Muhammad or Mohammed, who rose up in Mecca and proclaimed himself a prophet in the early part of the seventh century. He established the Islam religion which means "submission unto God." He taught that there is only one God, Allah, and that his disciples must abandon the many gods which the Arabs were then worshiping. He attributed his teachings to Adam, Abraham, Moses and Jesus. As part of the Islamic faith, Muhammad launched a vast social and religious reform in the dissolute pattern of life among the wild tribes of the Arab people.

When Muhammad died in 632 A.D., his domain extended over nearly all of the Arabian peninsula. Then one of his most devoted

---

[13] *History of Israel*, Keter Books, 1973.

disciples, Abu Baker, took over as *Caliph* and by 661 A.D. the Muslims had conquered Egypt, Iraq, Israel, Jordan, Lebanon, and Syria. They set up their capital in Damascus and later spread over most of the territory of the old Babylonian-Persian empires.

While all of this was taking place, the Jews were considered "a people of the book" (God's book of covenant people) by the Muslims, and during the first fifty years the Jews prospered under the Arabs. Then, as new rulers arose, there developed a severe antagonism toward all non-Muslims, including the Jews. Bitter persecutions ensued. To distinguish the Jews from their look-alike Arab cousins of the tribe of Esau, the Jews were required to wear identifying dress such as yellow turbans. Christians were required to wear blue.

All non-Muslims were required to pay extravagant land taxes, and this ultimately compelled the Jews to give up their farms and move to the cities where they could develop new occupations in order to survive. Dyeing and tanning became a major occupation of the Jews, while others became peddlers, small tradesmen, or developed the skill required for blowing glass.

III. THE CRUSADER PERIOD OF 1099 TO 1291

In 1095 Pope Urban II issued an appeal to the Christian kings to rescue the Holy Land, especially Jerusalem, from the Arabs. A mob of peasant crusaders were the first to set out. As they passed through southern Germany, Hungary, and the Balkans, they made war on every Jewish settlement that lay in their path. This genocidal destruction of whole Jewish communities was excused by these renegade Christians on the ground that the Jews were "Christ-killers." However, all this pillaging and slaughter of the Jews came to a halt when the Turks intervened and annihilated the First Crusade before it ever reached the Holy Land.

Two years later an army of Christian knights invaded the Holy Land, captured Jerusalem, and butchered between 20,000 and 30,000 people. Among these were many Jews who had recently restored the southwest section of Jerusalem with homes and synagogues. The Crusaders herded them into their various synagogues, and then set fire to the buildings. This resulted in the Jews concentrating in the coastal cities and setting up the strongest possible defenses. But the Crusaders maintained a continuous assault on these cities and after ten years they had conquered them.

Eventually, the Crusades failed. After years of extended campaigns, the kings of France and England made war on each other so that the support for the Crusaders virtually faded into oblivion. Under these circumstances, the Muslims in Egypt, called the Mamelukes, saw their opportunity, and began their assault on the Crusader strongholds. By 1291 the Crusaders knew they were finished. They gathered their tattered remnants, abandoned the field, and set out for home.

IV. The MAMELUKE PERIOD OF 1291 TO 1516

Originally the Mamelukes were Turkish prisoners who were captured by the invading Mongolians and sold as slaves to the sultan of Egypt. The Sultan had them trained as soldiers, and because of their diligence they were gradually promoted to high government positions. In 1250 the Mamelukes seized control of Egypt and ruled that country as a Muslim state for 250 years.

However, with the Crusaders gone and the Mamelukes in charge of the Middle East, the mood of the whole region dwindled into a listless existence of casual survival. The policies of the Mamelukes were particularly destructive to the economy of Palestine, where a few communities of Jews still remained. To discourage the Crusaders from returning, the Mamelukes methodically destroyed the coastal cities, and thereby eliminating the principal channels of trade along the eastern Mediterranean where many of the Jews had been making a meager living.

By 1488, the entire city of Jerusalem had only 4,000 households and among these were 70 struggling Jewish families. The Jews were among the most poverty stricken in the city because the Muslim rulers barred them from any realistic opportunity to earn a livelihood. The more ambitious Jews had moved to Egypt, Syria, or southern Europe, leaving only a handful of families in Jerusalem.

Meanwhile, a golden age for Jews had developed on the Iberian or Spanish peninsula where the Moors had developed a very advanced state of civilization and had provided the Jews with a haven of tolerance and prosperity. In fact, for a period of several centuries, the Moors allowed the Jews to develop one of the foremost intellectual and progressive communities that existed among the Jews anywhere in the world.

The Moors were originally rather primitive desert tribesmen of northwest Africa. However, when they became Muslims, the Moors joined the Arabs in conquering much of Spain in the 700s. Later, the Moors lost much of their territory in the 1200s. In 1492 they were defeated at the battle of Grenada by Ferdinand and Isabella, and were driven from the Spanish Peninsula altogether.

It is interesting that the Jews were also driven out of Spain along with the Moors, and many Jews settled in areas where Arab influence assured them hospitality and protection. It was one of those rare occasions when the tribe of Jacob and the tribe of Esau treated one another like cousins.

V. THE OTTOMAN TURKS OF 1516 TO 1913

The Turks, like the Moors, were Muslims but not Arabs. They took control of the Muslim world as the Mamelukes lost their grip on their vast holdings by pursuing conquests too far away from their logistical base of supplies.

Once the Ottoman Turks had taken over, they ruled the Muslim world with some of the most ruthless and capricious tactics in Muslim history. The Jews suffered right along with the rest of the population. At the height of their power, the Ottoman sultans had conquered Hungary, North Africa, Palestine and the eastern side of the Red Sea down to Yemen.

Constantinople, the capital of the old Byzantine empire, was conquered by the Ottoman Turks in 1453, and the name of the city was changed to Istanbul. It then became the capital of Turkey. I have visited the sultan's palaces in Istanbul where 10,000 members of the ruling class were fed by the sultan three times a day.

Probably nowhere in the world will one see such a display of huge diamonds, pearls, rubies, golden thrones, and extravagant wealth than is exhibited for the tourists in these palaces.

Outside the palace is the large flat stone where one could see—in the days of the sultans—the heads of those who had displeased the sultan during the previous week.

When World War I broke out in 1914, the Turkish sultan signed on with the German kaiser. When they lost the war, the whole Turkish empire, with all its Muslim holdings, disintegrated.

The end of World War I also marked the beginning of a whole new epoch for the Jews.

VI. THE JEWISH TRAIL OF TEARS FROM THE *PROTOCOLS* TO THE "HOLOCAUST"

Even before World War I, a major problem had developed for the Jews when a document was published which claimed to be the secret plans of the Jews to take over the world.

It was called *The Protocols of the Elders of Zion* and it contained many lurid passages of how the Jews would gradually starve, manipulate and intimidate the non-Jews until they gained control of every nation on earth.

It turned out that the document had been written by an agent of the Czar of Russia while he was serving in France. His purpose was to justify the confiscation of the estates of wealthy Jews in Russia. Originally, the document claimed the conspiracy was between the Jews and the Masons, but by 1905—when it was first widely published in Europe—the plans for a world takeover were attributed exclusively to the Jews.

Even after the courts in Switzerland had completed an investigation and pronounced the *Protocols* a complete fraud, there were strong anti-semitic groups all over Europe and America that continued to use this spurious publication to promote a militant hostility toward the Jews.

This became a major political issue in Germany when Hitler came to power in 1933. He called for the "physical extermination of the Jews" as "the final solution." Probably the best definitive history of this period is *The Course of Modern Jewish History,*[14] by Dr. Howard M. Sacchar, which says:

"April 4, [1933, a month after Hitler took over] the new Civil Service law barred Jews from all areas of public service."[15]

This removed the Jews from all the professions, the military, and government service. Soon after, all Jewish children were placed in segregated schools for indoctrination. Jews fled in all directions, taking what they could with them. By 1938, Hitler had confiscated all the wealth of the Jews by authority of the Reichstag. Then he abandoned "legal" action and instructed Joseph Paul Goebbels, the Nazi Propaganda minister, to announce that the Jews were part of a "conspiracy," and that violent action would follow.

Dr. Sacchar describes what the record shows:

"November 9 and 10 [1938] the Nazis conducted a nation-wide Pogrom [violent persecution of the Jews]. Nearly every Jewish home was smashed, while Jewish men, women, and children were savagely beaten. Some fifty thousand Jews were arrested and flung into concentration camps....Five hundred synagogues of Germany were burned and gutted with bombs and kerosene. Reichsmarshal Goering...fined the German-Jewish community the sum of one billion reichmarks [$400,000,000] to cover the cost of the damage—'for which,' he said 'the Jews are responsible.' In addition, Goering stipulated that on January 1, 1939, all Jewish businesses would be completely liquidated...."[16]

This was only the beginning. As the Nazis expanded into Czechoslovakia, Hungary, Poland, the Ukraine and other parts of Russia, death camps were set up in every region. There were also

---

[14]Dr. Howard M. Sacchar, *The Course of Modern Jewish History*, Cleveland: The World Publishing Company, 1958.
[15]Ibid., p. 428.
[16]Ibid., p. 430.

slave labor camps to help provide the manpower for heavy industry. However, on 800 calories per day, workers usually died off very rapidly from malnutrition and disease.

We spare the reader the testimony of eye witnesses at the Neuremberg trials who described the mass executions (7,000 per day in Poland alone), the gas chambers, the forced starvation, the bizarre medical experiments, the sexual abuse, the tortures and the beatings. When it was all over and World War II had come to an end, Allied officers attempted to assess the genocidal consequences of the Nazi extermination policy.

The first rough estimate provided the much publicized number of six million dead. However, Dr. Sacchar says:

"During the Nazi hegemony between 4,200,000, and 4,600,000 Jews were done to death. The figure of 6,000,000 released at the end of the war has since been discounted. Approximately a third died by starvation and disease, the rest by direct physical execution."[17]

And if we are shocked by the genocidal destruction of over 4.6 million Jews, think how the heavens must have wept over the estimated 80,000,000 of many ethnic groups who were killed by their own governments in Communist China and the Soviet Union.

When human beings are slaughtered in such gargantuan numbers the mind staggers trying to comprehend it. As Stalin is reported to have said, "When you kill one person, it is a tragedy. When you kill a million, it is merely a statistic."

During the final stages of the Nazi genocidal bloodbath, many Jews fled to Palestine and many more fled to the United States. The Jewish population in America rose to around five million. Many of these refugees were world-renowned chemists, physicists, and advanced mathematicians who enriched the technological resources of the United States in developing explosives, rockets, and the nuclear bomb that won the war.

---

[17]Ibid., p.457.

THE JEWS FINALLY ESTABLISH THEIR OWN ISRAEL

When World War I broke out, the Turkish Empire fought on the side of Germany. So when the British troops came out of Egypt to conquer the Turkish forces in Palestine, British leaders decided this would be a good time to give the Jews a homeland in Palestine, thus fulfilling the words of Isaiah who prophecied that the Gentiles would be the saviors of the Israelites in the latter days. Isaiah had written the word of the Lord as follows:

"Behold, I will lift up mine hand to the Gentiles, and set up my standard to the people: and they shall bring thy sons in their arms, and thy daughters shall be carried upon their shoulders."[18]

As early as 1897, Dr. Theodor Herzl had sponsored the first conference of the World Zionist Organization and presented his dissertation entitled, "The Jewish State." By the closing years of World War I, tens of thousands of Jews had been completely uprooted from Russia, Poland, and Eastern Europe. The urgent need for a Jewish homeland was strongly advocated among most of the western allies.

Finally, on November 2, 1917, the famous Balfour Declaration was issued by the British government which officially adopted the policy of establishing a national homeland for the Jews in Palestine. The British military forces captured Jerusalem on December 11, 1917, and a British Commission was immediately dispatched to Jerusalem to begin implementing the Balfour Declaration.

However, there was a long struggle ahead. The British were given a mandate to protect the interests of both Jews and Arabs in the Palestine area, but riots broke out when the Arabs heard a fabricated rumor that perhaps the Jews would tear down their sacred Dome of the Rock and build a temple there.

---

[18]Isaiah 49:22.

These riots continued off and on right up to World War II. At that point the Arab nations became allies of the Axis Powers, and the Jews volunteered for service with the British-American allies.

RESTORING A HOMELAND FOR THE JEWS

When the war was over, the United Nations partitioned Palestine and authorized the Jews to set up the area where most of them had located as the sovereign nation of "Israel." This became official on May 14, 1948, and the United States was the first nation to extend diplomatic recognition. However, six Arab nations immediately attacked Israel, and for a short time the outcome seemed dubious. However, when the conflict was over, Israel had not only survived, but had increased her territory by 50 percent.

The next attack came from Egypt in 1956 and during this conflict, Israel captured the Sinai Peninsula. As a peace gesture Israel surrendered the captured territory and withdrew her forces back to her original boundaries.

Once again, the Arab League prepared to attack Israel in June of 1967, but a few hours before the scheduled action, the Israeli air force made a preemptive strike against the air fields of the Arab League nations. With the air power of the Arab League demolished, Israel was able to end the war in six days. This increased the territory of Israel by 200 percent and moved the eastern border of Israel down to the Jordan River. Most of the captured territory, which is called the West Bank, has been furnished with irrigation water, and settlements have been set up with date farms, banana plantations, citrus groves and truck gardens.

Many Arabs now work at these farms and settlements along with the Jews.

In passing it might be mentioned that I was in Israel just before the "Six-Day War" broke out. The American press was predicting an unavoidable disaster for Israel, but the actual outcome shocked the world. It was so astonishing and the victory so sudden and complete that I wrote a book about it so Americans would understand what had happened. It was called *Fantastic Victory.*[19]

Almost immediately I received letters from military and political leaders of Israel commenting on the accuracy of the account as well as the historical analysis of the cause of the war.

Since I had sent no books to these men, I was surprised to hear from them. Later I learned from Dr. Joseph Ginat of the Prime Minister's Office that since this book was the first major work to come out on the war, the Israeli government had purchased large numbers of copies to distribute among their military and political leaders.

One of the generals later sent over a whole box of military reports to add to our files on the Six-Day War.

As time went by, there have been additional military clashes, but none as decisive as the Six-Day War.

During these conflicts, the most noble gesture from the Arabs occurred when the President of Egypt, Anwar el-Sadat, virtually risked assassination by extremists in his own country to fly to Israel for the purpose of negotiating with Israel for a long term peace.[20]

*　*　*　*

---

[19]Salt Lake City: Bookcraft, 1967.
[20]*Abba Eban, An Autobiography,* London: Futura Publications LTD., 1978, p. 610.

JESUS INTRODUCES THE ART OF DIVINE STORYTELLING AND THE SCIENCE OF SYMBOLISM

Jesus was at least a third of the way through his ministry before he introduced the fine art of divine storytelling. The apostles did not know it yet, but they were about to be sent out on special missions to defend the teachings of Jesus on their own.

No doubt Jesus felt that prior to their departure it would be appropriate to show the apostles how to answer difficult or obscure gospel principles with divine storytelling. So the scripture says:

"The same day went Jesus out of the house, and sat by the sea side.

"And great multitudes were gathered together unto him, so that he went into a ship, and sat; and the whole multitude stood on the shore.

"And he spake many things unto them in parables, saying, Behold, a sower went forth to sow...." [1]

Until this time the Savior had been so forthright and straightforward in his preaching and teaching that this new storytelling device puzzled his disciples. Therefore, they said:

---

[1] Matthew 13:1-3.

"Why speakest thou unto them in parables?"[2]

Certainly Jesus had not used this obscure storytelling style when he taught his apostles the Sermon on the Mount. Nor did he use parables when he taught the multitudes on the plain. Matthew says:

"He answered and said unto them, Because it is given unto you to know the mysteries of the kingdom of heaven, but to them it is not given....

"Because they seeing see not; and hearing they hear not, neither do they understand....

"But blessed are your eyes, for they see: and your ears, for they hear."[3]

Jesus called these stories "parables," but this simple name might be misleading. In reality, the Savior's parables were artistically contrived to allow a tiny fable to carry the heavy load of a very complex truth or series of truths.

Someone has said that parables are earthly stories designed to explain heavenly principles.

The fascinating thing about the Savior's parables is the fact that they seemed so simple; but after a little contemplation, the mind perceives a whole new horizon of understanding.

This brings us to the Savior's primary purpose in using parables. The light of the gospel does not open up in the mind of a new disciple like a flower in full bloom. From the beginning it is something beautiful, but it is only a bud. The flowering comes by opening it petal by petal, precept by precept, line upon line.

A well structured parable will do that.

---

[2]Matthew 13:10.
[3]Matthew 13:11-16.

However, the superb advantage of a parable is that it blossoms only as fast as the new disciple is able to absorb and appreciate it. For some individuals the blossoming will be very rapid. For others it will be painfully slow.

Telling gospel truths with parables protects the newcomer from being blinded by too much beauty or too much light too soon. It also protects the gospel from having its pearls desecrated by the unworthy before they have prepared themselves to recognize and appreciate the intrinsic beauty and value of pearls.

HEAVENLY SYMBOLS AND DIVINE ROLE PLAYING

Parables are closely related to all the ceremonies, ordinances, and even the most sacred rituals of the church.

Here again, the purpose of the Lord is to use a very simple ceremony or ordinance to illustrate a sacred and sometimes complex secret of heaven. As in a carefully structured parable, the ceremony opens up the understanding of the participant a petal at a time, and the simplicity of the ceremony protects its sacred meaning from the desecrating ridicule of the non-believer or the cynic.

In the days of the prophet Moses, the Lord undertook to teach a very rustic and volatile population of Israelites—recently liberated from slavery—the sacred meaning of the terrifying dimensions of the atoning sacrifice which would be made by the Father's Beloved Son.

The lesson began with the slaying of a precious and sometimes much loved possession of the family—a lamb or a calf. God's people had done this since the days of Adam.[4] The sacrifice of the lamb or calf was performed in remembrance of the Savior's sacrifice which was yet to come.[5]

---

[4]Moses 5:5-8, P. of G.P.
[5]Alma 34:14, B. of M.

The sacrifice was then used for a variety of purposes. Sometimes it was burned on the sacred altar,[6] sometimes it was eaten[7] after a portion had been contributed to the priests for their sustenance.[8]

It was used in connection with the consecrating of those who were to serve in the highest offices of the priesthood. First, there were washings of the candidate, then an anointing with sacred oil. This was followed by the candidates being dressed in the robes of the holy priesthood.[9]

Then a calf was slain as a "sin offering,"[10] representing the slaying of the Son of God for the sins of the world.[11]

Next a ram was slain as a burnt offering on behalf of those who had come to be set apart for their high calling.[12]

This was followed by the slaying of the ram whose blood was used for the consecrating of the men who were about to assume their high offices. Moses took a portion of its blood and consecrated these men in the following manner:

Moses dipped his finger in the ram's blood of consecration and touched the right ear, signifying the need to let only the principles of truth pass through the ear and into the mind.[13]

Then he touched the thumb of the right hand of the candidate, signifying that he must always have clean hands and a pure heart dedicated to the service of God and his fellow men.[14]

---

[6]Leviticus 1:6-13.
[7]Leviticus 7:15-16.
[8]Leviticus 7:28-34.
[9]Leviticus 8:1-13.
[10]Leviticus 8:14-17.
[11]Moses 5:7, P. of G.P.
[12]Leviticus 8:18-21.
[13]Psalms 78:1; Proverbs 23:12.
[14]Psalms 24:4.

Next, he touched the large toe of the right foot, signifying that his feet must always follow the strait and narrow pathway of truth and righteousness.[15]

Although blood sacrifices were done away with after the supreme sacrifice of the Savior in the meridian of time,[16] the washings and anointings, as well as the consecrating of God's servants to live the commandments of God on the highest possible level, continued as the central purpose of the Christian temples later set up by the apostles.[17]

THE SPIRITUAL ELEMENTS OF SYMBOLISM IN THE ORDINANCE OF BAPTISM

Baptism is a beautiful and simple ceremony, but filled with meaningful symbolism as one becomes better acquainted with the deeper gospel truths.

For example, the candidate enters into the water, which is the great universal element out of which everything was organized and made in the very beginning.[18]

The baptismal prayer, which was given by direct revelation, has two parts.[19] First, there is a declaration that the person officiating has been commissioned by Jesus Christ to act in his name. Second, this ordinance is performed in the name of the Father, the Son, and the Holy Ghost. Baptism is the beginning of the "new birth," and the Lord revealed to Adam that all three members of the Godhead are involved in the redemption process.[20]

The candidate is then completely immersed in the water. The word "baptism" comes from the Greek word "baptizo" meaning immersion or submerging. This is symbolic of death which comes to

---

[15]Proverbs 4:26; 1 Nephi 8:20, B. of M.

[16]3 Nephi 9:19, B. of M.

[17]Mosheim's *Ecclesiastical History*, London: Longman, Brown, 1850, vol. 1:105; Doctrine and Covenants 124:39-40.

[18]Genesis 1:1-7.

[19]3 Nephi 11:25, B. of M., Doctrine and Covenants 20:73.

[20]Moses 6:60, P. of G.P., plus Doctrine and Covenants 45:4-5.

all, and the burial in the grave. It also represents the death and casting away of our sins that will now be buried with the past and blotted out of the heavenly computer.[21] The burial in the water also represents the washing away of the sins and cleansing of the soul.[22]

The rising from the water represents the great resurrection which likewise comes to all. It also represents the coming forth in the "new birth" with a soul cleansed from all its infirmities of the past.[23]

Coming out of the water represents a re-entry into the world as the candidate steps on to the strait and narrow path which leads to the Savior's glorious redemption and the fullness of God's love as seen by Lehi and Nephi in their two remarkable visions.[24]

The witnesses constitute the Lord's representatives on this side of the veil certifying that the baptism was performed by an authorized servant of God, that the baptismal prayer was said correctly, and that the candidate was completely submerged in the water as the Lord requires.[25]

On the other side of the veil, this ordinance is witnessed by the Holy Ghost or his emissaries. The Holy Ghost performs three roles: First, to certify that the ordinance was properly and authoritatively performed; second, to certify that the candidate has demonstrated by "fruits meet for repentance" true sincerity; and third, to "justify" this person before the Savior so that the cleansing of sin can take place under the operation of the Atonement.[26] This will be achieved when the Savior goes before the Father and pleads on behalf of the candidate that his or her sins be remitted.[27]

Thus we begin to appreciate on a more profound level the sacred implications of ordinances, ceremonies, temple rites, and the superb

---

[21]Acts 3:19; Doctrine and Covenants 109:34.

[22]Acts 22:16; Doctrine and Covenants 39:10.

[23]John 3:3; 1 Peter 1:23; Mosiah 27:25, B. of M., Alma 5:49. B. of M, Moses 6:59.

[24]1 Nephi, chapters 8 and 11, B. of M.

[25]Doctrine and Covenants 127:6-7.

[26]Moses 6:59-60.

[27]Doctrine and Covenants 45:3-5.

artistry of divine story telling. It is our Heavenly Father's way of unfolding the budding beauty of gospel truths until we are able to enjoy the exhilarating fragrance of the full bloom.

We will now consider the broad ramifications of five famous parables which Jesus related one after another. These parables were each designed to answer a gospel question.

WHY DOESN'T EVERYBODY APPRECIATE AND ACCEPT THE GOSPEL?

Jesus possessed the gift of discernment, and many times he would read the hearts and minds of his disciples before they knew that he was aware of what they were thinking.[28]

Jesus had two reasons for telling parables. The first was to teach the gospel by illustrations, and the other was to keep the spies from Jerusalem confused. These paid informers were trying to gather evidence of some serious offense so they could have Jesus arrested. The plan was to ensnare Jesus by making him "an offender for a word."

Yet the parables seemed such innocent, childish stories. How could a prosecutor prove an "offense" with one of these?

Jesus also knew that preaching the gospel through parables had a tendency to filter out the unrepentant, the proud, the "fat hearted," and the dull of hearing.[29]

But at the time, even the apostles seemed dull of hearing. When Jesus had the disciples alone, he assured them he was not trying to hide anything from them. In fact, he wanted them to appreciate what a great privilege the Father had granted them by allowing them to be the Savior's intimate associates during his earthly ministry. When they had questions or doubts, they could ask.

---

[28]See Mark 2:8; Luke 5:22.
[29]Matthew 13:15.

Many of the ancient prophets,[30] even King David, were allowed to see a vision of the ministry of Christ,[31] and Jesus knew that many of these ancient servants of God secretly wished they could have been selected to be with Jesus during his earthly ministry. But it was the apostles who received this marvelous privilege. Therefore, he began by saying:

"Blessed are your eyes, for they see: and your ears, for they hear.

"For verily I say unto you, That many prophets and righteous men have desired to see those things which ye see, and have not seen them; and to hear those things which ye hear, and have not heard them."[32]

JESUS INTERPRETS THE PARABLE OF THE SOWER

But now Jesus was ready to explain the parable of the sower. Actually, this parable didn't turn out to be so much about a sower of seed, but about different kinds of soil. It is sometimes called the parable of the soil.

Jesus explained that the sower is the one who spreads the words of the gospel abroad in the earth.

The words or seeds that are cast helter-skelter along the highway are virtually dead on arrival, since they are plucked up by hungry birds and never allowed to germinate. Even if one of the seeds falls upon a ready listener, Satan is quick to pluck it out of his heart before the seed takes root.

The words of the gospel that fall on stony ground with scarcely any soil will often be "received with gladness," but the roots are shallow and their staying power is weak. The first high wind of criticism or persecution will blow them over, or the heat of the sun will shrivel them up.

---

[30]Helaman 8:19-20, B. of M.

[31]For example, see Psalms, chapter 22.

[32]Matthew 13:16-17.

Then there are the seeds of the gospel sown among thorns. In this case the soil is good, but it is crowded with a thriving crop of thorns and thistles. This is where the new converts are distracted by riches, pride, the lusts of the flesh, and the sophisticated deceit of what passes for "much learning." These lose their discipleship because their testimony is choked out by the things of the world.

Finally the word falls upon a mind and heart that is hungering and thirsting for the truth. The soil of the soul has been plowed, harrowed and prepared through humble, diligent study and prayer. The seed flourishes, grows and produces "much fruit." Sometimes it is thirtyfold, sometimes sixty, and occasionally as much as a hundredfold.

Every missionary or sower of the seed knows the joy of the harvest whether it is thirty, sixty or a hundred. In fact, it is difficult to describe the joy that comes with even *one* convert. Jesus said:

"And if it so be that you should labor all your days in crying repentance unto this people, and bring, save it be one soul unto me, how great shall be your joy with him in the kingdom of my Father!

"And now, if your joy will be great with one soul that you have brought unto me into the kingdom of my Father, how great will be your joy if you should bring many souls unto me!"[33]

WHY NOT SEPARATE THE GOOD PEOPLE FROM THE BAD?

One of the greatest trials and frustrations of good people is trying to live the gospel standards and raise their children according to righteous principles while living among "bad" people.

Of course "bad" is a relative term. So is "good." But having children come home saying four letter words, telling off-color stories or joking about getting high on drugs compels parents to wish the Lord would sort out the people into the "good" and the "bad" and keep them separate.

---

[33]Doctrine and Covenants 18:15-16.

The Lord did that once. In the days of Noah, the bad were all drowned after being duly warned. Furthermore, in the last days the bad will all be burned after being duly warned.[34] Meanwhile, there is a mixture of good and bad. Jesus decided to tell a parable to illustrate why the burning must not come prematurely. He said:

"Another parable put he forth unto them, saying, The kingdom of heaven [on earth] is like unto a man which sowed good seed in his field:

"But while men slept, his enemy came and sowed tares among the wheat, and went his way.

"But when the blade was sprung up, and brought forth fruit, then appeared the tares also.

"So the servants of the householder came and said unto him, Sir, didst not thou sow good seed in thy field? from whence then hath it tares?

"He said unto them, An enemy hath done this. The servants said unto him, Wilt thou then that we go and gather them up?

"But he said, Nay; lest while ye gather up the tares, ye root up also the wheat with them.

"Let both grow together until the harvest: and in the time of harvest I will say to the reapers, Gather ye together first the tares, and bind them in bundles to burn them: but gather the wheat into my barn."[35]

From the Lord's point of view this parable illustrates two problems.

To begin with, tares look exactly like wheat while they are growing up together. It is not until the heads of grain appear that

---

[34]Malachi 4:1.
[35]Matthew 13:24-30.

they become so obviously different. The lesson in this parable was quite clear to the apostles once it was explained.

The tares of that period are believed to have been a type of rye grass which was a terrible nuisance to the farmers in Palestine.[36] The seed of the tares is different in shape and size compared to wheat and is bitter to the taste. Nevertheless, they look a lot alike when they are growing up together.

The second problem which is illustrated in this parable is the fact that many billions of spirits prepared for this earth include large numbers who are entitled to have their earth-life experience even though the Lord knows they will not accept the gospel. So in this life they are tares. This means they respond to the temptations of the adversary and largely serve his purposes rather than the Lord's.

So the question arises, why not separate them from the wheat so that they do not grow up together? From the Lord's standpoint, the problem is not that simple so he explained the parable as follows:

"He that soweth the good seed is the Son of man;

"The field is the world; the good seed are the children of the kingdom; but the tares are the children of the wicked one;

"The enemy that sowed them is the devil; the harvest is the end of the world; and the reapers are the angels.

"As therefore the tares are gathered and burned in the fire; so shall it be in the end of this world."[37]

So at the end of the world there is a complete separation just as there was in the days of Noah. Only this time, instead of drowning, there will be a universal burning of the wicked.[38]

---

[36]James E. Talmage, *Jesus the Christ*, pp. 300-301.
[37]Matthew 13:37-40.
[38]Isaiah 24:6.

In the meantime, the Savior said the righteous must not pray for the burning prematurely because it is not yet time for the harvest. If the harvest came too soon, many of the righteous would be destroyed. Until that time, there must be patience, long-suffering, and endurance to the end by those who are the Lord's wheat.[39]

There is another lesson to be learned, and that is the fact that tares are different from people. Once the seed of the tare is planted it is doomed to grow up to produce tares. However, in the case of people, some can be changed into the Lord's wheat. Jesus wanted his disciples to know they were to achieve this whenever possible. The formula calls for good leadership and much patience.

HOW GOD SWEETENS THE BREAD OF LIFE

Jesus said:

"The kingdom of heaven is like unto leaven, which a woman took, and hid in three measures of meal, till the whole was leavened."[40]

In the days of Abraham, he became the leaven on which the Lord depended to preserve righteousness in the earth and instruct the tares of his day, which were the Egyptians and the people of Palestine.[41]

When the young prophet Jeremiah hesitated to respond to his call, the Lord revealed to him that he had been ordained before he was born to be the leaven of his generation. [42]

Thus it has been down through the ages. Great leaders have been raised up by the Lord to sweeten the meal of life and make tares into wheat wherever possible. In some ages this has been a very lonely assignment, as it was in the days of Isaiah and Elijah. But they kept the leaven of gospel fermentation alive. In other epochs

---

[39]Matthew 13:28:30.
[40]Matthew 13:33.
[41]Abraham 2:9; 3:15, P. of G.P..
[42]Jeremiah 1:5.

there have been leaders like Nephi IV in America, who saw every single person of his region converted to the gospel.[43]

It is important to emphasize how much the Lord depends upon leadership fermentation *within* the kingdom.

Many a ward, stake or mission has gone through a sleepy, lackadaisical episode until suddenly a small cadre of new priesthood leaven arrives with inspiration and enthusiasm. I have lived long enough in certain areas to see the poorest ward of a stake become the best, and to see a slow moving stake or mission become the leader of a region.

God's leadership leaven is a precious commodity. He depends upon it "until the whole is leavened."[44]

WHY DON'T THE MISSIONARIES JUST CONVERT THE GOOD PEOPLE?

When the gospel net is cast out by God's fishermen, it brings in all kinds of fish. The Savior illustrated why his disciples should not be too surprised with some of the strange varieties that are brought in. He said:

"Again, the kingdom of heaven is like unto a net, that was cast into the sea, and gathered of every kind."[45]

Sometimes the net brings some amazing people whose past reputations may be shocking to other disciples. What a stir it caused among the Pharisees when Jesus preached to the "harlots and publicans," and converted many of them.[46] Jesus had a ready reply for the Pharisees' complaints. He said:

"I came not to call the righteous, but sinners to repentance."

---

[43]4 Nephi 1:2, B. of M.
[44]Matthew 13:33.
[45]Matthew 13:47.
[46]Matthew 21:31-32.

And just to pour a little salt into their wounded pride, he made one of the publicans an apostle![47]

Think of the brilliant and truly great leaders the Lord would have lost, if he hadn't gathered up "all kinds"—including some sinners—in his net. Among those Jesus would have lost would have been Paul, Alma the Elder, Alma the Younger, King Lamoni, and a host of Lamanites who became the super-righteous Anti-Nephi-Lehies. All of these repented and became prophets or great priesthood leaders.

Of course, during the sorting out process, there are some who were gathered into the gospel net but lacked the quality to remain among the chosen. The scripture says they are like "the dog...turned to his own vomit again; and the sow that was washed [but turned] to her wallowing in the mire."[48]

Jesus finished this parable by saying that the fishermen:

"...gathered the good into vessels, but cast the bad away.

"So shall it be at the end of the world: the angels shall come forth, and sever the wicked from among the just,

"And shall cast them into the furnace of fire: there shall be wailing and gnashing of teeth."[49]

THE GOSPEL IS LIKE A PEARL OF GREAT PRICE

Jesus concluded this interesting series of parables with a strong emphasis on the supreme prize to be gained in this life. He said:

"The kingdom of heaven is like unto a merchant man, seeking goodly pearls:

---

[47]Luke 5:27-28; Mark 2:14-15.
[48]2 Peter 2:22.
[49]Matthew 13:48-50.

"Who, when he had found one pearl of great price, went and sold all that he had, and bought it."[50]

"Again, the kingdom of heaven is like unto treasure hid in a field; the which when a man hath found, he hideth, and for joy thereof goeth and selleth all that he hath, and buyeth that field."[51]

Such was the message of Jesus to his disciples. No task was to be too hard, no sacrifice—even to the laying down of their lives—was to be too great, if they ultimately gained the magnificent and precious pearl of great price, which is eternal life.

*   *   *   *

---

[50]Matthew 13:45-46.
[51]Matthew 13:44.

A SIMPLIFIED CALENDAR
BASED ON THE SCRIPTURES

The Fall				Meridian			Millennium
1,000	1,000	1,000	1,000	0	1,000	1,000	1,000

Students of the Bible are always frustrated by the fact that there is no standard calendar which they can comfortably use as a universal frame of reference in fixing the dates for Biblical events.

Many editions of the Bible set forth dates based on the calculations of Archbishop Usher, but he determined the beginning of human history to be 4004 B.C., and this is one of the factors that has led many chronologists to designate the date of Christ's birth as 4 B.C.

However, we have a number of modern scriptures which help us fix the important dates of the Bible with considerably more confidence. Let us begin with Adam.

ADAM'S CALENDAR

We have reason to believe that Adam's calendar began with the metamorphosis which is called "the Fall." This conclusion is drawn from the fact that the Lord has said that, before the Fall, "the Gods had not appointed unto Adam his reckoning."[1]

As human history began to unfold, the scripture says that Adam and Eve raised two generations (children and grandchildren), although none of their names are given.[2]

---

[1] Abraham 5:13, P. of G. P.
[2] Moses 5:2-3, P. of G. P.

After that, Cain and Abel were born. Following the murder of Abel, Eve gave birth to Seth when Adam was "a hundred and thirty years" old.[3]

This is the first date given in the Bible. Therefore, by this time it is apparent that the years were being calculated from some fixed date. The scripture in Abraham 5:13 would suggest that Adam's "reckoning" began with the Fall, not with Adam's birth, and we therefore assume that this became the fixed point for the measuring of the years on Adam's calendar.

This would further suggest that when Seth talked about his birthdate, he would say he was born in 130 A.F., meaning 130 years after the Fall.

THE THOUSAND-YEAR CALENDAR

The Lord indicates that the pattern of human history has been formulated in time slots of a thousand years each. One scripture suggests that this pattern was predetermined in the pre-existence.[4] Note that this advanced planning was done in the pre-earth life before Israel even existed.

Not only does it appear that the planning for human history would be in thousand-year segments, but the Lord says that when the final judgment comes, the history of the world will be revealed in terms of what happened in each of these thousand-year periods. For example, the Lord says:

"And then shall the first angel again sound his trump...and reveal the secret acts of men, and the mighty works of God in the FIRST THOUSAND YEARS.

"And then shall the second angel sound his trump, and reveal the secret acts of men, and the thoughts and intents of their hearts, and the mighty works of God in the SECOND THOUSAND YEARS.

---

[3]Genesis 5:3.
[4]Deuteronomy 32:7-9.

"And so on, until the SEVENTH angel shall sound his trump."[5]

THE MERIDIAN OF TIME ON GOD'S CALENDAR

Both history and scripture combine to indicate that the coming of Christ at the meridian of time occurred at the conclusion of four thousand years and the beginning of the two thousand years that would take place before the Millennium. Speaking of the meridian of time, Dr. James E. Talmage says:

"The term 'meridian' as commonly used, conveys the thought of a principal division of time or space....So the years and the centuries of human history are divided by the great event of the birth of Jesus Christ. The years preceding that epoch-making occurrence are designated as time *Before Christ* (B.C.); while subsequent years are each specified as a certain *year of our Lord*, or, as in the Latin tongue, *Anno Domini* (A.D.)."[6]

Typical scriptures referring to the coming of the Savior in the meridian of time include:

"...his Only Begotten Son, even him whom he declared should come in the MERIDIAN OF TIME, who was prepared from before the foundation of the world."[7]

And again:

"This is the plan of salvation unto all men, through the blood of mine Only Begotten, who shall come in the MERIDIAN OF TIME."

Assuming that the meridian of time occurred at the end of 4,000 years, it would mean that John the Baptist was born 3,999 A.F. (after the Fall) on Adam's calendar.

However, Jesus was born the following year, at the commencement of a new calendar. So how shall the birthdate of Jesus be

---

[5]Doctrine and Covenants 88:108-110 (emphasis added).
[6]Talmage, *Jesus the Christ*, pp. 57-58 (emphasis added).
[7]Moses 5:57, P. of G. P.

designated? Actually, he was born on the great neutral nodal date of
0 B.C. or 0 A.D. whichever way you may choose to say it. This left
Bible scholars who accept this dating system in a dilemma. As a
result, some ended up by saying Jesus was born in 1 B.C., while
others said it was 1 A.D. But both dates have proven unsatisfactory.

So how should the date of the Savior's birth be designated? The
answer is found in the method of calculation used in connection with
the Lord's calendar.

THE LORD'S CALENDAR

The Lord gave us a clear illustration of how his own calendar
works when he announced that he wanted his restored church to
commence its corporate existence on April 6, 1830. He said this date
was significant because it marked one thousand, eight hundred and
thirty years since he came "in the flesh."[8]

Assuming that the Lord literally meant what he said, this tells us
two things.

First, it suggests that in spite of all the adjustments and changes
that have been attempted in connection with our present secular
calendar, it fits the Lord's calendar.

Second, the Lord did not use 1 B.C. or 1 A.D. for his birth date.
Instead, he used the neutral nodal date of 0. Notice how neatly this
fits into the calculating of dates.

For example, when Jesus was one year old, the Lord's calendar
said it was 1 A.D. When he reached age two, the Lord's calendar said
2 A.D. Consequently, when our present secular calendar reached
1830, the Lord said it had been exactly one thousand, eight hundred
and thirty years since Jesus came into the world and was made
"flesh."

---

[8]Doctrine and Covenants 20:1.

THE NEPHITE CALENDAR

In ancient America, the Nephite calendar followed the same pattern as the Lord's calendar.

For example, the Nephites were told that the Savior would be born in Bethlehem 600 years after Lehi left Jerusalem.[9]

They were also told that they would know of his birth because there would be a day and a night and a day without any darkness.[10]

They also knew that when the normal nighttime returned there would be a new star in the heavens.[11]

However, when these marvelous signs occurred—just as the prophets had predicted—[12] the Nephites forgot to change their calendar.

In fact, it was 609 years after Lehi left Jerusalem before the Nephites suddenly awakened to the fact that even though the great sign of Christ's birth had occurred, they were still following their old chronology.[13]

They therefore began their new dating system, using the birth of Christ as the starting point. We note that under this system it would not be 1 A.D. until AFTER a year had passed since the sign was seen. In this way, the Nephite calendar harmonized perfectly with the Lord's calendar.

And strange as it may seem, the Lord's calendar—as we have seen—synchronizes with our own calendar in modern times.

* * * *

---

[9]1 Nephi 10:4; 19:8; 2 Nephi 25:19, B. of M.
[10]Helaman 14:3-4, B. of M.
[11]Helaman 14:5, B. of M.
[12]3 Nephi 1:19-21, B. of M.
[13]3 Nephi 2:6-7, B. of M.

WHAT DOES IT MEAN TO BE BAPTIZED BY THE HOLY GHOST AND WITH FIRE?

When John the Baptist launched his missionary program among the Jews, he said:

"I indeed baptize you with water unto repentance: but he that cometh after me is mightier than I...he shall baptize you with the Holy Ghost, and with fire."[1]

When Jesus came he said:

"Whoso cometh unto me with a broken heart and a contrite spirit, him will I baptize with fire and with the Holy Ghost."[2]

As we carefully study this element of the Gospel, we discover that the "fire" mentioned in these verses is actually the "power" of the Holy Ghost. It is appropriately identified with "fire" because its presence is manifest on a wide spectrum from "the burning in the bosom" to visible flames which were seen on the day of Pentecost.

The scriptures tell us that the "fire" of the Holy Ghost may reveal itself in either of two dimensions. One is the tangible dimension which manifests itself to the eyes, the ears, and the entire sensory system of the body. The other is intangible. As we shall see the scriptures verify that this dimension of the Holy Ghost often works as a refining fire within us without our even knowing about it or feeling it.

---

[1]Matthew 3:11
[2]3 Nephi 9:20.

THE TANGIBLE DIMENSION OF THE HOLY GHOST

The TANGIBLE dimension of the Holy Ghost is highly visible, sometimes even spectacular with a mighty wind and flames of fire resting on the recipients as it did on the Day of Pentecost.[3]

When this first dimension of the Holy Ghost rests upon individuals, they are filled with so much divine rapture that they see visions, prophesy, sometimes speak in tongues or interpret what someone else has said in tongues. They communicate with beings beyond the veil, and are visited by angelic personages who minister to them.[4]

These more spectacular manifestations of the Holy Ghost have always occurred during the opening scenes of each new dispensation. It is the Father's way of testifying to a new body of Saints that "he has made bare his mighty arm," and he has revealed himself with power.[5]

However, these glorious manifestations from the Lord automatically expose the recipient to the demands of Satan for "equal time." As Brigham Young said:

"When individuals are blessed with visions, revelations, and great manifestations, look out, then the devil is nigh you, and you will be tempted *IN PROPORTION* to the vision, revelation, or manifestation you have received."[6]

Sometimes Lucifer's "equal time" manifestations have been extremely spectacular and terribly frightening. The scriptures indicate that when Satan first manifests himself, he usually tries to convert. If that fails he then frequently resorts to violent intimidation. The scripture describes what it was like when Moses went through one of these ordeals. It says:

---

[3] Acts 2:2-4.

[4] *History of the Church*, Salt Lake City: Deseret News Press, 1904, vol. 2:428.

[5] Isaiah 52:18; 3 Nephi 28:25, B. of M.

[6] Brigham Young, *Journal of Discourses*, vol. 3, p. 206.

"Satan came tempting him, saying, Moses, son of man, worship me. And it came to pass that Moses looked upon Satan and said....Get thee hence, Satan; deceive me not....

"And now...Satan cried out with a loud voice, and rent upon the earth, and commanded, saying: I am the Only Begotten, worship me....Moses began to fear exceedingly; and as he began to fear, he saw the bitterness of hell....

"And Moses received strength and called upon God, saying: In the name of the Only Begotten depart hence, Satan....and he departed."[7]

Satan used this same routine on the Savior during the forty days in the wilderness.[8] He used it on Joseph Smith[9] And he did the same thing to the Savior's modern apostles in 1837 when they introduced the restored gospel in England. While administering to one of his associates, Heber C. Kimball, the apostle in charge of the mission, writes the following:

"While thus engaged, I was struck with great force by some invisible power, and fell senseless on the floor. The first thing I recollected was being supported by Elders Hyde and Richards, who were praying for me....Elder Hyde and Richards assisted me to get on the bed, but my agony was so great I could not endure it, and I arose, bowed my knees and prayed. I then arose and sat up on the bed, when a vision was opened to our minds, and we could distinctly see the evil spirits, who foamed and gnashed their teeth at us. We gazed upon them about an hour and a half....

"We were not looking towards the window, but towards the wall. Space appeared before us, and we saw the devils coming in legions, with their leaders, who came within a few feet of us. They came towards us like armies rushing to battle. They appeared to be men of

---

[7]Moses 1:12-22.
[8]Luke 4:1-13.
[9]Doctrine and Covenants 128:20.

full stature, possessing every form and feature of men in the flesh, who were angry and desperate; and I shall never forget the vindictive malignity depicted on their countenances as they looked me in the eye; and any attempt to paint the scene which then presented itself, or portray their malice and enmity, would be vain. I perspired exceedingly, my clothes becoming as wet as if I had been taken out of the river. I felt excessive pain, and was in the greatest distress for some time. I cannot even look back on the scene without feelings of horror; yet by it I learned the power of the adversary, his enmity against the servants of God, and got some understanding of the invisible world. We distinctly heard those spirits talk and express their wrath and hellish designs against us. However, the Lord delivered us from them and blessed us exceedingly that day."[10]

Orson Hyde was another apostle who was present and endured this same experience. In a letter to Heber C. Kimball, he later wrote:

"While you were apparently senseless and lifeless on the floor and upon the bed (after we had laid you there), I stood between you and the devils and fought them and contended with them face to face, until they began to diminish in number and to retreat from the room. The last imp that left turned round to me as he was going out and said, as if to apologize, and appease my determined opposition to them, 'I never said anything against you!' I replied to him thus: 'It matters not to me whether you have or have not; you are a liar from the beginning! In the name of Jesus Christ, depart!' He immediately left, and the room was clear. That closed the scene of devils for that time."[11]

When this incident was reported back to Joseph Smith in America, he wrote:

"When I heard of it, it gave me great joy, for I then knew that the work of God had taken root in that land. It was this that caused the devil to make a struggle to kill you."[12]

---

[10]Orson F. Whitney, *Life of Heber C. Kimball*, Salt Lake City: Stevens and Wallis, Inc., 1945, pp. 130-131.

[11]Ibid., p. 131.

[12]Ibid., p. 132.

Joseph Smith then related some of his own experiences in which he had several contests with Satan and his minions. He concluded by saying:

"The nearer a person approaches the Lord, a greater power will be manifested by the adversary to prevent the accomplishment of His purposes."[13]

THE "GENTLE" BAPTISM OF FIRE

In contrast to the strong, spectacular manifestations of the first dimension of the Holy Ghost which makes it possible for Satan to demand equal time, there is a second dimension. This is the manifestation of the Holy Ghost in a more quiet way that might be called the "gentle" baptism of fire.

It is often so gentle that the recipients may wonder if anything is really happening to them. Jesus had this in mind when he spoke to the people on the western hemisphere immediately after his resurrection and said:

"Whoso cometh unto me with a broken heart and a contrite spirit, him will I baptize with fire and with the Holy Ghost, even as the Lamanites, because of their faith in me at the time of their conversion, were baptized with fire and with the Holy Ghost, and *THEY KNEW IT NOT.*"[14]

There are several occasions when there were massive conversion of thousands of Lamanites, but the Savior does not indicate which incident he had in mind when he said the Lamanites "were baptized with the fire and Holy Ghost, and they knew it not."

Some have thought perhaps he may have been referring to a spectacular manifestation of the Holy Ghost described in the book of Helaman. On that occasion, Lehi and Nephi (the sons of Helaman) had been imprisoned and were being starved to death. When their

---

[13]Ibid.
[14]3 Nephi 9:20, B. of M.

captors came in to slay them they found the two prophets surrounded by fire and then a thick cloud of darkness filled the prison. In the midst of all this they heard the voice of the Lord calling them to repentance. The message was accompanied by three frightening earthquake shocks. The terrified captors pleaded with the Lord to spare them and when he did, they were visited by ministering angels.[15]

However, under these cataclysmic circumstances it seems as though the fire and the Holy Ghost was so vividly evident that Jesus would not be referring to this incident when he said, "and they knew it not."

It is this writer's belief that the Savior may have been speaking of an incident more than a hundred years earlier when vast hosts of Lamanites were converted by having a "change of heart" without visible manifestations of fire and earthquake and ministering angels.

This massive conversion of the Lamanites is described in Alma, chapter 23, where the four sons of King Mosiah—Ammon, Aaron, Omner and Himni—desired to go in peacefully among their Lamanite enemies and teach them the Gospel. As they did so, the people began to open their hearts so the Spirit could work upon them, and they were not only converted, but they began to change their entire outlook on life. It says:

"As many of the Lamanites as believed in their preaching and were converted unto the Lord, never did fall away.

"For they became a righteous people; they did lay down the weapons of their rebellion, they did not fight against God any more, neither against any of their brethren.

"And these are they who were converted unto the Lord: The people...in the land of Ishmael...the Lamanites in the land of

---

[15]Helaman 5:22-52, B. of M.

Middoni; and also...in the city of Nephi; and...the land of Shilom....Shemlon, Lemuel...and the city of Shimnilom."[16]

It is suggested that this incident fits the statement of Jesus more appropriately than the first where the fire of the Holy Ghost was so spectacular.

As mentioned a moment ago the "gentle" fire of the Holy Ghost takes over the beatification of the human spirit so gently that the individual may not even realize anything is happening. But the family and friends of the new believer will soon notice some remarkable changes beginning to take place. Even the new convert will eventually begin to recognize these changes.

When this gentle fire rested on the hearts of the people in the days of King Benjamin, the people began to realize that something wonderful was occurring. They said:

"The Spirit of the Lord Omnipotent....has wrought a mighty change in us, or in our hearts, that we have no more disposition to do evil, but to do good continually."[17]

The prophet Alma also described what it was like to have the Holy Ghost gently bestow its powerful influence over his people. He said the people found themselves:

"Becoming humble, meek, submissive [to God's requirements], patient, full of love and all long-suffering;

"Having faith on the Lord; having a hope that ye shall receive eternal life; having the love of God always in your hearts, that ye may be lifted up at the last day and enter into his rest."[18]

---

[16]Alma 23:6-13, B. of M.

[17]Mosiah 5:2, B. of M.

[18]Alma 13:28-29, B. of M.

This is the refining influence which Jesus called being "born again."[19]

THE GENTLE FIRE BRINGS NEW REVELATION

One of the most important functions of the Holy Ghost is to share with the Lord's servants a continuous endowment of new truth. After the restoration of the Gospel in modern times, Joseph Smith instructed the early members to watch for these manifestations of the Spirit which would broaden their understanding through new revelations from the Holy Ghost. He said:

"A person may profit by noticing the first intimation of the spirit of revelation; for instance, when you feel pure intelligence flowing into you, it may give you sudden strokes of ideas, so that by noticing it, you may find it fulfilled the same day or soon...and thus by learning [to recognize] the Spirit of God and understanding it, you may grow into the principles of revelation."[20]

When these experiences happen to us, it is appropriate to humbly kneel before the Lord and thank him for speaking to us through his Holy Spirit.[21]

WHY THE GENTLE CHANNEL OF THE HOLY GHOST HAS SOME UNIQUE ADVANTAGES

There is a great advantage to the Father and the Saints when the body of the church has developed a sufficiently mature spiritual channel of communication so that the quiet fire of the Holy Ghost can deliver its inspiration by this means.

This is usually achieved by engaging in frequent conversations with the Lord through prayer. The prophet Enos followed this pattern of spiritual refinement until he says the "voice of the Lord came into my mind."[22] This is one of the richest rewards of being "born of the Spirit."

---

[19]John 3:3.
[20]Smith, *Teachings of the Prophet Joseph Smith*, p. 151.
[21]Moroni 10:4, B. of M.
[22]Enos 1:10, B. of M.

However, new revelation seldom comes in a flood. The Holy Ghost shares eternal truths "precept upon precept, line upon line, here a little and there a little."[23]

One of the most significant aspects of this entire procedure is the fact that when God's servants use this quiet and gentle device for communication, Satan can only demand "equal time" through the same channel.[24] This being true, an individual can largely exclude Satan from having any significant influence in his or her life by filling the mind with righteous and virtuous thoughts. This is one way to bind Satan. Therefore the Lord said:

"Let virtue garnish thy thoughts unceasingly; then shall thy confidence wax strong in the presence of God; and the doctrine of the priesthood shall distil upon thy soul as the dews from heaven."[25]

Obviously, the distilling of God's doctrine upon the soul is a beautiful way of describing the quiet channel of the Holy Ghost.

THE GENTLE CHANNEL OF THE HOLY GHOST
USED EXTENSIVELY TODAY

In our present dispensation there has been a discernible transition from the more spectacular manifestations of the Holy Ghost during the early days of the church to the more quiet and safer channels of the Spirit in recent times.

This transition is demonstrated in the life of one of the early apostles, Wilford Woodruff, who later became president of the church. Here are several excerpts from Wilford Woodruff's journal:

"Joseph Smith visited me a great deal after his death, and taught me many important principles....Joseph Smith continued visiting myself and others up to a certain time, and then it stopped.

---

[23]Isaiah 28:10.
[24]Brigham Young, *Journal of Discourses*, Volume 3, p. 206.
[25]Doctrine and Covenants 121:45.

"The last time he visited me was while I was in a storm at sea....The night following this, Joseph and Hyrum visited me, and the prophet said...'GET THE SPIRIT OF GOD.'"[26]

Joseph Smith was simply telling this apostle to solve his problems by seeking the "gentle" fire of the Holy Ghost. It would put the answers in his mind as it did for Enos. Wilford Woodruff subsequently had other visitations, but not from Joseph Smith. For the most part, he solved his day-to-day challenges by depending upon the communications of the Spirit.

And that is largely the way the church is governed today.

A PERSONAL EXPERIENCE

This author was present on one occasion as an invited participant when a group of the General Authorities were seeking to determine the best way to present a series of twenty-six Sunday Evening Tabernacle Broadcasts which I had been asked to deliver for the Church Missionary Committee. After an extensive discussion, a unanimous decision was finally reached, and suddenly the Spirit rested upon every person in the room. I was so animated and filled with a sublime euphoria by that experience that I could scarcely believe what was happening to me. I then heard the presiding officer say, "Brethren, we have our answer. If we do it this way, the Lord will bless us."

An acquaintance of mine, who was serving as secretary to this group of Authorities (and who later became a member of the First Presidency), lingered with me after the meeting. When we were alone, I could not help but exclaim to him, "Did you feel *that?*" He said, "Is that new to you?" I replied, "Well, yes it is." He then said, "That is what we call, 'Waiting upon the Lord.'"

From that moment on, I never had any doubt as to the inspired method by which the church leaders "wait upon the Lord" as they solve vast, complex problems relating to the administration of the affairs of the church from day to day.

*   *   *   *

---

[26] *The Deseret Weekly News*, Nov. 7, 1896, and quoted in *Temples of the Most High*, by N.B. Lundwall, p. 291.

THE NEPHITE VERSION OF THE BEATITUDES

In the Nephite text we find that the Savior sets forth the first four principles of the gospel as a preface to the Beatitudes and the Sermon on the Mount.

He did this because no one can truly take advantage of the beautiful principles of the Beatitudes or the Sermon on the Mount unless they are first willing to "come unto Christ" through faith, repentance, baptism and reception of the gift of the Holy Ghost.

It doesn't matter whether one finds the gospel during the years of innocence in childhood or whether the gospel message comes during the later years, or even after a depraved and sinful life, the key to salvation is accepting the benevolent invitation of a loving Savior who says, "Come unto me."

To do this a person must turn away from evil, begin to overcome the instincts of the flesh, and resolve to follow in the footsteps of the Savior the rest of his or her life. This resolution should be certified in the form of a covenant by entering into the waters of baptism, followed by the laying on of hands for the gift of the Holy Ghost. It will be recalled that this sacred ordinance is pronounced in the form of a commandment, which says: "Receive the Holy Ghost!"

What follows is the *BEATIFICATION OF THE HUMAN SPIRIT.*

THE BEATITUDES

Jesus followed the same pattern in teaching his disciples in America as he did in teaching the Jews. Before going into the full text of his Sermon on the Mount, Jesus outlined this ascent along the narrow path that allows a person to come unto Jesus through the beatifying of the human spirit. As we have said before, it is not an event, it is a process.

As we mentioned, many do not hear or appreciate the message of the gospel until after they have become wicked reprobates and flagrant violators of the commandments of God. When people of this sort are converted, it is not unusual for them to feel overwhelmed, depressed, depraved, unworthy and discouraged. So this is where Jesus wanted to begin his sermon on the beatitudes. He said:

"Yea, blessed are the poor in spirit *WHO COME UNTO ME*, for theirs is the kingdom of heaven."[1]

Here is hope and comfort for the newly converted who find themselves bitterly remorseful and feeling unworthy of the Savior's love and forgiveness.

In this first beatitude, Jesus assures these sinners that it *is* possible for them to enter into the kingdom of heaven!

In this verse we also find the golden key to ALL of the beatitudes. It is the Lord's promise that these blessings are available to any and all sinners who are willing to "*COME UNTO CHRIST.*"

With this phrase the Savior indicates that not everybody who is discouraged and poor in spirit is going to enter the kingdom of heaven; but if they will "come unto Christ," the golden gates of the kingdom will swing open and they will be welcomed.

Notice that the next eight verses are all connected to this first verse by the word "and." This means that these eight verses are actually part of the same sentence. Therefore, the promises in the rest of these verses are also dependent upon a person coming unto Christ.

---

[1] 3 Nephi 12:3, B. of M. Notice that the words, "Come unto me," do not appear in the King James translation, but only in the more complete text given by the resurrected Savior to the Nephites..

WHAT DOES IT MEAN TO "COME UNTO CHRIST"?

Let us pause for a moment in our discussion of the Beatitudes, and ask ourselves whether we have ever searched the scriptures to discover what it means to "come unto Christ." The scripture makes it clear that coming to Christ is a well-defined procedure. Perhaps we should set forth this divine formula in more of our sermons and teachings. Briefly, the procedure is outlined by the Lord as follows:

1. In a sense, we come unto Christ on our knees. We need to come with a broken heart and a contrite spirit to talk with our Heavenly Father.[2]

2. When we talk to our Heavenly Father we need to have our sins itemized—the law calls it a bill of particulars. There is nothing automatic about forgiveness of sins. We do not simply "cast our sins on Jesus" in wholesale lots and walk away. When we are "confessing our sins" we need to be specific so that we can gain specific forgiveness. [3]

3. It is important to remember that secret sins will not be forgiven. We will discover this at our first judgment, which comes right after we die.[4] If we have tried to hide serious offenses of immorality, various types of crimes, crooked business deals, joining Satan's secret combination, or otherwise subverting the kingdom of God, Satan will have his minions there to lay claim on us.[5] They will joyfully expose our sins which we have failed to bring under the Atonement so they can haul us off to the spirit prison where "there is a fearful looking for the fiery indignation of the wrath of God."[6]

4. Any sins we do not confess and bring under the Atonement at the time "we come unto Christ" will not be blotted out. The offender must pay for those sins himself in the next life.[7]

---

[2] 2 Nephi 2:7, 3 Nephi 19-20, Ether 4:15, Moroni 6:2, B. of M.; Doctrine and Covenants 56:18; 59:8.
[3] Matthew 3:6; Mark 1:5; Mosiah 27:35, Helaman 16:5, B. of M.; Doctrine and Covenants 59:12.
[4] Alma 40:11-14, B. of M.
[5] 2 Nephi 1:13, 23; Alma 13:13, 34:35, B. of M.
[6] Alma 40:11-14, B. of M.
[7] Doctrine and Covenants 19:16-17.

The Lord assures us that this is not merely "a few stripes" as some have taught,[8] but it consists of tasting a "portion" of the second death with the "hypocrites and unbelievers; even in outer darkness where there is weeping and wailing and gnashing of teeth." The Lord says those who have to pay for their own sins do not come out until they have endured their portion of the "suffering of his wrath."[9]

When Alma the younger briefly tasted of this second death experience, he says "I was racked with eternal torment, for my soul was harrowed up to the greatest degree."[10]

5. When we have offended an individual, we are required to seek out that person and try to gain his forgiveness. As the Lord says:

"If thou bring thy gift to the altar, and there rememberest that thy brother hath ought against thee;

"Leave there thy gift before the altar, and go thy way; first be reconciled to thy brother, and then come and offer thy gift."[11]

Unless we have done our best to gain reconciliation, we are liable to pay for our offense in the next world "to the uttermost farthing."[12]

Gaining forgiveness requires a willingness to repair any significant damages which resulted from the offense.[13]

6. When we have committed an offense against God by involving ourselves in acts of immorality or committing serious crimes, then we must confess to God's servants who will evaluate the offense and outline the process by which forgiveness may be obtained.[14]

---

[8]2 Nephi 28:8, B. of M.

[9]Doctrine and Covenants 76:38.

[10]Alma 36:12, B. of M.

[11]Matthew 5:23-24.

[12]Matthew 5:26.

[13]Mosiah 27:35, B. of M.

[14]Doctrine and Covenants 42:79-92.

7. Forgiveness of sins requires a certification by the Holy Ghost that we are "justified." This means that we have sincerely repented and have followed the procedure outlined by the Lord or his servants. Only then can the Atonement blot out our offenses.[15]

In summary, perhaps we could say that when we "come unto Christ," we accept Jesus as our Savior. We confess our sins. We express remorse for what we have done. We try to repair any injury we have caused. We reform our lives to conform with the Savior's teachings. Then we make our covenants with him through the prescribed ordinances, and firmly resolve to endure to the end.

THE HEALING OF A BROKEN HEART

Next, Jesus addressed those who are not only discouraged and poor in spirit but are in deep, sorrowful mourning. The human capacity to suddenly suffer the trauma of a broken heart is the bitter cup out of which all of us must drink many times during the span of our mortal lives.

Some are found mourning because they feel crushed with sorrow as they hear the gospel and suddenly contemplate the evil of their past lives.

This happened to Alma the elder when he heard the prophet Abinadi bear his testimony just before Abinadi was burned at the stake. Alma was touched by Abinadi's inspired testimony, but when he tried to defend the prophet, the king's soldiers sought to kill him and he was forced to flee for his life.[16]

While Alma was in hiding, a horrible depression descended upon him as he contemplated the gross immorality and terrible sins he had committed as an apostate priest of King Noah. He longed for the gentle spirit of Jesus Christ to comfort him, and lead him back into the light.[17]

---

[15]Moses 6:6, P. of G. P.
[16]Mosiah, chapter 17, B. of M.
[17]Mosiah, chapter 18, B. of M.

To all such, Jesus said:

"And again, blessed are all they that mourn [who come unto me], for they shall be comforted."[18]

Alma was indeed comforted. As a result of his repentance and pleading with the Lord, he received the ministering of angels. Later he was ordained to the priesthood, and eventually he became the president of the church under King Mosiah.

In a season of mourning, there is no greater comfort than the soothing spirit of the Lord Jesus Christ. He can comfort those who have lost a loved one, those who are mourning because they are separated from home and family, or those who have been suffering the ravages of war. He can comfort those who have failed in their family business, suffered a broken marriage, or lost a rebellious runaway child. His comfort is also there for everyday things like a disappointment in love, failure to pass an exam, being dismissed from a job, or losing an election.

These are the heartbreaks of life, and if we will stay close to the Savior, they are the learning experiences that ultimately work for the good of all those who love the Lord.[19]

BLESSED ARE THE MEEK

Jesus gave the third beatitude as follows:

"And blessed are the meek [who come unto Christ], for they shall inherit the earth."[20]

The word "meek" has a special significance in this context. In the previous chapter Jesus had said that people must "repent, and become as a little child, and be baptized." Becoming as a little child is specifically identified with being "meek," and here Jesus is identifying meekness with the willingness to go down into the waters

---

[18]3 Nephi 12:4, B. of M.

[19]Romans 8:28; Doctrine and Covenants 90:24; 100:15.

[20]3 Nephi 12:5, B. of M.

of baptism and covenant with God that he or she will obey the commandments of God.

Notice that the meek shall inherit the earth. Baptism is the first step toward the celestial kingdom, and they who reach the celestial kingdom shall inherit the earth.[21] We therefore conclude that when Jesus associates meekness with inheriting the earth, he is saying it is essential that those who repent must be willing to enter the waters of baptism and receive a forgiveness of sins. No one will inherit the earth who has not taken that step.

Many of us who have been engaged in missionary work have had very promising contacts who turn out to be like Nicodemus. They are great people, well educated, possessing radiant personalities and undoubtedly would be a great asset to the kingdom. But they are not sufficiently meek or humble to be baptized.

These may accept the gospel in the next world when they come to their senses and realize what a great opportunity they rejected during earth life. However, they will not inherit the earth. They will go to a terrestrial glory on some other sphere.[22]

Note that this group had the privilege of accepting the gospel, but let it pass them by until they reached the spirit world. Even though they finally accepted it, the delay cost them a place in the higher kingdom. They receive a glory but not an inheritance on the celestialized earth.

Of course, if people have not heard the gospel in this life, they will get to hear it in the spirit world. If they accept it, they are treated as though they had accepted it "in the flesh."

---

[21]Doctrine and Covenants 88:17-19.
[22]Doctrine and Covenants 76:71, 74.

THE REWARD OF THOSE WHO HUNGER AND
THIRST AFTER RIGHTEOUSNESS

Jesus then introduced the fourth step in the sublimation and beatification of the human spirit. This turns out to be the endowment of the Holy Ghost with all the light, glory and joy that comes with it. The Savior said:

"And blessed are all they who do hunger and thirst after righteousness [who come unto me], for they shall be filled with the Holy Ghost."[23]

It is interesting that Jesus would emphasize the need to "hunger and thirst" after righteousness before members of the church will begin to feel the pure intelligence of the Holy Spirit penetrating their very being and flooding them with radiant enlightenment and a sweeping vista of new understanding.

Some people successfully navigate the preliminary steps to the kingdom of God, and then never hunger and thirst for the treasures of the gospel that lie beyond. As a result, there is no longer a longing or anxiety to go on toward perfection so the Holy Ghost can lead them toward more light and knowledge.

It was for this reason that Paul became so unhappy with the saints in his own day. They were too apathetic. Following their entry into the kingdom they went to sleep. There was no spark of spiritual hunger or vibrant intellectual curiosity to know more about the Lord and his purposes. Paul chastised them and said:

"Therefore *not* leaving the principles of the doctrine of Christ, let us go on unto *perfection*; not laying again the foundation of repentance from dead works, and of faith toward God."[24]

---

[23]3 Nephi 12:6, B. of M.
[24]JST Hebrews 6:1.

"Going on unto perfection" in our own day is like climbing a golden stairway of knowledge, self-improvement, and spiritual enhancement that leads toward the gates of heaven.

Early morning prayer followed by a session of scripture study is a good way to begin. If a person reads eight pages of scripture each day throughout the year, he or she can complete the entire standard works of the church in twelve months. This type of study program becomes even more profitable if it is repeated the next year—and the next.

In this connection, we are commanded to familiarize ourselves with the rich tapestry of our roots in the Old Testament, and relive the life and teachings of the Savior and his apostles in the New Testament.

We are also encouraged to study the history of the church so that we can become better acquainted with the opening scenes of our own great epoch, when the heavens were opened and modern men had the thrill of receiving direct revelations. Once again the Savior joined with ministering angels and began the restoration of the gospel of Jesus Christ for the last time.

The Lord has exhibited a keen anxiety to have his followers hunger and thirst after righteousness, that they might be filled with the Holy Ghost as they gain a warm familiarity with the scriptures and the history of the church.

THE IMPORTANCE OF MERCY
IN THE PLAN OF SALVATION

Surely all those who have received such a flood of mercy by having their own sins blotted out should be quick to be merciful to others. Therefore the Savior said:

"And blessed are the *merciful* [who come unto me], for they shall obtain mercy."[25]

---

[25] 3 Nephi 12:7, B. of M.

This beatitude clearly indicates that a basic principle of heaven requires those who seek mercy at the hands of our Heavenly Father to be equally merciful to their fellow men.

However, this is not as easy as it sounds. To illustrate the point, Jesus later told the parable of the king who forgave a huge debt of one of his servants. But, the scripture says:

"The same servant went out, and found one of his fellow servants, which owed him an hundred pence: and he laid hands on him, and took him by the throat, saying, Pay me that thou owest.

"And his fellow servant fell down at his feet, and besought him, saying, Have patience with me, and I will pay thee all.

"And he would not: but went and cast him into prison, till he should pay the debt.

"So when his fellow servants saw what was done, they were very sorry, and came and told unto their lord all that was done.

"Then his lord, after that he had called him, said unto him, O thou wicked servant, I forgave thee all that debt, because thou desiredst me:

"Shouldest not thou also have had compassion on thy fellow servant, even as I had pity on thee?

"And his lord was wroth, and delivered him to the tormentors, till he should pay all that was due unto him.

"So likewise shall my heavenly Father do also unto you, if ye from your hearts forgive not every one his brother their trespasses."[26]

---

[26]Matthew 18:28-35.

THE SUPREME VIRTUE—PURITY
IN HEART, MIND AND SPIRIT

With the beatification of the spirit there comes a sensitivity of heart and mind that quickly discriminates between that which is inspiring, pure and sweet compared to that which is debauched, ugly, filthy and unclean.

There is a glorious blessing awaiting those who cultivate this attribute in the heart, mind and spirit. Therefore the Lord said:

"And blessed are all the pure in heart [who come unto me], for they shall see God."[27]

From the most ancient times, the two most deadly weapons Satan has used to corrupt God's children and rob them of their salvation have been sexual sin and human greed. Both of these are products of impure minds.

Sexual sin includes fornication, adulterous relations, incest, homosexuality, bestiality, and pornography—which is committing fornication or adultery in the heart.

Then there are various forms of diabolical greed which corrupt the purity of heart with everything from cheating, lying, thievery, confidence schemes, crooked business deals, and fraudulent swindles. Worst of all are those nefarious perpetrators of calloused greed who carefully gain the confidence of widows, orphans and unsuspecting victims, and then deliberately defraud them of their meager savings.

In this Beatitude Jesus says that in the absence of repentance and complete forgiveness, none of these shall see God!

---

[27]3 Nephi 12:8, B. of M.

THE PEACEMAKER IS WORTH
MORE THAN PRECIOUS GOLD

The next quality is the ability to avoid quarreling and contention; to be known as one who is amiable, who is quick to pour oil on troubled waters, and who carefully steers a steady course in times of turbulence and stress. The Savior said:

"And blessed are all the peacemakers [who come unto me], for they shall be called the children of God."

Sometimes it is just as important to be a peace*keeper* as it is to be a peacemaker.

A peacekeeper is one who participates in a family, a community, or a classroom in such a way that it engenders harmony, security, obedience to rules of law, and protection of the innocent, while at the same time providing quick and appropriate punishment of the guilty.

King Benjamin was a just such a peacekeeper. Think how much more peaceful, happy, and secure all communities would be today if they had leaders who could say as King Benjamin said toward the close of his life:

"I have...not sought gold nor silver nor any manner of riches of you;

"Neither have I suffered that ye should be confined in dungeons, nor that ye should make slaves one of another, nor that ye should murder, or plunder, or steal, or commit adultery; nor even have I suffered that ye should commit any manner of wickedness, and have taught you that ye should keep the commandments of the Lord, in all things which he hath commanded you—

"And even I, myself, have labored with mine own hands that I might serve you, and that ye should not be laden with taxes, and that there should nothing come upon you which was grievous to be borne—and of all these things which I have spoken, ye yourselves are witnesses this day.

"Yet, my brethren, I have not done these things that I might boast, neither do I tell these things that thereby I might accuse you; but I tell you these things that ye may know that I can answer a clear conscience before God this day."[28]

Of course, being a peacekeeper or a peacemaker is especially challenging when a heated argument is already in progress.

This can sometimes happen in a classroom when everyone can sense that temperatures are rising. A wise teacher, or even a student, can create a more peaceful climate by simply requesting permission to ask a question. This tends to divert the discussion from a contest of personalities and introduces a slightly different perspective that calls for attention.

In contrast to this, a direct challenge to someone in a class usually precipitates an immediate debate. And of course a debate is a dialogue where someone must lose if someone else is going to win. Very often a simple question can result in a discussion while tempers cool, and in the end, everybody wins.

HOW STRONG IS YOUR TESTIMONY?

Finally we come to the two great tests that determine the mettle of a committed believer. The Savior said:

"And blessed are all they who are persecuted for my name's sake [who come unto me], for theirs is the kingdom of heaven.

"And blessed are ye [who come unto me] when men shall revile you and persecute, and shall say all manner of evil against you falsely, for my sake."

"For ye shall have great joy and be exceedingly glad, for great shall be your reward in heaven; for so persecuted they the prophets who were before you."[29]

---

[28]Mosiah 2:12-15, B. of M.
[29]3 Nephi 12:10-12, B. of M.

Thus we come to the end of these beautiful beatitudes. They are God's progressive degrees of refinement that lead to the eventual sublimation of the human spirit.

*   *   *   *

A PERSONAL SEARCH FOR THE MEANING OF THE ATONEMENT

Several years ago I wrote an article describing how my mission president, Elder John A. Widtsoe of the Council of the Twelve Apostles, took the time to guide this writer through the scriptures so I could understand the teachings of Amulek on the atonement.[1] This instruction became such a treasure of spiritual knowledge that down through the years I have been eternally grateful to Elder Widtsoe for his patience, his insights and his guidance.

Here is the story of how it happened.

Ever since I was a small boy, I always had a lot of questions about the crucifixion. On Easter I would listen to the story of the suffering of the Savior and wonder why all that torture on a Roman cross was necessary. In my mind, the reality of it was so terrible that it made me cringe to think about it, and it made me want to find out why Heavenly Father would ask Jesus to go through that horrible ordeal.

In fact, Jesus himself raised this very question with his Beloved Father when he prayed in the Garden of Gethsemane. He said:

"Father, ALL THINGS ARE POSSIBLE UNTO THEE; take away this cup from me!"[2]

It was as though he were saying, "Father, you are God. You are all-powerful. You must know of some other way to achieve your

---

[1]Skousen, *The First Two Thousand Years*, pp. 352-362.
[2]Mark 14:36.

righteous purposes without requiring me to be crucified and die on a Roman cross. Please take this cup from me."

In our mind's eye we can conceive of these words racing with the speed of thought to the Father's glorious habitation near Kolob.[3] And we can visualize the Father receiving it. But what Jesus did not know was the torturous truth that as he faced the terrible crisis of the cross, it was as agonizing to the Father as it was to the Son. Who will measure the anguish of our Heavenly Father or the compassion that throbbed throughout his very being as he sent the angel to say:

"My Son, there is no other way."

But why? Down through the corridors of time, this pitiful plea of the Savior echoes through the chambers of one's mind. One cannot help asking:

Why couldn't the Father work it out some other way? Even more important, why was this terrible ordeal considered necessary for the salvation of mankind? Did the Father require this sacrifice or was it required by somebody else? If it was somebody else, who was it? And in the final analysis, what did it accomplish? or, even more to the point, if it did prove important to accomplish something of eternal necessity, how was it done?

COULD A MISSION PRESIDENT ANSWER THESE QUESTIONS?

When I was called as a seventeen-year-old to serve as a missionary in England, these questions were still rumbling around in my mind. The spiritual leader in charge of all the European missions was an apostle named Elder John A. Widtsoe, and his headquarters were in England. Early in my mission I began to hope that sometime, somehow, I would be able to ask this apostle about the atonement.

Elder Widtsoe was not only a great religious leader, but he was one of the foremost secular scholars in the church. He had graduated from Harvard with highest honors and did his advance studies at the University of Goettingen in Germany. He had served as the president

---

[3]Abraham 3:3, P. of G. P.

of two universities, and was among the few Americans who belonged to the Royal Society of London. Within the church, he was considered to be one of the most profound scriptural and doctrinal scholars.

Finally, I had the opportunity to ask Elder Widtsoe my questions. However, his response was somewhat disappointing. He said:

"Oh, you would have to know a lot more about our Heavenly Father before you would understand the answers to those questions. In fact, you would have to spend several years laying line upon line and precept upon precept in order to get the whole picture."

But I was persistent. I promised to take the time. Finally, he decided to slowly guide me through the scriptures so I could find those concepts which would lay a foundation for what I needed to know. However, Elder Widtsoe turned out to be a most singular teacher. Instead of giving me the chapter and verse for each precept, he would describe the principle in general terms, and then tell me approximately where it was in the scriptures. After that, it remained my task to find it.

So it took a long time. In fact, it did indeed require "several years of study"—extending long after my mission—before Elder Widtsoe felt satisfied that I was beginning to understand the profound principles underlying the atonement of Jesus Christ.

Eventually, after hearing my final presentation, he suggested that it be written up in a carefully documented treatise and sent to him. This material was later published in the appendix of *The First 2,000 Years,*[4] and was entitled, "Why Was the Atonement Necessary?"

Anyone acquainted with the writings of John A. Widtsoe will recognize that some of the most fundamental principles underlying the necessity for the atonement are set forth in his books and articles. For example, the role of the organized intelligences—by which the Father rules the universe—is discussed in his book *Joseph Smith,*

---

[4]W. Cleon Skousen, *The First 2,000 Years*, Salt Lake City: Bookcraft, 1953.

Seeker After Truth, pp. 134-138,[5] and also in his book *Joseph Smith as Scientist*, pp. 150-152.[6]

The lifetime studies on the atonement by this distinguished apostle seemed to have grown out of the question raised by Jacob, the early Nephite prophet, who said:

"Why not speak of the atonement of Christ, and attain to a perfect knowledge of him?"[7]

Early in his life, Elder Widtsoe learned that each of us—with careful, prayerful study—can understand the atonement and make it a much more meaningful part of our lives. In the process, we can also come to know and love the Father and the Son in a much more personal way.

IT ALL BEGINS WITH UNDERSTANDING THE NATURE OF GODHOOD

The scriptures and prophetic teachings now available to us describe the marvelous pathway of eternal progression which was worked out aeons before we were born. This upward journey toward exaltation and a fullness of joy ascends heavenward through a whole series of distinctive phases.

PHASE I

IN THE BEGINNING ELOHIM WAS ORDAINED TO SET UP A NEW KINGDOM

The first phase is about our Heavenly Father himself. This phase requires a righteous, dedicated individual in the family of the Gods who will make the necessary preparations for the setting up of a whole new kingdom. In our case, this was our Heavenly Father, who is known as "Man of Holiness," or Elohim.[8]

---

[5]John A. Widtsoe, *Joseph Smith, Seeker After Truth*, Salt Lake City: Deseret News Press, 1952.
[6]John A. Widtsoe, *Joseph Smith As Scientist*, Salt Lake City: Bookcraft, 1964.
[7]Jacob 4:12, B. of M.
[8]Moses 6:57, P. of G. P.; *Teachings of Joseph Smith*, p. 371.

To prepare himself for Godhood, this noble, supremely intelligent being had to pass through exactly the same pattern of eternal progression we are now following. As the Prophet Joseph Smith said:

"God himself was once as we are now, and is an exalted man, and sits enthroned in yonder heavens. That is the great secret .... It is the first principle of the Gospel to know for a certainty the Character of God, and to know that we may converse with him as one man converses with another, and that he was once a man like us; yea, that God himself, the Father of us all, dwelt on an earth, the same as Jesus Christ himself did...."[9]

Once our Heavenly Father had attained exaltation under the guidance of his own Father he was ordained by his Father to begin setting up a new kingdom similar to those which the :family of the Gods had set up before him. It was a monumental honor to be loved and trusted to the extent that he would be ordained to organize or "create" a new kingdom. We are told:

"In the resurrection, men who have been faithful and diligent in all things in the flesh, have kept their first and second estate, and [are] worthy to be crowned Gods, even the sons of God, will be ORDAINED to organize matter."[10]

It will be immediately apparent that if the family of the Gods is continually ordaining numerous worthy individuals to organize planets, solar systems and galaxies, astronomers should find some evidence of this mammoth cosmic growth pattern. By 1929, the perfecting of the telescope permitted Edwin Hubble to make the landmark observation that "wherever you look, distant galaxies are moving rapidly away from us."[11] This means that we are at the core of the cosmos, or at least our Father's part of the cosmos, and the universe is expanding in all directions away from this core as new

---

[9]Smith, *Teachings of the Prophet Joseph Smith*, pp. 345-346.
[10]Brigham Young, *Journal of Discourses*, 15:137.
[11]Stephen Hawking, *A Brief History of Time*, New York: Bantam Books, 1988, p. 8.

kingdoms are formed and old kingdoms are pushed further out into space.

So instead of a "big bang" expanding the universe, there may be a different explanation. For example, we now know that behind the elaborate phenomena of our ever-expanding universe there is a family of highly intelligent and exhalted beings who are building galaxy upon galaxy. The Gods have provided a pattern of eternal progression for their worthy posterity, and as each individual attains the perfection of an exhalted, resurrected being, he can be ordained to begin organizing another kingdom. As we have already seen, one of those perfected resurrected beings was our Heavenly Father who was trained and ordained during phase 1 so He would be ready for the next step.

PHASE II

HOW THE FATHER ACQUIRED HIS POWER

Having been ordained from above, our Heavenly Father set about to build a power structure from below.

This is an interesting priesthood principle. It is the way a ward, a stake, or the church itself is set up. Take a bishop, for example. He is ordained from above, but his status as a great bishop depends upon the sustaining support he receives from his ward members. This means he must be trusted and honored in his calling or he will have little influence or power in his ward. Or, to say it another way, he was ordained from above but his POWER is from below.

Our Heavenly Father says the same is true of those who attain Godhood. Speaking of himself, the Father says in one scripture that his "honor," which emanates upward from those he governs, is his "power."[12] This explain why he would say in another place that he is from above, but "my power lieth beneath."[13]

---

[12]Doctrine and Covenants 29:36.
[13]Doctine and Covenants 63:59.

In order to appreciate this principle of "structuring power from beneath," it is necessary to realize that our Heavenly Father can only maintain the power and support of those he governs by submitting himself to the strictest discipline. He must absolutely avoid anything that might destroy the love, confidence, and trust of those over whom he exercises Godhood. This is a highly delicate and sensitive relationship because the vast host of intelligences that have been organized on various levels of his kingdom look to him as the great arbiter, the dispenser of justice, and the superintendent of that portion of the cosmos assigned to his jurisdiction.

But what if our Heavenly Father were like the supreme being envisioned by St. Augustine, the famous religious philosopher of the fourth century? He believed God could do anything he pleased, even going so far as to arbitrarily save some souls to suit his private whims, and then summarily consign the rest to eternal damnation and hell.

Our Heavenly Father says he could NOT do that. And he gives us a very impressive reason why. He says that if he were capricious, arbitrary or unfair, he would CEASE TO BE GOD. He would lose his influence, and with it his power. Those over whom he presides would cease to honor him, cease to believe in him, and cease to obey him.

Of course, our Heavenly Father is too wise to allow that to happen, but he wants us to know that it *could* happen. One of the most important principles to learn about Godly government is that those who occupy presiding positions must maintain the love and confidence of those they govern or they could fall.

THE RISKS OF GODHOOD

No one would dare to teach this doctrine unless God had revealed it himself. Therefore the scriptures state it so clearly, no one should miss its full implications. They tell us that:

Our Heavenly Father cannot be unjust or "he would cease to be God."[14] He cannot allow his compassion or love of mercy to rob the demands of justice, or "he would cease to be God."[15] He cannot lie or he would cease to be God."[16] He cannot vacillate and change or he would "cease to be God."[17] He cannot "look upon sin with the least degree of allowance," or he would cease to be God.[18]

This vividly establishes an ironclad principle of Godhood: the Father must accomplish his purposes within very strict parameters that insure the trust and love of those he governs, or he would "cease to be God."

This tells us that when Jesus asked the Father if it were *possible* for the Father to take us back into his presence without the atoning sacrifice he received the most explicit of all answers, "No." The Father did not have that option. There was something compelling about the Savior's crucifixion which made it absolutely necessary for the angelic messenger to tell Jesus, "There is no other way."

The scriptures reveal why this was so. To get a basic understanding of the big picture we must go back and trace the pattern of eternal progression from our earliest primal state up until now. We need to know how the Father built his power base from *beneath*, and how we got where we are.

THE FATHER BEGAN BY ASSEMBLING A VAST HOST OF PRIMAL INTELLIGENCES

When the prophet Lehi was explaining the creation to his sons he said everything in the universe is made out of just two things—something "to act" and something "to be acted upon."[19]

---

[14]Alma 42:13, B. of M.

[15]Alma 42:25, B. of M.

[16]Titus 1:2; Doctrine and Covenants 62:6.

[17]Mormon 9:19, B. of M.

[18]Doctrine and Covenants 1:31; Alma 45:16, B. of M.

[19]2 Nephi 2:14, B. of M.

A modern scripture tells us that the thing which acts is called an "intelligence,"[20] and that which is acted upon is called "element" or a particle of primal matter.[21]

These same passages tell us that both of these entities are eternal. They were not created, and they cannot be destroyed. They can only be organized, reorganized, or disorganized.

We are also told that these "intelligences" think and act independently.[22] They don't have to do anything. When the Father gives them a command, he must "wait" until they "obey."[23] They are very much like the members of a ward, and, like the bishop, our Heavenly Father sometimes has to be very patient "waiting to be obeyed."

We are not given any details concerning the long period of testing and training through which we passed as intelligences, but we are told that some of the intelligences progressed much faster than others during the testing period.[24] When Joseph Smith came to an understanding of this principle he recorded in his diary:

"...in the evening with the Twelve and their wives at Elder Woodruff's...I explained many important principles in relation to [the] *progressive improvement in the scale of intelligent existence.*"[25]

As a result, all of these intelligences had to be graded and prepared for assignments which would be appropriate for their individual abilities and inclinations. When the time was right our Heavenly Father prepared to usher these intelligences into their next stage of advancement or development.

---

[20]Doctrine and Covenants 93:29.

[21]Doctrine and Covenants 93:35.

[22]Doctrine and Covenants 93:30.

[23]Abraham 4:18, P. of G. P.

[24]Abraham 3:18-19, P. of G. P.; *Documentary History of the Church*, vol. 4, p. 519.

[25]*History of the Church* of the Church of Jesus Christ of Latter-day Saints, Salt Lake City: The Deseret Book Company, 1976, vol. IV, p. 519 (emphasis added).

PHASE III

THE SPIRIT CREATION, OR FIRST ESTATE

From our Heavenly Father's perspective, this next step involved a massive operation which is completely beyond our comprehension. The scripture says:

"The Lord God, created [in the Hebrew, "organized"] all things ... spiritually before they were naturally upon the face of the earth."[26]

To achieve this, here is what the scripture says he did.

The Father selected the most brilliant and progressive of all these intelligences and had him "begotten" into an embodiment of spirit matter "after his own image." This supremely intelligent being thereafter became known as the Firstborn. As Paul says:

"His dear son ... who is the image of the invisible God, the first born of every creature."[27]

The scripture says that he was then tutored, tested, and educated until he developed from "grace to grace" and received a "fullness of truth."[28] This is defined in scripture as "a knowledge of things past, present, and future."[29]

Elohim then made the Firstborn his general manager for the organizing of all the rest of the Father's kingdom.[30]

When John wrote his Gospel he captured the magnitude of this assignment when he said:

"In the beginning was the Word, and the Word was with God, and the Word was God. The same was in the beginning with God. All

---

[26]Moses 3:5, P. of G. P.

[27]Colossians 1:13.

[28]Doctrine and Covenants 93:11-14.

[29]Doctrine and Covenants 93:24.

[30]Moses 1:32-33, P. of G. P.

things were made by him; and without him was not any thing made that was made."[31]

Then, to make sure his readers would realize that he was talking about the Savior, John added:

"And the Word was made flesh, and dwelt among us, (and we beheld his glory, the glory as of the only begotten of the Father,) full of grace and truth."[32]

The fact that the Savior was put in charge of "our" creation is of particular interest to us because the scripture tells us that God's course is one eternal round,[33] and this brilliant individual who became the "Firstborn"—and who was given the name of Jehovah—was placed in charge of the round to which we belong. He worked under the direction of the Father and here is the scripture which tells us the vast dimensions of that which the Firstborn—or Jehovah—engineered, organized and ultimately accomplished:

"The worlds were made by him; *men* were made by him; all things were made by him, and through him, and of him."[34]

This means that the rest of us had to wait until the Firstborn was perfected and prepared to take over the organizing process. It also means that even though we were begotten as the spirit children of our Heavenly Father, the organizing and preparing of our spirit bodies was under the direction of the Firstborn.

This could only be accomplished by allowing Jehovah or the Firstborn to become as completely loved, honored, and obeyed as the Father, himself. The Firstborn thereby became the ONE personality among all of the intelligences assigned to our round who could later qualify for the role of our Redeemer. This led the prophet Nephi to write:

---

[31]John 1:1-3.
[32]John 1:14.
[33]Doctrine and Covenants 3:2; 35:1; 1 Nephi 10:19; Alma 7:20, B. of M.
[34]Doctrine and Covenants 93:10.

"There is none other name given under heaven save it be this Jesus Christ, of which I have spoken, whereby man can be saved."[35]

Peter said the same thing.[36]

The scriptures sometimes describe spirits as "intelligences that were organized before the world was."[37] This means that the intelligences were organized with particles of spirit matter and then structured into various planets, together with all the embellishments of plants, animals, and mankind to inhabit them. As we noted earlier, the Lord speaks concerning this spiritual creation and says:

"I, the Lord God, created all thing...spiritually, before they were naturally upon the face of the earth."[38]

From this we conclude that during the spirit creation all things were organized by combining intelligences with particles of primal spirit matter.

We should also mention that some scholars have thought that spirit is "immaterial" and without substance, but the prophet Joseph Smith explained:

"Spirit is a substance ... it is material, but ... it is more pure, elastic and refined matter than the [mortal] body."[39]

As we mentioned earlier when we were discussing the science of miracles in Chapter 7, the ingredient of "intelligence" which human beings possess is simply a very high order of the same family of intelligences that Jehovah implanted in everything that exists. We read:

"There is not a particle of element which is not filled with life [or intelligence] .... It is in the rock, the sand, the dust, in water, air, the

---

[35]2 Nephi 25:20, B. of M.
[36]Acts 4:12.
[37]Abraham 3:22, P. of G. P.
[38]Moses 3:5, P. of G. P.
[39]Smith, *Teachings of the Prophet Joseph Smith*, p. 207.

gases, and, in short, in every description and organization of matter, whether it be solid, liquid, or gaseous, particle operating with particle."[40]

As the intelligences differed in their various degrees of advancement, they were assigned to different levels of organized matter that represent all the wide variety of organized "things" which exist, from planets to people.

As the apostle John A. Widtsoe wrote:

"It was clearly comprehended by the Prophet [Joseph Smith] and his associates that intelligence is the vivifying force of all creation—animate or inanimate—the rock and tree and beast and man, have ascending degrees of intelligence."[41]

As Joseph Smith's close associate, Brigham Young, indicated, all matter is "capacitated to receive intelligence."[42]

It is also important to notice that as "things" were organized, God placed a governing intelligence in charge of each entity to superintend the vast order of intelligences and matter comprising that being or "thing." Each of us, for example, constitute the governing intelligence in charge of the billions of intelligences which are organized and functioning in our bodies. Even the earth has a governing intelligence which Enoch heard crying out to the Lord.[43]

It was a major surprise to scientists when they first began seeing evidence of individual intelligences exercising their own independent self-determination clear down among the most minute forms of organic substance.

By 1927, Werner Heisenberg, Nobel Prize winner and the father of Quantum Mechanics, was writing in scientific papers that the

---

[40]Brigham Young, *Journal of Discourses*, vol. 3:277.
[41]John A. Widtsoe, *Joseph Smith, Seeker After Truth*, Salt Lake City: Deseret News Press, 1952, pp. 150-151.
[42]*Journal of Discourses*, vol. 7, p. 2.
[43]Moses 7:48, P. of G. P.

particles of matter do not follow the precise pattern of mechanical operation. Then Dr. Robert A. Millikan, another Nobel Prize winner from the California Institute of Technology, isolated the electron for the first time and announced that electrons behave as though they were imbued with finite intelligence that makes them independent and individualistic. He was saying, in other words, that they do not follow precisely what had been assumed to be fixed and inflexible laws of physics.

Of course, these manifestations of individualistic intelligences, operating in particles of matter, came from a secular study of earthly substances. However, the Lord has indicated that the pattern for the organizing of "things" in our earthly existence is similar to the pattern followed in organizing intelligence with particles of spirit matter during our preearth existence. The scripture reads:

"That which is spiritual being in the likeness of that which is temporal; and that which is temporal in the likeness of that which is spiritual; the spirit of man in the likeness of his person, as also the spirit of the beast, and every other creature which God has created."[44]

Thus, by following principles that are now becoming more familiar to us, the elaborate spirit creation was finally completed and called, "the First Estate."[45]

MAJOR EVENTS DURING THE FIRST ESTATE

We now know that several major events occurred during the time we were in the spirit world or the First Estate. For example:

There seem to have been several great councils in which we all participated. At one of these councils the Firstborn, or Jehovah, explained the purpose of the First Estate. We were told that each intelligence or personality would be tested to see if he or she would do "all things whatsoever the Lord their God shall command

---

[44]Doctrine and Covenants 77:2.
[45]Abraham 3:25-26, P. of G. P.

them."[46] If so, those individuals would be "added upon" and have the blessing of passing on into the Second Estate or temporal world.[47]

However, it was not long before one of the early-born spirits—which we assume to be the meaning of the title, "Son of the Morning," or Lucifer—became very jealous of the Firstborn.

This became evident to all of us when a council was held to discuss the plans for the structuring of our present earth. In that council, the Father chose the Firstborn as the superintendent in charge, but almost immediately it became apparent that the "Second" was very angry and began to violate the laws of the First Estate. This resulted in considerable dissension because "many followed after him."[48] Nevertheless, at this council the contention gravitating around Lucifer did not erupt into a war in heaven. That came later.

Before going further, we should mention that this particular earth has great significance to the Firstborn or Jehovah. We are told that he had created a vast number of planets before this one,[49] but, as we know, it turned out that our earth was the one where he himself would live and have his mortal existence.

Furthermore, the scripture says that it will be on this very planet where the great last battle will be fought between the forces of the Firstborn and the forces of Satan. And it will be from this very planet that Satan and his hosts will be cast out of the Father's domain."[50]

This would seem to indicate that our present earth is the last of the creations belonging to this round, and that it will be on this planet that the great winding up scene for this round will take place.

---

[46]Abraham 3:25, P. of G. P.

[47]Abraham 3:26, P. of G. P.

[48]Abraham 3:27-28, P. of G. P.

[49]Moses 1:33, P. of G. P.

[50]Doctrine and Covenants 76:36-38; 88:112-115.

THE WAR IN HEAVEN

The crisis which is mentioned in scripture as "the war in heaven,"[51] occurred during a special council which was called by the Father to select the "Redeemer" who would be required for the perfecting of the Second Estate. Before any selection was made, Lucifer was the first to speak up. However, he did not volunteer to be the Redeemer because he said he had a new plan that would not require a Redeemer. He then presented a ridiculous scheme based on his recommendation that the Father set up a heavenly dictatorship that would not allow anyone to sin in the Second Estate.

He reasoned that if no one were allowed to sin during the Second Estate there would be no need for a redeemer with all of that terrible suffering connected with the atonement. Satan felt that the genius of his plan was the marvelous idea of temporarily suspending free agency during phase III of our eternal progression. If his plan had been adopted, here is what we assume would have happened:

Each person would get his or her assignment.
Each person would then be compelled to fulfill his or her assignment.
No disorder would be allowed.
No disobedience would be allowed.
There would be no sin.
There would be no injustice.
There would be no failures.

Under this plan, all would return to the Father untainted, therefore all would be saved. None would be lost. In short, this was a guaranteed, no-fault, eternal life insurance program.

It is interesting that the Greek philosopher, Plato, reflected some of these same ideas in proposing what he thought would be an ideal society. He said:

---

[51]Revelation 12:7.

"The greatest principle of all is that nobody, whether male or female, should be without a leader. Nor should the mind of anybody be habituated to letting him do anything at all on his own initiative; neither out of zeal; nor even playfully. But in war and in the midst of peace—to his leader he shall direct his eye and follow him faithfully. And even in the smallest matter he should stand under leadership. For example, he should get up, or move, or wash, or take his meals ... only if he has been told to do so. In a word, he should teach his soul, by long habit, never to dream of acting independently, and to become utterly incapable of it."[52]

Thomas Jefferson called Plato's theories "nonsense."[53] John Adams waded through all of his writings and said: "My disappointment was very great, my astonishment was greater, my disgust shocking."[54]

THE FREEDOM FACTOR

The Father's Firstborn held out for a Second Estate with everyone enjoying free agency. In fact, this was the Father's program similar to that which had been used throughout the eternities. That is why the Firstborn, or Jehovah, said: "Father, *thy* will be done."[55]

But a free society is a very risky society. If all are free to make their own choices, we are bound to have a certain amount of disorder, a certain amount of injustice, and a broad differential in obedience to God's commandments. To put it bluntly, some make it, some do not. That is why it is risky.

When the "freedom plan" of Jehovah (or the Savior) was chosen by the Father, Lucifer was outraged. He felt his 100 percent guaranteed, no-fault insurance program was so brilliant, innovative and efficient that he thought the Father would embrace it with

---

[52]Quoted by Eugene H. Methvin in *The Rise of Radicalism*, New Rochelle, N.Y.: Arlington House, 1973, p. 30.

[53]Andrew Allison, *The Real Thomas Jefferson*, Washington: The National Center for Constitutional Studies, 1981, p. 579.

[54]Quoted by Jefferson in *The Writings of Thomas Jefferson*, Albert Ellery Berg, ed., Washington: The Thomas Jefferson Memorial Association, 1907, vol. 15:156.

[55]Moses 4:2, P. of G. P.

animated enthusiasm. In fact, he wanted to be sure he got the credit for it and asked that the Father transfer his "honor" to him. "[56]

With so much arrogance and conceit festering within him it was almost predictable what would happen when Lucifer's plan was rejected. Lucifer rebelled. He tried to overthrow the Father from his throne and make himself the master of the Second Estate.[57]

So the battle was joined, and the conflict began. But the war in heaven was not fought with swords and spears. It was fought with polemics, debate, and testimony-bearing."[58]

In this contest Lucifer's plan was the easiest to sell because it offered a 100 percent guarantee of getting through the Second Estate unscathed—and all of this by merely giving up free agency for awhile!

On the other hand, the most important argument for the supporters of Jehovah was the fact that if Satan lost, none of his followers would participate any further in the Father's plan of eternal progression. They would not receive physical bodies, and they would be cast out of the Father's program of eternal progression forever.[59]

Finally, after a mighty struggle, there was a great victory by the Savior's righteous "soldiers of God"—which is one of the meanings of the word, Israel. Two-thirds finally ratified the Savior's plan, whereupon Lucifer and one-third of the Father's spirit children were cast out. However, it serves God's purposes to allow these rebellious spirits to operate on the temporal earth during part of the Second Estate.[60] Nevertheless, their doom is to eventually be cast into outer darkness and eternally suffer what is called "the second death."[61]

---

[56]Moses 4:1, P. of G. P.
[57]Isaiah 14:12-14; Doctrine and Covenants 29:36.
[58]Revelations 12:11.
[59]Doctrine and Covenants 76:44.
[60]Revelations 12:12; Jude, Verse 6.
[61]Doctrine and Covenants 76:36-37.

When the teaching and training of the First Estate were completed, we were ready for the plunge into the testing or probationary existence which is called the Second Estate.

PHASE IV

OUR PRESENT MORTAL LIFE, THE SECOND ESTATE

Our Heavenly Father set up our mortal life here on earth to accomplish three things:

First, to clothe our spirits with a temporal body without which we can never attain a fullness of joy nor inherit eternal life.[62]

Second, to learn the difference between good and evil by actually living in an environment where good and evil exist side by side.[63]

Third, to pass through a "probationary estate," where we can be tested to determine whether we will accept Christ as our Savior, repent of our sins, enter into a covenant with him and thereafter live the commandments of the Father to the best of our abilities.[64]

However, *this whole plan had one major problem.*

This is the problem mentioned by Paul when he said: "For all have sinned, and come short of the glory of God."[65]

How can our Father, who "cannot look upon sin with the least degree of allowance,"[66] take us back into his presence to be further trained for Godhood, when we are still tainted with the effects of learning the difference between good and evil while here on earth? Some of the evil inevitably rubs off on all of us, so that none of us can go out of this life as a creature of perfection. Only the Savior succeeded in doing that."[67]

---

[62]Doctrine and Covenants 93:33-34.

[63]2 Nephi 2:5, 26; Alma 12:31, B. of M.

[64]Alma 12:32-34, B. of M.

[65]Romans 3:23.

[66]Doctrine and Covenants 1:31; 1 Nephi 10:21, B. of M.

[67]Hebrews 15.

Meanwhile, the rest of us, no matter how diligent, have "fallen short of the glory of God," and are unworthy to return to the presence of the Father where no "unclean thing" is allowed."[68]

This brings us to a gigantic roadblock in the plan of eternal progression. We know our training for Godhood required that we learn the difference between good and evil. Having done so, is the Father to be robbed of the fruits of his great educational program just because of this technicality?

It might occur to us that the Father could take us back on his own initiative if he really wanted to. After all, he is God, and if he is satisfied that we have done our best, who can complain?

We have already seen that this option is not open to the Father. As the Supreme Administrator of justice and fairness in our universe, he could not take this arbitrary and unfair step in favor of those training for Godhood without an immediate outcry from all the other intelligences. No doubt Lucifer and his dark angels would be out in front, leading the revolt.

These potential protests are what the scripture calls, "the *demands of justice.*"[69] When we stop to think about it, many of these intelligences were held back and given lesser assignments as a result of their failure to comply with all of God's commandments, or because they were lacking the quality of genuine diligence in their performance. Because these were held back they would certainly object if they saw the Father arbitrarily taking back into his glorious kingdom a group who had fallen short of the glory of the Father during their training for Godhood. Their howl of objections could certainly be described as "the demands of justice."

So how does the Father get around this obstacle? How have the families of the Gods *always* gotten around the "demands of justice" so that these advanced graduates in Godhood training might be brought back into the presence of God?

---

[68] 1 Nephi 15:34, B. of M.; Moses 6:57, P. of G. P.
[69] Alma 34:16, B. of M.

OVERCOMING THE DEMANDS OF JUSTICE

The answer is found in the very nature of the intelligences themselves. Our Heavenly Father knows that all of the intelligences are endowed with a strong and compelling sense of compassion. When someone has suffered intensely, these intelligences are inclined to express their sympathy by granting certain things "for the sake" of that individual that would be otherwise refused.

Thus we are introduced to the principal ingredients required for the success of the atonement. These two elements are love and mercy.[70]

To make these operate so as to overcome the demands of justice, two things must be provided.

The first requirement is that there must be an individual for whom all of the intelligences have developed a compelling sense of love. We can now appreciate why the Father was so careful during Phase II to see that his Firstborn was placed in a central position where he could become the most loved of all the "organized intelligences" in our vast system—a love corresponding to that which is felt for the Father himself.

This love and trust was further enhanced by having the Firstborn select, train, and assign all of the intelligences to their respective places. This is why the Father made him the "creator" or organizer of all things.[71]

The second ingredient necessary to overcome the demands of justice is to have this much beloved leader undergo an experience of such excruciating agony that it would arouse a moving sense of compassion and mercy in every single intelligence belonging to the Father's kingdom.

---

[70]Alma 34:14-15, B. of M.
[71]John 1:3.

Amulek said the suffering had to be so terrible that it would have an "infinite" impact.[72] This means it had to reach the outermost regions of the Father's kingdom, and cause the intelligences to cringe with anguish and compassion as they saw what was happening to the Father's Firstborn.

This is what placed the Firstborn in an ideal position so that his suffering would arouse the flood of sympathy that would permit him to plead that for "his sake" he be allowed to take his "brethren" back with him into the presence of the Father. The Father could not do that on his own, or he would "cease to be God." However, the Father can do it—with no risk whatever—if the Savior has overcome the demands of justice through the merits of the mercy which he has engendered in the intelligences through his suffering.

This whole divine procedure is spelled out by the Savior himself in the following scripture where we notice that the entire petition is based on his suffering and for his sake:

"Listen to him who is the advocate with the Father, who is pleading your cause before him—saying: Father, behold the SUFFERINGS and DEATH of him who did no sin, in whom thou wast well pleased; behold the BLOOD of thy Son which was SHED, the blood of him whom thou gavest that thyself might be glorified;

"Wherefore, Father, SPARE THESE MY BRETHREN that believe on my name, that they may come unto me and have everlasting life."[73]

We notice that this personal supplication by the Savior is not for "just anyone." It is for those who "believe on my [his] name." It is a fundamental principle of the Gospel that the Savior's sacrifice can only overcome the "demands of justice" for those who have repented and done their best to qualify for this blessing. As Amulek has said:

---

[72]Alma 34:12, B. of M.
[73]Doctrine and Covenants 45:3-5.

"And thus he shall bring salvation to all those who shall believe on his name; [and] ... have faith unto repentance.

"And thus mercy can satisfy the demands of justice, and encircles them in the arms of safety, while he that exercises no faith unto repentance is exposed to the whole law of the demands of justice; therefore only unto him that has faith unto repentance is brought about the great and eternal plan of redemption."[74]

IS A SIN AN "OFFENSE" AGAINST GOD OR DOES IT CREATE A DEBT WE OWE TO GOD?

Some people like to think of Christ's suffering as undergoing the punishment that men and women should be receiving themselves because of their sins—sort of like paying another person's debts. This is called the "balancing of the books." Others call it the "compensatory" doctrine of *quid pro quo,* or "THIS much suffering for THAT much sin."

The concept of balancing the books is attractive because it is simple and therefore easy to understand. Gospel scholars have occasionally used this symbolism in order to make a point without going into the more precise but complex aspects of the atonement.

Nevertheless, as we mature in our understanding of the Gospel, we come to realize that Jesus could not pay for our sins the way someone might pay another person's debt. The scripture says that approach would be immoral and unjust.

As one prophet points out, it would never satisfy the demands of justice to have Jesus try to compensate for the wrongs committed by someone else. A sinner could not approach the gates of heaven and claim he was pure or guiltless because Jesus had paid the debt or suffered the penalty for sins which the sinner should have paid for himself.

The great Amulek explained the fallacy of this approach by saying:

---

[74]Alma 34:15-16, B. of M.

"Now there is not any man that can sacrifice his own blood which will atone for the sins of another. Now, if a man murdereth, behold will our law, which is just, take the life of his brother? I say unto you, Nay. But the law requireth the life of him who hath murdered."[75]

So one person cannot pay for the sins of another the way one might pay for the debts of another. Amulek is simply saying that where sin is concerned, the punishing of one person for the offenses of another would not satisfy anyone's sense of justice.

On the other hand, the atonement, as we have pointed out, is a procedure by which a glorious and sinless personage such as the Savior, builds up enough love and sympathy among the hosts of intelligences so that for "his sake" the offenses of the penitent sinner will be overlooked as a favor to him. It is important to appreciate that the intelligences do not feel any particular sympathy for the sinner who has fallen short of the glory of God and is asking for a blessing he doesn't actually deserve. It is because of their love and sympathy for Jesus that the "demands of justice" are satisfied, and the sin is overlooked.

What is particularly interesting is the scripture which says that past sins are only overlooked by the hosts of intelligences so long as the Savior intercedes because of that person's righteousness. The moment that individual discontinues being righteous, and the Savior stops interceding for him, ALL OF HIS FORMER SINS RETURN. Here is the way the Lord says it:

"...go your ways, and sin no more, but unto that soul who sinneth shall the FORMER SINS RETURN."[76]

Notice that this scripture which describes "former sins" returning, does not fit the "compensatory" theory of the atonement. Under the "compensatory" concept, a debt—once paid—is gone forever. Not so, the Lord says. The possibility of "former sins returning" is only

---

[75]Alma 34:11-12, B. of M.
[76]Doctrine and Covenants 82:7.

possible in a situation where the mediation of the Savior is dependent on a person repenting and trying to do his best. The moment there is backsliding, the former sins return because Jesus is no longer interceding in that person's behalf.

RESTRICTIONS ON THE ATONEMENT

From this we can see that, although the atonement is infinite, the Savior is nevertheless restricted as to those for whom he can plead. He can only use his good offices on behalf of those who have sincerely repented, otherwise the intelligences feel that justice is being cheated. In a modern revelation, the Savior says:

"Therefore I command you to repent—repent, lest I smite you by the rod of my mouth, and by my wrath, and by my anger, and your sufferings be sore—how sore you know not, how exquisite you know not, yea, how hard to bear you know not.

"For behold, I, God, have suffered these things for all, that they might not suffer if they would repent; But if they would not repent they *must suffer even* as I; Which suffering caused myself, even God, the greatest of all, to tremble because of pain, and to bleed at every pore, and to suffer both body and spirit—and would that I might not drink the bitter cup, and shrink."[77]

It is as though the Lord were pleading with us and saying, "Don't let my suffering be in vain. I was crucified for you, but you must qualify yourself or you will not receive it. I can become your Mediator only through your repentance and your obedience to the Father's commandments; otherwise, I cannot deny justice when it has its claim."[78]

Let us summarize by saying that the atonement of Jesus Christ is conditional. If he had paid a debt for us, it would be paid and the debt would be gone forever. But this is not true of sins. If we return to our sins after having been forgiven, the condemnation for our former sins returns with it.

---

[77]Doctrine and Covenants 19:15-18.
[78]See Mosiah 15:27, B. of M.

CONCERNING THOSE WHO REJECT
THE SAVIOR'S GRACIOUS GIFT OF GRACE

And what does the scripture say will happen to those who have an opportunity to hear the Gospel and repent, but reject it, and die in their sins? Alma describes what happens to them after they pass into the spirit world:

"The spirits of the wicked, yea, who are evil—for behold, they have no part nor portion of the Spirit of the Lord; for behold, they *chose* evil works rather than good; therefore the spirit of the devil did enter into them, and take possession of their house—and these shall be cast out into outer darkness; there shall be weeping, and wailing, and gnashing of teeth, and this because of their own iniquity, being led captive by the will of the devil.

"Now this is the state of the souls of the wicked, yea, in darkness, and a state of awful, fearful looking for the fiery indignation of the wrath of God upon them; thus they remain in this state, as well as the righteous in paradise, until the time of their resurrection."[79]

Of course, these two verses are talking about the multitudes who heard the Gospel and rejected it so that they died in their sins. As we have already explained in chapter 42, the Lord has a special program for those who never heard the Gospel in mortality. In fairness, they are taught the Gospel on the other side, and if they accept it, they are treated as though they had accepted the Gospel in the flesh.[80]

THE ATONEMENT IN PERSPECTIVE

As we reflect on what the Lord has revealed concerning the atonement, we have learned the following definitive principles:

1. Jesus did for us what no other being could have done, not even the Father.

---

[79]Alma 40:13-14, B. of M.
[80]1 Peter 4:6.

2. The Father positioned Jesus in the First Estate to organize everything in our part of the universe, thereby making him the most loved person in our round of God's kingdom, even equal to our love for the Father.

3. In order for us to advance toward Godhood, it was necessary for us to learn the difference between good and evil by passing through a probationary estate where good and evil exist side by side.

4. The very nature of this training experience does not permit any of us to go through this exposure to evil without becoming tainted by evil to some degree, thereby "falling short of the glory of God." Consequently, the Father cannot take us back into his presence where sin is not tolerated with the least degree of allowance. If he tried, the scripture says the Father would lose his Godhood.

5. The atonement plan required that the Savior pass through such a horrendous ordeal of suffering that it would arouse an immense feeling of compassion and mercy in all of the intelligences belonging to our part of God's great kingdom.

6. This made Jesus the recipient of the vast outpouring of mercy and compassion which flows up to him from the myriad of intelligences and allows him to plead with the Father that for "his" sake (not ours) let those who have qualified, through repentance, return to the mansions of the Father. Jesus calls this generous intercession his "free gift of grace." It is available to all of us if we repent and do our best to qualify for it.[81]

The best way to show our appreciation for the miracle of the atonement is to prayerfully and carefully use it every day. Sometimes our sins are in response to distress and anger. At other times our sins are a response to our lower instincts. Then there are times when our sins are the result of sheer neglect—indifference to loved ones, neighbors, the needy or someone we have offended. These daily deficiencies need repentance and reform. By this means these blemishes in our lives can be brought under the atonement and

---

[81]Acts 15:11; Romans 3:24; 1 Corinthians 1:4; Ephesians 2:8; 2 Nephi 2:6-8, 25:23, B. of M.

erased. If we use the Savior's "free gift of grace" on a daily basis, it will demonstrate the beautiful and pragmatic fact that it works!

We also show our appreciation for the Savior's sacrifice when we thoughtfully and prayerful partake of the sacrament. It is a good time to contemplate the feelings of the Savior when he collapsed beneath the trees of Gethsemane and said:

"Father, all things are possible unto thee. Take this cup from me."[82]

And we might ponder the anguish of the Father as he was compelled to send an angel to his son who was bleeding from every pore and tell him:

"My Son, there is no other way."

FOLLOW ME

Once Jesus had fulfilled that awesome assignment, he became the only way by which we can return to the glorious kingdom of our Father. Therefore:

We are baptized in his name.

We are confirmed in his name.

We are endowed with divine authority in his name.

We are sealed to our loved ones in his name.

We are resurrected in his name.

We are exalted in his name.

Each day, in the name of Jesus Christ, we thank our Heavenly Father that his Beloved Son had the magnificent courage in the Garden of Gethsemane to say: "Father, thy will be done."

---

[82]Mark 14:36.

Index

S

Z